CROSSING THE BORDER

New Relationships Between
Northern Ireland and the Republic of Ireland

Editors
John Coakley and Liam O'Dowd

Foreword by
Sir George Quigley

IRISH ACADEMIC PRESS
DUBLIN • PORTLAND, OR

First published in 2007 by Irish Academic Press

44, Northumberland Road,
Ballsbridge,
Dublin 4, Ireland

920 NE 58th Avenue, Suite 300
Portland, Oregon
97213-3786

www.iap.ie

British Library Cataloguing in Publication Data
An entry can be found on request

ISBN 978 0 7165 2921 7 (cloth)
ISBN 978 0 7165 2922 4 (paper)

Library of Congress Cataloging-in-Publication Data
An entry can be found on request

Typeset in 11/13pt Janson by FiSH Books, Enfield, Middx.
Printed by Biddles Ltd., King's Lynn, Norfolk

Contents

List of tables

List of figures

Contributors to this volume

John Bradley was formerly a professor at the Economic and Social Research Institute in Dublin, and now works as an economic development consultant. His published research explores the impact of the single European market, structural funds, and economic and monetary union on the less developed peripheral states and regions of the European Union as well as the transition of former COMECON countries to EU membership. He has carried out a wide range of international consultancy assignments for the Irish and other governments, the European Commission and other international organisations.

Patricia Clarke is the research manager for the Centre for Cross Border Studies, where she is engaged in research into a wide of range of aspects of North–South relations. Since returning from London in 2000 she has been central to the development of cross-border work in areas ranging across health services, educational disadvantage, telecom technologies, EU funding programmes, foot and mouth disease, mental health, information provision, sustainable development, and science and citizenship education.

John Coakley is an associate professor of politics at University College Dublin and director of the Institute for British–Irish Studies. He has edited or co-edited *The territorial management of ethnic conflict* (2nd edn., Frank Cass, 2003); *From political violence to negotiated settlement: the winding path to peace in twentieth century Ireland* (UCD Press, 2004); *Politics in the Republic of Ireland* (4th edn., Routledge, 2004) and *Renovation or revolution? New territorial politics in Ireland and the United Kingdom* (UCD Press, 2005).

Ivo Damkat is currently a PhD student in the School of Sociology, Social Policy and Social Work at Queen's University, Belfast. Formerly an assistant statistician at the Northern Ireland Statistical Research Agency, he was also a research assistant for the 'Mapping Frontiers, Plotting Pathways' project at Queen's University.

Kevin Howard is a lecturer in social studies at Dundalk Institute of Technology. He was formerly a researcher on the 'Mapping Frontiers, Plotting Pathways' project at the Institute for British–Irish Studies at University College Dublin. His research interests are in the general fields of ethnic mobilisation and the politics of identity. His most recent publication is 'Constructing the Irish of Britain: ethnic identification and the 2001 UK censuses', *Ethnic and racial studies* 29 (1) 2006, pp. 104–23.

Eoin Magennis is policy research manager with InterTrade Ireland. The research on which his chapter is based was completed while he was research and information officer with the Centre for Cross Border Studies, working on the 'Border Ireland' and 'Mapping Frontiers, Plotting Pathways' projects.

Cathal McCall is lecturer in European Studies at Queen's University, Belfast. Recent publications include *Identity in Northern Ireland: communities, politics and change* (Palgrave, 2001), and 'Shifting thresholds, contested meanings: governance, cross-border co-operation and the Ulster unionist identity', *European studies: a journal of European culture, history and politics* 19, 2003, pp. 81–103.

Brian Ó Caoindealbháin is research officer with Co-operation Ireland. He was formerly a research assistant on the 'Mapping Frontiers, Plotting Pathways' project at the Institute for British–Irish Studies, University College Dublin.

Liam O'Dowd is professor of sociology and director of the Centre for International Borders Research (CIBR) at Queen's University, Belfast. Recent publications include *Culture and cooperation in Europe's borderlands* [European Studies, 19] (Rodopi, 2003); *New borders for a changing Europe: cross-border co-operation and governance* (Frank Cass, 2003), both co-edited with James Anderson and Tom Wilson, and 'The changing significance of European borders', *Regional and federal studies* 12 (4) 2002, pp. 13–36.

Andy Pollak is the director of the Centre for Cross Border Studies, with offices in Armagh and Dublin. He is also secretary of Universities Ireland, which links the nine universities on the island. He is a former education correspondent, religious affairs correspondent and Belfast reporter with the *Irish Times.* With Ed Moloney, he co-authored a biography of Ian Paisley (Poolbeg, 1986). He was coordinator of the Opsahl Commission on Northern Ireland, and edited its report, entitled *A citizens' enquiry: the Opsahl Report on Northern Ireland* (Lilliput Press, 1993).

Etain Tannam is senior research fellow at the Dublin European Institute, School of Politics and International Relations, UCD, Dublin, and is the author of *Cross-border co-operation in the Republic of Ireland and Northern Ireland* (Macmillan, 1999). She has written various articles on the cross-border relationship, including, most recently, in *Public administration* 84 (2)(2006), and *British journal of politics and international relations* 8 (2) (2006).

Robin Wilson is a writer and policy analyst based in Belfast. He was formerly director of the think-tank Democratic Dialogue, and previously editor of the magazine *Fortnight.* He has written extensively on North–South relationships and is a member of a North–South forum organised by Co-operation Ireland.

Acknowledgements

Among the remarkable institutional changes that have formed the backdrop to political rapprochement in Northern Ireland in 2007, one of the more noteworthy has been the transformation in the North-South relationship. This book explores the unfolding character of this relationship over a long time-span, considering economic, social and political domains, and seeks to fill a vital gap by setting recent changes in their broader historical setting. The chapters which follow have emerged from a two-year research project entitled *Mapping frontiers, plotting pathways: routes to North-South cooperation in a divided island*, which sought to explore this relationship in depth from an interdisciplinary perspective. This was funded as part of an imaginative initiative by the Higher Education Authority, and we are grateful to Dr Eucharia Meehan and her colleagues in the HEA, who showed an active interest in the project from the beginning, and to the Special EU Programmes Body, the original source of the funding.

Our most obvious debt in this project is to the authors who have contributed to this volume; we are grateful for their commitment and for their patience in putting up with our many editorial demands. But behind them lies another body of researchers who contributed generously to the project, whose work has informed our contributions in this volume, and whose own contributions are themselves in the process of appearing in other outlets: James Anderson, Neale Blair, Alessia Cividin, Hastings Donnan, Terence Dooley, John Driscoll, Mary Gordon, Katy Hayward, Joe Heyman, Joan Henderson, Michael Kennedy, Sean L'Estrange, Judit Molnar, Ivo Nienhuis, Cormac Ó Gráda, Brendan O'Leary, Kieran Rankin, Stephen Roper, Ian Shuttleworth, Kirk Simpson, Paul Teague, Jennifer Todd and Brendan Walsh. We also wish to thank warmly other colleagues who offered vital administrative support: Hazel Moloney, Susan Muldoon, Aonghus Ó hAirt and Theresa O'Keefe. In particular, we would like to express our warmest appreciation of the joint coordinators of the project who held everything together, Patricia McCarron and Patrick McWilliams. Finally, we would like to pay tribute to our co-director in the project, Elizabeth Meehan, who not only helped to give coherence to the project but herself participated actively in all of its phases.

The *Mapping frontiers* project was not just an academic one; it engaged actively with the public sector, and in particular with those areas closest to its focus of study. We are grateful to the organisations that helped organise study groups: the Centre for Cross Border Studies, Clones Regeneration Partnership, InterTrade Ireland and the North-West Region Cross-Border Group. We would also like to record our thanks to the contributors to our opening project public conference: An Taoiseach, Mr Bertie Ahern, TD; Mr Tim O'Connor and Dr Peter Smyth, Joint Secretaries, North/South Ministerial Council; Mr Derick Anderson, Chief Executive, Loughs Agency; Mr Pat Colgan, Chief Executive, Special EU Programmes Body; Mr Martin Dennany, Director of Marketing and Communications, Waterways Ireland; Mr Niall Gibbons, Director of Corporate Services, Tourism Ireland; Mr Aidan Gough, Strategy and Policy Director, InterTrade Ireland; Mr Martin Higgins, Chief Executive, Safefood; Dr Seán Ó Ceárnaigh, Programme Manager, Corporate Planning, Foras na Gaeilge; Mr George Patton, Chief Executive, Ulster Scots Agency; and Lord Laird of Artigarvan. We are grateful to the four-member advisory group which offered a valuable external perspective on the project and assisted in other ways: Dame Joan Harbinson, Mr Walter Kirwan, Professor Brendan O'Leary and Dr Peter Smyth. Finally, our closing word of gratitude must be to Lisa Hyde and Irish Academic Press for the care with which they have prepared this volume for publication.

John Coakley
Liam O'Dowd
June 2007

Foreword

The political accord recently concluded by the political parties in Northern Ireland, with the active encouragement and support of the British and Irish Governments, must surely rank as the most significant development in the last 85 years of this island's history.

For Northern Ireland it ushers in an era of unprecedented political inclusiveness and, with the restoration of devolved institutions, there is opportunity for the policy creativity needed to forge the cohesive society which has proved so elusive. It also promises to open a new chapter in a North-South relationship marked more often by hostility and distrust than by fraternity and cordiality.

This book therefore appears at exactly the right time. Its contributors are to be congratulated on a searching analysis of the factors which have acted and interacted to change the significance of the border.

Whilst exploring the impact of the political dynamic within the island itself on this process, it rightly attaches importance to the role which changes in the global environment have played in reconfiguring cross-border relationships. There are so many examples worldwide now (not least the European Union) of communities of interest transcending political boundaries that it would be perverse to condemn this island to a suboptimal future by refusing to recognise that its potential can only be realised as a shared regional space.

Thanks to excellent work done by InterTrade Ireland and the business organisations, some of the most interesting developments reflecting this insight have occurred within the economic dimension. The book highlights the extent to which the two parts of the island are powered by very different engines – one private-sector-driven and very globalised and the other over-reliant on the public sector. However, while each economy is more open to the other than ever before, the existing patterns of trade do little to produce a recognizably all-island economy, where one would expect to find industrial clusters producing filaments of economic activity crisscrossing the island regardless of the border.

It is a major virtue of the book that its analysis constantly stimulates the reader to do more than merely contemplate the results and admire the elegance with which they are presented. Its findings in all the areas it examines challenge policy makers to be more creative about how the potential of this shared regional space can be fully exploited.

It points, for example, to the asymmetrical competencies of the two administrations (not least, in regard to fiscal matters) as a factor in the gross imbalance between the economies. The current debate about the alignment of corporate tax rates throughout the island addresses precisely that issue.

Drawing on research which deals with many facets of the North-South narrative, the book identifies the features which might lead one to pass an optimistic or a pessimistic verdict on the progress made in the journey from the zero sum politics of territorialism to the new positive sum relationships which can be of mutual benefit to people on both sides of the border.

I find it difficult, particularly in light of recent developments, to avoid the conclusion that the future lies with the optimists. The 'mood music' is so different. As the book shows, the rhetoric of hostility has been replaced by talk about reducing mutual ignorance, promoting shared benefits, and co-operating to meet global challenges.

This offers the hope that we can escape the entail of history, replacing prejudice with pragmatism and forging the bonds which make borders irrelevant.

Sir George Quigley
July 2007

Part 1

Introduction

1

The 'new' Irish border: changing political, economic and social dimensions

JOHN COAKLEY AND LIAM O'DOWD

INTRODUCTION

A twentieth-century visitor to Rathlin Island, the part of Northern Ireland most remote from the Republic, might have been taken aback at the symbolism of the island's most visible guardian. The dramatic East lighthouse on its north-eastern coast proclaimed its institutional links to Dublin: it was built, and it continues to be maintained, by a venerable public body, the Commissioners of Irish Lights, headquartered in Dun Laoghaire. As a rare body that continued undisturbed by the partition of Ireland in 1921, this ancient all-Ireland institution itself symbolises the complexity of the North–South relationship. It is indeed a particularly apt symbol. Not only was it an unusual surviving all-island body; it also formed part of a broader British–Irish marine protection network that had uniquely survived the end of the union.

By the middle of the twentieth century the Commissioners of Irish Lights was an even more exceptional state-sponsored institution. By that time, a huge gulf had opened up between the unionist North and the nationalist South. In the South, there was a growing, inward-looking preoccupation with the failures of the Irish state. These included mass emigration and unemployment, a declining rural economy, inability to revive the Irish language, and absence of progress in ending partition – perceived shortcomings which highlighted the fact that the major goals of the Irish nationalist project were further from realisation than ever.[1] In the unionist North, on the other hand, there was no sense of grand projects unrealised or expectations disappointed. On the contrary, Northern Ireland was benefiting from being part of the Allies' victorious war effort. Post-war economic reconstruction, the extension of a developing British welfare state to Northern Ireland, the firm alliance between the Ulster Unionist Party and the ruling British conservatives and the ineffectual nature of nationalist opposition to unionist one-party rule left unionists in little doubt about the merits of the union and partition: the economic and political case for these seemed to be self-evident.[2]

A striking indicator of the perceived irrelevance of the North–South relationship in the mid-twentieth century is evident in the *magnum opus* on the Northern Ireland economy produced by two Queen's University economists. The South merited only two minor and passing references (regarding cross-border labour migration) in 646 pages of text.[3] This is mirrored on the southern side, where standard texts on the economy were similarly sparing in their references to Northern Ireland.[4] Political analysis showed a similar pattern of divergence: the consciousness of the all-Irish dimension that is so clear in Nicholas Mansergh's texts on the politics and government of the Irish Free State and on Northern Ireland in the 1930s had evaporated thirty years later.[5] By mid-century, therefore, the two parts of Ireland had truly grown apart, each apparently preoccupied with its own problems and circumstances, each far more concerned with its relationship with Britain than with the other jurisdiction. Evolving forms of separate development were punctuated by periodic outbreaks of partitionist and anti-partitionist rhetoric, while the deep sense of grievance among northern nationalists continued to fester. Of course, the formal economic and political gulf between North and South in the 1950s was not the whole story. It seemed wider in Dublin- and Belfast-centred perspectives than in areas closer to the border. Cross-border ties survived in many areas of life. Yet we see the 1950s as an important benchmark against which later developments may be assessed – a point to which we return later in this chapter, and one which recurs in the rest of this book. This gulf between North and South – less visible, perhaps, to those living along the border – provides a useful benchmark for assessing contemporary relationships.

By the end of the century, a much more dynamic pattern of interaction between the two parts of the island had developed. Behind this change lay a combination of factors of varying significance: the prolonged violent conflict in Northern Ireland, membership of the European Union, and dramatic economic change most visibly represented by the 'Celtic tiger' phenomenon in the South. The object of this book is to explore precisely how the North–South relationship came to be transformed, while examining the extent and limits of this transformation in a number of key domains – politics and administration, the economy and civil society.

Two aspects of this relationship run through this chapter and the ones that follow. While these are analytically separate, the interaction between them provides some of the more fascinating paradoxes thrown up by the Irish border. The first theme is *North–South difference*: the impact of partition in accentuating those very divisions to which it was designed, at least in part, to respond. In this context, the border may be seen as a marker delineating the frontier between two quite different jurisdictions. The second aspect is the *North–South relationship* in the strict sense: the survival of all-Irish structures and cross-border interaction (whether informal or institutionalised) and, particularly, the appearance of new dimensions to this relationship. Some of these took surprising form: they represented not merely efforts to overcome obvious difficulties raised by the border but, ironically, attempts to exploit some of the new opportunities generated by partition, for example in the smuggling economy of the border region.

We begin to consider these themes of North–South differences and relationships in the present chapter, where we seek to amplify and refine the crude image just presented of the stand-off between the two parts of the island in the middle of the twentieth century. We do this in four stages. In the first three we look at broad sectors where the impact of partition was deep and distinctive: political life, economic activity and social behaviour more generally. In the fourth we indicate how the remaining chapters in this book propose to develop further the analysis of this important issue.

PARTITION AND IRISH POLITICS

The form that the partition of Ireland took was quintessentially the outcome of a political struggle. This arose from a profound cleavage between British imperial interests and Irish nationalist ambitions, the outcome of which was determined by an obvious mismatch in the political and military resources available to the two sides.[6] But it also reflected the disposition of forces and interests on the Irish battlefield where the outcome of the struggle was decided. This confrontation between mutually hostile forces on the island did not, however, point inevitably to the shape that partition was ultimately to take. It is true that there were important differences between North and South at the economic and social levels, as we will see in the next two sections; and the conflict between unionism and nationalism seemed so deep that, in the eyes of many, partition of the island was the only conceivable solution. In this section, we argue that a fuzzy political frontier was translated into a stark constitutional border which separated two increasingly differentiated administrative systems. We look at these three areas – the political, constitutional and administrative – in turn.

The political arena

Analysis of Irish electoral behaviour demonstrates clearly that interpretations which stress the distinctiveness of the six counties that now form Northern Ireland in the context of the rest of the island both oversimplify and distort the pattern in reality, projecting a retrospective, historically misleading logic. Since the mobilisation of unionism and nationalism as mass movements in the 1880s, it had been clear that party politics – reflecting deeply held political views, not least on the subject of the relationship with Great Britain – was powerfully territorial. Most of Ireland was strongly or even overwhelmingly nationalist, determined to achieve autonomy for the island; two counties, Antrim and Down, were overwhelmingly unionist, determined to resist Irish autonomy; and four counties (the remaining four now within Northern Ireland) were deeply divided, with a small nationalist majority in two and a small unionist majority in the other two.

This description, identifying two counties as orange, twenty-six as green, and four as chequered, of course oversimplifies the position. Furthermore, use of different territorial units (such as parliamentary constituencies, urban and rural districts, or poor law unions) would produce a different pattern; but the difficulty in drawing a 'fair' boundary between the two sides would remain. The principle adopted in 1921 (maximising the number of Protestants in Northern Ireland by including the four mixed counties, even though two of these had Catholic majorities) could well have been reversed if the same principle were given a different content (maximising the number of Catholics in Southern Ireland by including the four mixed counties, even though two had Protestant majorities).

The outcome of the partition settlement laid out in the Government of Ireland Act, 1920 and implemented in 1921 – a six-county Northern Ireland, rather than a two-county entity, or one with boundaries that sought to follow the line of political division as closely as possible – thus failed to separate a unionist North from a nationalist South; instead, it separated a divided South from an even more divided North. This point is more obvious from the perspective of pre-partition Ireland than from the vantage point of the early twenty-first century: now, the division between nationalism and unionism as articulated traditionally in the South has been obliterated, though that in the North has, if anything, intensified. Indeed, the spatial expression of nationalist–unionist conflict in the North has been transformed. Using the crude measurement instruments of the pre-partition period, the four 'mixed' counties of Northern Ireland are no longer divided between two with nationalist and two with unionist majorities; since at least 1991, all four have had nationalist majorities of varying sizes.[7]

Our concern here is not – at least directly – with the nationalist–unionist relationship in Northern Ireland, but rather with the North–South one. The discussion above nevertheless highlights a fact that can too easily be overlooked: in its indifference to ethno-geographical realities, the border not only imposed a barrier between unionism and nationalism but also left an unnecessarily large nationalist minority (35 per cent, rising to about 45 per cent by the end of the twentieth century) in the North, and a small unionist minority (initially 10 per cent, but subsequently dwindling demographically and disappearing politically) in the South. Since over time the majority–minority relationship turned out to be much more politically significant in the North, we may summarise the dilemma from the perspective of northern attitudes towards the South: partition 'saved' the northern majority from the fate it feared in a politically independent Irish nationalist state dominated by Catholic values and an agrarian economy, but it also 'condemned' the northern minority to exclusion from a meaningful role in the political life of the northern state, and from any role at all in the state to which its members overwhelmingly wished to belong.

In assessing the political factors that shaped the character of partition, then, we may identify two forces which collaborated in deepening it and two which saw it as damaging their interests. The obvious party with a vested interest in partition was northern unionism, preoccupied with the struggle to remain free of the influence of the southern state. The less obvious party was the southern state, preoccupied with the struggle to assert its independence of the United Kingdom: advancing independence and deepening the border were interdependent processes, as will be seen below.[8] The obvious party with a vested interest in opposing partition was northern nationalism, whose leaders continued to focus on demands for Irish unity. The less obvious party was the British state, the very author of partition. It should be recalled that the Government of Ireland Act, 1920 had not only separated Northern Ireland from 'Southern Ireland'; it had also cut Northern Ireland adrift from Great Britain, thrusting home rule on it and forcing it to retain loose links with its southern counterpart. From the perspective of the British, a deepening of partition represented not so much enhanced Northern Irish independence of Dublin as enhanced southern Irish independence of London – an unwelcome expression of centripetal forces in an empire already under strain.

The constitutional arena

The unfolding story of the Irish border is largely the story of the assertion of northern unionist independence of the South, the *de facto* endorsement of partition by British and southern governments (notwithstanding the latter's irredentist rhetoric) and the isolation of the northern nationalist community. This pattern had become clear already in the 1920s. In the political–constitutional domain, there were three decisive stages in this process. The first was the implementation of partition in 1921 under the terms of the Government of Ireland Act, 1920. The creation of two new jurisdictions within the United Kingdom, Northern Ireland (whose governing institutions survived until 1972) and Southern Ireland (whose institutions never functioned, and which was superseded by new arrangements in 1922), represented the original blueprint for division of the island, even though the two new entities were to be linked by certain all-Irish institutions. The second was the departure of Southern Ireland from the United Kingdom in 1922 as a British dominion, the Irish Free State, with the same status as Canada. This resulted in the eventual disappearance of those ancient island-level executive and judicial institutions that linked the two parts of the island even after partition (including the offices of Lord Lieutenant and Lord Chancellor, and the Irish Privy Council). The third stage was the agreement of 1925 that followed the Boundary Commission débâcle. This secured for Northern Ireland recognition of the existing six-county border as permanent, and for the Irish Free State a significant financial relief package. It also involved the scrapping of the proposed representative body that would link them both, the Council of Ireland – a body that found little favour with either government.[9]

Following the trauma of the early state-building process, the status of the Irish border continued to be shaped by broader international forces. From a British perspective, residual reluctance to concede the full implications of the partition of Ireland was reflected in the form taken in the royal title following the Irish Free State's departure from the United Kingdom. The King no longer reigned over 'the United Kingdom of Great Britain and Ireland and the British Dominions beyond the Seas' (the title adopted in 1801) but over 'Great Britain, Ireland and the British Dominions beyond the Seas', a subtle change which implied that the monarch's writ in Belfast ran as King of Ireland, not King of Great Britain – or even of the United Kingdom. The royal title was changed only in 1953 to designate 'the United Kingdom of Great Britain and Northern Ireland' as the principal territory over which the Queen's jurisdiction was to be exercised.

This constitutional posturing – primarily but not exclusively symbolic in significance – was matched on the Irish side. As is well known, the 1937 constitution renamed the Irish Free State 'Eire, or, in the English language, Ireland', and defined the 'national territory' as extending over the whole island of Ireland. But what is certainly not well known is that it also cleverly provided (in deep disguise, in article 29.4) for continued recognition of the King as head of state, consigning the state's new president to a purely domestic role, withholding from him not just the title 'head of state' but also the right to accredit Irish diplomats and receive letters of accreditation from foreign ambassadors. In one of the best-kept secrets in Irish political history, this continued to be a royal function until 1949.

These constitutional gestures were not merely exercises in flag-waving in Dublin and London. For the British, they probably provided until 1949 symbolic reassurance for the belief that Ireland had not been totally 'lost'. For the Irish, they arguably provided until 1999 reassurance that the problem of partition had been 'solved', in symbolic terms at least – after all, the constitution provided a comforting definition of an all-island national territory, parking the issue of unity and providing a formal excuse for not engaging further with it. In the world of 'high politics' and diplomacy, however, Ireland's departure from the Commonwealth and the transfer of the King's functions in the area of external relations to the President of Ireland in 1949 represented for the British government an unwelcome move towards complete independence on the part of Dublin, and opened a sustained period in which the very designation 'Ireland' was seen as embodying an unacceptable territorial claim over Northern Ireland.

The constitutional impasse, and its management by the two governments, was accompanied, and perhaps facilitated, by a *de facto* compartmentalisation of the internal politics of Northern Ireland from politics in Britain and the Republic. Constitutional posturing enhanced a tendency to ignore, or at least to fail to engage with, the evolving impact of the Irish border and the full working out of the consequences of partition. The eruption of violent political conflict in the late 1960s was a harsh reminder of the extent to which communal and political antagonism had become institutionalised within Northern Ireland, and how ill-prepared the British and Irish governments were to address the causes of the conflict and to advance effective solutions. As the conflict intensified into a three-cornered struggle between republicans, loyalists and the official security forces, a new partnership between the British and Irish governments evolved, albeit one subject to periodic tensions and setbacks. The result was an enhanced Dublin voice in Northern Ireland politics. This received formal recognition in the Anglo-Irish agreement of 1985, which gave the Irish government a consultative role in Northern Ireland's affairs, and it was given fuller expression in the Good Friday agreement of 1998, the most important portions of which came into effect in December 1999 – a development that is central to this book.

The administrative arena

Conflict over constitutional frameworks tells us relatively little about the real institutional or administrative significance of the Irish border. At the level of policy implementation, the new regimes in Dublin and Belfast faced major challenges, though these were of a contrasting character, as will be seen in chapter 2. The government of the Irish Free State inherited a whole network of existing Dublin-based 'Irish' government departments and agencies whose writ was island-wide – the Commissioners of National Education, the Department of Agriculture and Technical Instruction and the Local Government Board, for instance. Redefining these to have a slightly narrower remit (over twenty-six rather than thirty-two counties) was a manageable challenge, and the considerable numbers of civil servants who resigned or moved were replaceable. On the other hand, the state apparatus had to be created afresh in those areas where London-based 'imperial' departments had functioned in Ireland: external affairs, defence and the post office, for instance. In Northern Ireland, there was no comparable need for departments corresponding to these latter, but the new administration faced a much bigger challenge in setting up new departments in areas where Dublin rule now ended.[10]

In any case, what was striking about this process of the erection of separate states was its thoroughness: Dublin and Belfast built up distinct, parallel structures, between which contact was minimal, at some considerable cost. New and separate departments of Home Affairs, Agriculture and Education were obviously needed, but the speed and thoroughness with which such elderly, established and non-political bodies as the Public Record Office, the Registrar General's Office, the Valuation Office and the Ordnance Survey were partitioned was surprising, and suggested that enthusiasm for the process was lacking on neither side of the border.[11] Indeed, although there was contact subsequently between civil servants on the two sides, North–South links were kept to a minimum, confined to a few sectors where they could hardly be avoided.[12]

Politically and administratively, then, the border acquired a deep significance with surprising speed. The old unionist and nationalist parties retracted to Northern Ireland; the new party system of the South (dominated by Fianna Fáil, Fine Gael and Labour) was virtually unrepresented in the North.[13] Electoral law, the education system, the process of land reform, taxation principles and levels, public health administration, local government and other aspects of public sector activity steadily diverged, sometimes because of innovation in Northern Ireland but more commonly because of policy shifts in the South. In the Free State, new criteria for the registration of the legal and medical professions and diverging qualification standards in the area of teacher education (including new Irish language requirements) meant that these professions quickly became segregated along the line of the border, making cross-border mobility increasingly difficult.

In addition to the impact of change in constitutional and administrative provisions, there have been other major influences on the process by which the border was deepened. Some of these have evolved gradually in ways unforeseen, or unintended, by the architects of partition. One such influence was the expanding role of the state in general in shaping and regulating economy and society in the course of the twentieth century. Partially influenced by war-time mobilisation, and by popular demands for reform and greater citizenship rights, the remit of governments and state administrations expanded in areas such as health, education, welfare, and economic and cultural arenas. Thus, state-building in Ireland and elsewhere served to enhance the importance of national borders, in that the practical everyday significance of residence in a territorially delimited state increased. This effect was magnified in the Irish case as state-building took a different shape on either side of the border. North and South were not symmetric jurisdictions. The former was constituted by a peculiar form of regional devolution within a large, powerful and relatively prosperous polity – the United Kingdom. The South, on the other hand, was a relatively poor, heavily agricultural state, constructed around the remnants of an imperial administrative apparatus and still heavily influenced by its ex-imperial neighbour.

At the political level, then, we may summarise the position as follows. Divisions on the island were much more acute than has been acknowledged in traditional nationalist historiography. The British government was indeed the agent of partition and, like any other government, imperial or revolutionary, it sought to promote its own interests; but it was responding to certain realities on the ground (that British interests might have been instrumental in creating these is a topic on which we withhold discussion here).[14] On the other hand, though, differences and divisions on the island of Ireland were much more complex than revisionist critics of the traditional nationalist perspective have acknowledged. In its anxiety to debunk the myth of the all-island nation, anti-nationalist analysis, especially in its early stages, has tended to imply a monolithic Northern Ireland holding out against an alien south, a position that is myopic with respect to the large nationalist population in Northern Ireland.[15] More recent analysis has tended to stress the importance of intra-unionist class divisions.[16] Arguably these divisions encouraged the leaders of Ulster unionism to preserve unionist unity by regularly turning elections into plebiscites on the border, thereby stressing differences between North and South to a greater extent than if unionism was more socially homogeneous.[17]

The creation of the Irish border certainly strengthened the logic of separate development in the two parts of the island and pointed in the direction of increased differentiation – a process more visibly driven at the political level by southern secessionism (in relation to Great Britain) than by northern rejectionism (in respect of the South). It was not difference as such that undermined the quality of formal cross-border relationships as their complex and often malign interaction on the island and between Ireland and Britain. Ironically, though, it was precisely as this differentiation between North and South accelerated in the late twentieth century (with civil conflict in Northern Ireland driving the two jurisdictions further apart) that a new political relationship between the two entities acquired more concrete form.

PARTITION AND THE IRISH ECONOMY

The theme of difference emerges clearly also in the economic domain. Here, it is much more difficult to argue that the island of Ireland is the appropriate unit of analysis. We have clear reminders that economic relationships are seldom encompassed by state boundaries, although they are assuredly influenced by them: historically, the British empire and the economic area defined by the islands of Britain and Ireland; then the interplay – however limited – between economies on either side of the border created in 1921; and, most recently, the European Union. We consider these three rather different contexts in the next three subsections.

The emergence of separate economies

Traditional nationalist writing accorded primacy to politics or culture over economics, attaching little weight to sharply diverging patterns of regional economic development on the island. An autonomous Irish state was seen as the key to reversing a pattern of relative economic decline and exploitation linked to British imperial domination of Ireland. This view overlooked the benefits which north-east Ulster in particular derived from imperial free trade. Mirroring their nationalist counterparts, most unionist interpretations gave priority to political and cultural (including religious) factors, although they regularly pointed to the economic benefits of the union as objective proof of the validity of their claims.

Only a few analysts accorded primary importance to economic factors in explaining the desire of unionists to remain part of the UK by stressing the 'uneven economic development' of North and South under the union.[18] The school of thought developed by the British and Irish Communist Organisation in the 1970s, for instance, took the view that the border was based on a 'diametrical conflict of interests, resulting from the different stages of development of capitalism in the North and the South'.[19] As is well known, there were striking regional imbalances in the degree to which Ireland participated in the industrial revolution. It has been argued that the region around Belfast indeed acquired all of the characteristics of an 'industrial district', fully participating in the latter phases of the industrial revolution in a way in which the rest of the island did not.[20] It might also be argued that the economy of the island as a whole was fundamentally restructured within the dominant political economy of British imperialism in the nineteenth century, producing two separate but peripheralised economies in Ireland dependent on, and constrained by, the dominant core English economy. The structure of imperial relationships has been described elsewhere as a 'rimless wheel' where diverse parts are linked more directly to the centre in various ways than to each other.[21] Adapting the metaphor further, it might be suggested that Belfast and Dublin constituted two hubs of different, and smaller, rimless wheels on the island of Ireland, while each was linked in different ways to the core economy of England. Economic policy made in London continued to exert a powerful conditioning influence on both Irish economies long after 1921. It served to freeze their structural relationships to England, while providing little basis for creating mutually interdependent cross-border links between them on the island of Ireland.

Although the Belfast region was the most industrially developed part of the island, from its inception Northern Ireland struggled to combat the threat of mass unemployment, as the contraction of its industrial sector and increased competition from other countries took their toll. It relied on war-time demand and post-war booms (especially in the case of the two world wars) for short-term reprieves from the long-term pattern of contraction.[22] With the outbreak of the Northern Ireland 'troubles' another type of war-time economy emerged – encouraging heavy dependence on British state expenditure, public sector employment and security-related jobs. In the immediate aftermath of partition, Northern Ireland had been a net subscriber to the British exchequer and was expected to be financially self-sufficient. Mass unemployment between the early 1920s and 1939 put strains on this relationship. Whereas unemployment and pensions dominated the North's budget in the inter-war period, after the war expenditure on health, welfare and the promotion of economic development increased dramatically.[23] After 1972, civil conflict and accelerating de-industrialisation further increased the central state's financial control over Northern Ireland as the latter became heavily supported by subvention from Westminster.[24]

For much of the rest of its history, therefore, the Northern Ireland economy was one of the weakest regional economies of the UK, characterised by very high levels of unemployment and economic insecurity in its core industries – shipbuilding, engineering and linen. The economic differences between the two parts of the island were reflected in the fact that 73 per cent of Ireland's industrial workers were concentrated in the six counties that became Northern Ireland by 1912, with the remaining 27 per cent spread around the rest of the island.[25] After partition, the South was left with a largely agricultural economy, partly subsistence-based and partly commercial. The commercial sector was linked not to the North but to Britain, whose 'cheap food' policy encouraged the export of livestock rather than processed foods from Ireland, as well as the import of manufactured goods from Britain. Attempts in the South to develop an indigenous manufacturing sector behind high tariff barriers in the 1930s had some success, though limited by the small size of the southern market. One of its side-effects was to underpin the border as an economic barrier.

The different economic experiences of the two parts of Ireland were reflected in a big contrast between the demographic history of the North and that of the rest of the island: there was a decline of almost 55 per cent over the period 1841–1951 in the population of the twenty-six counties that now constitute the Republic of Ireland, but decline was much lower (17 per cent) in the six remaining counties, and the population of Belfast and its surrounding districts actually increased.[26] Differences persisted well into the twentieth century. Even in the economic sector most prominently associated with the south, agriculture, analysis of output and productivity suggests that northern farmers easily outperformed their southern counterparts between the 1930s and the 1960s (though the gap began to close after that point); and there were important differences in the sectoral distribution of agricultural output.[27] In these circumstances, it is not surprising that some economists have concluded that partition 'formalised an already dichotomised island economy'.[28]

Economic policy in a divided island

To the extent that economic factors are shaped by political ones, it is not surprising that North–South differences were accentuated by partition.

Despite the fiscal autonomy of the South, it was slow to develop an active programme of economic planning, and it chose not to establish a currency independent of sterling until 1979. Although Northern Ireland enjoyed some fiscal autonomy until 1972, its policies in the areas of taxation and public expenditure tended to follow UK norms.[29] The outcome over time was a sharp divergence both in instruments for revenue generation and in public expenditure patterns. Rates of income tax in the two parts of the island diverged, differences in property and other forms of taxation grew, and by the latter part of the twentieth century additional revenue in Northern Ireland tended to come from a large subsidy from the British exchequer, while the Republic relied on transfers from the EU. The Republic's industrial policy, once highly protectionist, in stark contrast to the open economy of Northern Ireland, moved rapidly after the 1950s to attract levels of inward investment that saw its economy eventually outstrip that of Northern Ireland.

Historically, though, as in the case of the political cleavage, the North–South contrast is not the full story. It is true that rapid industrialisation in the Lagan valley in the early nineteenth century set Belfast and its hinterland apart from the rest of the island, linking this area instead to the pattern of development in the industrial heartlands of Scotland and England – but it did so in a manner that accentuated the religious gap, since those involved in the leading industries were overwhelmingly Protestant.[30] In any case, the Lagan valley is not Northern Ireland; and if we look more closely at the geographical distribution of the indicators already mentioned, the current North–South border evaporates. Indeed, it has been argued that from an economic perspective there was an important east–west gradient, rather than a North–South one.

Of course, uneven patterns of economic development need not lead to any kind of economic partition. On the contrary, they may be compatible with a relationship of mutual dependence, with one region supplying raw products to the other in exchange for value-added goods. But this did not happen in Ireland. Instead, the two parts tended to export local products to Britain, and to import manufactured goods from there. Northern and southern economies were largely insulated from each other. In 1965 Lawrence was able to observe that cross-border trade between North and South was insignificant and that the northern economy was overwhelmingly oriented eastwards rather than southwards: 75 per cent of all the North's imports came from Britain, while its exports to Britain accounted for 90 per cent of the total by value.[31] Both parts of Ireland did share a common labour market with Britain, but the direction of labour mobility was overwhelmingly west–east rather than north–south.[32]

The communications infrastructure of the island reflected the movements of trade and people: canals, railways and roads radiating from Dublin linked it overwhelmingly with the west and south, and both Dublin and Belfast were linked to Britain by the Irish Sea more firmly than they were to each other by the North–South rail corridor.[33] For this reason, it has been concluded that partition had 'few consequences in terms of economic links between both parts of Ireland', apart from the fact that Derry city lost its Donegal hinterland, and similar but less significant consequences for Newry.[34] The subsequent economic development pattern of Northern Ireland indeed suggests that remaining within the United Kingdom, rather than being incorporated in the southern state with its protectionist policies, clearly served the interests of the northern agricultural and industrial sectors, as well as facilitating significant subsidisation of the local economy by its more powerful British parent.[35] Pessimism regarding the prospect of integrating the two economies more closely, and doubts about the desirability of doing so, persisted among many economists until the late twentieth century.[36]

By the mid-1960s, however, economic policy North and South had begun to move in parallel directions, albeit from very different starting points. Both jurisdictions now sought to capture mobile foreign direct investment. In the North, this was to replace declining manufacturing sectors such as shipbuilding, engineering and linen. In the South, it was aimed at stemming mass emigration, the contraction of agricultural employment and the lack of competitiveness of indigenous manufacturing industry. The South was also moving rapidly from protectionism to free trade. These processes were given further stimulus by British and Irish participation in the process of European integration after 1973.

The impact of the EU

Joint membership of the European Union underlined the common problems of competitiveness facing the two economies as the sectoral breakdown of employment became more similar on either side of the border. Within the European Union, the two parts of Ireland appeared to share common problems of peripherality and competitiveness in an increasingly European and global market place. Europe was to prove no panacea, however, for creating a more integrated and competitive island economy. Global recession due to successive oil crises restricted economic integration in the 1970s, and the Northern Ireland conflict undermined the policy of attracting inward investment. New forms of differentiation and divergence appeared between North and South. As the South began to successfully attract new foreign investment, and its agriculture began to benefit from the EU's common agricultural policy, it began to break out of its less than beneficial structural relationship with the British economy. The northern economy, on the other hand, became ever more dependent on its British parent.

Ironically, too, the process of European integration reinforced the economic salience of the border in certain respects. The British and Irish states had rather different agendas in Europe. Most obviously, the UK's decision to remain outside the process of monetary integration resulted first in a breach in parity between the Irish and British currencies (the first time this had happened since 1820), and then in the adoption of entirely different currencies on the two sides of the border.

The relaunch of the European Community in the 1980s, principally through the building of the single European market, did have a direct impact on the border. Most obviously, in 1992, it involved the abolition of the border customs posts which had been in place since April 1923. The single market was also accompanied by the Interreg initiative geared to adapting border regions to the single market. Although slow to develop genuine cross-border projects, Interreg began to highlight the need to build cross-border economic cooperation in order to compete in the European market. The thrust to encourage regional economic integration on the island of Ireland highlighted the anomaly of road closures, border fortifications and attacks on the Dublin–Belfast railway line in the early 1990s. Business organisations on either side of the border began to lobby the Irish and British governments to promote cooperation in physical infrastructure planning and marketing on an all-island basis.

At one level, European integration encouraged the 'internationalisation' of the Irish border. It now came to be treated not just as an idiosyncratic product of the long and involved history of British–Irish relations but as an international border like others in the EU. At a more subtle level, EU membership forced the two formerly rival states to recognise each other's frontiers and identities more fully than they had done in the past – and, by implication, to accept partition more completely than either might have wished to. At the same time, European integration transformed the meaning of 'internal' national borders, rendering them more permeable in economic terms. It also served to highlight the special characteristics of border regions, including the Irish border counties, marking a shift from the Dublin-, Belfast- or London-centred policy-making which tended to obscure their distinctive character and interests.

To the extent, however, that the EU influenced the emergence of the 'Celtic tiger' economy in the South, it generated a new balance of economic power on the island in favour of the South. This marked a historic reversal of a century and a half of Irish economic history. Driven by foreign (mainly US) investment and supported by EU structural funds and access to the single market, the southern economy developed more high-technology industries in modern manufacturing sectors, increased industrial productivity and developed a more globalised profile than its northern counterpart. By contrast, the North's non-market services (that is, the public sector) remained over twice as important in terms of both GDP and employment share, reflecting the overarching dominance of public funding in the northern economy.[37]

While these developments suggested new forms of differentiation, as the North remained tied to Britain and the South dramatically reoriented its economic relationships to the rest of the EU and the US, they also stimulated more demands, especially from the North, for stronger economic linkages with the South, and for a greater level of regional planning for Ireland as a whole. North–South trade remains relatively small, although more significant for the North, and particularly for its smaller companies. Exports from the South to the other jurisdiction account for only 3 per cent of the total; exports in the opposite direction account for 10 per cent of Northern Ireland's total exports. Trade with the South is even more important for small companies (employing 25–49 people), as they sell 13 per cent of their output to the South, compared to 7 per cent for all companies.[38] Cross-border trade, however, is only one element in new forms of cross-border economic interaction. Other elements include the building of cross-border, inter-firm linkages in production, research and development, and marketing, as well as the strengthening of physical and communications infrastructure links across the border to help further economic integration and competitiveness on the island as a whole.

PARTITION AND CIVIL SOCIETY

A focus on the political and economic domains has an inbuilt tendency to stress the separateness of North and South. Constitutions and political institutions generally have a clearly demarcated territorial remit determined by state borders. While economic relationships typically transcend national borders, economic statistics emphasise the state as the central unit of analysis, often obscuring the role of localities and sub-regions that cross state borders. While political jurisdictions undoubtedly help shape civil society, the latter's social networks and relationships frequently transcend or pre-date state borders (see chapter 4). The impact of partition on Irish civil society proceeded more slowly and was less intense than at the political and economic levels. Of course, much depends on how civil society is defined *vis-à-vis* the state and whether the economic sphere is deemed to be part of it.[39] Here, we look in turn at two major interpretations of civil society, which prioritise respectively the issues of societal communication and associational life. We also consider more briefly a third, metaphorical interpretation, which has direct implications for the peace process.

Communications

One way of assessing civil society is to see it as a public sphere characterised by shared structures of communication or, in the words of McClain and Fleming, a 'non-legislative, extra-judicial, public space in which societal differences, social problems, public policy, government action and matters of community and cultural identity are developed and debated'.[40] A shared language is one of the key components of a functioning civil society in this sense. In Ireland, language divisions played little part in distinguishing the two parts of the island. By the end of the nineteenth century, the surviving Irish-speaking districts all lay within the twenty-six counties, but they now accounted for only a small minority of the population. State language policy, however, was to become a marker of North–South difference as compulsory Irish became part of the southern education system and a requirement for many public service jobs. Nevertheless, in contrast with other parts of Europe, language played little role in the creation of the border, and English has for long been a common cross-border language.

In the case of the mass media, another key component of civil society as public sphere, the picture is complicated. Prior to partition, papers such as the Belfast *Newsletter* clearly articulated the Ulster unionist case for partition, while the *Freeman's Journal* supported the Irish Nationalist Party before becoming a supporter of the post-Treaty government in the South. As the newspaper media developed, they helped to constitute two separate public spheres on either side of the border, although in the North there was a further sub-division between unionist and nationalist papers at both regional and local level. In the South, local unionist newspapers disappeared, and the *Irish Times* reinvented itself in the mid-twentieth century as a voice of liberal rather than unionist opinion. Radio was less confined by the border, with Radio Éireann (founded in 1926) reaching across it, particularly to nationalist listeners. The BBC, in both its radio and television forms, served to integrate Northern Ireland firmly within a British frame of reference, while the foundation of RTÉ television in 1962 underlined the separateness of the South.[41] Of course, coverage did spill over the border, especially from North to South, and stations had cross-border audiences where they could access signals. However, the frames of reference constituted by TV stations served to 'externalise' the other jurisdiction.

The role of the mass media was to become a critical factor in the differential coverage of the Northern Ireland conflict. While many journalists sought to maintain 'objectivity', media coverage, and access to it, did become a major weapon in the arsenal of the protagonists of the conflict.[42] However, the mainstream British mass media, printed and electronic, continued to circulate in both parts of Ireland, shaping a common discourse in areas of popular culture in such areas as sport, entertainment, fashion and the activities of celebrities. In sum, the role of the mass media is complex and multi-faceted, in both constituting North and South as separate 'public spheres' and simultaneously spanning the border between North and South and between Ireland and Britain.

Institutions

A second understanding of civil society revolves around associational life, including social networks between the family and the state in which membership and activities are voluntary: formally registered non-governmental organisations of many different kinds, labour unions, political parties, churches and other religious groups, professional and business associations, community and self-help groups, sporting associations, social movements and the independent media. Some writers include economic organisations, such as firms, in this definition; others confine civil society to the 'third' or non-profit sector between the state and the economy.[43] Existing studies have provided sketchy and uneven evidence on the impact of the border on actual North–South interaction between third sector groups.[44] In sum, however, the effect of the border on civil society has attracted much less research than has its consequences in the political and economic domains (see chapter 4).

The relationship of the border to the churches illuminates its paradoxical and ambiguous impact on civil society. Religious differences were among the more important of the issues that underlay partition in the first place, and were central in the deliberations of the Boundary Commission. Yet the churches constituted important mechanisms for maintaining relationships across the border.[45] The fact that most churches – and, especially, the major ones – are organised on an all-island basis offers an important bridge between the two jurisdictions. Indeed, in their diocesan structure the two largest churches (the Catholic Church, with more than 4.1 million adherents in 2001–2, and the Church of Ireland, with 373,000) altogether ignore the border, and the Primacy of each is located in the city of Armagh in Northern Ireland.[46] The third largest church, the Presbyterian Church in Ireland, with 370,000 adherents, is also organised on an all-island basis.[47]

Trade unions also illustrate the survival of complex links across the border and between Ireland and Britain.[48] The Northern Ireland government refused to formally recognise trade unions under their jurisdictions until 1965 because of their affiliation to the (all-Ireland) Irish Congress of Trade Unions. A solution was reached through the framework of the Northern Ireland Committee of the Irish Congress of Trade Unions. This Committee has served as a bridge (even if tenuous at times), not only between trade unionists on either side of the border but also across the sectarian divide in Northern Ireland and between Ireland and Britain. The relationship of the border to the growing and increasingly diverse range of professional, cultural, sporting, community and voluntary organisations remains an under-researched area to which some of the chapters in this book make a preliminary contribution. Here, however, the impact of the respective states is highly significant in terms of statutory regulation and, in the case of community and voluntary associations, in terms of funding.

Civil society and the peace process

A third understanding of 'civil society' in the international literature should be noted. This sees it as a metaphor for the 'good society', characterised by positive norms and values and responsible citizenship. Here it is conceived as a repository of tolerance, non-discrimination, non-violence, trust and cooperation, freedom and democracy – in short, a society that is 'civil'.[49] This notion of civil society has become more prominent in Ireland in the context of the peace process, where civil society is seen to have the potential to offset or ameliorate 'uncivil' conflict in the political realm.[50] Examples here might include the work of various organisations to build bridges across the political divide in Northern Ireland and between North and South.[51] Some of those represented in organisations such as the Confederation of Community Groups in Northern Ireland and the Northern Ireland Council for Voluntary Action are confined to Northern Ireland; others, such as Co-operation Ireland and the Glencree Centre for Reconciliation, work on a cross-border basis, as do several international non-governmental organisations with an interest in promoting peace and reconciliation. The Good Friday agreement and the EU's peace programmes have explicitly sought to fund and support both cross-community and cross-border linkages between voluntary and community groups as a means of promoting trust and reconciliation (see chapter 6). This sector also reflects the impact of the North–South difference. In the absence of regional political institutions in the North, the British government encouraged the growth of a substantial voluntary sector dependent on state funding as a way of managing the conflict. Much of this sector remains relatively self-contained within the North. However, cross-border links have been fostered by independent voluntary action, by EU funding, and within the framework of the Good Friday agreement.

ADDRESSING THE LEGACY OF PARTITION

Our purpose in this chapter is not, of course, simply to document the past, but to provide a baseline against which more recent developments may be assessed. As we have seen, to the extent that the island of Ireland was a unified entity at political, economic and social levels before 1921 – and this unity was at best imperfect, especially in the economic and political domains – partition disrupted this. But it did so by dividing the island along a rather arbitrary geographical frontier that failed to match the deep political, economic and social dichotomies to which it was designed to respond. In many respects, it was political and administrative divisions on the island which articulated the most profound dichotomy. Much of the subsequent turbulent history of the border, up to and including efforts to address the issue once again in the Good Friday agreement, arose from this mismatch between state boundaries and underlying societal divisions. In a nutshell, partition produced in Northern Ireland an insecure majority, which saw reinforcement of the border as its own best protection, and an embittered minority, which saw the dismantlement of the border as the only solution.

The remaining chapters in this book seek to document and illustrate the outplay of this tension in the major domains already discussed – first, in Part 2, by looking at these domains and at interrelations between them in turn, then, in Part 3, by exploring developments in narrower sectors by means of specific case studies. Running through these chapters also are the two dimensions highlighted above: the North–South *difference* (reflected in contrasting patterns of development) and the North–South *relationship* (reflected in various forms of interaction or non-interaction between the two jurisdictions).

Since partition was ultimately a political decision, in chapter 2 John Coakley, Brian Ó Caoindealbháin and Robin Wilson look at the impact of the border in this area, and at the innovative efforts of the Good Friday agreement to reintroduce a significant Irish dimension. This is followed, in chapter 3, by an exploration by John Bradley of economic realities on the island of Ireland before and after the Good Friday agreement. The civil society context is so broad that any comparable treatment of this would be impossible; instead, in chapter 4 Kevin Howard looks at a specific aspect – organisational networks in the broadest sense – before and after the Good Friday agreement. These three sectors are, of course, very broad and overlapping. Both John Bradley (chapter 3) and Etain Tannam (chapter 5) examine the links between the political and administrative framework and economic activity, the latter stressing the impact of the EU in particular. Kevin Howard (chapter 4) and Liam O'Dowd and Cathal McCall (chapter 6) explore the links between the political framework and different aspects of civil society.

In Part 3, we move on to more specific case studies, selected to highlight issues arising in the general areas discussed above. chapters 7 and 8 address two areas where political decision making has particular importance for North–South cooperation: the education and health sectors, where the position is analysed respectively by Andy Pollak and Patricia Clarke. In chapter 9, John Bradley supplements his general economic overview in chapter 3 by considering two specific cases: the textile and information technology sectors. chapter 10 matches this in respect of the social sector: Kevin Howard explores the challenges raised by partition in the sport of competitive cycling. The two remaining sets of case studies look at cross-domain areas: in chapter 11, Eoin Magennis examines a specific area of public policy, the 'common chapter' in economic and social policy shared by the northern and southern administrations in recent years. In chapter 12, Liam O'Dowd, Cathal McCall and Ivo Damkat assess the changing character of cooperation in four illustrative areas: youth training, health, economic development and electricity generation. Here, they examine the different meanings of cross-border cooperation, and different capacities for sustaining it, across the state, market and voluntary sectors.

This book is intended, however, to be much more than a collection of isolated studies. In the conclusion (chapter 13) we seek to pull together the findings of our authors with respect to a set of common issues: in particular, how to characterise and explain the temporal and functional dimensions of the Irish border, and how to account for their interrelations. Weaving through all the chapters is the question of how evolving differences between the two parts of the island co-exist, and mutually interact, with the changing nature of the relationships between them. To different degrees, and in different contexts, the following chapters address the impact of key political and constitutional milestones which have marked cross-border relationships: the partition of Ireland in 1920–1, the fall of

Stormont in 1972 and entry into the European Community in 1973, and the Good Friday agreement of 1998. Cutting across the temporal phases of the North–South relationships, the functional dimensions of the Irish border are explored throughout this book within three key domains: politics and administration, the economy and civil society.

In a nutshell, the chapters that follow address in specific sectors the more general issue that we seek to tackle in this book: the degree to which the significance of the border has changed and, more specifically, the manner in which it has been redefined as a consequence of the dramatic socio-economic and political transformations that have occurred over the last four decades.

NOTES

1 These goals were articulated most explicitly in the party constitution of Fianna Fáil, adopted in 1926 and retaining this form until 1995.

2 For a discussion of the great reversal in the relative positions and ideologies of unionism and nationalism between the 1950s and the 1990s see L O'Dowd, 'The great reversal: nationalism and unionism, 1950–2000', in MP Corcoran and M Peillon (eds), *Ireland unbound: a turn of the century chronicle* (Dublin: Institute of Public Administration, 2002), pp. 260–77. The abject failures of the Anti-Partition League (1945–51) and the IRA campaign of 1956–62 seemed to underline the degree to which the Irish border had become rooted and institutionalised.

3 KS Isles and N Cuthbert, *An economic survey of Northern Ireland* (Belfast: HMSO, 1957). Isles and Cuthbert marshalled an array of evidence to support the view that 'full self government would be against Northern Ireland's economic interests' (p. 429) while arguing for closer alignment with the economic policy of the Westminster government. It is also noteworthy that Isles and Cuthbert completely ignored the economic dimension of the communal divide within the North.

4 See D O'Mahony, *The Irish economy: an introductory description* (Cork: Cork University Press, 1964), and J Meenan, *The Irish economy since 1922* (Liverpool: Liverpool University Press, 1970). References to Northern Ireland in the latter, longer work were confined to the area of demography, apart from a passing reference to North–South trade.

5 See N Mansergh, *The Irish Free State: its government and politics* (London: Allen and Unwin, 1934) and *The government of Northern Ireland: a study in devolution* (London: Allen and Unwin, 1936). By contrast, there are few references to the South in RJ Lawrence, *The government of Northern Ireland: public finance and public services, 1921–1964* (Oxford: Clarendon Press, 1965), nor to Northern Ireland in B Chubb, *The government and politics of Ireland* (Stanford: Stanford University Press, 1970).

6 Of course, the victory of Sinn Féin over the Home Rule party in 1918 greatly accentuated this cleavage. For the latter, Irish autonomy was quite reconcilable with Ireland remaining within the British Empire and playing an active role in it.

7 J Coakley, 'Religion, national identity and political change in modern Ireland', *Irish political studies* 17:1 (2002), pp. 4–28. Recomputing these data on the basis of the 2001 census shows the following as the proportion of the population of Catholic community background: Armagh, 54.9%; Londonderry (city and county), 59.4%; Fermanagh, 58.7%; Tyrone, 64.4%.

8 It has been argued that even in the early stages of the formation of the new Irish state, the only major nationalist leader with a considered commitment to Irish unity was Michael Collins; see E Phoenix, 'Michael Collins: the northern question 1916–1922', in G Doherty and D Keogh (eds), *Michael Collins and the making of the Irish state* (Cork: Mercier, 1998), pp. 92–116.

9 M Laffan, *The partition of Ireland, 1911–25* (Dundalk: Dundalgan Press, 1983), pp. 104–5.

10 For a general description of the process, see D Birrell and A Murie, *Policy and government in Northern Ireland: lessons of devolution* (Dublin: Gill and Macmillan, 1980), pp. 132–5.

11 But there is evidence of some foot-dragging in Dublin in a least the area of education; see D H Akenson, *Education and enmity: the control of schooling in Northern Ireland 1920–50* (Newton Abbot: David and Charles, 1973), pp. 39–45.

12 See M Kennedy, *Division and consensus: the politics of cross-border relations in Ireland, 1925–1969* (Dublin: Institute of Public Administration, 2000).

13 The closest any of the northern (or former all-Ireland) parties came to contesting an election in the south was in 1927, when the National League briefly sought to revive the support base of the old Nationalist Party. In Northern Ireland, where a separate Labour Party was established in 1924, loose links with the Dublin-based party were retained until 1949, and revived in 1968 under the umbrella of a 'Council of Labour', but this structure, never particularly effective, evaporated after 1970. During the 1950s Irish Labour candidates enjoyed limited success in Stormont and local elections in Northern Ireland; see M Gallagher, *The Irish Labour Party in transition, 1957–82* (Dublin: Gill & Macmillan, 1982), pp. 131–5. On one occasion, Fianna Fáil contested a northern election: Éamon de Valera was elected to represent South Down in the Northern Ireland House of Commons in 1933.

14 On the general issue of partition, see D Gwynn, *The history of partition, 1912–1925* (Dublin: Browne and Nolan, 1950); Laffan, *Partition* (1983); T Hennessy, *Dividing Ireland: World War I and partition* (London: Routledge, 1998).

15. For an early, lively challenge to the nationalist consensus which, however, set the tone for much later revisionist writing by ignoring northern nationalists, see M Sheehy, *Divided we stand: a study of partition* (London: Faber and Faber, 1955), pp. 21–37.

16 See, for example, P Bew, P Gibbon and H Patterson, *Northern Ireland 1921–1996: political forces and social classes*, rev. edn. (London: Serif, 1996).

17 When the Ulster Unionist leader, Terence O'Neill, attempted a *rapprochement* with the South in the mid-1960s, opposition from within unionism to his initiative was one of the key factors in the destabilisation of Northern Ireland and the ultimate breakup of the monolithic ruling party.

18 See, for example, P Gibbon, *The origins of Ulster unionism* (Manchester: Manchester University Press, 1975).

19 British and Irish Communist Organisation, *The economics of partition*, 4th edn. (Belfast: British and Irish Communist Organisation, 1972), p. 6.

20 Bradley, 'History', pp. 42–3. This is challenged by observers who argue that the British–Irish economic relationship as a whole may be characterised historically as imperial and colonial; consequently, in this view, Ireland endured a process of economic peripheralisation, manifested differently on either side of the border, which removed the capacity of the Irish economies to innovate or even to 'hook on' to innovation. At the height of its power, in the nineteenth century English industry 'captured innovations' as it sought to restrict competitors (including Irish ones) and retain access to key raw materials, markets and supplies of labour; see D O'Hearn, 'Global restructuring and Irish political economy', in P Clancy, S Drudy, K Lynch and L O'Dowd (eds), *Irish society: sociological perspectives* (Dublin: Institute of Public Administration, 1995), pp. 90–131, at p. 119, and R Crotty, *Ireland in crisis: a study of capitalist colonial underdevelopment* (Dingle: Brandon Press, 1986).

21 See A J Motyl, *Imperial ends: the decay, collapse and revival of empires* (New York: Columbia University Press), p. 4. It was not only economics which sustained the British empire in this way; D Cannadine, *Ornamentalism: how the British saw their empire* (London: Penguin, 2002) has shown how a hierarchical 'ornamentalism' centred on the 'imperialized monarchy' (1850–1950) tied together the extraordinarily diverse, often exotic, political elements of the empire. Such ornamentalism also bound Northern Irish unionists to the monarchy while, until recently, nationalists refused to comply by accepting titles of honour.

22 See D Johnson, *The interwar economy in Ireland* (Dundalk: The Economic and Social History Society of Ireland, 1985) [*Studies in Irish economic and social history*, 4], pp. 3–5, and L Kennedy, *The modern industrialisation of Ireland, 1940–1988* (Dundalk: The Economic and Social History Society of Ireland, 1989) [*Studies in Irish economic and social history* 5], pp. 6–8.

23 See Lawrence, *Government of Northern Ireland* (1965), pp. 74–102. While taxation under the control of Northern Ireland (estate, stamp, motor vehicle and other licences) accounted for 17.9% of total taxation on average between 1929 and 1938, it had shrunk to 5.9% of the total in 1963 (p. 85).

24 See B Rowthorn and N Wayne, *Northern Ireland: the political economy of conflict* (Cambridge: Polity Press, 1988), and L O'Dowd, 'Development or dependency? State, economy and society in Northern Ireland', in Clancy et al., *Irish society* (1995), pp. 132–77.

25 Calculated from M E Daly, *Social and economic history of Ireland since 1800* (Dublin: Educational Company of Ireland, 1981), p. 137.

26 Bradley, 'History', pp. 42–3; see pp. 35–46 for an overview of pre-1960 economic history.

27 C Ó Gráda, *A rocky road: the Irish economy since the 1920s* (Manchester: Manchester University Press, 1997), pp. 79–80.

28 J Bradley, 'Economic aspects of the island of Ireland: an overview of the two economies', in J Bradley (ed.), *The two economies of Ireland: public policy, growth and employment* (Dublin: Oak Tree Press, 1995), pp. 7–34, p. 7.

29 Bradley, 'Economic aspects' (1995), pp. 7–8.

30 See P Ollerenshaw, 'Industry, 1820–1914', in L Kennedy and P Ollerenshaw (eds), *An economic history of Ulster, 1820–1939* (Manchester: Manchester University Press, 1985), pp. 62–108, at pp. 62–6. But this difference was commonly masked to nineteenth-century observers by the overall pattern of poverty and underdevelopment in Ireland. In 1886, for instance, Charles Booth's careful analysis of census data described a cycle of impoverishment, and 'a demoralisation of industry likely to be the cause, as well as consequence, of poverty and waning trade, and certain to be the source of political discontent', without noting any regional differences; see C Booth, 'Economic distribution of population in Ireland', in Department of Agriculture and Technical Instruction (ed.), *Ireland: industrial and agricultural* (Dublin: HMSO, 1901), pp. 54–62, at p. 56.

31 Lawrence, *Government of Northern Ireland* (1965), p. 20.

32 See C Ó Gráda and B Walsh, *Did (and does) the border matter?* (Dublin: Institute of British Irish Studies, 2006) [IBIS Working Paper no. 60]; also available at www.qub.ac.uk/cibr/mappingfrontierswps.htm.

33 At partition dense networks of railways did span the border, which cut the existing railway system at fifteen points, traversing some lines more than once. By the late 1950s, all cross-border rail lines had been closed except for the main Dublin–Belfast line. Sixteen cross-border roads were officially approved for customs purposes in 1923, but these co-existed with a complex network of approximately 180 unapproved cross-border roads; see L O'Dowd and J Corrigan, 'Securing the Irish border in a Europe without frontiers', in L O'Dowd and T Wilson (eds), *Borders, nations and states: frontiers*

of sovereignty in the new Europe (Aldershot: Avebury, 1996), p. 120.

34 Daly, *Social and economic history* (1981), pp. 137–8.

35 D S Johnson, 'The Northern Ireland economy, 1914–1939', in Kennedy and Ollerenshaw, *Economic history* (1985), pp. 184–223, at pp. 188–90.

36 See, for example, R O'Donnell and P Teague, 'The potential and limits to North–South economic cooperation', in P Teague (ed.), *The economy of Northern Ireland: perspectives for structural change* (London: Lawrence and Wishart, 1993), pp. 240–70, at pp. 265–6.

37 D Hamilton, 'Economic integration on the island of Ireland', *Administration* 49:2 (2001), pp. 73–89.

38 Hamilton, 'Economic integration' (2001), pp. 81–4.

39 For a discussion of various ways of defining civil society, see M Edwards, *Civil society* (Oxford: Polity, 2004). He distinguishes three dominant conceptions of civil society: (1) as public sphere; (2) as associational life; (3) as a metaphor for the 'good society'. In practice, these conceptions are often interwoven in empirical analyses of civil society.

40 L McClain and J Fleming, 'Some questions for civil society revivalists', *Chicago-Kent law review* 75:2 (2000), pp. 301–54.

41 See R Cathcart, *The most contrary region: the BBC in Northern Ireland 1924–1984* (Belfast: Blackstaff Press), and M McLoone and J Macmahon (eds), *Television in Irish society: 21 years of Irish television* (Dublin: RTE, 1984).

42 See, for example, D Miller, *Don't mention the war: Northern Ireland propaganda and the media* (London: Pluto Press, 1994), and B Rolston, *War and words: the Northern Ireland media reader* (Belfast: Beyond the Pale Publications, 1996).

43 Edwards, *Civil society* (2004), p. 20. J Keane, *Civil society: old images, new visions* (Stanford: Stanford University Press, 1998) is an example of a writer who incorporates the economy or the market into the concept of civil society. There is much debate in this tradition on what might be included in, and excluded from, the concept of civil society. American writing, on the whole, tends to conceptualise civil society as the non-profit sector.

44 One study found that 74% of voluntary organisations south of the border had 'contact' with counterpart organisations in Northern Ireland; F Powell and D Guerin, *Civil society and social policy: voluntarism in Ireland* (Dublin: A & A Farmar, 1997); another found that 60% of third-sector groups were 'involved in cross-border activities'; E Quinlivan, *Forging links: a study of cross-border community co-operation in the Irish border region* (Belfast: Co-operation Ireland, 1999). However, it has also been maintained that the number of such groups in the Republic of Ireland that are involved in 'promoting North–South dialogue and understanding' is relatively small, 'not much more than 20 organizations altogether'; B Harvey, *Rights and justice work in Ireland: a new base line* (York: Joseph Rowntree Charitable Trust, 2002), pp. 85–6.

45 D Ó Corráin, *The Irish churches and the two states in Ireland, 1949–73* (Manchester: Manchester University Press, 2006).

46 Both the Catholic Church and the Church of Ireland designate the Archbishop of Armagh as 'Primate of All Ireland', but each also recognises the Archbishop of Dublin as 'Primate of Ireland' – an ancient distinction that appears to follow that in the neighbouring island, where the Archbishop of York is 'Primate of England' and the Archbishop of Canterbury 'Primate of All England'. Notwithstanding long-running tussles between Dublin and Armagh, no clear distinction between the roles of the two offices has emerged. In the Catholic Church, recent developments suggest that the Dublin Primacy may now be the more important of the two.

47 The Republic accounted for 84% of all Catholics in the island in 2001–2; the corresponding figures for the Church of Ireland and the Presbyterian Church were 31% and 6%; calculated from Census of Ireland, 2002, and Census of Northern Ireland, 2001.

48 For a historical account, see C McCarthy, *Trade unions in Ireland 1894–1960* (Dublin: Institute of Public Administration, 1977), and T Cradden, *Trade unionism, socialism and partition: the labour movement in Northern Ireland, 1939–53* (Belfast: December Publications, 1993).

49 This conception is represented in works such as R Putnam, *Making democracy work: civic traditions in modern Italy* (Princeton: Princeton University Press, 1993), and A Etzioni, *The spirit of community* (London: Fontana, 1993).

50 See, for example, A Guelke, 'Civil society and the Northern Ireland peace process', *Voluntas* 14:1 (2003), pp. 61–78, who argues that republican and unionist accounts fail to accord a positive role to civil society in the peace process, in contrast to 'metropolitan' accounts.

51 See A Pollak (ed.), *A citizens' inquiry: the Opsahl Report on Northern Ireland* (Dublin: Lilliput Press, 1993).

Part 2

Parameters of the North–South relationship

2

Institutional cooperation: the North–South implementation bodies

JOHN COAKLEY, BRIAN Ó CAOINDEALBHÁIN
AND ROBIN WILSON

INTRODUCTION

On 2 December 1999, an unprecedented political event took place in Ireland: after almost eighty years of fully fledged partition, a set of public sector bodies whose writ extended over the whole island came into existence. This radical departure from the practices of the past formed part of the complex architecture of the 1998 agreement, and the new bodies had a clearly defined role within this. But, as is well known to policy analysts, the creation of new institutions by legislative fiat is no more than that: formal existence on paper must be followed through by the establishment of functioning bodies, with buildings, staff, budgets and clearly defined goals. Moreover, new institutions of the kind that appeared in 1999 offer an additional challenge to governments; they present a particular coordination dilemma to the extent that they straddle conventional departments. Quite apart from these institutional difficulties, though, the new bodies were caught in the middle of a long-term political standoff that seriously compromised their capacity to respond to change.

Our object in this chapter is to assess the progress made since 1999 in giving life to the new North–South bodies in circumstances which have been particularly challenging. We do this by providing first an account of the broad political background to institutional North–South cooperation in Ireland. We then examine the more specific context within which the bodies appeared – the 1998 agreement, which continues to define their mode of operation. We follow this with a general overview of the functioning of the bodies, including not just the six established explicitly by the agreement but also a *de facto* seventh body, Tourism Ireland. We explicitly exclude the important area of policy cooperation outside the framework of the implementation bodies for which the agreement also made provision;

we discuss it briefly below, but detailed discussion would lie beyond the scope of this chapter.

THE CONSOLIDATION OF PARTITION

The partition of Ireland in 1921 may have been intended as a pragmatic political solution to apparently irreconcilable demands by the two main communities on the island of Ireland, but it undoubtedly led to a degree of administrative disruption that was intended by no one and that can have been welcomed by very few. As we have seen in chapter 1, partition had profound implications for Ireland's network of public bodies, which up to that point fell into two categories. First, several important bodies forming part of the 'imperial' civil service were managed directly from London under the political direction of UK cabinet ministers: the Post Office, the foreign service and the military, for instance. Second, an impressive range of bodies formed a separate 'Irish' civil service, under the political control of the Chief Secretary for Ireland (who was also a UK cabinet minister): education, health, local government and policing, for instance.

The implications of partition were different for these two sets of bodies, and were made yet more complex when the symmetrical arrangements of the Government of Ireland Act which had ushered in partition in 1921 were overturned in 1922. The replacement of 'Southern Ireland' by the Irish Free State – no longer an autonomous part of the United Kingdom, but a separate British dominion with the same status as Canada – was important for post-partition institution building. First, it meant that the 'imperial' services would simply retract to the new, rather smaller surviving (Northern) Irish portion of the United Kingdom, leaving the Irish Free State to set up its own postal system, diplomatic service and defence forces entirely separate from those of the United Kingdom.[1] Second, the 'Irish' civil service would be partitioned, leaving Northern Ireland to set up entirely new bodies that would in general duplicate functionally those in Dublin. It might have been thought that this common background would at least have fostered informal North–South cooperation after partition, based on personal ties and associations among officials, but in practice contacts were minimal in the ensuing decades.[2] Separatist zeal in the two parts of the island extended also to what would have been the only surviving political link between the two jurisdictions. Specific provision had been made for an inter-parliamentary Council of Ireland linking North and South, politically important as an embryonic Irish parliament, but with responsibilities confined to a small number of areas:

private bill legislation, railways, fisheries and infectious diseases of animals. Even these modest functions disappeared in 1925, when a tripartite agreement between the Irish, Northern Irish and British governments scrapped the council, dividing its few functions between the Dublin and Belfast administrations.

For four decades after 1925, a frosty political atmosphere between North and South inhibited administrative cooperation. For many on the southern side, working with the northern authorities implied acceptance of partition, while, from a unionist point of view, closer interaction was feared as a potential mechanism for furthering Irish unity. Although the 1925 agreement had provided for continuing interaction between the northern and southern governments, and the two premiers, William Cosgrave and James Craig, appear to have envisaged some degree of cooperation on matters of common concern, tentative early contacts petered out.[3]

Relations between Dublin and Belfast underwent further strain following the 1932 general election in the South and the formation of a Fianna Fáil government under Éamon de Valera, who was committed to revision of the 1921 Anglo-Irish treaty and who compounded unionist insecurity by engaging in periodic rhetorical attacks on partition. His protectionist economic policies further angered the northern authorities, with exports from Northern Ireland to the Irish Free State suffering disproportionately under a new tariff regime. Nor did de Valera's departure from office in 1948 improve matters. The formation in that year of an all-party anti-partition movement and the new coalition government's decision to declare Ireland a republic and withdraw from the Commonwealth raised tensions further. London responded swiftly by passing legislation which reinforced Northern Ireland's position in the United Kingdom, making its future status dependent on the will of the Northern Ireland parliament.[4]

Where cooperation did occur during this period it was largely mediated through contacts between civil servants, and then only when this could hardly be avoided. While the archives show that issues of mutual concern such as fishing rights, river drainage and electricity interconnection were discussed with pragmatism at 'semi-official' level (thus fostering good and enduring working relationships between those involved), the benefits of joint action were insufficient to overcome the suspicions of the political authorities on the two sides. Over the whole period from partition to the outbreak of the 'troubles', indeed, there were only four areas of significant cooperation between the two administrations: electricity transmission, electricity generation, railways, and fisheries (interestingly, in the last two of these areas such cooperation had been envisaged in the Government of Ireland Act). It is worth examining these further, as they illustrate both the pressures that inhibited cooperation and the pitfalls that obstructed its efficient operation.[5]

The first steps towards North–South electricity cooperation developed in the late 1930s under the pressure of increasing international tensions. Civil servants on both sides had intermittently floated the idea of a cross-border electricity interconnector, but the political climate ensured that this had never progressed beyond vague proposals. With the outbreak of war, however, the protection of electricity supplies became a key strategic issue. By November 1940 the Irish government was actively considering an electricity connection in the context of wartime emergency planning, but the issue was not sufficiently compelling to overcome unionist suspicions until the Luftwaffe raids of April 1941 brought home to the Stormont cabinet the vulnerability of Northern Ireland's electricity supply, given its dependence on a single power station located in the heavily targeted docklands area. After much debate, and under pressure from London, it was reluctantly agreed to proceed with a stand-by electricity connection between North and South. Crucially, the link-up was realised through a commercial agreement between the electricity companies in the two jurisdictions, and the details were worked out by public officials on both sides without any formal intergovernmental contact.[6]

The second issue was a distinct but related one. In the early 1940s, electricity generation in the South was operating at full capacity and the Electricity Supply Board (ESB) began planning for the expected post-war surge in demand. One option was a hydroelectric power station on the river Erne between Belleek and Ballyshannon, which could generate between 50 and 80 megawatts of power and allow a surplus to be sold to Northern Ireland. However, for this scheme to achieve its maximum potential it would be necessary to carry out engineering works across the border around the Erne lakes. The ESB was willing to finance these works, which would also, as a by-product, alleviate the long-standing flooding problem in the area. This proposal was particularly attractive to the northern government, which was being offered a solution to the Erne drainage problems at no cost to itself. Notwithstanding reservations in the northern cabinet, the plan's supporters, who included influential civil servants and, significantly, the prime minister, Brooke, won through.[7] As in the case of the emergency electricity interconnector in 1941–2, the actual details were worked out between officials, with no direct contact between the two governments, but in 1950 identical bills were passed in the Irish and Northern Irish parliaments, providing a legislative basis for the scheme, which was finally completed in 1957.

The third instance of cross-border cooperation arose from the threatened closure of the Great Northern Railway Company. The company operated a number of cross-border lines, including the important Dublin–Belfast service, but its viability was in doubt in the context of increasing competition from road transport. Neither government was willing to see the rail link severed, or to accept the economic and employment consequences of closure. In August 1950 the Northern Ireland Minister of Commerce, William McCleery, travelled to Dublin to negotiate a possible solution with the Republic's Minister for Industry and Commerce, Daniel Morrissey – the first direct ministerial contact since 1925. It was finally agreed in early 1951 that the governments would jointly purchase the company as a going concern. But this first North–South intergovernmental experiment in joint authority proved not to be a success. Weakened by political disputes, declining revenue, and restrictive political controls, the company was finally wound up in 1958 and its assets were divided between Córas Iompair Éireann (CIÉ) and the Ulster Transport Authority.[8]

The fourth example provides an illustration of a more successful form of cooperation. Lough Foyle had been a source of dispute between Dublin and Belfast since partition, with both sides claiming jurisdiction over the strategically important waterway. The issue was further complicated by a dispute over fishing rights in the lough, with the historical claims of the Irish Society (a body dating from the plantation of Ulster in the seventeenth century) to ownership of the fishery contested by the South. The issue was brought to a head in 1948 when the Irish Society took legal action in the southern courts to establish its title to the fisheries. The two governments agreed in 1950 to buy out the Irish Society. Legislation was passed in Dublin and Belfast, and in 1952 the Foyle Fisheries Commission came into being, with a remit of managing and developing the fishery on behalf of the two governments. The commission was to prove one of the most enduring examples of North–South cooperation, functioning successfully up to 1999 when it was absorbed into the Foyle, Carlingford and Irish Lights Commission (see below).

While the above examples of cooperation in the 1950s were problem- rather than policy-driven, there emerged in the South in this decade a much more pragmatic approach to cross-border relations. Against a background of new outward-looking economic policies and growing functional cooperation on the continent, anti-partition rhetoric was slowly displaced. Cooperation on matters of common concern was now advocated in the Republic as the most effective route to eventual unity. This new thinking was strongly supported by Lemass and, following his appointment as taoiseach in 1959, he sought to establish a productive working relationship with Stormont.[9] Contacts increased at an administrative level and, following the historic exchange visits between Lemass and the new northern prime minister, Terence O'Neill, in 1965, cooperation was placed on a more structured basis, with ministerial meetings becoming common.

However, this new *rapprochement* was overtaken by the outbreak of civil unrest in 1968. It was only following the installation of direct rule from London in 1972 that formalised North–South cooperation once again found a place on the agenda. As is well known, the Sunningdale agreement of December 1973 made provision for a new, interparliamentary Council of Ireland, though the details of the areas over which it would exercise jurisdiction were not specified (the provisional list included natural resources and environment, agriculture, trade and industry, electricity generation, tourism, roads and transport, advisory health services, and sport, culture and the arts; and, at a later stage, possibly policing). But elaboration of a detailed blueprint was overtaken by political events. Following a general strike in May 1974 that attracted massive support from the unionist community, the new power-sharing executive in Belfast collapsed, and with it disappeared for the time being the prospect of new North–South institutions.

Another significant development at this time was Ireland's accession in 1973 to membership of what is now the European Union.[10] The EU's focus on the need to transcend borders and promote free movement of people, goods and services encouraged a particular interest in funding border-related projects. Under the umbrella of the regional development fund, a special border-area programme was launched in 1980 and renewed in 1985, though it provided for separate funding on the two sides of the border rather than an integrated approach linking the two. Later EU initiatives in the area of regional policy provided stronger incentives for cross-border cooperation and promoted much higher levels of contact in border regions (the most important was the Interreg programme, 1989–93, which was followed by Interreg II in 1994–9 and Interreg III in 2000–6; see chapters 6 and 11).[11]

Notwithstanding the hostility of unionist leaders to southern involvement in the North, the Dublin–Belfast axis was increasingly bypassed by a Dublin–London one which acknowledged the interest of the Irish government in Northern Ireland. This culminated in the Anglo-Irish agreement of 1985, a landmark innovation that was important from two perspectives. First, with a view to giving the Irish government a voice in the running of Northern Ireland, it provided for an inter-ministerial Anglo-Irish Intergovernmental Conference with a standing secretariat made up of civil servants from the two jurisdictions. Located in Maryfield near Stormont, the secretariat gave the Irish government a direct presence in Northern Ireland, with the capacity to provide information on matters of central interest, particularly in the area of security. Second, the agreement offered a powerful incentive to unionists to negotiate with a view to replacing an arrangement which they found profoundly objectionable – an incentive finally realised in a new agreement in 1998.[12] It is to this agreement, and the North–South bodies for which it made provision, that we now turn.

THE 1998 AGREEMENT AND THE NORTH–SOUTH BODIES

As is well known, the 1998 agreement covered a very wide range of areas, including three 'strands' which made provision for new institutions: strand one dealing with institutions within Northern Ireland, strand two covering the North–South relationship and strand three focusing on the Irish–British relationship.[13] Our concern here is with the second strand – or, rather, with one element of this. Strand two made provision for a redefinition of the arrangements made in 1985, replacing the 'Anglo-Irish' secretariat in Maryfield by a 'British–Irish' secretariat which now has its headquarters in central Belfast, but whose areas of responsibility are restricted to those not allocated to devolved institutions in Northern Ireland. But it also made provision for more explicit, bilateral North–South cooperation. Under the umbrella of a North/South Ministerial Council, formal cooperation would occur in six areas where existing agencies North and South would collaborate, and special implementation bodies would be established in a further six areas (the twelve areas were animal and plant health, teacher qualifications, transport planning, environment, inland waterways, cross-border workers, tourism, EU programmes, inland fisheries, aquaculture, emergency services, and urban and rural development). This list represented a significant victory for Ulster Unionist leader David Trimble in the late stages of the negotiation of the agreement, as the original blueprint for cooperation had offered a much longer list, extending over sixty areas for cooperation or for implementation bodies.[14]

The details as to how the new bodies were to come into existence were left to negotiations, and an agreement was finally reached between the Irish government and the northern parties on 18 December 1998. This provided that the first four areas listed above, together with tourism and health, would be subject to formal North–South cooperation between existing agencies. In three further areas (inland waterways, EU programmes and aquaculture) special implementation bodies would be established. The three remaining areas (cross-border workers, inland fisheries and urban and rural development) were set aside, but implementation bodies to replace these were to be established for food safety, trade and business development, and language (Irish and Ulster Scots).[15] Legal provision for these initiatives was made by a British–Irish agreement on 8 March 1999.[16]

Even though all arrangements for this new initiative were in place by early 1999, it was not until December 1999 that the bodies were formally launched. This long delay was caused by the fact that the North–South dimension formed part of a much broader political framework of interlocking institutions, and none could come into existence until agreement on the details of all had been reached. The most difficult issue was that of IRA disarmament. It was only by fudging this that the agreement came into force on 2 December 1999; and the dissatisfaction of the Ulster Unionist First Minister, David Trimble, with progress in this area caused him to procure the suspension of the devolved institutions from 11 February to 30 May 2000, and again, this time in the long term, on 14 October 2002. Given the interdependence of the institutions, this posed particular difficulties for the North–South bodies. The original hostility of the Democratic Unionist Party to the North–South dimension was a further obstacle, though it later became clear that the party would indeed accept the North–South bodies; it did so, subject to certain assurances regarding accountability, in the St Andrews agreement of 13 October 2006.

The North–South bodies need to be seen in the context of the political arrangements that oversee their operation.[17] As provided by the agreement, the bodies operate under the oversight of the North/South Ministerial Council (NSMC). This body met in full plenary format on four occasions before the devolved institutions were suspended in October 2002, the meetings being attended in each case by most members of the Irish government and of the Northern Ireland executive: on 13 December 1999 in Armagh, on 26 September 2000 and 30 November 2001 in Dublin, and on 28 June 2002 in Armagh. But it is at sectoral meetings of the NSMC that most of the decisions regarding the establishment and development of the bodies have been made. Before the suspension of devolution, sixty such meetings had taken place, each involving the relevant southern minister for the area in question, his or her northern counterpart, and another northern minister from the 'other' political tradition.

Of the sixty meetings, thirty-six dealt with the operation of the implementation bodies: eight with the Foyle, Carlingford and Irish Lights Commission, seven each with the trade body and with the Special EU Programmes Body, five each with Waterways Ireland and with the Food Safety Promotion Body, and four with the language body. A further five meetings addressed the area of tourism, in which a *de facto* seventh body appeared. These proved sufficient to cover the early stages in setting the bodies up, but this level of political oversight came to an end in October

2002 with the suspension of the Northern Ireland executive. Since the stakes were so high (with the status of several hundred employees of the implementation bodies being potentially called into question), special arrangements were then made by the two governments. An agreement on 19 November 2002 provided that the oversight responsibility from the northern side could be exercised by the British government and parliament until such time as devolution was restored. It was, however, provided that no additional functions would be conferred on the bodies through these arrangements, meaning that they would operate essentially on a 'care and maintenance' basis.[18] Between 6 December 2002 and 13 October 2006, 167 formal agreements between the two governments were made in respect of the six implementation bodies and Tourism Ireland, covering areas ranging from budgets and board appointments to specific administrative matters.[19]

Table 2.1. North–South implementation bodies: staffing levels and budgets, 2006

Body	Staff, 2006	Budget, 2006	*%NI*	*%RI*
Waterways Ireland	347	47.84	27.5	72.5
Safefood	34	10.06	30.0	70.0
InterTrade Ireland	45	14.81	33.8	66.2
Special EU Programmes Body	45	3.22	56.2	43.8
Language Body	62	22.95	32.2	67.8
Foras na Gaeilge	*52*	*19.86*	*25.4*	*74.6*
Ulster-Scots Agency	*10*	*3.09*	*75.5*	*24.5*
Foyle, Carlingford and Irish Lights Commission	48	5.28	50.0	50.0
Tourism Ireland Ltd	152	63.60	28.7	71.3
Total	733	167.76	30.5	69.5

Note: Staffing levels refer to the position on 5 October 2006, and include temporary and seconded as well as permanent staff. Budget figures are expressed in millions of euro. The third and fourth columns of figures indicate the proportion of the budget of each body that is due from the Northern Ireland and Irish exchequers respectively. The staff and budget of the Commissioners of Irish Lights are not included in this table. In the case of the Special EU Programmes Body, the great bulk of revenue and expenditure relates to programmes administered by the body, and is not reflected in this table; in 2005, for instance, its total revenue amounted to €175m.

Source: Information provided by the North/South Ministerial Council secretariat.

The overall staffing levels and budgets of the bodies are summarised in Table 2.1, which makes clear their considerable variation in size (the large field staff of Waterways Ireland dwarfs the employee base of the other bodies). The column dealing with budgets may be misleading: the body with the smallest allocation, the Special EU Programmes Body, is in fact responsible for administering by far the largest tranche of funds, but these monies – mainly from the EU – are not included in the table.

The bodies also have distinctive management arrangements – reflecting, apparently, compromises designed to ensure that none of the bodies would embark on an excessively independent course (which unionists might fear as leading potentially to an erosion of the border). The two bodies where these concerns were largely absent, Waterways Ireland and the Special EU Programmes Body, have a straightforward structure: they are run by a chief executive appointed by the NSMC. Two other bodies, Safefood and InterTrade Ireland, also have chief executives appointed by the NSMC, but in each case there is a board (called an 'advisory' board in the case of Safefood) which is required to have between eight and twelve members. In the case of Safefood, the NSMC appoints an additional scientific advisory committee, made up in 2005 of eighteen members representing scientific expertise and food safety interests. The two remaining implementation bodies have a more complex make-up. The language body is managed by a twenty-four-person board appointed by the NSMC, but this comprises two sets of members, sixteen representing Irish language interests and eight representing Ulster Scots. This reflects the division of the body into two agencies, one now known as Foras na Gaeilge, the other as Tha Boord o Ulstèr-Scotch. Each has its own chairperson, who acts as joint chairperson of the language body. The board appoints two chief executives, one for each agency, subject to NSMC approval. It was provided that the Foyle, Carlingford and Irish Lights Commission would be similarly divided into two agencies, the Loughs Agency (with responsibility for Lough Foyle and for Carlingford Lough) and the Lights Agency (which would take on the functions of the Commissioners of Irish Lights), but, as discussed below, only the first of these agencies has come into existence. Its chief executive is appointed by the board, subject to the approval of the NSMC.

The conditions governing board membership are the same in all cases. The initial boards were appointed for three-year terms, but provision was made that later terms might be varied by the NSMC, provided none exceeded five years. No one was to serve for more than two consecutive terms, and provision was made for the dismissal of board members by the NSMC. The NSMC appoints the two chairs of the language body, and appoints the chair and vice-chair in the case of the three remaining bodies. Board members themselves are selected to maintain an appropriate North–South balance, and the composition of the boards reflects the kinds of political compromise that were integral to the agreement itself.

The position in the tourism sector is rather different. There, agreement was reached by the Irish government and the Northern Ireland executive that a publicly owned limited company would be established by the two existing tourism agencies (Bord Fáilte in the Republic and the Northern Ireland Tourism Board) to promote the island as a tourist destination in an integrated way. The new body, Tourism Ireland, has a twelve-person board representing its stakeholders, and selects its own chief executive.

THE NORTH–SOUTH BODIES AT WORK

Although the new bodies have been at least formally in existence since 1999, for political and other reasons most of them experienced significant start-up difficulties, and all have suffered from a leadership vacuum at the political level since 2002. A full review of their operation and of their success in tackling their objectives might thus be premature, but it is nevertheless worth reviewing their work briefly. We may do this by considering the bodies in turn.[20]

Waterways Ireland

In many respects, Waterways Ireland has been the most visible of the bodies: its specific but broad mandate, impact on the landscape, large staff (the largest of all the bodies, by far) and high profile in the leisure sector have given it a positive and relatively uncontroversial image among the public at large. Its programme also attracted an unusually wide degree of cross-party support, with even DUP politicians endorsing its proposed restoration of the Ulster Canal. The importance of the all-Ireland dimension was reflected in the fact that there already existed an important civil-society body, the Inland Waterways Association of Ireland, founded as a lobby group in 1954 and currently with seventeen branches, twelve in the Republic and five in Northern Ireland.[21]

The body is run by a chief executive appointed by the NSMC, without the kind of board that is typical of the other bodies. Its formal terms of reference were defined as follows (it should be noted that in practice the emphasis on the Lagan system has been dropped, and the body has responsibility for two other areas, the Lower Bann and the Shannon Navigation):[22]

> Management, maintenance, development and restoration of the inland navigable waterway system throughout the island, principally for recreational purposes: immediately in respect of the Shannon–Erne Waterway and of the possible restoration and development of the Ulster Canal; progressively thereafter, in respect of the wider Shannon–Erne system and the island's other waterways (principally the Royal Canal, Grand Canal, Barrow and Lagan). The Body would take on the functions, together with the appropriate support functions, exercised in that regard by the Waterways Service of the Department of Arts, Heritage, Gaeltacht and the Islands and the Rivers Agency of the Department of Agriculture in Northern Ireland, and would also take over the functions of Shannon–Erne Waterway Promotions Ltd.

The new body appeared to provide sensible rationalisation of a waterways network in respect of which island-level planning made sense. Up to that point, the planning and management of Ireland's waterways was disjointed. The major waterways of Northern Ireland, such as the Erne system and the Lower Bann, were managed by the Rivers Agency of the Department of Agriculture. In the South, the Office of Public Works (established in 1831 to manage, *inter alia*, state property in Ireland) had controlled the Shannon navigation since the nineteenth century and was given charge of the other waterways in 1986. Responsibility for all of these was transferred to the Waterways Service of the Department of Arts, Heritage, the Gaeltacht and the Islands in 1996. The waterways included two large navigable river systems that had been developed for commercial traffic, the Shannon and the Barrow; the Grand Canal, opened in 1804 to link Dublin with the Barrow and the lower Shannon; and the Royal Canal, opened in 1817 to link Dublin with the upper Shannon (the two canals, by then controlled by the state railway company, CIÉ, had been closed since 1961). There was also a newcomer: the old Ballinamore–Ballyconnell Canal, opened in 1860 to link the Shannon and Erne systems but closed only nine years later, had been redeveloped and reopened for leisure traffic in 1994 with funding from the British and Irish governments and from the International Fund for Ireland. A new company, Shannon–Erne Waterway Promotions Ltd, had been set up to manage and market the canal.

The new body was set up with an interim chief executive and an interim headquarters in Dublin, and was given the name 'Waterways Ireland'. Within a short time, it had moved to its permanent headquarters in Enniskillen and a permanent chief executive had been appointed. Regional offices were opened in Dublin, Scariff and Carrick-on-Shannon, reflecting the wide spatial span of the new body's responsibilities. Since its establishment, its main work has been in the area of managing and upgrading existing facilities (including continuing work on the restoration of the Royal Canal, and extension of the Shannon navigation from Lough Key to Boyle). The principal new area of potential activity is the restoration of the Ulster Canal, which would link the Shannon–Erne system with Lough Neagh and the Bann – a considerable engineering challenge, but a project to which the Irish government expressed its renewed commitment in late 2006.

Safefood

Although there was a tradition of cross-border interaction on food safety, albeit on an informal case-by-case basis, it was not included on the initial list of subjects marked for cooperation in the Good Friday agreement. It was, therefore, something of a surprise when it was agreed during the December 1998 negotiations that a North–South implementation body was to be established in this area. The Food Safety Promotion Board, which operates under the name Safefood, has a broad range of responsibilities, embracing both the promotion of food safety on the island and North–South scientific collaboration in the area of food-borne diseases. Its full formal remit is as follows:

- promotion of food safety
- research into food safety
- communication of food alerts
- surveillance of food-borne diseases
- promotion of scientific cooperation and linkages between laboratories
- development of cost-effective facilities for specialised laboratory testing.

Despite the clear rationale for cross-border cooperation on food safety, the new body was entering a rather crowded institutional landscape. In the North, the Food Standards Agency Northern Ireland (FSANI) oversees the enforcement of food safety legislation, while its parent body, the Food Standards Agency (FSA), has a UK-wide remit to protect consumers from food-related health risks and to provide information on food safety and healthy eating issues. The Food Safety Authority of Ireland (FSAI) has a similar role in the South, with an overall responsibility for coordinating enforcement and setting standards for food safety.

Safefood thus faced a key challenge of finding a niche for itself which would complement, rather than duplicate, the work of the existing bodies.

Its founding legislation set out some parameters, making clear that the existing arrangements for enforcement and inspection would continue to apply and, interestingly, that the prior bodies would retain their promotional roles in relation to compliance issues. However, there remains a degree of uncertainty about the exact division of labour between the agencies, and this, in practice, is worked out on an *ad hoc* basis.[23] Structures have been established for sharing information and coordinating activities, in particular public campaigns, with regular bilateral meetings between Safefood and the other two agencies, and frequent contact at all levels of the organisations. Interaction between the bodies has also been facilitated by the appointment, in a personal capacity, of senior technical staff members from the FSAI and FSANI to Safefood's scientific advisory committee and by the establishment, in 2005, of an All-Island Food and Nutrition Forum, which provides a platform for collaboration and exchange of information on nutrition issues.

Safefood's initial efforts to define its role were not helped by political events in Northern Ireland. Apart from the general difficulties faced by all the North–South bodies as a result of the suspension of the devolved institutions in the period February–May 2000, it was faced with an additional obstacle when the ongoing dispute over IRA decommissioning resulted in UUP First Minister David Trimble refusing to nominate Sinn Féin ministers to attend North–South meetings from October 2000 to November 2001. As Safefood fell within the responsibilities of Sinn Féin Health Minister Bairbre de Brún, the NSMC was unable to give direction to the body's activities in this period, with the result that it could not make permanent appointments or finalise its structures. The new organisation therefore faced considerable start-up challenges, having no pre-existing structures to draw on and having an initial complement of only seven temporary staff. It was nevertheless able eventually to establish a headquarters in Littleisland, Cork, and the November 2001 sectoral meeting of the NSMC finally approved the body's management and staffing structure and put it on a permanent basis.

The body has been active in carrying out its scientific remit and in encouraging North–South collaboration. It has commissioned numerous research projects and has attempted to foster greater interaction and information exchange between food science laboratories on the island, for example by developing research networks, staff mobility programmes, and an all-island directory of laboratory services. It has also sought to improve cross-border cooperation in the event of food disease outbreaks, organising training programmes for health professionals in border areas and seeking to ensure North–South coordination in disease surveillance and communication of food alerts.

As a new arrival in the food safety field, one of the body's priorities has been to create awareness of its role and to establish itself as an authoritative source of information. It has been highly visible in the media, carrying out a number of food safety campaigns which have sought to develop the 'Safefood' brand and promote its consumer helpline. In seeking to pursue its promotional role on an all-island basis, Safefood has had to tailor its communication strategies to the different media markets, with radio advertising not as effective in Northern Ireland due to the dominance of the non-commercial BBC. Its campaigns there are further complicated by the need to have regard to UK-wide campaigns run by the FSA, and by a perception that it is a 'southern' body. In common with the other North–South bodies it faces the administrative burden of dealing with two different sets of legislative requirements and two different bureaucracies, each with their own cultures and priorities.

InterTrade Ireland

The creation of a body dealing with business cooperation was another of the surprises in the December 1998 agreement. Initially named the Trade and Business Development Body, it was given a wide mandate to promote North–South cooperation in business-related matters. Its formal terms of reference are:

> To exchange information and coordinate work on trade, business development and related matters, in areas where the two administrations specifically agree it would be in their mutual interest. The specific areas of implementation would include:
>
> - cooperation on business development opportunities, North and South;
> - devising new approaches to business development in a cross-border context, in such areas as research, training, marketing and quality improvement;
> - supporting business by making recommendations to increase enterprise competitiveness in a North–South context in areas such as skills availability, telecoms, IT and electronic commerce;
> - promotion of North–South trade and supply chains, including through business linkages and partnerships;
> - promoting cross-border trade events and marketing initiatives;
> - identifying new areas of trade between North and South;
> - promoting market awareness and trade development in a North–South context;

- undertaking specific projects and events in relation to trade promotion, when tasked jointly on a project by project basis;
- providing advice on specific aspects of trade promotion, when tasked jointly to do so.

The new body began its operations in an entirely new area, where no body had existed previously (though substantial voluntary efforts to promote North–South business cooperation had taken place, and existing economic agencies North and South would continue). As its name suggests, an underlying assumption of its foundation was that trade between the two jurisdictions was less than optimal. Indeed, trade with Northern Ireland as a proportion of Republic of Ireland trade has been in long-term decline since around 1960, remarkably unaffected by the pattern of civil unrest.[24] A further assumption was the notion that mainly Protestant northern businesspeople, already cooperating with their southern counterparts through their respective organisations, the Confederation of British Industry (CBI) and the Irish Business and Employers' Confederation (IBEC), would set political differences aside to realise economic gains. IBEC's predecessor, the Confederation of Irish Industry, had indeed produced a study in 1992 which suggested that an additional £3 billion could be generated from North–South trade, leading to predictions of a large expansion in employment.[25]

On the other hand, as the information revolution has replaced industrial capitalism in a globalised environment, the key to economic performance is the network rather than the individual firm.[26] The challenge facing InterTrade Ireland is thus not to match firms in one jurisdiction with consumers in the other, but to develop collaborative partnerships which ensure that the border is traversed by networks operating seamlessly throughout the island. Examples already in existence include the IBEC–CBI Joint Council, the Chamberlink network of chambers of commerce and the Irish Congress of Trade Unions (all-Ireland body). Indeed, the very existence of these prior civic connections, paving the way for InterTrade Ireland as an organic, facilitating development, goes some way to explaining the success of this body.

The centrality of this point to InterTrade Ireland's thinking was made clear in its 2002–4 corporate plan, where it described its economic rationale in sophisticated terms, connecting the economic and the political via the related notions of trust and 'social capital':

> The political imperative is clearly the consolidation of the peace process in a manner that will facilitate the development of networks of trust across the island. The implicit economic rationale is that increased

> coordination of trade and business activity can help engineer the realization of economic spillovers and synergies that will mutually benefit both the North and the South … The realisation of economic spillovers and synergies may also generate higher volumes of trade between the two jurisdictions but increasing the volume of trade per se should not be regarded as the main performance measurement of the effectiveness of InterTrade Ireland. Quite apart from the fact that simply measuring the flow of trade poses methodological difficulties, the total volume of trade is predominated [*sic*] by low-technology products … The future competitiveness of the island economy and of both jurisdictions which comprise it, will depend upon coordinating and exchanging information and knowledge which will improve the capability of indigenous businesses to trade higher up the value chain.[27]

Brokering supply-chain networks in or around transnational companies in Ireland is one specific way of doing this.[28] By the end of 2005, InterTrade Ireland had already created sixty North–South partnerships and eight new facilities, an achievement that bodes well for the future work of the body, but many obstacles remain in the path of promoting Ireland as a single investment location (the absence of a single, island-wide rate of corporation tax is just one of these, though a very important one).

The Special EU Programmes Body (SEUPB)

This body was initially given very specific and, indeed, time-bound functions: to supervise and administer existing EU programmes, such as Interreg and Peace, and to assume similar responsibilities in respect of new programmes over the period 2000–6 – in particular, in respect of policies covered by the 'common chapter' shared by development plans over this period in Northern Ireland and the Republic (see chapter 11). Its formal terms of reference are defined as follows:

> Until the conclusion of the current Community Initiatives:
>
> - the central secretariat, monitoring, research, evaluation, technical assistance and development roles currently exercised jointly in respect of Interreg and Peace by the Department of Finance and the Department of Finance and Personnel;
> - administration of certain sectoral sub-programmes under Interreg and Peace (interest rate subsidy and cross border cooperation between public bodies).

In relation to post-1999 Structural Funds:

- advising North/South Ministerial Council and two Departments of Finance on negotiation with the EU Commission of post-1999 Community Initiatives and of Common chapter;
- preparing, for the approval of the two administrations in the Council and in close consultation with the two Departments of Finance and other relevant Departments, detailed programme proposals under the new Community Initiatives (likely to be Interreg III, Leader+ and Equal, and possibly a successor to Peace);
- central secretariat, monitoring, research, evaluation, technical assistance and development roles in respect of these Initiatives;
- grant-making and other managerial functions in respect of Interreg III and of North–South elements of programmes under other initiatives, within the framework of the relevant overall policies of North and South respectively, and subject to the expenditure allocations and specific programme parameters agreed between the two administrations and with the EU Commission;
- monitoring and promoting implementation of the Common chapter, which would have a specific budgetary allocation.

The body essentially gave a more institutionalised structure to earlier arrangements for cooperation in respect of the administration of joint North–South interests in EU-funded programmes. By embracing a range of programmes, it has allowed a more integrated approach to the various sources of EU funding, moving away from the earlier dispersal of management capacity throughout the two administrations.

The largest programme under the aegis of the body by far is Peace II, which had spent €978 million on 6,500 projects by November 2006. The spatial focus of certain of the more central instruments in this programme (on Northern Ireland and the six border counties of the Republic, or only twelve counties in all) has, however, been of long-standing concern.[29] While the case for regeneration of the border counties is overwhelming, many aspects of the associated reconciliation process have a clear island-wide (and not merely cross-border) dimension, one which is hampered by the narrower geographical structure of the programme. The only source of funding for broader activities of this kind, other than that privately raised by such bodies as Co-operation Ireland, would be the Reconciliation Fund operated by the Department of Foreign Affairs – modest in scale, and therefore with limited capacity to fill the gap that will increasingly loom as EU support diminishes.

The SEUPB also has responsibility for the Interreg programme, which to an extent offsets 'back to back' development on the island. Within this programme, the body has favoured a more consistent approach to cross-border cooperation. In December 2000, for instance, the European Commission sent back the draft Irish Interreg III programme, on the grounds that it offered little practical support to the SEUPB and reflected only weak cooperation between Belfast and Dublin.[30] The commission also sought more recognition for the three local authority-based cross-border networks; as with InterTrade Ireland, the success of the SEUPB depends on moving away from the hierarchical approach conventionally favoured by government towards one of managing the networks in its domain.[31] The value of this 'network-based' approach to cross-border development is clear, as is the need for links between local authorities, the private sector and non-governmental organisations.[32] But, as with Peace, Interreg is bound by the twelve-county restriction. Here too there is a cogent argument for genuinely all-Ireland spatial planning, a need acknowledged not just by the Irish and British governments (which commissioned a study of the island economy, and published it in association with the British–Irish Intergovernmental Conference in October 2006) but also by the Irish Labour Party.[33]

The language body

While language was not one of the original areas identified for cross-border cooperation, it was agreed during the December 1998 negotiations that there would be an all-island agency to promote the Irish language and, in what was widely perceived as a quid pro quo, a parallel agency would be created to cultivate Ulster Scots. The disparity in the relative strength of the languages was reflected in the terms of reference of the two agencies, which were defined as follows:

> One body, with two separate parts, with the following functions:
> *Irish Language*
> - promotion of the Irish language;
> - facilitating and encouraging its use in speech and writing in public and private life in the South and, in the context of Part III of the European Charter for Regional or Minority Languages, in Northern Ireland, where there is appropriate demand;
> - advising both administrations, public bodies and other groups in the private and voluntary sectors;
> - undertaking supportive projects, and grant-aiding bodies and groups as considered necessary;

- undertaking research, promotional campaigns, and public and media relations;
- developing terminology and dictionaries;
- supporting Irish-medium education and the teaching of Irish.

Ulster Scots

- promotion of greater awareness and use of Ullans and of Ulster Scots cultural issues, both within Northern Ireland and throughout the island.

In the South, Irish language activities had previously been shared among a number of state bodies, and these were now integrated in Foras na Gaeilge. The moulding of these disparate groups into a unified organisation has been a challenge for the new agency, which is now responsible for a greatly expanded remit and budget, and the organisational memory of its inherited staff has been of great importance in maintaining continuity.

Foras na Gaeilge has pursued a wide range of activities on both sides of the border, including the production of educational materials and language resources, the funding of Irish medium schools and Irish-language media, and the commissioning of research. Its headquarters are in Dublin, and it has opened a sub-office in Belfast to facilitate interaction with Irish language interests in Northern Ireland. One of the key challenges it faces in working on an all-island basis is the differing status of Irish in the two jurisdictions, a predicament recognised by its founding legislation, which instructs it to have regard to this differing status in carrying out its functions. Foras na Gaeilge, with its southern background, has also been challenged to adapt to the different administrative and educational structures in Northern Ireland and to develop working relations with a civil service which did not, historically, have a tradition of engagement with the Irish language.[34]

The Ulster Scots Agency came into being in a very different context. From its inception its bona fides was challenged by a debate over the linguistic status of Ulster Scots, with its detractors arguing that it was a 'mere' dialect, or, more polemically, a 'DIY language for Orangemen'. While interest in Ulster Scots cultural activities has increased over the years, the language is confined to marginal areas with dwindling numbers of native speakers, and enjoyed no official recognition in either jurisdiction prior to the Good Friday agreement. The inclusion of Ulster Scots in the Agreement, and the subsequent creation of Tha Boord o Ulstèr-Scotch, was widely seen as 'balancing' those elements which recognised Gaelic and nationalist culture, thereby reinforcing the identification of the language with the Protestant community. Against this background, the Ulster Scots Agency faced considerable challenges in getting off the ground: in contrast to Foras na Gaeilge, it had neither a template to follow nor organisational experience on which to draw.

Despite these obstacles, the Ulster Scots Agency has been quite active, particularly in the area of cultural promotion and raising awareness. It has provided finance and support for groups involved in activities such as traditional music and dance, assisted in the organising of festivals and established an Ulster Scots periodical.[35] Efforts have been made to encourage academic study of the language, with the establishment of an Institute of Ulster Scots Studies in partnership with the University of Ulster, and the agency has also funded the development of educational materials for use in schools. Although perceived as a 'northern' body, the agency has taken its all-island remit seriously and has opened a sub-office in Raphoe, County Donegal, with a development officer for Donegal, Cavan and Monaghan, counties with an Ulster Scots tradition.

While the composite structure of the language body holds potential for internal tensions and rivalry, the two agencies report good working relationships. They have engaged in a number of joint projects, including, for example, a celebration of the island's shared musical heritage, and they cooperate regularly on corporate and everyday matters. However, the considerably higher funding level of the Irish language agency has attracted political criticism in Northern Ireland,[36] and the Ulster Scots agency's first chairman, Lord Laird, resigned in April 2004 complaining of a lack of government support for Ulster Scots culture.[37]

The creation of an all-island body for language has obvious advantages for Irish and, to a lesser extent, Ulster Scots, in terms of the benefits of cross-border language planning and the dissemination of best practice. However, its greatest significance may actually lie in its bringing together of the island's opposing cultural traditions. Both agencies are aware of the powerful symbolism of their cooperation and of its potential to increase awareness and acceptance of the island's linguistic and cultural diversity. While peace and reconciliation work is not explicitly part of their remit, they recognise that, uniquely among the North–South bodies, they are 'operating in the area of hearts and minds', and aim to break down barriers and displace exclusivist notions of identity and culture. However, if they are to fulfil this potential, a key task for both agencies will be to counteract the politicisation of Irish and Ulster Scots and to work against their identification with a particular community or religion.[38]

The Foyle, Carlingford and Irish Lights Commission

This body was unusual in that it was the only one where there already existed a considerable level of institutionalised North–South activity. But the area was also a complex one, and this was reflected in the dual-agency structure proposed – one which bore some similarity to the structure of the language body. Like the language body, as we have seen, the board was given responsibility for appointing two chief executives, one for the loughs agency, the other for the lights agency. Its formal terms of reference reflected this dual set of responsibilities:

> A body with the following functions:
> *Lough Foyle and Carlingford Lough*
> - promotion of development of Lough Foyle and Carlingford Lough, for commercial and recreational purposes;
> - existing functions of Foyle Fisheries Commission in regard to inland fisheries conservation, protection, management and development, and equivalent functions in respect of Carlingford Lough;
> - development and licensing of aquaculture;
> - development of marine tourism.
>
> *Lighthouses*
> - existing functions of the Commissioners of Irish Lights in respect of providing and maintaining aids to navigation along the coast of the whole island of Ireland and its adjacent seas and islands. Given that the CIL functions in an East–West context, arrangements to maintain linkage with the relevant British authorities.

The significance of pre-existing structures in this area became apparent at an early stage. The Foyle Fisheries Commission was a rare example of early North–South cooperation, and it became the core of the new Loughs Agency, which was given equivalent responsibilities in respect of Carlingford Lough. The commission had been established by statute in 1952, and consisted of two members each from Northern Ireland and the Republic, appointed respectively by the Minister for Commerce and the Minister for Agriculture. It was aided by an advisory council comprising representatives of fishing interests. Its functions of preserving and protecting fish stocks were simply continued by the new body, which inherited a staff of twenty-one (a further sixteen were quickly appointed). Its headquarters were established at Prehen on the Foyle. Its work includes the monitoring and preservation of fish stocks with, inevitably, a strong emphasis on the Foyle, though this is likely to change with the acquisition of an inshore patrol vessel for use in Carlingford Lough.

The story of the proposed lights agency indicates the kind of unexpected difficulties that can arise. An old body, the Commissioners of Irish Lights, had for long been responsible for the upkeep of all of the lighthouses around Ireland. Established originally under legislation of the Irish parliament in 1786, its functions were amended by UK legislation and it acquired its present name in 1867. It represents an unusual survival of a body whose status is still in part governed by UK legislation (for example, the UK Merchant Shipping Act 1995 confirmed it as the body responsible for the maintenance of Northern Ireland's lighthouses). This is illustrated in the arrangements for its financing: 'light dues' collected at Irish ports are supplemented by an Irish exchequer contribution and pooled with British dues in a 'general lighthouse fund' administered by the UK Department of Transport. The commissioners themselves are twenty-two in number, including six senior executives who are employees of the body.[39]

The complex legal status of the Commissioners of Irish Lights posed particular problems for the creation of a new body to replace it. Since the normal template was that an implementation body would occupy an area where a southern government department or agency functioned parallel to a similar body in Northern Ireland to which power had been devolved, there would obviously be difficulties if the area was one that under long-standing terminology was an 'excepted' one – one over which power would not be passed to a devolved administration. Indeed, this was an 'exceptional exception': not only had responsibility for lighthouses never been ceded to the 'home rule' institutions set up in Belfast in 1921, it had never been completely ceded to independent Ireland either. For this reason, at a plenary meeting of the NSMC on 28 June 2002 it was agreed that the relevant northern and southern departments would consider 'alternative possibilities', and come back with a recommendation on these. The most obvious possibility was simply to abandon the idea of establishing an implementation body in this area and instead to replace it by another area where a body could be established without raising such ancient legal hares – an outcome ultimately endorsed in the 2006 St Andrews agreement.

Tourism Ireland

Tourism Ireland is a 'compromise' not only in the same sense as Safefood – that two tourism agencies remain, North and South – but also in that while it looks like an implementation body its provenance comes under the policy cooperation area of the December 1998 agreement. The agreement specified the roles of the agency as follows:[40]

- planning and delivering international tourism marketing programmes, including programmes in partnership with the industry North and South;
- publication and dissemination in overseas markets of information of a balanced and comprehensive nature on the island of Ireland as a tourist destination, which must reflect the diverse traditions, forms of cultural expression, and identities within the island;
- market research, provision and information and other appropriate assistance to help the industry develop international marketing expertise;
- cooperation with, consulting, and assisting other bodies or associations in carrying out such activities;
- carrying out surveys and collecting relevant statistics and information.

There were clear sensitivities in this area. At a symbolic level, it was overshadowed by the 'shamrock affair'. In 1996, Tourism Brand Ireland had been established as a joint initiative of Bord Fáilte and the Northern Ireland Tourist Board (NITB), with a common logo replacing Bord Fáilte's long-established shamrock and the NITB's old red hand of Ulster. But following the general election of 1997 in the Republic, the new Minister for Tourism, Jim McDaid, demanded that the shamrock be reinstated, resulting in a stand-off when this was rejected by the NITB.[41] There have also been concerns in the industry in the Republic about association with Northern Ireland's image (with memories of the 'troubles' still vivid), and there is a genuine conflict of interest. Since most visitors to Northern Ireland enter the island via the Republic, the more days they spend in the North, the fewer they will spend in the South.[42] For unionists, the notion of marketing the island as a single entity is also an uncomfortable one at the symbolic level.

In addition to political difficulties, there are institutional ones. The new arrangement separates destination and product marketing (the first a task for Tourism Ireland, the second for the two pre-existing boards). As one newspaper feature on Tourism Ireland commented shortly after its establishment in 2000: 'Where there were two tourism bodies, there will now be three. Some industry figures believe this is a farcical scenario due only to political expediency since a full integration of the two bodies would not have been acceptable to unionists in the North.'[43] It could also be argued that the post-agreement North–South architecture, rather than 'joining up' activity on tourism, in a way chops it up, as three of the implementation bodies – Waterways Ireland, the Loughs Agency and the language body – all address features amenable to tourism attraction. Nevertheless, a significant growth in tourist numbers to the island in recent years has been recorded: in the three years to 2004, visitors rose by 11 per cent in the Republic and (from a much lower level) by 29 per cent in Northern Ireland; and Tourism Ireland dealt with a total of half a million phone and email inquiries.[44] As 2006 closed, Tourism Ireland was recording a bumper year, with an estimated 8.8 million visitors having been attracted to the island, bringing revenue of €4.2 billion, albeit the vast bulk of it (€3.7 billion) going to the republic.[45]

CONCLUSION

The prolonged 'care and maintenance' status of the implementation bodies imposed constraints on all of them. While it allowed them to continue on their existing trajectory, it set in train an inertia which became more restrictive over time. Writing before suspension of the devolved institutions in 2002, Laffan and Payne argued that 'functional North–South bodies are crucially dependent on a political layer to give them direction and legitimacy'.[46] This is true; and we propose in conclusion to address two questions: how effective a role did the NSMC play in the past in providing guidance to the implementation bodies, and what does the future hold, given uncertainty over the future of the devolved institutions in Belfast on whose existence the North–South bodies depend?

Two aspects of the relationship between the NSMC and the implementation bodies are worth considering: the mechanics of administrative control, and the extent of political oversight. First, the principle of 'no surprises' which officials applied to NSMC meetings had mixed consequences (this was based on the notion of maximising agreement in advance on issues on which decisions would be taken). On the one hand, it gave North–South cooperation a remote, technocratic air, akin to the process of European integration – and therefore subject to the same threats of public *ennui* evident since Maastricht and culminating in the collapse of the European constitution project. Furthermore, it did nothing to foster political risk-taking or policy innovation, or indeed to promote broader public discussion about what was taking place. On the other hand, particularly in the light of unionist coolness about the whole enterprise, it may well have been the case that it was precisely this level of caution and careful pace of development that secured so wide a measure of acceptance for the implementation bodies and the whole process of North–South cooperation – an image that may, ironically, have been enhanced by the survival of the bodies in the prolonged absence of political direction.

On the other hand, the second issue is precisely that of political oversight of the North–South process in the Northern Ireland Assembly and the Oireachtas. In neither case was there a dedicated committee to provide scrutiny, though the Oireachtas Joint Committee on Foreign Affairs could have chosen to take a more active interest. In Northern Ireland, the 'external' aspects of the work of the Office of the First and Deputy First Minister were deemed to be accountable to the Assembly as a whole, rather than to any of its committees. But this created an obvious dilemma of collective action: as everyone was responsible, no one was really responsible. Consequently, neither the Assembly nor the Dáil had any real prior input into NSMC meetings, and no cadre of parliamentarians developed the expertise required to ask searching questions of ministers. One pro-agreement assembly member, interviewed by one of the authors while the NSMC was functioning, said she was 'very concerned' about the lack of accountability and the 'superficial' statements made by ministers to the Assembly after its meetings.[47] This issue has been addressed head-on by the Democratic Unionist Party, which moved towards acceptance of the bodies provided they were appropriately overseen by the Northern Ireland Assembly.[48]

What of the future? Not least of the successes of the experiment in North–South cooperation we have described above has been the extent to which it has, by and large, been politically uncontroversial. For nationalists it is of course welcome and, for many of them, insufficient – they envisage a far greater measure of North–South collaboration. But even unionists formerly strongly critical of the process are prepared to accept the case for pragmatic collaboration that does not compromise constitutional principle: it may bring gains, but in any case it does not entail significant losses. This calls to mind the claim by Brian Faulkner, the unionist chief executive of the former power-sharing administration (1973–4), that the then North–South arrangements represented 'necessary nonsense'.[49]

In her introduction to the story of North–South cooperation up to the 1998 agreement, Tannam wrote: 'As with many land borders, there is scarcely a physical difference between towns and villages which lie on either side of the border. Yet the conflict in Northern Ireland has both reflected and reinforced the significance of the land border, making it more than a physical line, rather a line which represents deep and old political division.'[50] This line will, of course, continue, but its political significance may well alter fundamentally. Change will certainly be promoted by developments within the European Union; and a restructuring of local government in Northern Ireland may have further far-reaching implications. It is also clear that long-term economic, social and physical planning on an all-island basis will create further space for institutionalised North–South contact. In this process, the existing implementation bodies have already forged a path, helping to undermine the arbitrary barriers that history imposed on the administrative structures of a small island.

NOTES

1 UK ministries retained an involvement in a few areas – a military presence at certain ports until 1938, and management of Ireland's lighthouses by the Commissioners of Irish Lights, a body funded to the present through the UK Department of Transport.

2 E Tannam, *Cross-border cooperation in the Republic of Ireland and Northern Ireland* (Basingstoke: Macmillan, 1999), p. 45.

3 M Kennedy, *Division and consensus: the politics of cross-border relations in Ireland, 1925–1969* (Dublin: Institute of Public Adminstration, 2000), p. 15.

4 For background, see B Barton, 'Northern Ireland, 1925–39', in J R Hill (ed.), *A new history of Ireland: VII: Ireland, 1921–84* (Oxford: Oxford University Press, 2003), pp. 199–234, and C O'Halloran, *Partition and the limits of Irish nationalism: an ideology under stress* (Dublin: Gill & Macmillan, 1987); different northern reactions are recorded in P Bew, K Darwin & G Gillespie, *Passion and prejudice: nationalist/unionist conflict in Ulster in the 1930s and the origins of the Irish Association* (Belfast: Institute of Irish Studies, Queen's University Belfast, 1993), and in D Kennedy, *The widening gulf: northern attitudes to the independent Irish state, 1919–1949* (Belfast: Blackstaff, 1988).

5 For the definitive account, see Kennedy, *Division and consensus* (2000), on which the rest of this section is mainly based.

6 Kennedy, *Division and consensus* (2000), pp. 83–9.

7 Brooke had a personal political interest in finding a resolution to the Erne drainage problems as he was MP for the area and the issue had been a long-standing grievance among local farmers. The broader issue is discussed in M Kennedy, *The realms of practical politics: North–South co-operation on the Erne hydro-electric scheme, 1942–57* (Dublin: Institute for British Irish Studies, 2006) [IBIS Working Paper no. 75]; also available www.qub.ac.uk/cibr/mappingfrontierswps.htm.

8 Kennedy, *Division and consensus* (2000), pp. 137–46.

9 J H Whyte, 'Reconciliation, rights and protests, 1963–8', in J R Hill (ed.), *A new history of Ireland: VII: Ireland, 1921–84* (2003), pp. 309–16.

10 See Tannam, *Cross-border cooperation* (1999).

11 B Laffan and D Payne, *Creating living institutions: EU cross-border co-operation after the Good Friday agreement* (Armagh: Centre for Cross-Border Studies, 2001); available at www.crossborder.ie/pubs/creatingliving.pdf [accessed 30-11-2006].

12 The main architect of the agreement, the then Taoiseach, Dr Garret FitzGerald, argued that its central rationale was to tackle nationalist alienation in the wake of the 1981 hunger strikes and to bolster the position of constitutional nationalism; see G FitzGerald, *Ireland in the world: further reflections* (Dublin: Liberties Press, 2005), p. 143.

13 For overviews of the agreement and discussion of the background, see J Ruane and J Todd (eds), *After the Good Friday agreement: analysing political change in Northern Ireland* (Dublin: UCD Press, 1999); R Wilford, ed., *Aspects of the Belfast Agreement* (Oxford: Oxford University Press, 2001); R Wilson (ed.), *Agreeing to disagree? A guide to the Northern Ireland Assembly* (Norwich: The Stationery Office, 2001); J McGarry and B O'Leary, *The Northern Ireland conflict: consociational engagements* (Oxford: Oxford University Press, 2004).

14 See D de Bréadún, *The far side of revenge: making peace in Northern Ireland* (Cork: Collins Press, 2001), pp. 120–6, and Dean Godson, *Himself alone: David Trimble and the ordeal of unionism* (London: Harper Perennial, 2004), pp. 327–37.

15 See *Report from the First Minister (Designate) and Deputy First Minister (Designate)*, New Northern Ireland Assembly report no. 7 (Belfast: Northern Ireland Assembly, 1999), annexes 2 and 3; available at www.niassembly.gov.uk/reports/nnia7.htm [accessed 07-12-2006].

16 *Agreement between the Government of Ireland and the Government of the United Kingdom of Great Britain and Northern Ireland establishing implementation bodies* (Dublin: Department of Foreign Affairs, 1999); also available www.dfa.ie/home/index.aspx?id=8740 [accessed 09-01-2007].

17 See J Coakley, 'Northern Ireland and the British dimension', in J Coakley and M Gallagher (eds), *Politics in the Republic of Ireland*, 4th edn. (London: Routledge, 2004), pp. 407–29; J Coakley, 'The North–South relationship: implementing the agreement', in J Coakley, B Laffan and J Todd (eds), *Renovation or revolution? New territorial politics in Ireland and the United Kingdom* (Dublin: UCD Press, 2005), pp. 110–31.

18 See *Exchange of notes between the Government of the United Kingdom of Great Britain and Northern Ireland and the Government of Ireland concerning certain decisions of the North/South Ministerial Council* (London: HMSO, 2002); also available at www.north-southministerialcouncil.org/pdf/ cmnd_5708.pdf [accessed 30-11-2006].

19 The texts of communiqués relating to these decisions may be accessed at www.north-southministerialcou ncil.org/ip.htm [accessed 12-12-2006].

20 In addition to other sources listed below, this section relies on contributions made by representatives of the implementation bodies at the conference 'The North–South bodies five years on', Institute for British Irish Studies, UCD, 27 May 2005. This included presentations by Mr Martin Dennany, Director of Marketing and Communications, Waterways Ireland; Mr Martin Higgins, Chief Executive, Safefood; Mr Aidan Gough, Strategy and Policy Director, InterTrade Ireland; Mr Pat Colgan, Chief Executive, Special EU Programmes Body; Dr Seán Ó Ceárnaigh, Programme Manager, Corporate Planning, Foras na Gaeilge; Mr George Patton, Chief Executive, Ulster Scots Agency; Mr Derick Anderson, Chief Executive, Loughs Agency; and Mr Niall Gibbons, Director of Corporate Services, Tourism Ireland. Copies of the presentations are available at www.ucd.ie/ibis/conference2005.htm. We are grateful to each of these, and to the staff of the NSMC secretariat, for additional assistance in compiling this chapter. Further information on the bodies is available from their websites; see the glossary at the end of this book.

21 See the association's website at www.iwai.ie; this also contains a great deal of information about all aspects of the waterways.

22 In this and in dealing with the other bodies, we quote the terms of reference from the text of the formal UK–Irish treaty establishing the bodies; see *Agreement* (1999), annex 1. Annex 2 describes the structure and function of each body.

23 This, and much of the rest of this subsection, is based on an interview with Mr Martin Higgins, Chief Executive, Safefood, 20 October 2005.

24 C Ó Gráda and B Walsh, *Did (and does) the border matter?* (Dublin: Institute for British Irish Studies, 2006) [IBIS Working Paper no. 60]; also available www.qub.ac.uk/cibr/mappingfrontierswps.htm.

25 Tannam, *Cross-border cooperation* (1999), p. 143.
26 M Castells, *The rise of the network society* (Oxford: Blackwell, 1996); P Cooke and K Morgan, *The associational economy: firms, regions, and innovation* (Oxford: Oxford University Press, 1998).
27 InterTrade Ireland, *Corporate plan 2002–2004* (Newry: InterTrade Ireland, 2002), p. 17.
28 InterTrade Ireland, *Supply chain logistics and transportation on the island of Ireland: an integrated study* (Newry: InterTrade Ireland, 2002).
29 R Wilson (ed.), *No frontiers: North–South integration in Ireland* (Belfast: Democratic Dialogue, 1999).
30 Laffan and Payne, *Creating living institutions* (2001), p. 117.
31 Laffan and Payne, *Creating living institutions* (2001), p. 136.
32 John Driscoll, International Centre for Local and Regional Development, Harvard University, addressing the 'North–South makes sense' conference organised by the SDLP in Derry, 7 Oct. 2005.
33 See *Comprehensive study on the all-island economy* (Dublin and Belfast: British and Irish Governments, 2006); available www.nics.gov.uk/press/ofmdfm/final271006.pdf [accessed 07-12-2006] and *Towards a national spatial plan 2001–2015* (Dublin: Labour Party, 2001); available at www.labour.ie/download/pdf/spatial_plan.pdf [accessed 07-12-2006]. In addition, InterTrade Ireland publicised its own perspective: *Spatial strategies on the island of Ireland: development of a framework for collaborative action* (Newry: InterTradeIreland, 2006); available at www.intertradeireland.com/module.cfm/opt/29/area/Publications/ page/Publications [accessed 07-12-2006].
34 Interview with Dr Seán Ó Cearnaigh, Programme Manager, Foras na Gaeilge, 7 Oct. 2005.
35 Interview with George Patton, Chief Executive, Ulster Scots Agency, 11 Oct. 2005; other information in this subsection is derived from this interview.
36 The Irish language agency receives approximately 88% of the budget, to 12% for the Ulster Scots agency. The DUP has been especially vocal on this issue, accusing the Northern Ireland Department of Culture, Arts and Leisure of 'cultural discrimination', and it has demanded that the funding differential be bridged within three years (*News Letter*, 19 Oct. 2005).
37 See news.bbc.co.uk/1/northern_ireland/3652193.stm [accessed 30-11-2006].
38 Examples of ground-level difficulties (which reflect the much more intense politicisation of the language issue in Northern Ireland than in the Republic) include the tearing down of Ulster Scots street signs in Castlereagh (the loyalists who did so apparently believing them to be in Irish); news.bbc.co.uk/1/hi/northern_ireland/478513.stm [accessed 30-11-2006].
39 See the Commissioners' website, www.cil.ie/.
40 See 'Joint statement issued by the First Minister, Mr David Trimble, and the Deputy First Minister, Mr Seamus Mallon on the accommodation reached regarding future Northern Ireland Government Departments, and cross-border bodies, 18 December 1998', available cain.ulst.ac.uk/events/peace/docs/tm181298.htm [accessed 30-11-2006]. The formal provisions for the establishment of this body were not outlined in the British–Irish agreement of 1999, which covered only the six areas in which implementation bodies had originally been agreed.
41 *Irish Times*, 19 and 20 Sept. 1997.
42 C Ó Maoláin, *North–South co-operation on tourism: a mapping study* (Armagh: Centre for Cross-Border Studies, 2000); available at www.crossborder.ie/pubs/tourismmappingstudy.pdf [accessed 30-11-2006], p. 2.
43 *Sunday Tribune*, 18 February 2001.
44 See J Henderson and P Teague, *The Belfast agreement and cross-border cooperation in the tourism industry* (Dublin: Institute for British Irish Studies, 2006) [IBIS Working Paper no. 54]; also available at www.qub.ac.uk/cibr/mappingfrontierswps.htm.

45 *Irish Times*, 5 December 2006.
46 Laffan and Payne, *Creating living institutions* (2001), p. 133.
47 R Wilford and R Wilson (2001) *A democratic design? The political style of the Northern Ireland Assembly* (London: Constitution Unit, University College London, 2001), p. 36.
48 Democratic Unionist Party, *North, south, east, west: Northern Ireland's relationship with the other regions of the British Isles* (Belfast: DUP, 2004).
49 P Bew and G Gillespie, *Northern Ireland: a chronology of the troubles* (Dublin: Gill & Macmillan, 1999), p. 74.
50 Tannam, *Cross-border cooperation* (1999), p. 1.

3

The island economy: Ireland before and after the Belfast agreement

JOHN BRADLEY

INTRODUCTION

As we have seen in chapter 1, the partition of Ireland had immediate and exceptional significance for the two parts of the island in the economic domain, and differences between the two regions were accentuated over time. The logic in favour of deepening North–South economic linkages, thus making the two Irish regional economies less peripheral to each other, is partly economic (dealing with cross-border policy externalities and spillovers), partly geographic (close proximity and land borders have inescapable consequences), partly cultural (although this aspect is not without its negative side), and partly political (deeper economic links might aid the consolidation of peace and political stability within Northern Ireland and greater North–South trust and harmony). The unfortunate reality since 1922 has been that policy makers in both Northern Ireland and the Republic of Ireland attempted to improve their competitive advantages almost in complete isolation from each other. Given the political climate that prevailed both before and after the outbreak of civil unrest in 1968, this process of separate development (or economic *apartheid*) is easy to understand. The level of public and private sector planning and consultation needed to build a joint competitive strategy would have demanded degrees of trust and of cooperation that were never realistically going to be politically feasible prior to the Belfast agreement of 1998.

In a global economy, with no barriers to the movement of goods, factors of production or capital, small nations and regions are forced to specialise, since they cannot efficiently support a very wide range of different industries.[1] During the nineteenth century, the area that is now Northern Ireland came to specialise mainly in textiles and clothing, ship-building and light engineering.[2] The area that is now the Republic had radically different areas of specialisation, almost entirely in agricultural production and associated basic food processing. In the case of Northern Ireland, manufacturing experienced difficulty in diversifying during the twentieth century and still retains a relatively high concentration in sectors like textiles and clothing. However, in the case of the Republic there was a dramatic switch from the end of the 1950s, signalled by the publication of a new blueprint for the economy, *Economic development*, in 1958, away from the weak, traditional industries that had been fostered behind protective tariff barriers from the early 1930s, towards modern high-technology sectors such as electronics, computers, software, pharmaceuticals and chemicals.[3]

Today, both regions of the island have a relatively narrow portfolio of sectoral specialisation: Northern Ireland to a large extent in mature or declining sectors, the Republic in a range of modern sectors (or, rather, in specific products within such sectors) that are, however, rapidly moving towards maturity and could conceivably soon enter their decline phase. Thus, the perspective provided by industrial strategy frameworks such as Vernon's product life-cycle, Porter's diamond of competitive advantage or Best's productivity triad has implications for the economy of the whole island of Ireland that complement the more conventional economic aspects of international cost competitiveness.[4] The same may hold for the design of industrial policy in many of the smaller newly liberalised economies of Central and Eastern Europe and for some of the smaller Asian economies.[5]

We can characterise the key challenge of policy making in any small nation or region as that of blending the techniques and insights of the *economic* analysis of what one might call the 'outer' business environment with those of the *business* analysis of the middle ground of strategy. These two areas are often studied in isolation from each other by non-overlapping groups of researchers.[6] When cross-references are made between the two areas of research, each separate group tends to focus on the inadequacies of the other's methodology.[7] Seldom if ever are the two different perspectives looked at as being entirely complementary and mutually supportive.

The chapter is organised as follows. In the next section we set the context for the present state of the two economies on this island in terms of their previous histories. Our focus is on the manufacturing sector, in particular, since this can be regarded as the 'engine' of growth. The following section explores the implications of some of the most commonly used industrial strategy frameworks for the island economies, as policy makers in Northern Ireland attempt to address an imbalance in the regional portfolio of businesses caused by declining sectors, and as policy makers in the Republic face up to the likelihood of a rapid onset of maturity and decline of the computer and software sector. The wider challenges faced by policy makers in small peripheral regional economies in competing to attract replacement for maturing sectors are examined, and suggestions are made about the role of all-island policy cooperation. The last substantive section concludes with a reflection on the island economy of the future.

THE HISTORICAL ISLAND CONTEXT

After partition in 1920, the island of Ireland was a striking example of highly uneven industrial development. The South was poor and overwhelmingly agricultural. By contrast, the North – in particular the north-east region centred on Belfast – was heavily industrialised and relatively prosperous. The sectoral distribution of total employment, North and South, in the year 1926 is shown in Table 3.1. Manufacturing employment in the Irish Free State in 1926 accounted for 7 per cent of overall employment and only 13 per cent of total employment was in the broader classification of industry (consisting of manufacturing, building and construction and utilities). In contrast, the share of manufacturing employment in Northern Ireland in 1926 was over four times that of the Irish Free State.

Table 3.1. Sectoral employment, Northern Ireland and the Irish Free State, 1926

	Agriculture	Industry	(of which manufacturing)	Services
Irish Free State	54	13	(7)	33
Northern Ireland	29	34	(29)	37

Note: figures refer to percentage distribution by sector.

Source: R Munck, *The Irish economy: results and prospects* (London: Pluto Press, 1993).

The initial state of manufacturing on the island can be examined using data starting from the 1924 census of production for Northern Ireland and data from the 1926 census of industrial production for the Irish Free State, the first such data available (Table 3.2). Such comparisons confirm the

Table 3.2. Output in manufacturing, Northern Ireland and the Irish Free State, 1924–35

Sector	1924 £000	Share (%)	1930 £000	Share (%)	1935 £000	Share (%)
Northern Ireland						
Textiles and clothing	32,758	54.1	21,105	41.3	22,466	43.1
Food, drink, tobacco	15,036	24.9	13,876	27.1	16,146	31.0
Boot, shoe and apparel	2,944	4.9	3,458	6.8	2,934	5.6
Shipbuilding, engineering, metal	6,540	10.8	9,601	18.8	7,649	14.7
Paper and printing etc.	1,690	2.8	1,656	3.2	1,486	2.8
Timber	761	1.3	699	1.4	761	1.5
Miscellaneous	769	1.3	718	1.4	704	1.4
Total manufacturing	60,498	100.0	51,113	100.0	52,146	100.0
Irish Free State						
Textiles and clothing	1,179	2.4	966	2.2	2,146	3.2
Food, drink, tobacco	38,850	79.3	33,320	76.2	43,398	65.5
Boot, shoe and apparel	1,523	3.1	1,990	4.5	5,607	8.5
Shipbuilding, engineering, metal	1,543	3.1	1,838	4.2	5,283	8.0
Paper and printing etc.	1,917	3.9	2,098	4.8	2,947	4.5
Timber	1,347	2.7	1,472	3.4	2,395	3.6
Miscellaneous	2,630	5.4	2,071	4.7	4,444	6.7
Total manufacturing	48,990	100.0	43,754	100.0	66,220	100.0

Note: During this period, the Irish pound and sterling were at a fixed 1:1 parity.

Source: Report on the census of production for Northern Ireland (Belfast: Northern Ireland Statistical Agency, various years); *Census of industrial production* (Dublin: Central Statistics Office, various years).

dramatic difference between the two regions and serve to establish the full extent to which the Irish Free State had to evolve if it was to converge towards the higher level of industrialisation and economic welfare of Northern Ireland.

Immediately after independence in 1922, the manufacturing sector in the Irish Free State was not only a tiny part of the total economy, but it was almost completely concentrated in the food processing area. Northern Ireland, on the other hand, had three areas of concentration: textiles and clothing, transport equipment (shipbuilding, engineering and metal –

relatively modern capital-intensive sectors), and a less modern food processing sector. Very little fundamental sectoral change took place during the following decade, although the northern textiles and clothing sector declined somewhat, and there was modest growth in a range of other sectors in the Irish Free State.

Industrial and trade policy in the South

Inward orientation, 1932–60. From the early 1930s to the late 1950s high tariff barriers and a strict prohibition on foreign ownership of firms operating in the Republic were the cornerstone of policies designed to promote growth of indigenous manufacturing from the very low base shown in Tables 3.1 and 3.2.[8] The high tariffs succeeded in stimulating growth in local manufacturing but by the late 1950s it was clear that protectionism had long outlived its usefulness and that few of the so-called infant industries had matured and become sufficiently competitive to generate much by way of exports.

The changes forced on Irish policy-makers by economic collapse in the late 1950s were fundamental and far-reaching. The Control of Manufactures Act, 1932, which prohibited foreign ownership, was abolished and replaced by a policy that systematically cultivated inward investment. A key incentive was a zero rate of corporate tax on profits arising from manufactured exports. After accession to EEC membership in 1973, the government was obliged to change this policy, and from 1980 onwards a flat rate of 10 per cent was applied to all profits arising in manufacturing. As the benefits to business activity of low corporate taxation became apparent, and as an incentive to building an international banking sector, the low rate was gradually extended beyond manufacturing, and a flat rate of 12.5 per cent is now applied to the whole corporate sector. In addition, attractive investment and training grants were offered, as well as a complete dismantling of most tariff barriers within less than a decade.

Much of the history of the economy of the Republic during the following four decades can be explained in terms of the rapid growth of export-oriented foreign direct investment in manufacturing, from a very low base in the late 1950s to a situation in the late 1990s where two-thirds of gross output and 47 per cent of employment in manufacturing was in foreign-owned export-oriented firms.[9] US investment had always been at the very core of this process: by the late 1990s, almost one-quarter of total Irish manufacturing employment was in US-owned firms, and US ownership continues to be a vital factor in the Irish economy.

The new era of outward orientation in the Republic. The economic and industrial development dilemma of the Republic was that it was confronted by two conflicting options. One was to stay close to UK economic policy and institutional norms and attempt to track the UK's average performance over the business cycle. However, Irish policy-makers took a strategic decision in the late 1950s that the dominance of the UK market was unlikely to provide a suitable context for Irish development, modernisation and faster growth. Tax varying (or, more precisely, tax re-balancing) powers were a crucial element of policy making, especially with regard to the attraction of inward investment, and the centrepiece of the incentive system in manufacturing – initially a zero rate of corporation tax – required continued high rates of personal income tax and indirect taxes to balance the wider public finances. However, equally important were reforms in education, progressive improvement in infrastructure, evolution of social partnership arrangements, enthusiastic embracing of EU initiatives (the European monetary system, the single market, the social chapter, economic and monetary union), and – after many false starts – the creation of fiscal stability.[10]

The reduction of exposure to the UK market as a destination for Irish exports is illustrated in Figure 3.1. Thus, in the Republic's 'world' the United Kingdom was utterly dominant from the 1920s to the 1950s, with an export share of 90 per cent or above. The turning point came in the late 1950s, and while it was not dramatic, it led systematically to a fall in the UK export share to below 20 per cent by the early years of the twenty-first century. Most of the decline in the role of the UK market was compensated for by a rise in trade with the rest of the EU, against a background of a massive increase in the overall level of exports. With no other changes, a shift in export destinations to faster growing and more dynamic European markets would be expected to ease the constraint on the Irish manufacturing expansion.

Sources of inward investment. The detailed census data for manufacturing classified by nationality of ownership for the year 1996, the height of the high-technology boom, are shown in Table 3.3. Although only 16 per cent of local plants were foreign-owned, they produced just over two-thirds of gross output and made up nearly half of total manufacturing employment. The importance of the US connection was illustrated by the fact that almost 40 per cent of the foreign plants were US-owned, with 16 per cent British and 13 per cent German. More recent census data for manufacturing (available up to the year 2004) confirm that these shares have remained very steady during the following eight years.

A striking difference between locally owned and foreign-owned plants is that the indigenous ones exported on average just over one-third of their

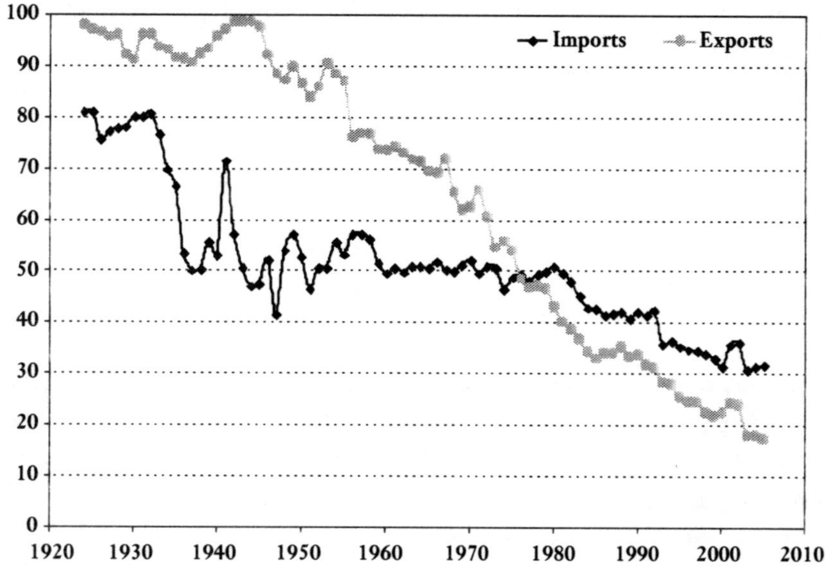

Figure 3.1. UK share of Republic of Ireland imports and exports, 1924–2005

Note. The lines represent percentages of all imports and exports. In 1936 the criterion for determining source of imports was changed from country from which consigned to country in which originated, resulting in a lower attribution of imports to the UK.

Source. for 1924–71, *Statistical abstract of Ireland*, various years; for 1972 and later, Central Statistics Office, *External trade statistics: database direct*, available at www.cso.ie/px/pxeirestat/database/eirestat/Trade/Trade.asp [08-01-2007].

output, while the foreign-owned ones exported almost 90 per cent, rising to above 95 per cent for US-owned plants. Thus, by the late 1990s the domestic market was of little or no significance to the owners of foreign plants. They located in the Republic to produce for export. It was and remains the competitive characteristics on the supply side of Irish manufacturing that attract inward investment: corporate tax rates, labour costs, skill levels and infrastructure.

Some further differences between foreign and indigenous plants are illustrated in Table 3.4. Foreign plants tended to be larger (measured in terms of gross output, or in numbers employed, per plant); they were more productive (measured in terms of net output per person engaged); and consequently they were more profitable, since they faced similar wage costs to local firms. In terms of these proxy measures, US-owned plants

Table 3.3. Total manufacturing, Republic of Ireland: general characteristics, 1996

Nationality of ownership	No. of plants	Total persons engaged	Gross output (£m)	Materials purchased: % imported	Gross output: % exported
Irish	3,871	120,224	12,188	25.1	34.0
Other EU	344	37,114	4,765	65.2	70.5
(of which UK)	*117*	*12,283*	*1,960*	*52.9*	*53.5*
(of which German)	*98*	*10,684*	*855*	*80.3*	*93.3*
Non-EU	384	69,296	19,343	65.7	93.9
(of which US)	*286*	*54,167*	*15,814*	*61.6*	*95.3*
Total foreign	728	106,410	24,108	65.6	89.3
Total	4,599	226,634	36,296	47.0	70.7

Note: Gross output is measured in Irish pounds.

Source: *Census of industrial production*, 1996.

were over seventeen times larger than indigenous-owned plants, over five times as productive, and almost eight times as profitable. Once again, these characteristics have remained very steady in more recent years.

Table 3.4. Manufacturing plants, Republic of Ireland: characteristics by ownership, 1996

Plant ownership	Gross output per plant (£000)	Net output per person engaged (£000)	Destination of exports (per cent)			
			UK	*other EU*	*USA*	*rest of world*
Irish	3,149	34.6	42.2	32.2	8.2	17.3
Other EU	13,851	65.3	36.8	46.8	6.8	9.6
(of which UK)	*16,750*	*87.4*	*74.3*	*10.9*	*5.4*	*9.3*
(of which German)	*8,724*	*35.9*	*12.3*	*72.7*	*6.4*	*8.6*
Non-EU	50,372	166.7	19.9	50.6	11.4	18.1
(of which US)	*55,293*	*177.9*	*20.1*	*52.5*	*9.5*	*17.9*
Total foreign	33,115	131.3	22.6	50.0	10.7	16.8
Total	5,481	80.0	25.7	47.1	10.3	16.9

Notes: monetary values are in Irish pounds.

Source: *Census of industrial production*, 1996.

Since the foreign-owned manufacturing sector is so large in the Republic, it has economy-wide as well as sectoral implications. Thus, the overall health of the economy has come to depend on the performance of this sub-sector. However, the mainly tax-based industrial incentive system, and the fact that the Republic features as a production platform rather than as a market, means that opportunities exist for transfer pricing. A much larger distortion concerns profit repatriation, since foreign firms tend not to reinvest a high proportion of their profits in the local economy. The resulting outward flows of profits show up in the Irish balance of payments statistics, where there is a large deficit on net factor income. This introduces a wedge of some 10–15 per cent between gross domestic product (GDP) and gross national product (GNP).[11]

The balance sheet. The experience of the Republic has been that a crude erection of trade or other barriers in order to 'protect' weak regions was ultimately damaging to economic welfare. A blind belief in competition policy and the forces of market liberalisation was never subscribed to, but it was also feared that this would be inadequate. Reviewing the ways in which poorer regions can seek to accelerate their growth rate in order to catch up, Krugman suggests that the Irish experience is essentially a working out of Marshallian externalities:[12]

1. An initial clustering of similar industries (often foreign owned and in high-technology areas such as computer equipment, software and pharmaceuticals) takes place, supported by local suppliers of specialised inputs subject to economies of scale.
2. These clusters generate a local labour market for skilled workers, further facilitating the growth of the cluster. At this stage, the training and human resource policies of the EU structural funds were crucial aid in ensuring elastic labour supply.
3. Spillovers of information further encourage growth in the high technology sectors and provide the basis for additional clustering effects, often in traditional areas that can benefit from new technologies in their supply chains (such as food processing). Here, the improvements in physical infrastructure and in the productive environment supported by the structural funds were crucial.
4. Finally, a consensual process of social partnership needs to be put in place to ensure that there are as few losers as possible in the economic restructuring that accompanies such a virtuous circle, with the result that growth is less likely to be choked off by industrial unrest.

However, Krugman also draws attention to some of the risks to which a country like the Republic is exposed as it follows this growth process. First, the dynamic foreign manufacturing base is concentrated in a narrow range of technologies that can quickly move through maturity and into decline, an issue that will be taken up again in the next section. Second, the policy initiatives that ensured that the Republic enjoyed an advantageous 'first mover' status in the early 1960s may not be sufficient to guarantee success in making the transition to the next wave of technological inward investment when the key electronics, software and pharmaceutical sectors enter their maturity and/or declining phase. Indeed, the Irish industrial incentive package may not even be able to retain the original maturing sectors, which may move to lower-cost locations.

Industrial and trade policy in Northern Ireland

Although radical changes have taken place in Northern Ireland manufacturing during the past three decades, in some important ways these developments can be seen as a continuation of an historical evolution that started after the First World War.[13] The first annual census of production taken in 1924 in Northern Ireland showed that one sub-sector of manufacturing (textiles, including textile products) accounted for 64 per cent of total manufacturing employment and produced 54 per cent of gross output. At the start of the outbreak of civil unrest in 1969, the share had declined to 41 per cent. A similar census taken just before the Belfast agreement (for the year 1996) showed the continued important role of textiles, which still accounted for about 23 per cent of total employment in manufacturing.

The evolution of an index of aggregate Northern Ireland manufacturing employment over the three decades from the 1960s (the period that coincided with the initiation of modernisation in the Republic of Ireland) to 2005 (spanning a period of major civil unrest) is shown in Figure 3.2, in comparison with indices for the aggregate UK and for the Republic. A large element of the northern manufacturing decline can be put down to the inability of the North to attract inward investment to anything like the extent of Scotland or the Republic of Ireland due to the uncertainty and disruption caused by the conflict as well as by world economic conditions.

While Northern Ireland tracked a wider decline in UK manufacturing, it did not experience the parallel strong growth of private services that occurred in the more prosperous core regions of southern England. A rigorous analytic study by Borooah and Lee interpreted the northern decline in manufacturing employment over the 1970s and early 1980s

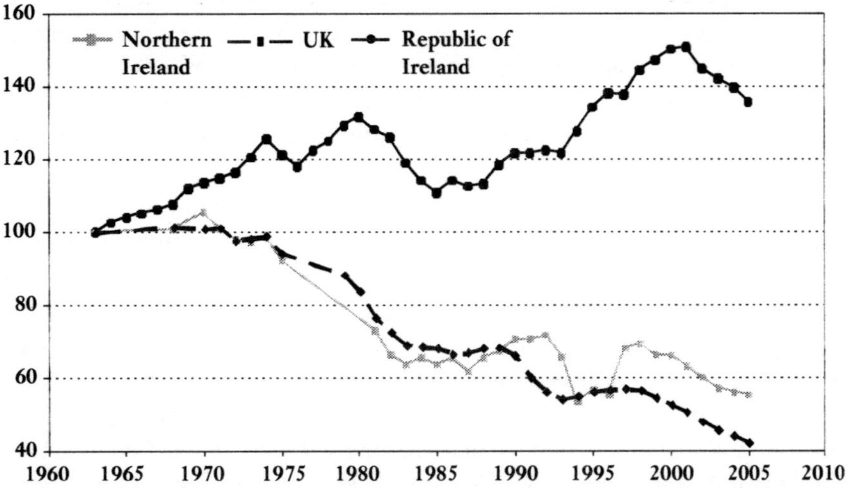

Figure 3.2. Evolution of manufacturing employment, Republic of Ireland, Northern Ireland and UK, 1963–2005

Note: index: base 1963 = 100. Sectoral employment definitions changed over the period 1963–2005, making the compilation of consistent data difficult, but the broad pattern of UK and Northern Ireland de-industrialisation is captured correctly.

Source: Regional trends, various years, for Northern Ireland; European Commission, Directorate General for Economic and Financial Affairs, AMECO Annual Macroeconomic Database (AMECO), for the UK and the Republic of Ireland; available at ec.europa.eu/economy_finance/indicators/annual_macro_economic_database/ameco_en.htm.

mainly in terms of a systemic loss of regional cost competitiveness, and showed that growth of total factor productivity in Northern Ireland during the 1960s and 1970s was at a rate substantially below that of the UK, but at the same time wage rates in Northern Ireland converged rapidly on the UK average.[14]

Recent industrial strategy in Northern Ireland. The most recent comprehensive report on industrial strategy in Northern Ireland – *Strategy 2010* – was published in March 1999.[15] The debate around industrial strategy in Northern Ireland has paralleled the experience of the Republic. The overriding emphasis in strategy from the mid-1980s was on the need for improved competitiveness as the key driving force behind industrial policy, with a consequential reduction in the level of financial subsidisation of industrial activities. However, the necessary changes in policy were implemented only to a very limited extent.[16] There seems to have been a clear lack of success on the part of the agencies in Northern Ireland, whether due to implementation difficulties or reluctance to wean industry away from high levels of subsidisation. For example, the average rate of financial support to industry in 1996–8 made up 5 per cent of manufacturing GDP and more than 20 per cent of manufacturing investment, values which are very high in comparison with other UK regions and with the rest of the EU.[17]

Strategy 2010 correctly identified the rapid globalisation of economic activity as the primary factor that will set the future context for accelerated growth and restructuring of manufacturing in Northern Ireland. Although the opportunities offered by globalisation are obvious, with international trade growing at over twice the rate of local GDP, these benefits can only be realised if the local economy can obtain access to export markets by having a high degree of competitiveness, measured in the very widest sense. For a regional economy like Northern Ireland, a local concern for the health and dynamism of the external economy will always have two distinct but complementary aspects:

1. how external markets are going to sustain buoyant demand for exports from Northern Ireland, and
2. where foreign direct investment (FDI) into Northern Ireland is likely to come from.

In a short- to medium-term perspective, the list of dominant export destinations and sources of foreign direct investment is unlikely to switch dramatically from the position today. Consequently, the British market must continue to be of central concern for Northern Ireland producers, since it is the destination of over half of external sales and is the source of the bulk of inward investment.

The size and persistence of British exchequer financing (the so-called 'subvention') serves to influence and colour every aspect of the northern economy. Efforts to pin down the precise causes and extent of the subvention are often frustrated by lack of appropriate data. The subvention directly supports employment in the northern public sector, which (based on studies of the period immediately before the Belfast agreement) made up about 33 per cent of total employment. This compares with 22 per cent in the UK as a whole (and about the same in the Republic). The subvention also directly supports incomes of the unemployed, the retired and the sick, as well as providing a high level of public housing, health and education (over and above direct public employment aspects). These might be termed the primary impacts of the public sector.

However, secondary impacts of Northern Ireland's public sector activity on the structure and behaviour of the local manufacturing and market service sectors are of equal, if not greater, importance relative to the above primary impacts. For example, subvention finance sucks in imports, and explains much of the buoyancy of the retail sector.[18] Northern manufacturing has come to be made up predominantly of small firms, oriented mainly to supplying the domestic market, which is in turn sustained to a great extent by direct and indirect demand arising from public sector activity. The fact that the northern economy emerged relatively unscathed from the last British recession of the early 1990s was due in the main to the large size and cushioning effects of automatic and discretionary public expenditure stabilisers. The buoyancy of activity in the northern manufacturing sector relative to Britain was also largely due to the much higher level of subsidies and grants, and, therefore, almost certainly had little to do with local competitiveness in any underlying sense.

Explaining Northern Ireland's performance. Perhaps the greatest success of the northern economy was that it functioned in a relatively normal fashion in spite of prolonged and severe disruption from civil unrest. In part, this can be explained by the availability of financial transfers to boost public sector activities so that the negative consequences of the inevitable decline of private sector activities were mitigated. In the 1950s and 1960s, Northern Ireland had attracted a substantial level of foreign direct investment to replace the shrinking (but still important) textiles and heavy engineering sectors.[19] This investment was predominantly in sectors where the North already had a comparative advantage, such as artificial fibres. Unfortunately, this advantage effectively vanished with the onset of the oil price rises of the 1970s, and a wide range of labour-intensive industries across northern Europe in general migrated to the low-cost centres of Southern Europe and Asia.

Current policy proposals on manufacturing incentives have focused on the perceived need to rebalance and reform priorities for financial support. Unfortunately, with regard to the provision of incentives for inward investment, current thinking remains very conservative. With regard to direct financial assistance, it was suggested that 'the existing grant regime for inward investment should be maintained unless and until new measures become available'.[20] Moreover, the possibility of targeting grants at specific sectors or of determining differential rates of assistance on a sectoral basis were ruled out, for reasons that were not made explicit. Rather, the document recommended that grant applications be prioritised on the basis of a series of specific company characteristics, such as commitment to research and development or export orientation. However, this raises serious questions about the state's ability to identify successful firms, and about how the necessary rebalancing of industry from low to high value-added activities can take place. In effect, it is a continuation of the present subsidy regime that has proved singularly unsuccessful in the past. Alternative policies are difficult to find. For example, with regard to attempting to match the Republic's low rate of corporation tax, Northern Ireland has no policy-making powers in fiscal matters and must implement UK-wide rates.[21]

STRATEGIC MARKETING AND FUTURE IRISH INDUSTRIAL STRATEGY

Past and present industrialisation on the island of Ireland has displayed a curious asymmetry. In the late nineteenth century, the north-east region – centred on Belfast – displayed phenomenal growth in a range of what were then modern high-technology industries (ship-building, engineering and textiles), while the rest of the island stagnated. Almost exactly one hundred years later, the southern part of the island – centred to a large extent on Dublin – displayed phenomenal growth in a range of high-technology industries (computers, software, chemicals and pharmaceuticals), while the northern part of the island displayed little or no dynamism and retained a dependence on declining industries.

Explanations for this behaviour require economic as well as business perspectives. Research suggests that development is most active where two conditions hold:[22]

1. A sufficient degree of policy autonomy is available that permits freedom of action to address local problems.
2. Economic and business policy are designed and implemented in tandem, the first to design an attractive environment for business to flourish, the second to recognise and exploit profitable opportunities where they exist, and to feed back information to policy-makers where problems and obstacles are identified.

Is economic development on the island a competitive, zero-sum game? In other words, must the success of one region of the island of Ireland always be accompanied by failure and decline in the other? At the peak of the early twentieth-century success of the northern region of the island, the southern region remained chronically underdeveloped. At the peak of the early twenty-first-century triumph of the southern 'Celtic tiger', the northern region had lapsed into a post-industrial dependency on state subventions. In what follows, we examine issues related to business and policy cooperation on the island.

Industrial policy in regions and states

At various times in the life of a country or region, often when the economy is performing particularly poorly or is facing major new challenges, state and regional governments and agencies carry out in-depth reviews and re-evaluations of economic and business strategy. To the extent that the focus is on problems and challenges that are regarded as 'strategic' rather than 'tactical' in nature, such policy reviews are only carried out infrequently, and have a medium- or long-term orientation. The capacity of such reviews to improve economic and business performance depends both on the extent and quality of the review of past policies and future options, as well as on the extent to which any policy prescriptions are systematically implemented.

Table 3.5. Policy focus in regions and states

Domain	Region	State
Economic policy	Derivative focus	Primary focus
Business policy	Focus on differentiation	Institutional and regulatory focus

The key differences in policy emphasis as between states and regions are summarised in Table 3.5. In the case of a state (such as the Republic), there is a primary focus on economic policy, since states have considerable freedom of action in setting policies in the fiscal and monetary areas. A region (such as Northern Ireland), on the other hand, has little or no freedom in this area, and its policies derive from the larger state (in this case, the UK) of which it is a part. When it comes to business policy, regions have – or at least usually seek – some freedom of action which they can attempt to use to differentiate their business environment from other regions of the state. In the case of Northern Ireland, an example of business policy differentiation has been the use of higher rates of grant aid than apply elsewhere in the United Kingdom. States also need to focus on business policy initiatives, but in the wider context of institutional and regulatory arrangements that promote greater efficiency of their firms as they compete within the international marketplace.

States can use economic policies to attempt to influence the environment within which businesses can function efficiently, even though their freedom of action has diminished as supranational organisations like the European Union take on more power as a result of policy harmonisation. Regions have far less power, and must take most aspects of the economic policy environment as set externally by the state to which they belong.

But regions are not completely powerless when it comes to policy making, and they can use business policies to distort conditions in their favour relative to the other regions of their state. Nevertheless, policy makers in regions still need to understand how national economic policies affect them differentially, even though there is little that they can do to influence policy other than to call for some form of 'compensation' to offset actual or perceived disadvantages. Unfortunately, such 'compensation' often comes in the form of financial transfers from the core regions to the peripheral regions that can blunt competitiveness and engender dependency.[23]

The dilemma facing regional policy-makers requires them to strike a balance between the knowledge that national policies can have regionally asymmetric negative impacts, and the extremely constrained scope for designing off-setting region-specific policies within the context of the nation state.[24] Thus, regional policy has a built-in tendency to become inward looking, and this is sometimes difficult to counteract. National policy-making, on the other hand, tends to be more outward looking and is constrained only by the more complex, political and diffuse rules of the global marketplace as it seeks to optimise local gains from policy initiatives.

These policy dilemmas have been summarised by Kenichi Ohmae as follows:

> The world economy today represents a simultaneous shift of power from the traditional national government down to region-states, and up to super-national economic blocs. Governments in tune with this change will seek economic stability through the latter, and prosperity by means of the former.[25]

With the regional devolution measures affecting Northern Ireland, Scotland and Wales within the UK, some elements of power have begun to shift from the centre (London) to the regions (Edinburgh, Cardiff and, more unevenly, Belfast). Simultaneously, increasing integration tendencies within the European Union are resulting in some powers that were previously the prerogative of nation-states passing to supranational agencies such as the European Central Bank and the European Commission. In certain respects, the policy environment of regions is coming to resemble that of small states, while the policy environment of small states is coming to resemble that of regions. Indeed, according to Ohmae, the world economy has become a series of interacting regions, where national boundaries have lost much of their previous economic and business significance.[26]

At the risk of oversimplification of what are very complex issues, the comparison between the Republic and Northern Ireland shows that the intelligent combination of economic policy and business strategy can generate huge synergies in terms of rapid national growth and convergence. To achieve these synergies requires a degree of economic policy autonomy that can be used to protect workers who lose their jobs in declining sectors and who require extensive retraining for other occupations. But more importantly, policy autonomy can be used to address weaknesses shown up by frameworks such as the competitiveness diamond of Michael Porter or the capability triad of Michael Best. Regions simply do not have sufficient economic policy autonomy and are heavily restricted in the extent to which they can intervene to support individual sectors and subsectors.[27]

Wider strategic policy issues on the island of Ireland

In a wide strategic context, the two regions of the island appear to be characterised by very different economic policy environments as they plan for their future. In the case of the Republic, strategic policy orientation towards the future is relatively benign at present and could be characterised by reference to five key issues.

1. The continued creative use of modest but significant scope for national policy-making autonomy against a background of a progressive ceding of elements of macroeconomic fiscal and monetary policy autonomy to the institutions of the EU.
2. The continuation of the crucial policy orientation of the past decades concerning openness to inward investment using a mainly tax-based system of industrial incentives and associated improvements in physical infrastructure and human capital.
3. Further modernisation of the industrial base through targeted foreign direct investment in high-technology areas as well as through steady expansion of indigenously owned industry (see chapter 9 for an extended treatment of this issue).
4. A probable continuation of the process of 'decoupling' of the economy away from the earlier heavy dependence on the UK as a result of

its sustained systematic and pro-active orientation towards participation in EU policy initiatives.
5. The pursuit of steady improvement in economic performance with the aim of building on the recent rapid convergence in order to sustain a standard of living equal to that of wealthier core economies of the EU as well as bringing about greater social equity.

The strategic policy context for Northern Ireland is more difficult to characterise with any degree of precision since the region has only recently experienced a sustained period of peace and is mired in a protracted process of designing and implementing major changes to its system of political and economic governance. Nevertheless, from a strategic point of view the region faces major policy challenges and will have to address some potentially serious issues.

1. The continuation into the medium term of a situation where the region has limited regional policy-making autonomy, combined with a lack of political consensus as to the wisdom of seeking out and using greater policy autonomy in the context of the Belfast agreement.
2. The continued dependence on a narrow range of policy instruments (particularly in the area of indiscriminate grant-based industrial incentives) that have not proved effective in the past.
3. Difficulties in modernising its manufacturing base away from its traditional specialties, such as textiles and clothing, towards higher value-added products (this issue is also discussed in detail in chapter 9).
4. A continuing dependence on Britain as the main external sales destination. Although this has been a benefit around the turn of the century, when the major economies of the EU suffered slow growth, it may prove to be potentially undesirable in the longer term if the UK remains outside the euro zone.
5. Economic peripherality within the UK, a relatively low standard of living among the UK regions, combined with the possible perpetuation of dependence on external financial aid in the form of the 'subvention', with consequential lack of dynamism in the regional economy (that is, a Mezzogiorno problem, see note 23).

The fact that the northern and southern strategic policy orientations are so out of alignment is likely to continue to have disruptive consequences for planning and executing any proposals to 'complete' the island's economy. While there are likely to be many positive aspects to the evolution of North–South relationships over the coming years, there will be negative aspects as well. In very general terms, the strategic policy environment of the Republic would appear to be much more favourable at present than the situation facing Northern Ireland. There remains the possibility that, in the absence of explicit, concerted and profitable North–South cooperative initiatives, there will be a tendency for a continuation of the previous process of essentially separate development of the two regions and an inability to complete the island economy, even as conventional North–South trade continues to expand. In the absence of appropriate island-wide policy-making forums, there is likely to be a lack of focus and urgency in addressing the related problem and consequences of policy mismatch.

Industrial structure and North–South business links

Overall manufacturing employment shares in Northern Ireland and the Republic are now fairly similar, though the South has a far higher concentration in high-productivity, high-technology industries. This reflects the much more significant contribution of foreign direct investment, which has raised productivity and profitability substantially. Indirect information on the indigenously owned sectors suggests greater similarity between the two island economies. A key relationship between the economies of Northern Ireland and the Republic involves North–South trade. The ability to sell outside a regional economy requires the ability to produce a range of goods and services that are in demand elsewhere. The characteristics of the northern and southern productive structures – with the South having a more modern industrial base – have important implications for internal trade.

Table 3.6 shows southern exports to the North, to Britain and to the entire EU, disaggregated using the standard industrial trade classification (SITC), with specific details of some sub-divisions. The table highlights some striking facts. By the late 1990s, exports from the South to the North were heavily concentrated in food and live animals (SITC 0), accounting for 25 per cent of total southern exports to Northern Ireland. For the same product category, this compares with 17 per cent of total exports to Britain and only 11 per cent of total exports to the EU as a whole. There is a very high concentration of southern exports in the categories of machinery and transport equipment (SITC 7) to Britain and the EU as a whole, accounting for over a third in each, but it accounts for only 12 per cent of total southern SITC 7 exports to the North. More notably, almost 25 per cent of southern exports to Britain and to the EU but less than 2 per cent of total exports to the North fall into the important category of office and auto-

Table 3.6. Export shares by SITC sections, Republic of Ireland, 1997

SITC section	Northern Ireland	Great Britain	Rest of EU
0 (Food and live animals)	24.5	16.9	11.3
1 (Beverages and tobacco)	6.6	1.7	1.6
2 (Crude materials, inedible, except fuels)	2.8	2.2	1.8
3 (Mineral fuels, lubricants, related materials)	1.1	1.0	0.6
4 (Animal and vegetable oils, fats)	0.0	0.2	0.1
5 (Chemicals and related products)	9.3	15.9	24.4
(54) Pharmaceuticals	*(0.8)*	*4.2*	*(5.6)*
6 (Manufactured goods classified by materials)	17.4	5.6	4.4
7 (Machinery and transport equipment)	12.1	36.8	35.6
(75) Office and ADP machines	*(1.8)*	*(25.1)*	*(23.8)*
(77) Instruments	*(1.9)*	*(5.9)*	*(6.4)*
8 (Miscellaneous manufactured articles)	12.0	14.8	15.0
9 (Other commodities and transactions)	0.0	3.1	3.9
Residual (other)	15.3	1.8	1.3

Source: Trade statistics, December (Dublin: Central Statistics Office, 1997).

matic data processing machines (SITC 75).[28]

Thus, the composition of bilateral trade between the North and the South is very different from bilateral trade between Britain and the South, as well as between the EU as a whole and the South. North–South trade – in both directions – is predominantly in traditional, low-technology products with an exceptionally high weight for food, drink and tobacco (SITC 0). Of course, this phenomenon simply reflects the underlying industrial structure in Northern Ireland compared with that of the Republic. However, the most important dynamic promoting increased intra-EU trade in the single market of the EU is associated inter-firm trade in similar product areas rather than trade in finished consumer goods. This two-way trade simply cannot easily take place between North and South, given the contrasting production structures.

The potential gains from greater North–South trade interaction, given existing northern industrial activity, may be modest relative to the potential gains from greater penetration into wider world (including British) markets. Nevertheless, there are gains to be made from intra-island trade in circumstances that could assist in strengthening the competitive performance of all businesses on the island. North–South trade improvement is not an *alternative* to east–west trade improvement, but is entirely *complementary* to it. It is a transitional process that has the potential to produce gains in the short term and, by strengthening its supply side, could help to position the island economy to make further advances in world markets. But North–South trade will be able to reach its potential if and only if the structure of manufacturing in Northern Ireland can be modernised and brought into line with that of Wales, Scotland and the Republic of Ireland.

CONCLUSION

Industry in Northern Ireland has yet to develop dynamic, self-sustaining characteristics, especially in terms of clusters of related and supporting industries. It remains heavily subsidised by public funding and is mainly concentrated in the low-technology sectors of traditional industries such as food processing, textiles and clothing. The situation in the Republic is somewhat healthier, but industrial development there has been heavily driven by foreign direct investment, which does not always lay down the full range of developmental roots in the domestic economy that are usual in locally owned firms. As time passes, a range of key interconnections and spillovers between related firms and industries is taking place, but this remains an area of concern for policy-makers in both parts of the island.

How might this situation be improved? Both regions are individually small, with populations of only 1.6 and four million. Northern Ireland is not only separated geographically from Britain, but, importantly, also appears to be very weakly integrated into the supply side of the British economy, even when demand for northern output is driven by the British market. For example, Northern Ireland is almost never central to strategic planning by British firms, and risks becoming both geographically and economically peripheral to Britain. However, recent improvements in access to transport and a more positive political situation should help to alleviate this over time. But Northern Ireland is unlikely ever to be placed on a par with the rest of the British economy, at least from the supply-side perspective. In contrast, there is less geographical or economic logic to Northern Ireland remaining peripheral within the island of Ireland.

The situation in the Republic, relative to the countries that provide the bulk of its foreign direct investment (predominantly the USA, but also Britain and the rest of the EU), has some analogues with the position in Northern Ireland. For example, just as Northern Ireland is not strategically central to externally owned (mainly British) firms located there, neither is the economy of the Republic always central to the strategic planning of many of its (mainly US-based) plants. Rather, the Republic is often seen merely in terms of a highly profitable location for production of goods mainly designed, developed, tested and marketed elsewhere, and a location where a very high-quality labour force is available at reasonable cost. As already argued, the branch plant nature of foreign firms located in the Republic does not always encourage the establishment of strong economic performance built on competitive advantage. Heavy dependence on foreign investment makes it harder to generate the type of cumulative self-sustaining indigenous growth that is a characteristic of successful European regional economies such as Emilia-Romagna in northern Italy and Baden-Württemberg in Germany.[29] This is a major preoccupation of Irish policy-makers.

Michael Porter has suggested that four interacting characteristics are essential for competitive success: factor conditions, demand conditions, related and supporting industries, and firm strategy, structure and rivalry. It might be suggested that in order to upgrade these four competitiveness factors on the island, policy makers in the two regional economies should not plan for separate development as two competing regions, but should facilitate a coming together in order to build on natural island economic strengths and remove barriers and weaknesses so that genuine synergies can be realised for the mutual benefit of both economies. Such synergies would ultimately be reflected in the formation and development of deeply embedded, inter-connected and supportive island industrial activity. This would be seen in the emergence of industrial *clusters* of firms and industries feeding backwards and forwards off each other, industrial *districts* centred around specific industries in specific geographic regions and with the potential to increase local sourcing, and industrial *networks* involving the exchange between firms and industries of mutually supportive information and knowledge.[30]

The unfortunate reality is that both North and South are attempting to improve their competitive advantages largely in isolation from each other.[31] Given the political climate of the last few decades, this process of separate development is easy to understand. The type of public and private sector planning and consultation needed to build a development strategy based on dynamic clusters of fast-growing, export-oriented firms (drawing on the research of Michael Porter and Michael Best) would have demanded levels of cooperation that were never realistically going to be politically feasible as long as the conflict in Northern Ireland continued.[32]

However, what of the post-Belfast agreement period? Based on research carried out during the 1990s, one was led to the conclusion that

North–South market imperfections were a serious constraint on cross-border cooperation, and that this was restricting the development potential of both regions.[33] It might appear that many of these imperfections have been addressed, and that cross-border institutions are now in place. But as Tannam notes in chapter 5, cross-border business cooperation has remained at a rather narrow level that has left the underlying development processes of both regions untouched.

In the Republic, the state's development strategy is kept constantly under review by government and by business and is debated widely and constructively in the public media. Untroubled by the political and community divisions that beset the North, policy-makers in the South, in both the public and private sectors, can focus on tuning and optimising a strategic approach to development that has attracted admiration across the world.

Policy-making for promoting and sustaining inward investment in Northern Ireland is less actively debated, and needs to be based on a comprehensive, critical and realistic evaluation of the present endemic lack of underlying competitiveness of the region, as documented, for example, in the regular Department of Trade and Industry publications on *Regional competitiveness indicators*. The faster growth of manufacturing output and employment in Northern Ireland relative to Britain is sometimes presented as a sign of underlying competitiveness rather than as an indication that very high grant rates serve to attract a certain type of labour-intensive, low-profit manufacturing and service activity to Northern Ireland before it leaves the UK and the EU for lower wage locations in Eastern Europe and elsewhere.[34] Such myopia amounts to denial of the seriousness of the situation, and is unlikely to deceive analysts of global economic trends, upon whom multinational companies rely for advice on their future investment strategies. These issues are further examined in two case studies elsewhere (see chapter 9).

As years pass, and few changes are implemented in Northern Ireland, it is easy to lose the optimism of the post-ceasefire period leading up to the Belfast agreement. In the cold light of day, after the collapse of early post-Belfast agreement attempts at devolved administration, the economic and business cross-border institutions of the agreement took on an appearance of negative, grudging, minimalist concessions to an 'Irish' dimension of the inter-communal problems of Northern Ireland that fundamentally rejected the concept of an island economy. Praise for modest progress made by these bodies tends to conceal the lack of any movements of a more strategic island importance.

Remaining as part of the UK under direct rule will probably doom

Northern Ireland to play out the process of continued industrial decline, stagnation and dependency that we described above.[35] Devolved government, even under the most optimistic of circumstances, is unlikely to be more beneficial to Northern Ireland than it is at present to Scotland, where the local administration finds it difficult to design and implement distinctive Scottish development policies.[36] There do not yet appear to be any other options that would command the enthusiastic support of both communities in Northern Ireland and their political representatives.

Future generations may have to look back on the Belfast agreement as a missed opportunity to put history behind us. And this may not – as the neo-functionalists claim – have been uniquely due to a failure of the political elite to react to market-led pressures emanating from the business communities. At a deep psychological level, perhaps both business communities may be found to have been reasonably happy to function within their separate spheres on this contentious island? Far from urging greater co-operation on the politicians, perhaps their actions (or lack of actions) may represent a subliminal desire to prevent the agreement from encroaching on the economic tranquillity of their lives?

NOTES

1 G Stigler, 'The division of labour is limited by the extent of the market', *Journal of political economy* 59 (1951), pp. 185–93.

2 For explanations of the late nineteenth-century sectoral specialisation in Ireland, see C Ó Gráda, *Ireland: a new economic history 1780–1939* (Oxford: Clarendon Press, 1994).

3 *Economic development* (Dublin: The Stationery Office, 1958) (Pr. 4803)

4 R Vernon, 'International investment and international trade in the product cycle', *Quarterly journal of economics* 80:2 (1966), pp. 190–207; R Vernon, 'The product cycle hypothesis in a new international environment', *Oxford bulletin of economics and statistics* 41:4 (1979), pp. 255–67; M Porter, *The competitive advantage of nations* (London: Macmillan, 1990); M Best, *The new competitive advantage* (Oxford: Oxford University Press, 2001).

5 J Bradley, 'The Irish economy in comparative perspective', pp. 4–26 in B Nolan, P O'Connell and C Whelan (eds), *Bust to boom* (Dublin: Institute of Public Administration, 2000), pp. 22–6.

6 Economists tend to be the worst offenders, and seldom if ever can bring themselves to acknowledge the existence of the contributions of, say, Vernon and Porter. However, only in his most recent work has Porter acknowledged the economic research on spatial issues and clustering by Krugman and others, and even then inadequately. See M Porter, *On competition* (Cambridge, MA: Harvard Business Review Press, 1998); for an attempt to synthesise, J Kay, 'Economics and business', *Economic journal* 101 (1991), pp. 57–63.

7 Business researchers tend to disparage as irrelevant the older approaches to trade and growth theory and to ignore the major advances that have been made in recent decades. Economists tend to criticise the lack of formal testing of the validity of business frameworks; see N Kay, 'Multinational enterprises: a review article', *Scottish journal of*

political economy 30:3 (1983), pp. 304–12.

8 The material in this section draws selectively from material contained in J Bradley, *An island economy: exploring long-term consequences of peace and reconciliation in the island of Ireland* (Dublin: Forum for Peace and Reconciliation, 1996); F Barry and J Bradley, 'FDI and trade: the Irish host-country experience', *Economic journal* 107:445 (1997), pp. 1,798–1,811; J Bradley, 'Foreign direct investment: implications for Irish economic development and wider lessons', *Rassegna economica: quaderni di ricerca* 3 (2000), pp. 97–138.

9 *Census of industrial production, 1998* (Dublin: Central Statistics Office, 1998).

10 The one EU initiative that Ireland did not adopt was the Schengen agreement, since the UK opted out, and Irish participation would have required the re-establishment of border controls between the Republic and Northern Ireland. The extra time required to pass through the Schengen border controls in European airports is a constant and irritating reminder of this opt-out.

11 Hence, although Irish GDP per head has now exceeded that of the UK, GNP per head – a more accurate measure of performance – is still very similar to that of the UK.

12 P Krugman, 'Good news from Ireland: a geographical perspective', in A Gray (ed.), *International perspectives on the Irish economy* (Dublin: Indecon Economic Consultants, 1997), pp. 38–53.

13 In this section we draw selectively on material from J Bradley and D Hamilton, 'Strategy 2010: planning economic development in Northern Ireland', *Regional studies* 33:9 (1999), pp. 885–902, and J Bradley, *The island economy: past, present and future* (Cork: Cork University Press, 2001) [*Cross currents* series].

14 V Borooah and K Lee, 'The regional dimension of competitiveness in manufacturing: productivity, employment and wages in Northern Ireland and the United Kingdom', *Regional studies* 25:3 (1991), pp. 219–29.

15 *Strategy 2010, a report prepared by the Economic Development Strategy Review Steering Group* (Belfast: Department of Economic Development, 1999). Although this document came under fierce criticism from the media, from the Northern Ireland Economic Council and from academics (including the present writer), it was never revised, has a life after death, and appears to continue to supply whatever strategic logic there is to northern industrial strategy; see Bradley and Hamilton, 'Strategy 2010' (1999).

16 Northern Ireland Economic Council, *The implementation of Northern Ireland's development strategy in the 1990s: lessons for the future* (Belfast: Northern Ireland Economic Council, 1999) [Report No. 131].

17 *Strategy 2010* (1999), p. 113.

18 The existence of subvention finance means that Northern Ireland households can enjoy a very high rate of consumption spending without this causing any problems for the current account of the balance of payments. The balance of payments constraint only matters at the UK national level, and not for its constituent regions – unlike the position in a sovereign state such as the Republic of Ireland, where it can operate to constrain consumer spending.

19 N Farley, 'A comparative analysis of the performance of the manufacturing sectors, North and South: 1960–1991', in J Bradley (ed.), *The two economies of Ireland: public policy, growth and employment* (Dublin: Oak Tree Press, 1995) [Irish Studies in Management]. See chapter 9 for a more extended treatment of the Northern Ireland clothing and textiles sector.

20 *Strategy 2010* (1999), pp. 168–9.

21 We return to the issue of all-island corporate tax rate harmonisation in the concluding section.

22 M Dunford and R Hudson, *Successful European regions: Northern Ireland learning from others* (Belfast: Northern Ireland Economic Council, 1996).

23 The Mezzogiorno region of southern Italy has given its name to a phenomenon of underdevelopment and dependency that arose originally when the much richer north-

ern Italian regions gave generous long-term income transfers to the south, which had an unintended side-effect of locking the south into a low-efficiency, low-productivity, low-entrepreneurial dependency; 'Annex III: Regional disparities: the Southern issue', *The economic and financial situation in Italy* (Brussels: EU Commission, 1993) [European economy, reports and studies, no. 1].

24 A recent example of an asymmetric shock that had a negative impact on Northern Ireland was the refusal of the UK government to join the European Monetary Union at its inception in January 1999. The subsequent strengthening of sterling relative to the euro had a more serious impact on the weaker Northern Ireland economy that on the more prosperous and stronger core British regions, particularly due to its trade exposure to the Republic, a eurozone member; see J Bradley (ed.), *Regional economic and policy impacts of EMU: the case of Northern Ireland* (Belfast: Northern Ireland Economic Council, 1998) [Research Monograph 6].

25 K Ohmae, *The invisible continent* (London: Nicholas Brealey, 2000).

26 K Ohmae, 'Putting global logic first', in K Ohmae (ed.), *The evolving global economy* (Cambridge, MA: Harvard Business Review Books, 1996), pp. 129–37.

27 An example of the limits to discretionary policy making in Northern Ireland is the case of the high level of aid promised in the mid-1990s to a Taiwanese textiles plant (Hualon), which sparked off protests from rival textiles companies in England and had to be adjudicated (in favour of Northern Ireland) by the European Commission. In the event, Hualon changed its plans and never came to Northern Ireland.

28 The situation for chemicals and related products (SITC 5) is also anomalous, with 24% of total exports to the EU in this category, 16% to Britain, but only 9% to the North. One should note a residual category – 'other' – which makes up 15% of total Southern exports to the North, and is negligible to anywhere else. This category consists of goods whose trade volume is at too low a threshold to be accurately recorded, and almost certainly consists of traditional rather than high-technology products.

29 M Best, *The new competition: institutions of industrial restructuring* (Cambridge: Polity Press, 1990); Porter, *Competitive advantage* (1990)

30 An interesting European case is the recent decision of Peugeot to relocate out of Britain to Slovakia. Bidding for the plant was intense, in particular between Slovakia, the Czech Republic and the Polish region of Dolnoslaskie (Lower Silesia). Slovakia won, but the adjoining Czech, Slovak and Polish regions are becoming a cluster within the automotive sector.

31 *Strategy 2010* (1999); *Enterprise 2010* (Dublin: Forfas, 2000); *Ahead of the curve* (Dublin: Forfas, 2004).

32 Porter, *Competitive advantage*, Best, *New competitive advantage.*

33 Bradley, *Island economy* (1996).

34 Data presented in the *Strategy 2010* working paper on the textiles and clothing sector (unpublished) show that wage rates in Northern Ireland are almost nine times higher than in Estonia (for textiles) and nine times higher than in Romania (for clothing). The ratios for Bangladesh and Vietnam are in the region of thirty times higher.

35 Northern Ireland's economic dependency is presently, of course, of the comfortable variety, since the British subvention ensures that living standards do not fall too far below national levels.

36 See D Coyle, W Alexander and B Ashcroft (eds), *New wealth for old nations: Scotland's economic prospects* (Princeton: Princeton University Press, 2005).

4

Civil society: the permeability of the North–South border

KEVIN HOWARD

INTRODUCTION

In 1983, John Whyte published a preliminary overview of associational life in Ireland which drew attention to the negligible impact of partition on its organisational structure.[1] Whyte's article implied that civil society retained a border-transcending dynamic that might be counterposed to the border-reinforcing dynamic of separate state development. He was writing sixty years after partition, and in the period between when his data were sourced and the appearance of his article Northern Ireland experienced the most intensive and destructive political violence of the entire troubles. It is widely recognised that the 'troubles' reinforced the saliency of the political boundary; the southern government in particular sought to insulate its people from any possibly destabilising involvement in the north. Yet Whyte's preliminary conclusion was that the strength of the linkages across the Irish–UK land border was rare by international standards.[2] In all sorts of ways, across a range of diverse organisations, all-island and indeed all-archipelago associational life went on, in a sense, outside the line of sight of academic analysts and politicians. The general thrust of Whyte's analysis is that politics and associational life are distinct spheres. While this is a classical liberal position, it raises compelling questions about the nature of civil society on the island of Ireland. Looked at from one perspective, his findings point to the limited impact of political partition on all-island civil society; looked at from another perspective, they point to the limited impact of civil society on political partition.

This chapter is based on a follow up study twenty-two years later which aimed to revisit Whyte's tentative hypotheses. In the first section below, the concept of civil society, its contested meanings and its applicability to Whyte's study are discussed in the context of the partition of Ireland. The second section provides an overview of the data in the current study and describes how it relates to Whyte's earlier work. It provides a tabular summary of the territorial structure of the organisations surveyed and concludes with a general discussion of the problems of nomenclature – the lack of clarity over what precisely people mean when they refer to 'Ireland'. The third section is devoted to a detailed discussion of each of seven categories of civil society organisations: churches and church-related organisations, sport, cultural and scientific bodies, professional associations, social welfare and voluntary organisations, trade unions, and trade associations. The findings are compared to Whyte's earlier observations in each case. Finally, the conclusion draws together the findings of the current study and attempts to assess the nature of civil society on the island of Ireland in the light of John Whyte's earlier work.

CIVIL SOCIETY AND PARTITION

It is worth pointing out that Whyte does not use the term civil society at all, referring instead to private and voluntary organisations. This is particularly interesting from the perspective of the history of ideas. Whyte was writing in the early 1980s, before the resurgence of interest amongst academics and politicians in the notion of civil society. Michael Edwards provides a useful overview of the disparate conceptualisations of civil society that have emerged in the extensive subsequent literature.[3] He differentiates between civil society as 'associational life', as the 'good society', and as the 'public sphere'. These conceptualisations are analytically and practically distinct. Civil society understood as associational life corresponds to Whyte's notion of private and voluntary associations, and is central to the conceptual framework of liberalism. Civil society is the realm of personal freedom upon which the state seeks to encroach. The perceived triumph of liberalism that marked the end both of the Soviet Union and the Cold War stimulated a renewed interest in civil society as a necessary bulwark against the state, which, above all, is regarded as a coercive institution. Whyte's study, though articulated outside the terms of this debate, shows that the relationship between the public realm of the state and the private realm of associational life is more complex than that.

While there are different understandings of the role of civil society as well as of the term itself, the notion of civil society as associational life is closely related to that of social capital. This is another term of recent vintage, even if the idea encapsulated is as old as political thought.[4] The increased popularity of both concepts correlates with the decline of neo-liberalism which, since the mid-1990s, has been replaced by ill-defined 'third ways'. Central to this is the need to reinvigorate 'the community' – another equally fuzzy concept.[5] The British Office for National Statistics, for example, defines social capital as 'the pattern and intensity of networks among people' and its effects as 'the shared values which arise from those networks', thereby generating 'a greater sense of community spirit'.[6] The Taoiseach, Bertie Ahern, offered this definition:

> The concept of Social Capital relates to networks, relationships and feelings of belonging, of trust and a sense of civic responsibility. These are things which shape the spirit of co-operation and quality of life in local communities and groups, and enables wider society to achieve desired policy goals more effectively. I suppose you could describe Social Capital as a kind of glue that holds society together.[7]

As stated, the terminology Whyte uses corresponds to the notion of civil society as associational life. In this sense, it is a classic liberal conception of civil society as the realm of individual freedom and action separate from politics. For instance, Whyte highlights the apparent anomalies of unionists' vigorous support for all-Ireland sporting teams and nationalists' membership of British trade unions. At one level, individual pragmatism and/or social and cultural interests can be kept distinct from political preferences.

OVERVIEW OF THE DATA

Whyte found that, of the organisations he studied, 'a substantial minority ... 21% of the total operate across the international frontier, either on an all-Ireland or an all-archipelago basis'.[8] It is worth exploring this further by seeking to establish if this figure has changed and what, precisely, determines the shape of an organisation's territorial structure. Two key variables seem to have an impact on this: the nature of the organisation's activity, and its date of foundation. Given the lapse in time since Whyte's original overview, and the fact that this did not provide sufficient data on when organisations were established, the idea of conducting a new survey seemed a compelling one.

A new study

The rest of this chapter is based on a short survey of organisations listed in the Institute of Public Administration's 2005 *Yearbook*.[9] In the case of each organisation, the survey sought to establish its territorial area of operation and its date of foundation. The organisations were grouped to correspond closely to the categories used in Whyte's original study: churches and church-related bodies; youth and sporting organisations; cultural and scientific bodies; charitable and welfare organisations; professional associations; trade associations; and trade unions. Of course, we acknowledge an inescapable element of subjectivity in the allocation of organisations to these categories. However, it was not our intention to replicate exactly the original study. The aim was to revisit the general hypotheses that the type of activity in which an organisation is involved and its foundation date have an impact on its territorial parameters. Of the 622 organisations surveyed, 418 responded either to the original request or to a follow-up prompt – a response rate of 67 per cent.

Table 4.1. Territorial structure of associational life in Ireland, 2005

Category	Rep. of Ireland	All-Ireland	All-archipelago	NI/UK	other	No. of responses	No. of bodies
Churches and church-related	13	78	0	0	9	22	38
Youth and sporting	14	72	3	5	6	74	116
Cultural and scientific	25	59	9	0	7	64	77
Professional associations	34	41	25	0	0	59	97
Social welfare/ voluntary	50	38	4	0	8	57	96
Trade unions	62	5	14	19	0	43	63
Trade associations	67	21	6	6	0	99	135
All	42	43	6	3	6	418	622

Note: all figures except those in the last two columns are percentages, and total 100 horizontally. The last column reports the number of bodies surveyed, and the penultimate column the number responding to the survey.

Source: mail survey by author of organisations taken from IPA *Yearbook*, 2005, corresponding to the categories mentioned above, December 2004 to February 2005.

Table 4.1 provides an overview of the territorial structure of civil society organisations in Ireland classified by the seven categories mentioned above. It should be noted that the organisations vary greatly in size and relative importance, a consideration that needs to be borne in mind in interpreting the quantitative discussion below. Civil society organisations can be arranged along a spectrum. At one end would be organisations confined solely to one side or other of the border and which were established after partition. In other words, the international boundary delimits these organisations temporally and spatially. At the other end of the spectrum would be organisations established before partition which continue to be organised on an all-Ireland or an all-archipelago basis. The first are paradigmatic national organisations; they are constrained by, and they reinforce, the boundary; the second are paradigmatic boundary-transcending transnational organisations in that they continue to operate as they have always done, despite the international boundary.

As can be seen from Table 4.1, the striking feature of our research is that the percentage of bodies organised transnationally is even greater than in John Whyte's preliminary survey. The least 'partitionist' category is the 'churches and church-related' one, followed closely by the 'youth and sporting' category. The most 'partitionist' categories are the trade association one, followed by the trade unions and then the social welfare and voluntary groups. The 'cultural and scientific' and the 'professional association' categories occupy a middle ground between the religious and the material, between the sacred and the profane, so to speak.

What's in a name?

One of the striking features of organisational nomenclature in Ireland is the way in which an organisation's territorial parameters cannot be read off from its name. The significance of this is that the usage of terms such as 'Ireland' and 'national' in the organisational nomenclature of entities that are confined to the twenty-six counties serves to elide the island's separation into two jurisdictions.[10]

At one level the mismatch between territorial structure and organisational nomenclature could be regarded as trivial, but naming conventions are heavily laden with political and historical symbolism even if those constructing them are not fully aware of their significance. The dispute over the decision to discard the territorially ambiguous organisational title 'Royal Ulster Constabulary' for the more accurate 'Police Service of Northern Ireland' is just one recent and high-profile example. The 'Belfast' or 'Good Friday' agreement of 1998 is another. This applies equally to civil society institutions and associations. Organisational nomenclature is heavily laden with political symbolism; naming conventions 'flag' far more than mere function.

Naming conventions can be seen as either consciously or unconsciously recycling territorial claims. In this sense they constitute a form of what Michael Billig describes as banal nationalism, defined as consisting of:

> ideological habits which enable the established nations of the West to be reproduced. It is argued that these habits are not removed from everyday life, as some observers have supposed. Daily, the nation is indicated, or 'flagged', in the lives of its citizenry. Nationalism, far from being an intermittent mood in established nations, is the endemic condition.[11]

Central to this process of inculcating and maintaining 'nation-ness' is the homeland's map-image. The outline of the state is widely disseminated; as an image it is instantly recognisable; it functions as an iconic logo – no words are necessary. Yet in the map-image of Ireland the state is hardly ever used; it jars the sensibilities of even the most partitionist twenty-six county nationalists. This contrasts with the practice of Scottish nationalists, Welsh nationalists and even Northern Irish unionists of representing their 'homeland' as disembodied from the territory of adjacent political entities. The styling of the map-image in the twenty-six-county state is one example of how, despite the partition of the island of Ireland, ambiguity over what constitutes 'Ireland' remains endemic.

Similarly, the usage of the term 'Ireland' to describe the twenty-six-county state is constitutionally validated and thoroughly entrenched in the greater part of the island, while there is a correspondingly ambiguous – if less widespread – usage of the term 'Ulster' when what is being referred to is Northern Ireland. It is this ambiguity in naming conventions that is one of the most obvious results from our survey of the territorial structure of civil society organisations. Of the organisations we surveyed, the majority (66 per cent) began their titles with 'Irish' or with 'national', or ended with 'of Ireland'. Consider, for example, the 'Irish Rugby Football Union' or the 'Irish Bankers' Federation'; the 'National Dairy Council' or the 'National Women's Council of Ireland'; the 'Statistical and Social Inquiry Society of Ireland' or the 'Teachers' Union of Ireland'. Alternatively, included amongst the organisations that responded to our survey are the Ulster Teachers Union, the Ulster Clay Pigeon Association and the Ulster Rifle Association. The territorial area of organisation for all these organisations was given as Northern Ireland. Indeed, we found no correlation between name of organisation and territorial structure with the exceptions of when title and territory were unambiguously flagged, for example, the 'Northern Ireland Athletic Federation', or the 'Republic of Ireland Snooker and Billiards Association'.

SEVEN CATEGORIES OF CIVIL SOCIETY ORGANISATIONS

We turn now to analyse each of the organisational categories, following the structure as set out in Table 4.1, moving from the least to the most partitionist, and comparing our findings with Whyte's original study.

Churches and church-related organisations

Whyte argued that of all the categories this is the one in which the border is least observed. This is clear in Table 4.1. More than in any other category, organisations of this type ignore the political boundary at least as far as the land boundary is concerned. We did not identify any all-archipelago church organisations. This is also the category in which we find the largest organisations. The major churches pre-date partition by many centuries; indeed, the Church of Ireland regards itself as the 'descendant of the Church founded by St Patrick in the fifth century AD, which embraced the whole island'.[12] The Catholic Church remains the largest of any all-Ireland organisation in terms of members, that is, people born into and brought up in the Catholic faith while not necessarily being practitioners or even believers. Defined in this maximal fashion, there are 4.2 million Catholics on the island of Ireland. At the opposite end of the spectrum there are fewer than 800 Bahais.[13] In terms of both sociological and political importance, the Catholic Church and the organisation representing the Bahais are radically different; nevertheless, both stress their all-Ireland orientation. Of the organisations that responded to the survey, 83 per cent described themselves *de facto* as boundary transcending, either as all-Ireland organisations (61 per cent) or, alternatively, as functioning on a worldwide basis (22 per cent). Some organisations are territorially structured in accordance with the political boundary. For example, the Jewish Representative Council of Ireland confines its activities to the Republic; Northern Ireland is organised separately. The Islamic Council of Ireland described itself in similar terms. Nevertheless, these are the exceptions. As Whyte indicated, there appears to be something about the nature of religious organisations, irrespective of their scale and or foundation date, that is, literally, transcendent.

Sport in Ireland

This study differs significantly from Whyte's in the greater emphasis given to the youth and sports category. The reason for this is that in the five years between 2001 and 2006 sport moved to centre stage in state projects of invigorating social cohesion on the island of Ireland. According to a 2005 study, published jointly by the Republic's Economic and Social Research Institute and the Irish Sports Council, the value of sporting bodies is that:

> They bring people together, help build communities, and provide a focus for collective identity and belonging. The collectivities affected by sport in this way can range from the small community that supports a local club team to an entire society following the fortunes of an individual or national team in major international competition.[14]

Partition has had an impact on sporting activity in Ireland in diverse ways. Ireland has thirty-two-county national teams in some sports and twenty-six-county national teams in others that compete on the world stage in their various disciplines. At the same time, the largest, richest sporting organisation of all, the Gaelic Athletic Association (GAA), does not engage in any serious international competition. Nevertheless, it is a border ignoring organisation, with the largest number of active voluntary members of any sporting organisation. It has been estimated that the GAA has 300,000 adult members, which contrasts with the association's own estimate of 700,000 members (the latter figure includes children).[15] It is an indigenous civil society association that has flourished in spite of partition, yet, as we will argue, political division on the island has parallels even in the GAA.

The organisation of sport on the island of Ireland falls between the two ideal types suggested above. Whyte identifies nineteen sports that are organised on an all-Ireland basis, and twenty-one organised on a Republic or Northern Ireland basis (he does not classify nine-county Ulster sporting organisations separately). This is an area in which there has been an explosion of interest and corresponding organisational development. The website of the Irish Sports Council lists sixty-two governing bodies for the various sports in Ireland.[16] The equivalent website of the Sports Council of Northern Ireland lists ninety organisations described as 'Northern Ireland/Ulster governing bodies of sport'.[17] However, some of these are the same organisations as posted on the Irish Sports Council's website; others are the northern branches of all-Ireland organisations, while still others are the Northern Ireland branches of UK organisations.

Association Football, or soccer, is the world's most popular sport. The Irish Football Association is a useful example of a pre-partition all-island organisation retrenching to one side of the line after partition. Its website describes the organisation's trajectory:

> On the 18th November 1880 … the Irish Football Association [came into being]. Its aims were to promote, foster and develop the game throughout Ireland … The IFA's first International venture was against England at the Knock Ground, Bloomfield in East Belfast, in 1882. Ireland lost 13-0 … however success was to come eventually, on a worldwide stage through qualification for the World Cup Finals in 1958 (Sweden), 1982 (Spain) and 1986 (Mexico).[18]

The website glosses over the transmutation of the thirty-two-county Ireland soccer team into the six-county Northern Ireland team. This studied indifference to the existence of the 'southern' and far more successful Football Association of Ireland was helped by the fact that the two 'Ireland' teams did not contest a competitive match against each other for fifty years after partition.[19] Both teams continued to describe themselves as the 'Ireland' national team, an anomaly that was not fully resolved until the 1970s; indeed neither team now describes itself solely as 'Ireland'. According to soccer's international governing body, FIFA, the twenty-six-county team is the 'Republic of Ireland'; the six-county team is Northern Ireland.

Whyte highlights a class dimension that might have impacted on the organisation of sport. He suggests that:

> By and large, the more middle-class games (golf, polo, lawn tennis, rugby) seem more likely to be organised on an all-Ireland basis than the more proletarian sports (cycling, soccer, wrestling). This may be because political feelings in the past tended to run higher in working-class circles.[20]

While acknowledging that his analysis was preliminary, the above observation requires a degree of qualification. It implies that the working class is more likely to be nationalist and that proletarian sportspeople are less likely to organise on an all-Ireland basis than the middle classes. In the case of rugby union, Whyte suggests that 'on neither side [of the politico-religious divide] was there a desire to make an issue about symbols such as flags and anthems'. The perception that rugby is a more middle-class activity is widespread. Yet the 'proletarian' enthusiasm for rugby in working-class Limerick is an exception to this generalisation. Moreover, recent claims of intra-provincial sectarianism in the organisation of rugby in Ulster have shone a light beneath the veneer of apparent all-Ireland unity, exposing to some extent the artificiality of an all-Ireland national team with two 'national' anthems. More problematic again are coarse fishing, by definition a proletarian sport and organised on an all-Ireland basis, and boxing – the quintessential proletarian sport. Competitive cycling also falls into this category, as discussed in chapter 10.

Moreover, 'class' as a determinant in whether or not particular sports are organised nationally or transnationally cannot really explain the GAA – the paradigmatic all-Ireland body. Yet, even here, there are indications of emerging North–South divisions. Hassan has argued that these divisions were brought into sharp relief during the GAA's internal debate during 2001 over whether or not to abandon the association's rule 21, the prohibition on members of the 'crown forces' in Northern Ireland from being GAA members.[21] When rule 21 was debated in November 2001, every one of the Republic's 301 delegates voted in favour of its repeal; delegates from the six northern counties overwhelmingly voted to retain it. These divisions in turn correlate to radically divergent experiences of what it means to be a member of the GAA. In the North it was potentially dangerous, an experience that has no parallel in the South of Ireland. GAA members in the Republic have not been targeted and killed by pro-state terrorists, nor have their sports grounds been used as bases by state security forces. The 'rule 21' controversy could be seen as indicating that as far as southerners are concerned, the North is settled business. Intra-GAA political divisions were revisited in 2005 during the run-up to the vote on whether or not to open Croke Park, the GAA's showcase stadium, to 'foreign games', namely rugby and soccer. What in effect was a private matter for the GAA on how it should use its assets was recast as a debate over the nature of contemporary Irish identity. In the end, the vote was overwhelmingly in favour of allowing a temporary derogation from the rule prohibiting these sports. The territorial divisions almost mirrored those over the rule 21 controversy; no northern county was in favour of the derogation.

Cultural and scientific bodies

In this category, organisations established prior to partition continue to be territorially structured on an all-island basis. This includes the well-known peak organisations such as the Royal Irish Academy (established in 1785), the Royal Hibernian Academy (1823), the Statistical and Social Inquiry

Society of Ireland (1848) and the Royal Irish Academy of Music (1856), but also lesser-known organisations such as the Water Colour Society of Ireland (1870). The Esperanto Association of Ireland (founded in 1907 as the Irish Esperanto Association) is the only pre-partition organisation in this category identified as based solely in the Republic. Even for those organisations established after partition, all-island, all-archipelago, and/or international structures predominate. Indeed, only a minority (16 per cent) are described as based solely in the Republic. The most common reported structure is all-Ireland (60 per cent). What the responses to our survey indicate, and what Whyte signalled, is that the impact of partition on the cultural unity of the island has been limited.

Professional associations

The cross-border compatibility of professional accreditation is crucial to the creation and maintenance of a mobile transnational labour market. It has become a pressing issue for the EU as it seeks to harmonise the internal commodification of labour. Yet the example of Ireland and the UK foreshadows what the EU is working towards, in that there is a significant amount of all-archipelago recognition of professional qualifications. Of those professional associations that responded to our survey, 66 per cent were transnational organisations, and only 34 per cent were confined solely to the Republic. Of these, only two were established before partition. The first, Veterinary Ireland, is an amalgam of five smaller veterinary organisations that existed in the twenty-six counties prior to 2000. The Veterinary profession after partition retrenched to either side of the border, though under bilateral agreements veterinary surgeons qualified in the UK or Ireland can practise across the border as long as they register with the governing body of the other state. In 2006, for example, nine Northern Ireland surgeons registered to practise across the border. The second organisation, the Association of City and County Councils, was established in 1899, before partition, in the wake of the seminal 1898 Local Government (Ireland) Act.[22] It was restructured in 1922 following the breaking off of contact by the northern county councils.

Although there are a 'bewildering variety of units of territorial organisation', there is a significant presence of all-archipelago bodies (25 per cent of our survey respondents). For Whyte, one possible explanation of this is the mobility of professionals: 'For professional people above all, the archipelago is one market. Irish doctors, engineers, architects, surveyors and so on have gone in large numbers to Britain, and are anxious to avoid taking any step which would make that freedom of movement more difficult.'[23] The foundation dates of professional associations would appear to bear out Whyte's suggestions. For instance, the Association of Surgeons of Great Britain and Ireland was established in 1920.

Yet not all professional qualifications are mutually recognised across the archipelago. The teaching profession, for instance, offers a well-known counter-example. Traditionally throughout the archipelago, different teaching regimes applied; Scottish schools would not recognise any qualifications other than their own. The issue is further complicated in Ireland in that some professions are regulated, while others are not. For example those working in the fields of law, finance/taxation, and teaching are regulated; architects are not – at least not in Ireland.[24] Nevertheless, the general claim that professional associations are comparatively more likely to be organised internationally is borne out by the responses to our findings.

Social welfare and voluntary organisations

The difficulty in achieving conceptual precision is not confined to defining civil society or social capital. We referred above to a similar difficulty in defining voluntary activities. These difficulties stem from the same problem: how to draw a clear line between the public and the private that differentiates publicly funded from voluntary activity in the sphere of social welfare provision. The term voluntary can appear slightly misleading. As Edwards puts it, 'the word "voluntary" here needs a little explanation, since many associations are run by paid professionals as well as volunteers'.[25] When voluntary social welfare activity took off in the nineteenth century, the boundary between publicly funded state activity and privately funded voluntary activity was easier to draw. The enormous growth in state provision has blurred the boundary, as voluntary associations have been incorporated into mechanisms of social administration and provision. The classic liberal definition of civil society rests on the distinction between public and private; the value of this is now questionable.[26]

The intimate relationship between the state, as the source of funding and support, and voluntary associations helps us to make sense of some of our seemingly anomalous survey responses. High-profile organisations such as the Irish Society for the Prevention of Cruelty to Children, the National League of the Blind of Ireland and St John Ambulance Brigade were founded before partition, in 1880, 1898 and 1903 respectively. Yet all three describe themselves as based solely in the Republic, though in each case they report warm relationships with their parallel organisations in the North. In some instances, however, respondents regarded the North as a shared British–Irish space; for instance, since 1972 the United Kingdom's

National Union of Students and the Republic's Union of Students of Ireland have shared an office and worked together closely. More indicative of southern ambivalence about the North were the responses from the Disabled Drivers' Association of Ireland and Rural Resettlement Ireland, formed in 1970 and 1990 respectively. The first organisation reported a resistance on the part of their members, particularly older ones, to engage in any cross-border activity. Rural Resettlement Ireland reported that they had never considered working in Northern Ireland, because of concerns around perceived cultural differences. In this category, therefore, our responses suggest that the key independent variable is the type of organisation rather than date of foundation. Different projects of state- or nation-building shaped the possibilities for voluntary action.[27]

Trade unions

As indicated in our table, the impact of the state is even more apparent on trade union activity. While it remains the case that 14 per cent of those unions that responded to our survey are organised on an all-archipelago basis, there has been a significant degree of retrenchment to either side of the line. For example, the foundation date of the National Association of Teachers in Further and Higher Education was given as 1904; at the time it was a UK-wide (all-archipelago, pre-1922) organisation that withdrew from the Free State post-1922. Nearly half (48 per cent) of union respondents dated their foundation to the period before partition. Three of these, the Transport Salaried Staffs Association, the National Union of Journalists and the Amalgamated Transport and General Workers Union, remain all-archipelago based; one, the Irish National Teachers Organisation (established in 1868) remains organised on an all-Ireland basis. All the rest are confined to one side of the border or another, either solely in the Republic (50 per cent), in the United Kingdom as a whole (20 per cent), or solely in Northern Ireland (10 per cent), although the Ulster Teachers Union claims twenty members living in the Republic.

For those unions established after partition, only one, the Services, Industrial, Professional and Technical Union (SIPTU, founded in 1990), is organised on an all-Ireland basis, while three are organised on an all-archipelago basis: the British Equity Actors Union (founded in 1929); the manufacturing and public sector union Amicus (2001); and the Union of Construction, Allied Trades and Technicians (UCATT, 1971). However, the roots of SIPTU, Amicus and UCATT are in the trade union movement of the nineteenth and early twentieth centuries (indeed, UCATT dates back to the 1820s, and Amicus to the 1850s). SIPTU is an amalgam of the Irish Transport and General Workers Union (founded in 1909) and the Federated Workers Union of Ireland (founded in 1924). The amalgamations that took place to create Amicus (predominantly engineering) and UCATT (solely construction) had nothing to do with partition. In other words, these amalgams are composites of pre-partition unions, and not post-partition boundary-transcending organisations. The rationale for consolidation seems to be economy of scale. In relation to territorial structure, the state context appears to be a far stronger factor than date of origin. As would be expected, then, the overwhelming majority (83 per cent) of the unions that responded to our survey with post-partition dates of origin are organised on one or other side of the border. Foundation dates range across thirty years: from 1930 (Teachers Union of Ireland) up to 1999 (National Association of Principals and Deputies). Once again, as with those respondents in the voluntary category, what comes out of the research is a sustained pattern of organisational consolidation on either side of the boundary.

Trade associations

The relevance of the political boundary is even more marked in relation to trade associations. Whyte argues that these are the most partitionist of all, something which is to be expected in that 'a large proportion of the business of a trade association is with its government ... it is only common sense to have one trade association facing one government'.[28] This is borne out by our own research as shown above. The impact of the state could help explain some of the anomalous responses to our survey. The date of origin of the Licensed Vintners' Association, for instance, is given as 1872, yet its territorial parameters are described as the Republic of Ireland. In other words, whatever about its origins, the relevant territory is the twenty-six-county state. Of those trade associations founded before partition, the majority (64 per cent) described themselves as based solely in the Republic. Some all-Ireland trade associations established before partition continue to operate; these include the Farm Tractor and Machinery Trade Association (established 1912); the Irish Timber Council (1918); and the Irish Thoroughbred Breeders' Association (1920). The only all-archipelago entity still in existence that was established before partition is the National Federation of Retail Newsagents (founded in 1919). For the post-partition period, Whyte's conclusion is largely borne out: the overwhelming majority of organisations are confined to one or other side of the boundary. Yet, even for those organisations established before partition, the imposition of the political boundary and the evolution of different legal, regulatory and social administrative environments on either side have had a curling effect – associations have re-orientated towards the centre of political and administrative power in their respective jurisdictions.

CONCLUSION

In broad terms, we have found Whyte's tentative conclusions to be supported by this research. A significant minority of the civil society organisations we surveyed (20 per cent) were founded before partition. As Whyte predicted, many of these (indeed the majority – 58 per cent) have remained cross-border entities. However, within this category the type of organisation represented varies significantly; sporting, cultural and religious organisations make up 62 per cent of the total. Correspondingly, and as Whyte further predicted, there is a wide variation in the degree to which partition impacts on organisational territorial structure. As can be seen above, religious, sporting, cultural and professional associations transcend the border most, and this follows irrespective of foundation date. Social welfare and trade organisations follow the boundary more frequently than other categories, and again this follows irrespective of date of foundation. It is also important to remember that none of these categories is static. Expansions and retrenchments are ongoing, though, as we show in chapter 10, the territorial organisation of the seemingly most apolitical activities can easily come to symbolise ethnonational tensions and divisions.

Of perhaps greater significance is how Whyte's research and the follow-up survey reported here suggests that associational life has had a limited impact on the shape, policies and practices of the state. In Northern Ireland, Christopher Farrington argues that civil society – despite all its supposed bridge-building potential – remains divided along ethno-sectarian lines.[29] In the North, social capital, both a basis for and a consequence of associational life, appears to be of the strictly intra-communal 'bonding' variety rather than the inter-communal 'bridging' variety. Moreover, this is a situation that reflects profoundly the division and ethnically exclusivist nature of the state and its peak social institutions. In relation to the island as a whole, Acheson and his colleagues capture it well in their observation that: 'the Irish case shows that the dispositions, types of networks and institutional arrangements of communities (the forms of bonding and bridging capital available to them) do matter, but they matter much less than the processes of state and institution-building in which they are situated'.[30]

In the above definition, the state is the matrix within which civil society operates; it is the state that shapes civil society rather than, as in classical liberalism, civil society being 'outside' the state. The voice of business in the form of trade associations and the voice of workers in the form of trade unions are very much directed towards their respective centres. The parameters of the state constrain these organisations as evidenced by their territorial structures, which have become state-centric even for those unions founded before partition. Yet religious, sporting and cultural organisations are the most likely to be organised transnationally. So, while the centralised nature of the two states in Ireland affects the territorial shape of civil society, the extent of this depends on the type of organisation. Our analysis of Whyte's findings and our follow-up investigation lend support to Edwards' argument that 'major social transformations or systemic changes in politics and economics have rarely been achieved by associations acting alone, even when channelled through broad-based social movements'.[31] When looked at this way, associational life clearly has a boundary-transcending potential, but in and of itself its impact on partition has been limited.

NOTES

1 J Whyte, 'The permeability of the United Kingdom–Irish border: a preliminary reconnaissance', *Administration* 31:3 (1983), pp. 300–15.
2 Whyte, 'Permeability' (1983), p. 314.
3 M Edwards, *Civil society* (Oxford: Polity, 2004).
4 The concept was popularised in particular by R Putnam, *Bowling alone: the collapse and revival of American community* (New York: Simon and Schuster, 2000). For a critical review of the notion of social capital see A Portes, 'Social capital: its origins and applications in modern sociology', *Annual review of sociology* 24 (1998), pp. 1–24.
5 F W Powell and M Geoghegan, *The politics of community development: reclaiming civil society or reinventing governance?* (Dublin: A & A Farmar, 2004).
6 Office of National Statistics, *Social capital: measuring networks and shared values* (London: ONS, 2005); available at www.statistics.gov.uk/cci/nugget.asp?id=314 [accessed 18-07-2006].
7 The Taoiseach, B Ahern, from his speech given at the launch of the National Economic and Social Forum's report, *The policy implications of social capital* (Dublin: NESF, 2003); available www.taoiseach.gov.ie/index.asp?locID=365&docID=1719 [accessed 09-01-2007]
8 Whyte, 'Permeability' (1983), p. 302.
9 *Administration yearbook and diary 2005* (Dublin: Institute of Public Administration, 2004).
10 Use of the term 'Ulster' in the titles of organisations confined solely to the six counties of Northern Ireland, similarly, serves to elide the northern province's partition. Indeed, the description of the archipelago as the British Isles has a similar consequence; it presents these islands as 'British' and ignores independent Ireland's status as a sovereign state. For a discussion of the historical contingency of territorial nomenclature in these islands, see N Davies, *The isles* (London: Macmillan, 1999).
11 M Billig, *Banal nationalism* (London: Sage, 1995), p. 6.

12 Whyte, 'Permeability' (1983), p. 303.
13 In the Republic, the 2002 census recorded 3,462,606 Catholics, the Northern Ireland 2001 census identified 737,412 Catholics; the Bahais were 490 and 254 respectively.
14 L Delaney and T Fahy, *Social and economic value of sport in Ireland* (Dublin: Economic and Social Research Institute and Irish Sports Council, 2005), p. 1.
15 Delaney and Fahy, *Social and economic value* (2005) pp. 11–12.
16 www.irishsportscouncil.ie/developing–ngb–contacts.aspx [accessed 18-07-2006].
17 www.sportni.net/links/ni_gov_body.htm [accessed 18-07-2006].
18 www.irishfa.com [accessed 10-10-2004].
19 Two years later, the association's potted history had been amended to refer to partition: 'Up until partition in 1921 the IFA governed football across the entire island but a decision by the Dublin clubs to form their own association led to the formation of the FAI (Football Association of Ireland). Nowadays the IFA looks after the interests of the game in the six northern counties: Antrim, Armagh, Down, Fermanagh, Londonderry and Tyrone', available at www.irishfa.com/the–ifa/about–the–ifa/ [accessed 10-04-2006]. There is an intriguing parallel between the Free State's enthusiasm for the League of Nations and the FAI's support for and membership of FIFA, the world governing body of soccer, boycotted by the IFA between 1928 and 1946; see G Fulton, 'Northern Catholic fans of the Republic of Ireland soccer team', pp. 140–56 in A Bairner, ed., *Sport and the Irish: histories, identities, issues* (Dublin: UCD Press, 2005), p. 145.
20 Whyte, 'Permeability' (1983), p. 305.
21 D Hassan, 'Sport, identity and Irish nationalism in Northern Ireland', pp. 123–39 in Bairner, *Sport* (2005).
22 See the association's website at www.councillors.ie/Home/tabid/36/Default.aspx [accessed 12-11-2006]
23 Whyte, 'Permeability' (1983), p. 308.
24 See the Department of Education and Science www.education.ie/servlet/blob-servlet/mrpq_contact_list.htm [accessed 10-12-2006].
25 Edwards, *Civil society* (2004) p. 20.
26 The divergence between North and South in this respect began before partition and increased further subsequently, especially after the Second World War, when the relationship between the state and the individual developed in very different ways. The development of comprehensive, universally accessible, cradle to grave, welfare structures provided by the state applied more fully to Northern Ireland, as part of the UK, than it did to the South. By the time partition was imposed there had been at least 200 years of voluntary action in Ireland, carried out by organisations from either of the two major religious denominations, leaving 'little space between them for a pillar of secular action'; see N Acheson, B Harvey, B Kearney and A Williamson, *Two paths one purpose: voluntary action in Ireland, north and south* (Dublin: IPA, 2004), p. 24.
27 As Acheson and his colleagues put it, 'in both Irish jurisdictions the development of the voluntary sector has been closely aligned with the approaches taken to citizen welfare by government in each jurisdiction … [post-partition] these processes dragged the two apart and emphasised differences that were already evident before partition … the factors that underpinned the divergence between the two Irelands are still very much in play'; see Acheson et al., *Two paths* (2004), pp. 321–2.
28 Whyte, 'Permeability' (1983), p. 310.
29 C Farrington., *Models of civil society and their implications for the Northern Ireland peace process* (Dublin: Institute for British Irish Studies, 2006) [IBIS Working Paper no. 43].
30 Acheson et al., *Two paths* (2004), p. 319.
31 Edwards, *Civil society* (2004), p. 52.

5

Public policy: the EU and the Good Friday agreement

ETAIN TANNAM

INTRODUCTION

The aim of this chapter is to examine the question of whether the cross-border relationship has been transformed by EU membership, and if so to determine the limits of such change. The end of the century did indeed witness a more dynamic interaction between Northern Ireland and the Republic of Ireland and the EU played a part in this dynamism, as the other chapters in this book show. However, there were also limits to this transformation, complicating any attempts to present a stark, unambiguous portrait of the border in the twenty-first century.

Previous research has examined the impact of the European Union (EU) on economic and political cooperation between Northern Ireland and the Republic of Ireland.[1] The theoretical framework used in this work was that of neo-functionalism, where the hypothesis was that common economic interests would lead to cross-border economic cooperation, and that this would eventually spill over to cross-border political cooperation. The conclusion drawn ten years ago was that actors adopted a rationalistic, economic cost-benefit analysis to apparent incentives for cross-border cooperation. However, in many areas, agencies in Northern Ireland and the Republic of Ireland perceived each other as rivals for resources, rather than as cooperators. Political intervention by both Irish and British governments, rather than the existence of common economic interests, was found to be the most important explanation for cross-border economic cooperation. Nevertheless, in certain sectors, perceptions of common economic interests had led to cross-border cooperative initiatives, particularly in aspects of business.

This chapter thus proposes to examine:

- whether the establishment of cross-border institutions under the Good Friday agreement of 1998 and the EU's dynamism in encouraging cross-border cooperation have led to new dimensions in cross-border cooperation with implications for politics and economics; and
- the relative significance of intergovernmental factors and supranational factors (under the frameworks of the Good Friday agreement and the EU respectively) in advancing cross-border cooperation.

Of course, the impact of recent changes needs to be assessed in the context of earlier developments, and these are reviewed in the first section of this chapter. This is followed by a general overview of the implications of the Good Friday agreement and the new EU role in promoting cross-border cooperation. The last three sections before the conclusion evaluate patterns of North–South cooperation in three domains: public administration, politics and business. The methodology draws on primary reports from key organisations involved in advancing cross-border cooperation or in administering EU money, on interviews with key actors involved in the administration of cross-border initiatives, and on secondary research on the Good Friday agreement and the EU dimension.[2]

CROSS-BORDER COOPERATION BEFORE 1998

As we have seen in chapter 1, the North–South relationship was for long a rather tense one. The sensitivity of cross-border cooperation arose from the perception among unionists that such cooperation was one step on a slope towards a united Ireland. Indeed, for some nationalists, cross-border cooperation was embraced as a tool to achieve precisely this. But there was a second theme to nationalist attitudes towards cross-border cooperation: for many, it represented an unwelcome recognition not just of partition but of a northern administration that was strongly disliked by most nationalists. In any case, talks between Sean Lemass, Irish prime minister, and Terence O'Neill, Northern Irish prime minister, foundered as the general political situation in Northern Ireland deteriorated in 1966–9.[3] Similarly, the Sunningdale Agreement of 1973 collapsed under the weight of unionist opposition to its cross-border executive council.

However, in the aftermath of the Single European Act of 1986, calls for increased economic cooperation to maximise markets on either side of the border increased, led by members of both unionist and nationalist business communities in Northern Ireland, as well as by business leaders in the Republic. For the period 1988–94, cooperation was modest, with a few flagship joint projects or programmes, such as the opening of the Ballinamore–Ballyconnell canal which straddled the border.[4] Cross-border business conferences spearheaded by the joint council of the Irish Business and Employers Confederation and the Confederation of British Industry in Northern Ireland, and also by the Irish and Northern Irish Chambers of Commerce, were oft-mentioned examples of cross-border cooperation.[5]

Similarly, the creation of the single European market provided incentives for administrative cross-border cooperation. The administration of EU cross-border programmes financed by Interreg involved membership of monitoring committees to oversee the implementation of the programmes on the part of both the Republic and Northern Ireland.[6] Moreover, the EU's tourism, agriculture and transport programmes all had implications for administrative cross-border cooperation, emphasising the development of Northern Ireland and the Republic of Ireland as an island economy seeking to overcome its peripheral status.

There were thus obvious incentives for local cross-border cooperation. 'Europe of the regions', and the concepts of subsidiarity and partnership, appeared to provide incentives for increased local community cross-border cooperation. Subsidiarity implied that decisions would be made at the lowest administrative level at which it was efficient to do so. Partnership implied that decisions would be made jointly by local actors, politicians and business groups, as well as by central government and the EU Commission. In practice, the role of the EU was predominant in advancing localised cross-border cooperation (see below), and Anglo-Irish policy initiatives played the most important role overall in developing such cooperation.

For the two civil services, in Northern Ireland and in the Republic of Ireland, there were perceptions of conflicts of interest, and of compartmenalisation of interests. Therefore, the impact of EU cross-border programmes, or of other EU programmes with implications for cross-border cooperation, was limited to a handful of officials who were involved in a given scheme. Membership of monitoring committees administering EU programmes differed according to each policy area, but also each section of a policy area. Overall, there was very limited coordination between programmes. The breadth of cross-border administrative cooperation was thus impeded.

In addition, competing economic and political interests impeded cross-border administrative cooperation. Tourism and investment (including inward investment, investment in Irish ports and investment in transport generally) were two key areas of conflict – for example, investment in Dublin–Belfast road links threatened to be at the expense of developing

Dublin–Cork links. For Northern Irish civil servants, it was clear that EU funding was dwarfed by British funding, and Northern Irish policy on the EU was governed by the Conservative British administration (1979–97), whose priorities differed significantly from the Irish position on the EU. Thus, many civil service departments saw cross-border cooperation as bringing few short-term benefits. The Anglo-Irish division of the Irish Department of Foreign Affairs was the main civil service department seeking to advance cross-border cooperation.

Divisions over political ideology ensured that nationalist parties, the Social Democratic and Labour Party (SDLP) and Sinn Féin, supported and welcomed cross-border cooperation, but unionist parties, the Ulster Unionist Party (UUP) and the Democratic Unionist Party (DUP), opposed it. The DUP particularly painted cross-border cooperation as 'sinister' and an 'evil genius' and opposed the Haagerup Report, a document produced by the European Parliament in 1984 which called for political reform and economic development in Northern Ireland. However, in practice, Irish MEPs cooperated to receive EU funds and to lobby against reform of the EU's common agricultural policy. The UUP adopted a more moderate response to the EU and to cross-border cooperation, and its position shifted subtly after 1994. However, all unionist parties opposed institutionalised cross-border cooperation as envisaged by the British–Irish Joint Framework Document in 1995.

A noteworthy feature of cross-border political cooperation was evidence of increased local political cooperation between unionist and nationalist politicians along the border area. Special cross-border committees received fresh dynamism from EU regional policy to advance local economic development. These committees increasingly provided forums for meetings between unionist and nationalist councillors on both sides of the border. Cross-border conferences were well attended by all parties, and preparation of joint studies and of project proposals became a large focus of cross-border activity. Local councillors observed a growing consensus among all councillors on cross-border economic issues, but again coordination problems and an absence of information weakened opportunities for such cooperation.

The business sector also provided evidence of increased, albeit limited, cross-border cooperation. Cross-border business conferences and an atmosphere of change permeated accounts of the cross-border business relationship in the early 1990s. The Northern Ireland section of the Confederation of British Industry, the Irish Business and Employers Confederation and the Irish and Northern Irish Chambers of Commerce all lobbied for and organised cross-border initiatives, seeking to maximise market benefits for the two parts of the island. For example, Chamberlink was established in 1994 to develop a joint economic strategy for the border area. Trade between Northern Ireland and the Republic enjoyed a gradual increase in 1989–96, as did North–South mobility as measured by numbers of passengers crossing the border. Moreover, the Irish and Northern Irish tourist boards began to cooperate closely to increase numbers visiting each jurisdiction. However, there were obvious limitations to cross-border business cooperation (see chapter 3). Trade still constituted only 5 per cent of total trade for both sides; large firms were found to look to bigger markets, not to an 'all-island' economy; and different exchange rates hindered trade.[7] Thus, economic obstacles to cross-border cooperation existed, and it was agreed that government intervention was necessary if such cooperation were to increase.

Overall, continuity and some change characterised the cross-border relationship, but its most striking feature was the impetus provided not by the EU, nor significantly by businesses, nor by civil servants in general, but by the British and Irish governments. The European Commission itself followed the lead of the two governments and was willing to provide financial support. In 1994, it established a task force to investigate the issue of practical assistance to the southern Irish border counties and Northern Ireland. The Peace I programme provided €300 million under the structural funds umbrella, initially for a three year period. Fifteen per cent of the total allocation was reserved for cross-border development. The new structures to deliver the funding were described as 'a major development in terms of the level of devolved responsibility which it created'.[8] This was a highly significant development, notwithstanding uneven familiarity within the commission with the nuances of the Irish conflict and a certain reluctance towards getting involved in it.

In 1998, the political and economic landscape of cross-border cooperation altered dramatically with the inclusion of cross-border institutions in 'strand two' of the Good Friday agreement. Simultaneously, the Irish government was forced to introduce a new regional structure in response to commission demands, with a view to optimising funding prospects from the EU. In the remainder of this chapter the effect of the Good Friday agreement and of the recent EU dimension is assessed. In the next section the new arrangements for cross-border cooperation under the Good Friday agreement and the EU's new provisions are examined before their impact on the Irish–Northern Irish relationship is considered.

THE GOOD FRIDAY AGREEMENT AND THE EU

The Good Friday agreement provided for a power-sharing executive and assembly within Northern Ireland, with devolved powers over specified areas. Strand two of the agreement was of key relevance to cross-border cooperation, as described in chapter 2 above. The North/South Ministerial Council (NSMC) was established to develop 'consultation, cooperation and action within the island of Ireland, including through implementation on an all-island and cross-border basis – on matters of mutual interest within the competence of Administrations, North and South'. A British–Irish Council was also established, comprising representatives of the British and Irish governments and devolved institutions in Northern Ireland, Scotland and Wales and, if appropriate, elsewhere in the United Kingdom, and in adjacent crown dependencies. There was a new British–Irish Intergovernmental Conference which would subsume both the Anglo-Irish Intergovernmental Council and the Intergovernmental Conference established under the Anglo-Irish agreement of 1985.

The NSMC resembles the EU in its style of policy-making in some respects. Its plenary meetings are headed by the Taoiseach, the Northern Irish First Minister and the Deputy First Minister. Like the EU, emphasis is on reaching decisions in designated areas by consensus. Sixty areas of cooperation were discussed in the negotiations which preceded the Good Friday agreement, but only twelve of these were agreed upon. In six of these, implementation bodies were established, as described in chapter 2. The areas of cooperation comprised areas where an economic or other need for cross-border cooperation was recognised, but where various obstacles existed to establishing implementation bodies. Some objections were driven by unionist alarm at an excessively large Irish dimension. As one observer summarised it, 'the unionist concern has been to ensure that the North–South or Irish dimension does not acquire a momentum of its own that will undermine the union'.[9]

Thus, the negotiations which preceded the Good Friday agreement highlighted accountability and legality issues in respect of the new institutions. There was also bureaucratic resistance in civil service departments in both Dublin and Belfast.[10] However, as the next section shows, civil service involvement in cross-border cooperation was generally more significant than in the period before 1998. Two bodies are of particular significance for purposes of this chapter. One is the Special EU Programmes Body (SEUPB), which continues to be subject to monitoring committees, comprising commission officials as well as business and governmental representatives. The creation of the SEUPB implies that there are overlaps between the British–Irish dimension of cross-border cooperation and the EU dimension. The second is InterTrade Ireland, a body seeking to promote business contacts between the two jurisdictions.

Two main factors potentially altered the significance of the EU in the North–South relationship. First, the amount of money provided by the EU to foster cross-border cooperation and to underpin the peace process generally increased. Second, in response to Commission criteria for regional funding, the six counties in the Republic which adjoin the border were designated as having 'objective one' status, implying an entitlement to dedicated funding. In order to receive maximum funding from the EU, administrative arrangements to ensure partnership and subsidiarity were demanded.

Before 1999, the Irish state constituted a single 'objective one' region, under EU GDP criteria. However, the increased economic prosperity enjoyed in the 1990s led to the Commission altering this status. Thus in 1999 it was decided that only the Border–Midlands–Western region met objective one criteria. The rest of the state and all of Northern Ireland were subject to transitional arrangements whereby they would have access to objective one funding, but on a gradually reducing basis until 2006.[11] The identification of the Irish border region as 'objective one' increased the incentives for the Irish government to adhere to commission requests for partnership and for evidence of subsidiarity. The identification of a separate region within the Republic of Ireland ended the congruence of central administration and regional status in the Irish case. Thus, changes in Irish objective one status had potential implications for the border regions and for cross-border cooperation. Moreover, under the EU's peace programmes, the financial incentives to increase cross-border cooperation multiplied.

Central government departments were involved in administering the money, but so too were district partnerships and intermediary funding bodies, comprising eleven voluntary organisations working to foster economic and social development. Both the partnerships and the intermediary funding bodies 'were seen … as bringing an element of "bottom-up development"'.[12] Funding was allocated according to economic need and population size. The monitoring committee comprised twenty-two civil servants from the two jurisdictions and nine commission officials.

The EU dimension was further strengthened financially when it was agreed that Peace I would be continued until 2004 (as Peace II), providing €500m to the border regions (€400m to Northern Ireland and €100m to the six Irish border counties). In addition, Interreg, Leader and other community initiatives provided funding to Northern Ireland and the Republic of

Ireland. Northern Ireland was allocated €890m and the Republic of Ireland €3,200m under EU initiatives, some of them specifically for cross-border cooperation (see chapter 11). A consultation process with local partnerships began about how EU money should be allocated.

The main difference in the administration of Peace I and Peace II was that under the new Good Friday agreement arrangements a new implementation body, the SEUPB, would be responsible for administering the programme and for liaising with the monitoring committee and the European Commission on managing Peace II. The SEUPB chairs the monitoring committee, which comprises members of the Irish Department of Finance, the Northern Irish Department of Finance and Personnel, and business, voluntary sector, trade union and agricultural representatives. Overall, as part of strand two of the Good Friday agreement, the SEUPB is accountable to the central authorities in Northern Ireland and the Republic, and it represents a far more centralised form of managing EU money than the arrangements under Peace I. It constitutes a forum for civil service cross-border cooperation and for increased coordination of policy across the two jurisdictions.

Moreover, local partnerships are still perceived to play an important role in economic development, but in Northern Ireland the role of local councils was enhanced at the behest of the new Assembly and of local councils in Northern Ireland. The role of community or voluntary sector organisations was reduced. Thus the new partnerships comprised primarily local government actors, and second the social partners, including the voluntary sector. In the Irish border region county council-led task forces exist, comprising state agencies, local development bodies, social partners and local government.

Overall, changes in the Republic of Ireland's objective one status, increases in EU funding and the creation of new administrative structures to administer EU money potentially affected the cross-border relationship. The Good Friday agreement both overlaps with this EU dimension (through the creation of the SEUPB) and also potentially provides an independent effect on cross-border cooperation. In the next section the impact of both the Good Friday agreement and the EU on cross-border cooperation is assessed.

THE ADMINISTRATIVE DIMENSION

The provisions for cross-border cooperation under the Good Friday agreement had large potential implications for administrative, political and business behaviour.[13] Administratively, the establishment of the NSMC and the joint secretariat in Armagh had obvious implications for cross-border civil service cooperation. The heads of the joint secretariat work closely together and are dedicated to coordinating and implementing cross-border initiatives in specified areas. Similarly, the staff based in Armagh are by definition involved in cross-border administrative cooperation.

The implementation bodies work closely with relevant civil service departments in Northern Ireland and the Republic. For example, InterTrade Ireland 'works in close collaboration with the Department of Trade and Investment, Belfast, the Department of Enterprise, Trade and Employment, Dublin and with the existing development agencies, North and South'.[14] Similarly, the SEUPB comprises members of the Department of Finance and Personnel and the Irish Department of Finance. It works closely with a wide variety of civil service departments, such as agriculture, trade and enterprise, and with local economic and political actors, and encourages local communities to discuss future areas of local cross-border cooperation. Overall, the SEUPB coordinates the activity of various actors involved in administering EU funds to Northern Ireland and the Republic, providing greater coordination of the various monitoring committees involved in each EU programme.

The implementation bodies broaden levels of cross-border administrative cooperation by working with relevant civil service departments and divisions and other relevant actors. Such broad cooperation is central to their work. The areas of cooperation highlighted by the Good Friday agreement (as opposed to the implementation bodies) provide a further basis for extended cross-border administrative cooperation. For example, Tourism Ireland's budget is subject to Department of Finance approval in Northern Ireland and in the Republic. Its activities are closely engaged with the departments with responsibility for tourism on either side of the border.

Sectors for development in the specified cooperation policy areas are agreed by the NSMC. Thus, EU common agricultural policy issues, animal and plant health policy and research and rural development were approved by the NSMC for initial consideration. Again, the agricultural departments from both jurisdictions are involved in developing this area. Overall, sixty-five NSMC meetings, including four plenary meetings, occurred from 1999 to 2002, covering all areas of cooperation and the implementation bodies.[15]

A key finding of this study is that the administrative cooperation precipitated by the Good Friday agreement is not restricted to a few civil servants involved in specific policy areas, as in the early 1990s (see above). Under the new administrative arrangements, each Dublin-based civil service department of relevance to the NSMC's activities has a specific cross-border unit dedicated to liaising and coordinating activity with the NSMC and internally. This change was driven by the Good Friday agreement requirement that Irish and Northern Irish ministers are responsible for designated areas of cross-border cooperation, necessitating wider civil service departmental involvement. These units act as clearing houses for cross-border issues. They are chaired by senior civil servants and are intended to meet once a month to discuss cross-cutting issues with their Northern Irish counterparts.

In addition, there is an overarching coordinating group in the Republic of Ireland, chaired by the Department of Foreign Affairs. Thus, knowledge of cross-border schemes and initiatives is not confined to those directly involved, but is a broader part of departmental activity. The two departments of finance play a key role in ensuring that the implementation bodies can operate effectively, by overseeing their operation. They are currently involved in setting out the accountability system underpinning the NSMC and its main bodies.

The establishment of the North–South units and the emphasis on engaging with cross-border issues is driven politically from the highest level. Both governments closely monitor cross-border cooperation in civil service departments to ensure that such cooperation is prioritised. Thus, departmental perceptions of cross-border economic conflicts of interest, or reticence about developing cross-border cooperation, should not impede the aims of the Good Friday agreement. Nor has the suspension of the Assembly reversed the cooperation already achieved. However, in response to unionist concerns, it was agreed in 2002 that only policies and actions already mandated by the NMSC would be pursued, a policy of 'care and maintenance' of cross-border cooperation. Since December 2002, about 170 joint government decisions have been taken to ensure that the North–South bodies and Tourism Ireland can continue to carry out their important work (see chapter 2). Despite the suspension of the Assembly, exploratory work continues to take place in departments in Northern Ireland and the Republic on cross-border cooperation and on the EU dimension of cooperation.

Moreover, in 2003 a review of corporate governance of the North–South bodies was initiated, to ensure that the new bodies are fulfilling the highest levels of regulatory and financial compliance. It was also designed to fully address the unique all-island nature of the bodies and the climate within which they operate. Two cross-border civil service conferences have been held on the topic. A series of corporate governance facilitation meetings was agreed upon, comprising the implementation bodies, their sponsor departments, each finance department and the joint secretariat.

Thus, the Good Friday agreement, despite the suspension of the Assembly, has succeeded in achieving and maintaining coordination and cooperation between the two civil services. Momentum has been provided at the highest level. This high-level intervention and management as well as the establishment of the NSMC and secretariat have all reduced problems of information gaps and poor coordination among civil servants. Cross-border cooperation is part of the broader remit of civil service departments in the Republic of Ireland. Moreover, it has been observed that the NSMC secretariat is perceived as the relevant institution in many of the Good Friday agreement's policy areas, if an Irish or Northern Irish civil servant has a matter to raise or needs advice on a certain issue. Goodwill among civil servants on both sides of the border has been one of the major causes of optimism for those working in the NSMC secretariat. However, despite this improvement in the administration of cross-border cooperation, there are still some problems in the administrative cross-border relationship.

The existence of more extensive civil service cooperation and coordination procedures does not imply that there are no longer conflicts of interest between civil service departments. Thus, there is commonality, but also tension about certain issues, where economic priorities between civil service departments on either side of the border differ. The implementation bodies found themselves hamstrung at times because of their obligation to report back to their sponsor departments. There was a potential trade-off between coordination and stimulating innovative cross-border work. While there is greater networking at higher level to overcome conflicts of interest, cross-border sponsor department meetings occur only once a year approximately.

Moreover, while Irish departments have established North–South units, Northern Irish departments have not done so. Thus, one person interviewed for this study found that coordination and leadership problems existed in Northern Ireland, though the situation had improved in the Republic.

> No actor plays a coordinating role to ensure that all departments (north and south), North–South implementation bodies and other partnerships at the statutory level are working towards a single overarching objective and the impact of policies are compatible with this objective.[16]

While there are improvements in coordination arrangements governing cross-border administrative cooperation, its quality and coherence have been criticised. There is still, according to this view, 'a lack of sharing of information between policy-makers involved in promoting cross-border cooperation in different spheres ... lack of coordination and joined-up policy-making'.[17]

Thus, 'emphasis ... on partnership, genuine contact and exchange between promoters and beneficiaries and between bodies, organisations and networks on both sides of the border' is needed.[18] As regards Interreg specifically, 'projects tended to be appraised and agreed within the department working group and according to the policy priorities for that administration'.[19] Therefore, joint cross-border management of Interreg was relatively weak.

Moreover, political obstacles to cross-border cooperation affect levels of bureaucratic cooperation. For example, it was particularly difficult to establish cross-border promoters and beneficiaries; and cooperation between bodies, organisations and networks in the transport sector was impeded because the Northern Irish Minister for Transport was a member of the DUP and opposed cross-border cooperation on ideological grounds. His department was apparently not free to engage with the work of the NSMC. Similarly, the suspension of the Assembly and the new political landscape in Northern Ireland, where the DUP has the largest proportion of political support, have meant that the NSMC cannot play a proactive role in developing cooperation for fear of invoking a negative political response. The current difficulties have had a slight effect on levels of enthusiasm for cross-border cooperation.

Overall, in administrative cooperation, there is evidence of improvements derived from the NSMC's establishment and from high-level governmental impetus, but there is still some criticism of strategic vision, of only moderate coordination, and of ideological or political obstacles to developing cross-border cooperation. Neither the Good Friday agreement's institutions nor the EU have overcome these obstacles. Indeed, the EU's role in civil service cooperation has been far less central than the Good Friday agreement's impact. However, as the next section shows, the EU's impact on local border region cooperation has been greater. Moreover, there is a possible trade-off between coordination at central level and achieving local cross-border cooperation and partnership.

THE POLITICAL DIMENSION

While civil service behaviour is primarily governed by the impetus received from the Good Friday agreement, local cross-border cooperation has been influenced by both the Good Friday agreement's institutions and by the provision of EU funding to underpin the peace process and to advance regional development, though such funding of course predated the agreement. Thus, cross-border political cooperation is assessed in this section by examining local cross-border relations and also by examining the political parties' attitudes to cross-border cooperation as demonstrated in party manifestoes. Only the DUP and Sinn Féin manifestoes are examined, since each of these explicitly linked cross-border cooperation to their political ideologies, and these were the two parties which, as the largest and most militant within their respective communities, ultimately became the key players in negotiating long-term implementation issues.

Local cross-border cooperation

The above EU initiatives as well as strand two of the Good Friday agreement have had implications for local cross-border cooperation. Three border groups established before the agreement – the Irish Central Border Area Network (ICBAN), the North West Border Region Group and the East Border Region Group – have all received impetus from the new administrative arrangements and increased funding. These groups are stronger because of their inclusive political dimension, whereby local councillors from all parties are actively involved. Moreover, local cross-border cooperation is more difficult to construe as a step towards a united Ireland than more centralised approaches. ICBAN, though the third network to be created, may now be considered a prototype for all the cross-border bodies' operation (its area overlaps with that of the two other networks).

ICBAN comprises representatives of ten local authorities (five in the North and five in the South) from a wide range of parties, and its decisions are reached by full consensus. It has participated in transport projects, sales and marketing projects, and information provision networking projects. The relevant groups are actively engaged in lobbying the EU and national authorities. The border groups also meet as a partnership with social partners and county development board representatives. The partnership has three sub-committees, dealing with business and economic development, knowledge economy and human resources. Thus, in the submission of programmes or projects to be funded and in the allocation of funding, NGOs, local authorities and local businesses are all involved.

This broadly follows the model established for Peace I, in respect of which a joint management committee was established to oversee the programme's implementation. This comprised five members from the southern border counties and five from Northern Ireland as well as NGO representatives.[20] In addition, seminars and conferences were held with wide participation marking 'the development of strong working relationships with a wide variety of stakeholders. Local advisory committees were established to identify gaps in practical administration of cross-border programmes and to identify "best practice" in the area'.[21] Under Peace II, local council involvement was even greater as a consequence of the Good Friday agreement and political parties' desire to increase local power. Thus, practitioners have observed that through ICBAN, the North West Border Region Group and the Eastern Border Region Group, local cross-border political cooperation has increased. Moreover, the activities of these local cross-border groupings and networks are not hindered by Northern Irish party leaders, as an examination of election manifestoes shows.

Party manifestoes

Practitioners have observed that the DUP does not express opposition to strand two of the Good Friday agreement, unless efforts are made to link economic cooperation to unification. In its recent manifestoes, the party criticises the NSMC and implementation bodies, but in a relatively measured manner. The 2003 manifesto focused more strongly on the NSMC, accusing the UUP of giving Dublin unaccountable powers over affairs in Northern Ireland.[22] This point was reiterated in the DUP's review of the Good Friday agreement, in which it alleged that the UUP had allowed the NSMC to operate despite the suspension of the Good Friday agreement.[23] Moreover, the DUP states that 'un-controllable all-Ireland bodies are the starting point for a united Ireland'. However, among its recommendations is not that the NSMC be abolished, but that 'any relationship with the Republic of Ireland must be fully accountable to the Assembly'.[24] Civil servants interviewed observed that in DUP–Irish government negotiations, no insurmountable opposition to the NSMC has emerged to date. Overall, while the DUP clearly states its criticisms of the implementation bodies, its opposition to cross-border cooperation in general has weakened. Moreover, since its success in the 2003 elections, it has had a strong incentive to negotiate a successful settlement if devolved government is to be restored.

In Sinn Féin's manifestoes, emphasis on cross-border cooperation as a means to achieving a unified Ireland has lessened. Thus, in 1997, its section on cross-border economic development focused on the economic merits of cross-border cooperation.[25] In its 2001 manifesto it stresses its status as an 'all-Ireland party',[26] but again its emphasis on the NSMC is on its economic benefits and it refers frequently to the 'island economy' and the economic distortions of partition. Similarly, in its 2003 manifesto, it asserts the aim of developing 'all-Ireland structures to foster an Ireland of equals'.[27] It aims to use the NSMC 'to effect coordination and integration of policy-making and programmes of work across the border and throughout Ireland'.[28] In discussing local cross-border cooperation, again, it emphasises the economic need for such cooperation. While clearly Irish unity is the aim of Sinn Féin, in recent manifestoes it never explicitly links unity to the NSMC or to cross-border cooperation, but instead emphasises the economic rationale for cooperation.

Thus, the issue of cross-border cooperation *per se* has become less politicised for both the DUP and Sinn Féin, a trend which emerged in the early 1990s. The DUP exhibits more evidence of explicit issue-linkage of the NSMC to Irish unity than does Sinn Féin. However, its language is more measured than in previous documents. The NSMC's accountability is emphasised by the DUP, but not its status as such. For Sinn Féin, an expansion of the NSMC's policy areas is favoured, but not linked to unity explicitly. This economic emphasis contrasts with its earlier statements, but again continues a trend which became evident in the early 1990s.

Overall, political cross-border cooperation has increased at the local level, and party attitudes to cooperation are less subject to positions supporting or opposing the Irish border. However, the Good Friday agreement, and the EU's initiatives since 1999, have provided a further stimulus for attitudinal change. In the next section, the response of the business community to the Good Friday agreement and the EU is assessed.

THE BUSINESS DIMENSION

There are various areas of potential business cooperation, of which two are considered here. As the next subsection shows, tourism cooperation has proved relatively successful since the Good Friday agreement, but trade promotion has been more problematic.

Tourism

The establishment of Tourism Ireland following the Good Friday agreement represented the cornerstone of tourism cross-border cooperation.[29] The aim is to increase numbers visiting Northern Ireland and the Republic and to allow Northern Ireland to increase its overall number of tourists.

The overall goal is to double overseas spending by 2012.[30] The main means of achieving these aims is through provision of information, hosting of cross-border seminars and conferences and facilitation of marketing endeavours.

The creation of Tourism Ireland coincided with a particularly turbulent international environment (September 11, the Iraq war and foot and mouth disease in the UK). Therefore, it is difficult to measure its success in terms of statistical outcomes. Indeed, data over the period 1998–2003 demonstrate only marginal change in the numbers of overseas visitors.[31] However, 2003 figures were greeted favourably by tourism leaders. Of the total number of visitors to the 'island economy', approximately 80 per cent visited the Republic of Ireland only, 16 per cent visited Northern Ireland only and 4 per cent visited both areas.[32] Thus, given the difficult international climate, tourism figures fared relatively well, although they had not increased dramatically.

Moreover, neither bureaucratic, business nor political conflicts of interest have proved an obstacle to tourism cooperation. Indeed, levels of agreement have been described as 'excellent'. However, as the system of policy formulation is relatively new, the decision-making process is under constant review. For example, Tourism Ireland is subject to controls from its two sponsoring departments, the two finance departments and the NSMC, which in turn includes a broader set of departments. The bureaucratic process of finding approval for a given project is thus complicated. However, the NSMC's corporate governance project (see above) is perceived as providing an effective means of overcoming these practical problems. As regards conflicts of economic interest, Tourism Ireland, by increasing overall figures to both areas, avoids perceptions that one jurisdiction is gaining at the expense of the other – the total size of the pie is bigger. Nor has the DUP opposed cross-border tourism cooperation; thus political obstacles have been minimised. Overall, tourism cooperation has succeeded relatively well, given the international obstacles it faced, in increasing numbers of visitors to Northern Ireland and the Republic of Ireland, but particularly in increasing communication channels and in facilitating harmonious agreement. In contrast, efforts to increase trade promotion have been less successful to date.

Trade and business development

InterTrade Ireland has aimed to promote trade and business development by providing information to businesses on both sides of the border about business opportunities, a strategy adopted by the joint council of the Irish

Business and Employers Confederation and the Confederation of British Industry in Northern Ireland in the early 1990s. Approximately thirty initiatives have been launched by InterTrade Ireland, most of which seek to establish new networks in various areas – for example equity, science and technology, marketing, business information and digital technology.[33] Business interest in many of the ventures is said to be high. Thus, the Fusion programme, bringing businesses, research centres and graduates together on a cross-border basis, initially financed forty projects and currently finances 140. The key difference between InterTrade Ireland and the joint council of the Irish Business and Employers Confederation and the Confederation of British Industry in Northern Ireland is that the former organisation is far larger and has a budget of €40m. Moreover, there is much larger public sector involvement in InterTrade Ireland. Thus, its scale and potential are far greater. For practitioners, the key importance of these initiatives is their ability to bring business people from Northern Ireland and the Republic of Ireland together to discuss practical problems and to exchange expertise. For members of the NSMC secretariat, InterTrade Ireland is succeeding in opening communication channels to an ever-increasing number of business people. Moreover, the administration of Peace I and II involves local business actors from both sides of the border who meet regularly to devise and monitor development plans.

Thus, cooperation is fostered through information provision at seminars and conferences. As in the early 1990s, these seminars, conferences and joint promotion ventures constitute the main examples of cross-border cooperation, but activity has increased in scale: joint promotions of Irish products overseas have been organised and strategic alliances are being encouraged between northern and southern firms.[34] However, in terms of tangible results, levels of cross-border trade have not increased, as chapter 3 has shown. Not only have imports as a percentage of the total not increased; they have fallen marginally, indicating that the logic of cross-border trade does not provide a compelling framework for businesses on the two sides of the border – particularly large businesses.

There are several possible reasons for the absence of an increase in cross-border trade. Physical peripherality and transport problems provide obstacles to cross-border business development. The problems in achieving closer transport cooperation spill over to the cross-border business relationship. Moreover, differences in industrial structure between Northern Ireland and the Republic of Ireland limit cross-border trade (see chapters 3 and 9). The Republic has a more modern industrial base, specialising in high-technology areas. In contrast, Northern Ireland has a greater concentration of industry in traditional manufacturing. The most important factor in explaining EU trade patterns is the existence 'of inter-firm trade in similar product areas, rather than trade in finished consumer goods'; thus 'trade simply cannot easily take place between North and South, given the contrasting production structures'.[35] Another reason for low levels of trade is that small firms tend to have closer cross-border links, but constitute a smaller share of total trade. Moreover, British self-exclusion from the eurozone hinders the gains from trade for these small firms.

Hence, there are market-driven factors that help to explain why cross-border trade is low. A key debate is whether or not governmental intervention can overcome these obstacles. Thus, 'semi-political interventions do not necessarily follow market signals … The intervention which has occurred has been directed almost exclusively towards North–South trading links as opposed to those between Northern Ireland and Great Britain', implying a political, rather than economic, motivation.[36]

The question whether institutional change can foster bottom-up cooperation 'on the ground' in a situation of historical conflict, or whether bottom-up initiatives must precede or coincide with institutional change, is at the centre of assessing the impact of 'top-down' initiatives such as the Good Friday agreement and the EU's policies on the Irish border. In the conclusion an attempt is made to determine to what extent patterns of cross-border cooperation have been transformed since 1998.

CONCLUSION

In the case of the Irish border, calls for overarching institutions to foster cross-border cooperation were dominant in the years preceding the Good Friday agreement. The economic argument was that market imperfections which hindered cross-border cooperation could be overcome by the creation of cross-border institutions, such as the NSMC. The implication of this argument was that 'bottom-up' cooperation would not occur in the absence of political institutional change.

The period 1998–2003 was characterised by dramatic and innovative institutional change and by significant financial aid from the EU. These changes have had various effects. The most dramatic has been the response of civil services on both sides of the border. The highest degree of cross-border cooperation occurs at the administrative level. Thus an important indicator of cross-border cooperation (over-arching institutions to administer cooperation) has occurred. This cooperation was politically driven by the British and Irish governments. Cross-border tourism cooperation has proved successful, but, in general, levels of cross-border business cooperation have not altered significantly. However, the politics of cross-border political cooperation has become more benign both in terms of parties' attitudes and at local level. This local cross-border cooperation is predominantly a result of EU funding and monitoring mechanisms.

Moreover, the monitoring and partnership systems with commission involvement are viewed as the legitimate locus of authority for designated policy issues. Similarly, civil service departments on both sides of the border look to the NSMC and its secretariat in agreed areas as being responsible for specific policy issues. One of the most surprising results, according to participants, has been the degree of civil service goodwill and support for the NSMC since its creation. The operation of the NSMC secretariat has been compared to the EU model of political behaviour, whereby members behave consensually and seek to resolve conflicts of interest through communication. Moreover, like the EU example, the communication process itself has improved bureaucratic relations since 1999, and lessened information gaps and mistrust. However, overall, while participants in the cross-border process have been impressed by the NSMC and EU's achievements, concern has been expressed that linking the activities of the NSMC to 'people on the street' has been more problematic. Apart from cross-border cooperation between local councils involving local business communities, bottom-up cooperation has not occurred in general, as indicated by business behaviour in Northern Ireland and the Republic.

The differentiated effect of the EU and the Good Friday agreement on cross-border cooperation implies that specific strategies are needed for different levels of society and for different sectors. This multi-pronged strategy will ensure widespread cooperation so that 'the involvement of numerous actors ensures synergies between the different levels of integration and positive pullovers from one domain to another'.[37] By definition, high-level intergovernmental institutional change will lead to increased administrative or bureaucratic cooperation. Thus, civil service cooperation has been governed by intergovernmental Anglo-Irish policy, not by supranational influences. Similarly, different groups of actors respond to different incentives for change, some local, some centralised, some supranational. A mixture of incentives is required to increase cross-border cooperation, combining local, centralised and supranational factors. The Good Friday agreement has facilitated increased cooperation and coordination. The EU has also played a key role at the local level. But in all of this we need to note an important caveat: since the collapse of the devolved institutions in 2002 political uncertainty has clouded the development potential of the North–South bodies, and the manner in which the blueprint provided by the Good Friday agreement will evolve in the long term remains unclear.

Overall, though, this study shows that the relationship between Northern Ireland and the Republic of Ireland has been altered and has been influenced by the Good Friday agreement and the EU in politics and in business. The limits to and the opportunities for cooperation have been highlighted. Clearly, the Irish border lies at the heart of a complex relationship, further complicated by the co-existence of new incentives and disincentives to change. In this way the 'crude image' of the stand-off between the two parts of the island described in chapter 1 has been amplified and refined by this chapter's conclusions.

NOTES

1 E Tannam, *Cross-border cooperation in the Republic of Ireland and Northern Ireland* (London: Macmillan, 1999).
2 Interviews took place between February 2004 and April 2004 with officials from the Anglo-Irish division of the Irish Department of Foreign Affairs, the Irish Department of Finance, the Irish joint secretary of the North/South Ministerial Council secretariat in Armagh, and the chief executives of Tourism Ireland, Co-operation Ireland and the Northern Ireland office in Brussels.
3 M Mansergh, *Cross-border bodies and the North–South relationship: laying the groundwork* (Dublin: Institute for British–Irish Studies, University College Dublin, 2001) [IBIS Working Paper, no. 12], p. 3.
4 The rest of this section is based substantially on Tannam, *Cross-border cooperation* (1999).
5 The joint council of the Irish Business and Employers Confederation and the Confederation of British Industry in Northern Ireland comprised four members from each employers' union and worked intensively towards the aim of achieving closer cross-border economic cooperation to maximise the potential markets on either side of the border.
6 Tannam, *Cross-border cooperation* (1999), p. 157.
7 Tannam, *Cross-border cooperation* (1999), pp. 146–50.
8 Special EU Programmes Body, *Building on peace: supporting peace and reconciliation after 2006* (Monaghan: ADM/CPA, 2003), p. 104.
9 Mansergh, *Cross-border bodies* (2002), p. 4.
10 J Coakley, *The North–South institutions: from blueprint to reality* (Dublin: Institute for British–Irish Studies, University College Dublin, 2002) [IBIS Working Paper, no. 22], p. 10.
11 SEUPB, *Building on peace* (2003), p. 124.
12 SEUPB, *Building on peace* (2003), p. 105.
13 This section is based on interviews with civil servants and NGOs (see note 2).
14 North/South Ministerial Council, *Annual Report* (Armagh: NSMC, 2002), p. 19.
15 Department of Foreign Affairs, Anglo-Irish division, *North/South cooperation: overview* (Dublin: Department of Foreign Affairs, 2004), p. 1.
16 Co-operation Ireland, *Current need* (2003), p. 9.
17 Co-operation Ireland, *Current need* (2003), p. 14.
18 B Laffan and D Payne, *Creating living institutions: EU cross-border cooperation after the Good*

Friday Agreement (Armagh: Centre for Cross-Border Studies, 2001), p. 139.
19 Laffan and Payne, *Creating living institutions* (2001), pp. 76–7.
20 Special EU Programmes Body, *Building on peace* (2003), p. 119.
21 Special EU Programmes Body, *Building on peace* (2003), p. 121.
22 Democratic Unionist Party (2003) *Fair deal manifesto* (Belfast: DUP, 2003).
23 Democratic Unionist Party (2003) *Towards a new agreement* (Belfast: DUP, 2003), p. 8.
24 DUP, *Fair deal manifesto* (2003), p. 13.
25 Sinn Féin, *Six-county assembly election manifesto* (Dublin: Sinn Féin, 1997), p. 5.
26 Sinn Féin, *Westminster election manifesto2001: building an Ireland of equals* (Dublin: Sinn Féin, 2001), p. 2.
27 Sinn Féin, *Agenda for government* (Dublin: Sinn Féin, 2003), p. 20.
28 Sinn Féin, *Agenda* (2003), p. 21.
29 For further discussion of this issue, see J Henderson and P Teague, *The Belfast agreement and cross-border cooperation in the tourism industry* (Dublin: Institute for British–Irish Studies, UCD, 2006) [IBIS working papers 54]; also available at www.qub.ac.uk/cibr/mappingfrontierswps.htm
30 Tourism Ireland, *Marketing strategy, 2004–06* (Dublin: Tourism Ireland, 2004), p. 9.
31 E Tannam, 'Cross-border cooperation between Northern Ireland and the Republic of Ireland: neo-functionalism re-visited', *British journal of politics and international relations* 8:2 (2006), pp. 256–76, at p. 270.
32 Tourism Ireland, *Facts and figures* (Dublin: Tourism Ireland, 2002), p. 2.
33 North/South Ministerial Council, *Annual Report* (2002), p. 20.
34 J Bradley and E Birnie, *Can the Celtic tiger cross the Irish border?* (Cork: Cork University Press, 2001), p. 33.
35 Bradley and Birnie, *Celtic tiger* (2001), p. 32.
36 Bradley and Birnie, *Celtic tiger* (2001), p. 74.
37 Co-operation Ireland, *Interreg IIIA Ireland–Northern Ireland programme: principles for the consideration of projects* (Belfast: Co-operation Ireland, 2003), p. 6.

6

The voluntary sector: promoting peace and cooperation

LIAM O'DOWD AND CATHAL McCALL

INTRODUCTION

Much of the debate about cross-border cooperation tends to concentrate on its political and economic aspects. Rather less attention has been devoted to the role of civil society in cross-border relationships and in particular to the role of the voluntary (including the community) sector.[1] This chapter focuses directly on the role of the latter in cross-border relationships and explores its significance in the promotion of peace and reconciliation. It is based empirically on a study of new patterns of cross-border cooperation within the voluntary sector supported by the EU under the Peace II programme.[2]

The central argument advanced below is that prosecution of cross-border cooperation involving the voluntary sector has the potential to undermine the territorial 'caging' which has been so central to the conflict in Northern Ireland. While the chapter is primarily concerned with co-operation across the state border, it also raises the question of links between the state and the internal borders which separate Catholics and Protestants within Northern Ireland. It suggests that the contribution of cross-border cooperation to conflict resolution must not be seen in isolation from the building of bridges between both communities in the North. The thrust of the peace process has been to separate two sets of issues, the first to do with North–South (cross-border) relations, the second to do with cross-communal relationships within Northern Ireland. This separation can be justified pragmatically on a political level and is a major part of the architecture of the peace process and the Good Friday agreement. This chapter argues, however, that the relationship between cooperation across the external and internal borders of Northern Ireland needs to be explored and developed, as it is critical to furthering peace and reconciliation. The voluntary sector provides an important context for exploring how this relationship might develop.

The cross-border dimension has come to be accepted by all sides as part of the framework for resolving the Northern Ireland conflict, even if they differ over its content and significance. From its early, and contentious, manifestation as the 'Irish dimension' in the Sunningdale agreement (1973), it was to re-emerge formally in the early 1990s as strand two in the peace process and the Good Friday agreement. From the Anglo-Irish agreement (1985), cross-border cooperation has been strongly supported by the US and the EC/EU.[3] The emphasis has been on promoting economic cooperation of mutual benefit to the peoples on the island, with the understanding that peace-building and reconciliation will be a by-product of such cooperation. The thirty-year maturation of the North–South intergovernmental relationship has been fundamental to the development of the cross-border dimension and the EU has provided contextual, ideological and substantive support.

The cross-border dimension was built into the EU's Peace I (1994–9) and Peace II (2000–6) programmes, which were designed to underpin the paramilitary ceasefires, and the Good Friday agreement respectively. Part of the distinctiveness of these programmes was the inclusion of voluntary sector agencies and grassroots community groups in multi-level partnerships with the EU Commission, government departments on either side of the border and latterly the Special EU Programmes Body (SEUPB) – a cross-border implementation body set up under the Good Friday agreement. The Peace programmes were designed to build bridges between the two communities in the North and with those across the border counties of the Republic.[4] Of course, voluntary sector bridge-building across the border did not begin with the Peace programmes. As chapter 4 indicates, the all-Ireland orientation of many voluntary bodies survived partition, while others such as Co-operation North/Co-operation Ireland and the Glencree Centre for Reconciliation were set up to promote peace and reconciliation in response to the outbreak of the 'troubles'. The Peace programmes provided, however, a new funding impetus to voluntary action, even if the voluntary sector attracted less funding than state or economic organisations.

The Peace programmes have been heavily criticised, sometimes on grounds of sectarian imbalance, but more often on the basis of their funding priorities, excessive bureaucracy and effectiveness.[5] Yet few of those involved question their net benefit – for example, the prospect of a Peace III programme was supported by the voluntary sector, all the political parties in Northern Ireland and the government in the Republic.

The chapter begins by making the case that borders and border change are integral both to ethnonational conflict and to conflict resolution, and thereby shape the capacity of the voluntary sector to promote peace and reconciliation. The second section traces how the recent reconfiguration of cross-border relations has challenged the architecture of containment which has helped to limit and intensify communal conflict in Ireland. The third section draws on empirical research into transnational cross-border cooperation based on interviews with voluntary sector activists funded under Peace II. The fourth section offers a preliminary interpretation of the distinctiveness, strengths and weaknesses of the new forms of cross-border cooperation within the voluntary sector. It indicates its potential in undermining the territorialist zero-sum conflict which has long characterised Northern Ireland and which now assumes its most visible and antagonistic form at the interfaces bordering the two communities *within* Northern Ireland. A concluding section underlines the distinctive capacity of the voluntary sector in promoting peace and reconciliation, while acknowledging its relative lack of resources in the overall context of cross-border cooperation in Ireland.

CHANGING STATE BORDERS AND CONFLICT RESOLUTION

The growing international and interdisciplinary literature on borders and border change helps illuminate the connection between state borders, border change, violence and conflict resolution.[6] Ironically, the stimulus for this new interest in borders has been the challenge posed by new forms of economic, political and cultural globalisation to existing territorial borders. 'Strong' theories of an increasingly 'borderless' world have been confronted by the empirical recognition that borders are not so much disappearing as being reconfigured in new ways.[7] There has been a simultaneous occurrence of 'de-bordering' and new forms of demarcation.[8] General accounts have noted that the declining salience of national borders and interstate conflicts have often coincided with the increased salience of internal borders and intrastate conflicts.[9] New forms of globalisation have unsettled and reconfigured national borders, creating opportunities and rationales for ethnonational groups wishing to challenge existing state borders – often demanding their own states in the process.[10] Similarly, the changing role of borders has encouraged many states to try to reassert control over forces and groups threatening the integrity of their territories.[11] Contemporaneous with these intrastate developments, a patchwork of international and transnational organisations seeks to develop, however imperfectly, a form of governance aimed at managing global trade, violent conflicts and boundary disputes, and at promoting human rights and ecological protection.[12]

Border change has assumed two forms which occasionally coincide – geographical or locational, and functional. The geographical boundaries of states are variable. Lustick observes that 'no fact about states is more obvious than the impermanence of their boundaries'.[13] He writes in the aftermath of the implosion of the Soviet Union but is also registering the replacement of great empires by the interstate system in the twentieth century and the burgeoning intrastate tensions generated by ethnonational secessionists and nationalists defending the boundaries of the existing state.[14]

The long history of state formation reveals no universally agreed criteria, imperialist, nationalist or ethnic, of where and how state borders should be drawn, and who should draw them.[15] Neither are there agreed guidelines for how many states should exist or on what basis groups might affiliate to, or secede from, existing states. The absence of such guidelines ensures a standing invitation to powerful groups to coerce others and impose their preferred borders. Border creation, therefore, is frequently arbitrary and intimately connected with violent conflict. As national states have proliferated in the twentieth century, border questions have become more rather than less pressing. At this level, border conflict in Ireland is scarcely unique. In 1920–1, it ended in partition – a form of conflict resolution imposed by the British government of the time. What is more remarkable, perhaps, is the subsequent longevity of the UK-Irish border, which now qualifies as one of the oldest state borders in Europe, despite being continually contested by its opponents since its inception.

The variable territory demarcated by state borders, however, is only one form of border change. While misplaced or displaced groups may contest border lines, even more pervasive, and certainly more continuous, is the change in the function and meaning of state borders. These changes often supersede the positions and intentions of protagonists in border conflicts. Like many other state borders, the function and meaning of the Irish border has changed in tandem with the decline of imperial power, the growth in the institutional power and infrastructure of states within a globalised interstate system, and new forms of economic, political and cultural globalisation over the last four decades. In one sense, the functions of state borders have become more specialised and less all-embracing even if they still remain symbolic markers of collective identity in a nationalistic age. The meaning and salience of territorial borders varies, however, across states, time periods and social groups. The capacity to cross state borders, either as migrants, tourists or workers, also varies greatly across time periods. It also varies significantly by income, occupation, class, and racial group or nationality. Information and finance capital cross borders more easily than goods and people. Borders, therefore, are regulators of movement and make movement possible, although often in a highly restricted and structured manner. It should not be surprising, therefore, that it is the most disadvantaged communities, including those in Northern Ireland, which are most constrained by internal and external territorial borders.

Any approach to understanding borders in general, and the Irish border in particular, must develop a framework which recognises their highly complex, ambivalent and changeable nature.[16] At the same time, it must acknowledge that groups, nations and states invest heavily in the permanence of borders even as they remain contested in one form or another as people try to create, maintain and transcend them. However, popular conceptions of the Irish border have tended to see it in rather one-dimensional and static terms – as marking competing and exclusivist claims to territory and as a barrier between 'us' and 'them'. Scholarly studies of the nature and the impact of the Irish border have been remarkably scarce. In part, this is due to a broader tendency of history and the social sciences to take state borders for granted as units of analysis, thereby equating state and society. Academic avoidance may also have something to do with the emotions and myths generated by the Irish border and the almost sacred place it has assumed in the contending ideologies of Irish nationalism and Ulster unionism.[17] Those studies which have been undertaken have been quickly assimilated into traditional unionist or nationalist positions on partition without addressing the broader dynamics of border change.

RECONFIGURING THE IRISH BORDER

The conflict in Ireland and attempts to resolve it since 1970 may be understood in terms of the dynamics of border change. By the 1960s, the architecture of containment designed in 1920–1 was beginning to be undermined. This architecture involved a particular configuration of relationships between the interstate border and the internal borders between the two communities in Northern Ireland. While 'the border' remained a matter of dispute *de jure* between the British and Irish governments, they had come to take it for granted, *de facto*, in that it served to 'cage' competing ethnonational and territorial demands within Northern Ireland. The arrangement seemed to deliver stability for long periods and, for the most part, served as a *cordon sanitaire* which prevented overspill of the conflict from Northern Ireland to the twenty-six-county state and the rest of the UK. This stability was achieved without ethnic cleansing or a mass displacement of populations. But stability was also dependent on a highly systematic form of internal 'caging' which caused the conflict to fester. Within Northern Ireland, 'caging' embraced a micropolitics of territorial control involving elections, government policies, popular intimidation and cultural practices. It sustained, and was sustained by, a culture of voluntary apartheid between the two communities. The zero-sum politics of territorial control were privileged while the occupation and control of territory was the ultimate metaphor for, and measure of, the state of the conflict between the two sides.

From the 1960s onwards a great variety of often contradictory developments began to disrupt the form of territorialist politics which had stabilised the conflict for fifty years. These developments included elite-level negotiations on North–South cooperation in the 1960s, the emergence of the civil rights movements and popular unionist attempts to regain control of the streets, the growth of communal conflict, the imposition of direct rule, the militarisation of the conflict, which further enhanced the internal borders within Northern Ireland, the growing intergovernmental partnership between the British and Irish governments, and the eventual involvement of the EC/EU and the USA in the search for a new solution. As the outline of such a solution emerged, it became clear that it would involve a reconfiguration of the state border and of its relationship to the internal borders within Northern Ireland.

The Good Friday agreement was designed to reduce the problematical territorialism at the root of the conflict by multiplying the arenas for dialogue, interaction and persuasion, and thereby circumscribing the zero-sum politics which has characterised Northern Ireland. The agreement seeks to transform the external and internal borders of Northern Ireland from coercive to contractual or negotiated relationships. At its heart is a consensus among all the parties that the line of partition be accepted unless there is a majority in both jurisdictions on the island to bring about a single Irish state.[18] This provision and the power-sharing, cross-border and equality dimensions of the agreement provide a possible peaceful and democratic way forward to bring about border change and some form of Irish unity in the future through dialogue and persuasion. On the other hand, it provides similarly for the same means to be used to confirm the union.

The Good Friday agreement provided for the revision of articles 2 and 3 of the Irish constitution by removing their territorialist claims and replacing them by a more voluntarist conception of Irish nationhood. This was informed by an explicit recognition that Irish culture does not map precisely onto the borders of the Irish state. The removal of the so-called constitutional claim, while hardly embraced enthusiastically by unionists as a major concession, given that they argued it should not have been there in the first place, nevertheless may have had a long-term and subtle effect on unionist elites' views of the South and of cross-border relations. The agreement included explicit recognition of partition by both the Irish government and northern republicans and nationalists, while acknowledging that change could come about only by a majority voting for change in both parts of Ireland.[19]

More general processes of change also shape unionists' perceptions – notably the rise of the 'Celtic tiger' and the loss of influence by the Catholic Church in the South. The impact of these factors is difficult to measure or quantify, but this does not mean that they are insignificant. Even a cursory survey of unionists' traditional perceptions of the South reveals the emphasis placed on factors such as economic retardation, the pervasive influence of the Catholic Church, the 'inward and backward looking' romanticism of Irish nationalism, and the territorial claim on the whole island. While all these factors have been cited as markers of difference by Ulster unionists, their removal or diminution does not herald a desire to join the Republic. Indeed, this narrowing of differences, strongly supported by northern nationalists, may feed a 'narcissism of minor differences',[20] and be compatible with the increased tendency of unionists since the 1960s to see themselves as British – as part of an imagined British nation and as identifiers with the historic and ceremonial aspects of the British state. Nevertheless, the changes arguably do improve the climate for cross-border cooperation for mutual benefit.

Debates remain over cross-border cooperation, especially at the political level, as the DUP tries to ensure a form of accountability that gives the unionist majority a veto on North–South cooperation. But the low-key and low-profile nature of cross-border cooperation has proved not to be politically controversial. The EU in particular has played a significant role in creating a more favourable context for cross-border cooperation by funding multi-level partnerships involving governments, voluntary sectors and community groups.[21] Research in the early 1990s by one of the authors in the border region revealed a remarkable degree of support for cross-border economic cooperation among border councillors, including 86 per cent of nationalists and 47 per cent of unionists.[22] Unionists were less actively engaged in local authority networks and insisted that cross-border economic cooperation should have no political agenda of creeping unification. They cited the Republic's constitutional claim, the IRA campaign and the Anglo-Irish agreement of 1985 as inhibitors of practical cooperation, but were more favourably disposed towards EU-sponsored cooperation. Unionists were insistent that cross-border economic cooperation or integration should have no political agenda or spillover into closer political ties. Nationalist representatives in the border region, on the other hand, saw economic cooperation as a means towards closer political links.

There are signs that, at a number of levels, the Irish border is now less of a barrier to cross-border cooperation, while it is also less highly charged as a stake in the conflict. The 'completion' of the single European market meant the removal of the customs posts which had been *in situ* since 1923, and military installations began to be removed as part of the peace process. The invisibility of much of the border suggests that it is now less of a territorial marker than before. By contrast, internal borders within Northern Ireland, and particularly in working-class parts of Belfast, have become more visible and more clearly marked by separation walls, so-called 'peacelines'. They have seemed to be emblematic of deepening intercommunal divisions, something which can also be gauged from evidence of increased spatial segregation, opposition to the Good Friday agreement, and growth of intercommunal distrust.

A conventional analysis of the peace process (including the Good Friday agreement) would be that it has improved cross-border relations and brought about enhanced cross-border cooperation while either sharpening internal borders between the two communities or, at least, failing to provide any impetus for their amelioration. At one level, this interpretation seems to support international research findings on the reduced salience of interstate conflict generally and the increased prominence of intrastate conflicts. One consequence is that the cross-border dimension to conflict resolution has been downplayed in an understandable desire to prioritise the improvement of intercommunal relations within Northern Ireland. Both governments seem to have agreed that the future development of the peace process is now dependent on agreement between the political parties representing both traditions in the North. While clearly such agreement is critical, what seems to be lacking is an adequate appreciation, or a sense of urgency, *vis-à-vis* the role of the cross-border dimension in building peace and reconciliation and in facilitating the improvement of intercommunal relations within Northern Ireland.

A plausible reason for this relative neglect of the cross-border dimension is that the North–South strand of the Good Friday agreement has been on the whole less controversial than strand one – the working of the Northern Ireland Assembly and Executive. However, this lack of controversy should not be taken to mean that the cross-border dimension to peace-building is non-problematical or less urgent. Indeed, its low profile may have something to do with the institutionally fragmented cooperation envisaged under the agreement – cooperation further disrupted thereafter by suspensions of the agreement's key institutions.[23]

As the Good Friday agreement remained becalmed, both governments fell back on a new version of containment policy by placing the onus on the Northern Ireland parties to resolve the deadlock as if they had little to do with interstate or cross-border relations. Unionist opponents of the Good Friday agreement have sought to reinterpret the peace process in the zero-sum terms of internal territorial conflict. Thus, they see the peace process, and the agreement in particular, as marking a series of gains for nationalists at the expense of unionists.[24] According to this view, a new agreement is needed to provide fairness for both communities – hence the importance of the St Andrews agreement of November 2006 in softening DUP hostility to the compromises agreed in 1998. This narrowing focus on internal communal borders, however, rather obscures the potential of the cross-border dimension in building peace and reconciliation.

EU involvement in the peace process, and its sponsorship of the Peace programmes in particular, allows us to probe further the links between cross-border cooperation and cooperation across the internal borders within Northern Ireland. Most of the EU Interreg and Peace funds have been channelled into supporting cooperation between the two states and governments on the island. While this has promoted a considerable co-operative agenda, it has certain built-in limitations to do with the territorial imperative of the two jurisdictions, the mismatched competencies of different institutional structures and the different orientations and priorities of both governments *vis-à-vis* the EU. The process tends to be heavily biased towards 'economic' cooperation and has been characterised by elite-level contacts at governmental and business levels.[25] While the 'trickle-down' or informal effects of this form of cooperation remain to be explored fully, it is in general more border confirming than border transcending. In other words, it advances a more benign territorialisation of divisions on the island based on the two governments dividing up the 'fixed cake' of EU funding between them.[26]

The distinctiveness of the EU's contribution, however, lies in the extent to which it seeks to deterritorialise the conflict – to build cross-border networks of cooperation around issues of common interest. In this sense, it seeks to move beyond bounded territory to the creation of a cooperative transnational space. This form of cooperation is more transnational than international or intergovernmental.

CROSS-BORDER COOPERATION: INTERVIEW EVIDENCE

Several aspects of the Peace I and Peace II programmes have sought to involve the voluntary sector in attempts to build multi-level partnerships around cross-border issues.[27] A research study undertaken by the authors explored cross-border cooperation under the Peace II programme focusing in particular on measure 5.3, which aimed to build cross-border peace and reconciliation via the voluntary and community sector. While the vast bulk of Peace I and II funding was allocated to building peace and reconciliation between the two communities in Northern Ireland, 15 per cent was allocated for building cross-border partnerships between North and South (see chapter 11).[28] The discussion below draws on findings which help illustrate the importance of the voluntary sector in 'transnational' cross-border cooperation aimed at ameliorating communal divisions in Northern Ireland.

At one remove from the state, the voluntary sector might be expected to be less 'territorial' than state agencies and more likely to escape the exclusivist politics of territorial control. Measure 5.3 was one of the few measures in the overall Peace programme concerned with building peace and reconciliation directly rather than as a by-product of economic development or social inclusion. As such, it was close to the ideological heart of the Peace programmes.[29] Its cultural and educational focus meant that it had to grapple directly with the meaning of peace *and* reconciliation, and it brought into focus the relationship between cross-community links in Northern Ireland and cross-border links between North and South. Translated into the parlance of the Good Friday agreement, it interfaced strand one issues and strand two issues, cross-community relations within Northern Ireland and North–South relationships. It also had a history as a direct descendant of measure 3.4 on cross-border reconciliation under Peace I, where the same voluntary sector intermediary funding bodies – Area Development Management/Combat Poverty Agency (ADM/CPA), Co-operation Ireland and Community Foundation Northern Ireland – also played a leading role. Our research on measure 5.3 draws primarily on evidence gathered from interviews with EU and member state government officials, Peace programme managers and voluntary sector intermediary actors, as well as with the providers of twenty-seven projects funded under the measure.

Limitations

Before presenting the research findings and analysis, however, a few prior caveats must be entered. First, the relatively narrow focus and short time-span of this research project is an inadequate basis for generalising about the overall impact of the Peace programmes. It is not, therefore, an 'evaluation' as understood in the parlance of EU, government and voluntary sector programmes.[30] Second, funded voluntary sector activity is not confined to this measure, and hence it would be misleading to claim that our study provides a sufficient basis for assessing the success or otherwise of the voluntary sector as a whole in advancing peace and reconciliation. Finally, building peace and reconciliation is a long-term process that continues to be contested. The projects researched here are relatively small-scale and time-limited by the Peace II funding regime; hence it would be unreasonable to expect immediate and tangible outcomes or, much less, to expect them to provide a stand-alone alternative to a stalled peace process.

Nevertheless, despite the relatively narrow focus of our research, our interviews with those involved at various levels in the process revealed glimpses of the potential for cross-border cooperation in building peace and in creating conditions for ameliorating communal division within Northern Ireland. It also illustrated a whole range of issues about the meaning of cross-border cooperation, partnership and sustainability, much of which is outside the scope of this chapter. In particular, our findings suggest that alongside border-confirming practices, there need to be border-transcending strategies – international (or interstate) cooperation needs to be supplemented by transnational cooperation if the rigid zero-sum mindset fuelling division in Northern Ireland is to be moderated.

Projects

The projects we examined were predominantly related to a variety of cross-border educational and cultural exchanges, community arts training initiatives, multi-media projects and recreational programmes aimed at increasing mutual understanding and promoting reconciliation. All had a track record in that they had been funded under Peace I, while many had also secured funding from other sources, notably the International Fund for Ireland. Uptake of Peace I's measure 3.4 had been slow initially, with unionist groups reluctant to become involved. By 1999, however, unionist involvement had increased, in part due to a determined promotion by the intermediate funding bodies and the optimism generated by the 1998 agreement.

One of our more interesting findings was that some unionist groups seemed to prefer cross-border projects to cross-community ones with neighbouring groups in Northern Ireland.[31] One member of a unionist project provider based in Belfast described the exchanges with groups in Drogheda, south of the border, established to discuss the meaning of the Somme and the 1916 Rising for unionists and nationalists:

> People in Belfast are comfortable to go south and talk about their history and their culture and their heritage and so on. Absolutely no worries. Largely because they're received as such. You know they're accepted as such … they're accepted by people who basically do want to explore, that haven't been caught up in the immediacy of what was, what's been going on here. But they do want to explore it and they're interested and that debate goes on and friendships are created, positions are stated and accepted but the friendships go on, you know. Here, the end result of a debate has to be a victor, has to be a winner … in fact it's comforting to, you know, even stand back and hear someone from the South articulating, you know, your rights to Republicans here.[32]

Another unionist group was heavily involved in bringing children from working-class areas of Belfast to Sligo, where they had taken part in St Patrick's Day parades and been duly impressed by the profusion of flags and other cultural paraphernalia:

> …you've seen kids leaving Belfast with a, like, protective shield around them, the wee hard man image, and they get down to the South it basically falls away. I suppose it's like going on holiday anywhere you come away from a territory where you've … it's a bit like an animal in the jungle, you protect your territory. Once you go down somewhere where you don't have to protect this territory you become a different person in a sense and the shell falls away. I watch most of the kids come back to Belfast on the bus I can see the attitude will change, and their behaviour, and they start punching each other and pulling each other by the hair. They're reverting back to the people they were when they left, 'I'm still a hard man now so don't you come to my street', and then they get punched in the face. So you can see the attitudinal change in the kids when they come back to Belfast that the shield's gone back up again.[33]

This respondent was realistic, however, about the limits of holiday-type exchanges and argued that the development of the project's work meant that sustainability needed to be a priority:

> OK, you can take kids down to Sligo but unless it's an ongoing, week to week, community relations programme with them, this notion of taking kids for ten weeks as a project it's useless … you need to take them for a year or two or three year programme where you are going to work with them kids every couple of years cause it's what you have to do. It can't be … cross-border stuff will not work in isolation. You need to do some sort of link in with other organisations where once you do the cross-border work with like the kids down the South, there should be then some sort of follow up of things where you actually work with the kids from Belfast. So there needs to be some sort of link. But again that involves man hours and people being involved and volunteering and doing things so it's a lot of heavy work you know. I think the funders must need to have a look at that. That's something they need to have a look at in the future.[34]

Another interviewee working with youth exchanges agreed that it was easier, initially at least, to bring people from Northern Ireland together in the South, for sporting and other informal events. Nevertheless, the stalled peace process also complicated Protestant unionist attitudes to cross-border and cross-community cooperation at the grassroots level. One respondent from a project provider observed that 'there is apathy here with the way Stormont has failed – the Protestants would be more keen to keep to themselves'.[35] Another commented:

> … there definitely has been resistance to cross-border linkages and that resistance remains, to a point. I don't think it's as strong as it was because they are able to see that it's not a political thing – we try to avoid talking politics. I think it is a little bit easier but it changes from time to time depending on what's happening on the political scene.[36]

Several reflected the reluctance of Protestant schools to become involved in certain projects. Opposition to such contact was influenced by factors such as the breaking of links between loyalist and republican ex-prisoners groups in the wake of 'Stormontgate', by disputes over marches, and the Holy Cross School issue.[37] However, many Protestant respondents also displayed an attitude of perseverance exemplified by the comment:

> The most comfortable place to be if there's a row going on is among your own people and agreeing with your own people and keeping your door closed and stuff like that … a lot of people who are

> committed and do want to see change can be coaxed out, you know, and we do that, but it takes time.[38]

There was some evidence of different attitudes between minority Protestant groups in rural and border areas and those in more homogeneous urban areas. Confirming other research findings, we found some sense that rural Protestants believe Catholics to be more proficient at community development and perceived such activity to be 'largely a Catholic thing'. Urban working-class groups, on the other hand, have a track record in community development projects and involvement in cross-border links and have gained confidence as a result. More defensive attitudes persist in rural border areas that have experienced high levels of politically motivated violence. In a report by the Rural Community Network on the attitudes of South Armagh Protestants one respondent commented: 'If you are the bog standard Protestant and you see the word "reconciliation" in the paper, it's off-putting; that's mixing and we don't want to do it.'

However, in other rural areas the situation is changing. According to one respondent from a rural Protestant group on the Tyrone–Donegal border:

> … the Protestant community is at a totally different position from where it was at in 1997 in terms of community development. I could have counted on my hand how many groups there were in Tyrone. Now we have a lot of groups. People said that we need this for our young people, for women, for whatever. There is a lot more things happening now so it is a lot easier.[39]

A respondent from a nationalist project provider claimed that there was as much need to reconcile North and South as there was to reconcile Catholic and Protestant communities in Northern Ireland, mentioning, in particular, the apprehension of southerners at the prospect of coming north of the border. This grassroots view was confirmed by one intermediate funding body leader recalling his attempt to engage in an exercise of prejudice reduction with a cross-border group comprising twenty-six nationalists from either side of the border. The result led him to abandon the discussion having elicited the following: 'Northerners leave dirty nappies on our beaches'; 'Southerners are over here taking our jobs and working for buttons'; 'Southern drivers are Padre Pio drivers, they close their eyes and trust to God'; 'Derry women wear too much make-up'.[40]

This respondent, one of the main managers of the 5.3 measure, emphasised the distinct value and need for cross-border reconciliation both in its own right and as a detour on the way to better cross-community relations in the North. He also stressed his experience of the lack of enthusiasm on the part of the southern establishment in seeing the Peace programme as a challenge to southern society.

The Irish border created economic, political, social and cultural schism between North and South, and eighty years of partition culminating in thirty years of violent conflict has served to exacerbate such schism. One intermediate funding body leader commented that: 'partitionism ... is extremely deep-rooted in the Republic of Ireland, arguably as much as or even worse than in Northern Ireland'. There is some evidence to suggest that political elites and sections of society in the Republic of Ireland now imagine North and South as economically, politically and culturally separate. For example, in *Through Irish eyes: Irish attitudes towards the UK*, a 2004 report commissioned by the British Council in Ireland and the British Embassy in Dublin, one southern respondent went so far as to comment: 'Northern Ireland is just different. Everything about it – the people, the infrastructure, even their clothes, their way of life, they are different people.' However, geographical location and historical relationships can impact upon southern perceptions of northerners. According to one project provider in Dundalk, 'people [in Dundalk] are closer mentally [to Newry] than they are to Drogheda ... there is a mind set there that is much more similar to Newry than Drogheda'. He believed that his cross-border project, linking the museums in Dundalk and Newry, helped cement historic ties.[41]

There can be no doubt that the border has acted as an effective barrier between North and South and engendered a sense of estrangement between northern and southern co-nationals and between the two communities in Northern Ireland. However, this sense of estrangement seems to be weaker in the Irish border region. Arguably, the border appears more of a barrier the further people are removed from it, while it tends to dissolve at close quarters. It is important also not to underestimate durable cultural ties, especially those that bind the Irish national imagined community island-wide. The Catholic Church, the Irish language, Irish music and the Gaelic Athletic Association (GAA) are key cultural resources that continue to be identified with an Irish nation. These common identifications remain, despite evidence of prejudice between northern and southern nationalists in ways that are not readily available or accessible to Ulster Protestant unionists. However, the creation under the 1998 agreement of bodies such as Tourism Ireland Ltd, for the promotion of tourism on an all-Ireland basis, supports the representation abroad of North and South as one and the same place rather than as separate places. This represents a transcending of internal borders and the North–South border simultaneously, and constitutes a transnational rather than international form of cooperation.

One of the features of the projects researched here was the emphasis on innovative and creative ways of engaging people in joint projects. Thus one Strabane–Lifford project used the medium of drama 'to bring people out of their box, in terms of their thinking and outlook'. Another Belfast project was using photography, video, multimedia and the internet to empower people to campaign on issues that affected them. These projects, while developing methods of cross-border and cross-communal communication, were less concerned with product or outcome than with process. One project, in seeking to involve young people from the South with both communities in the North and an immigrants' centre in Dublin, felt constrained by the territorial limits of the Peace programme, which embraced only six of the twenty-six southern counties.[42] Many of the projects employed innovative means of cooperating while 'expressing difference' by creating new spaces for interaction and dialogue across the border. Both the relevant intermediate funding bodies and the grassroots organisations involved in measure 5.3 tended to emphasise the acceptance of difference and the promotion of diversity as a prelude to building trust, confidence, respect, understanding and reconciliation. To this end, storytelling emerged as a key activity.[43] Storytelling has been identified by Rothman as a particularly important mechanism for reconciliation in identity-based conflicts – self-perceptions being constructed through stories.[44] Developing a peace-building strategy based on local expertise and storytelling enables it to become embedded in the local community.

Such a strategy requires 'space' beyond the sometimes claustrophobic structures of intercommunal interaction in Northern Ireland, yet a context in which some of the stories resonate. Here the opportunities provided for transnational, cross-border networks are valuable. This research and previous examinations of cross-border cooperation suggests that it may be worth making a distinction between territory and space. Territory involves the bordered geography of both states and the communities within Northern Ireland. Space, on the other hand, is the space of networks, and may refer to Northern Ireland and the border counties, to the all-island context, or to a British–Irish, European or more global context. Space has elastic boundaries, depending on the reach of the networks involved – networks which may be concerned with specific functional interests that are economic, political, or cultural. Networking projects in cross-border space, like many of those studied here, are conducive to escaping the zero-sum nature of territorially based conflict. They represent a shift away from state-centred activities – the island of Ireland as a space is not a territorial state but it is an arena conducive to developing networks of cooperation. Cooperation across borders is also a growing necessity with respect to human rights, the global economy, environmental issues and new forms of communication which have in large part escaped the containers of territorial state boundaries.

ROLE OF THE VOLUNTARY SECTOR

Two types of cooperation

Cross-border networking as practised by intermediate funding bodies and grassroots voluntary and community bodies under measure 5.3 is, however, much less prominent than the other form of cooperation between states and state agencies. The latter has been territorial rather than spatial, and intergovernmental or international rather than transnational, in character. Intergovernmental cooperation marks a major advance on the decades when formal cross-border contacts were almost non-existent. It renders the border more permeable by building linkages across it. However, as argued above, these activities are also border confirming. Cooperation between, for example, government departments and local authorities serves to remind participants of their differences as well as their similarities, and exposes the different competencies, cultures and practices of accountability which have developed throughout over eighty years of separate state development in the UK and the Republic. These differences can be inbuilt inhibitors of flexible and creative forms of cross-border cooperation – serving to maintain borders as much as to transcend them. As such, territorial forms of cooperation may be a necessary but insufficient element in promoting peace and reconciliation.

Cross-border networking, the other form of cooperation, involves the creation of common rules, discourses and practices geared to a common functional purpose. It is thus less state-centred, less border confirming and more directly focused on transcending territorial borders in pursuit of shared objectives. While the first (international) form of cooperation can underline and preserve differences, the transnational form may remind people of what they share – of their similar characteristics, interests and opportunities in a broader context. The first form of cooperation may involve 'mutual recognition' and the second, a degree of harmonisation. The distinction we make here is analytical – neither form of cooperation may exist in a pure form. In practice both of these forms of cooperation can co-exist with and complement each other.

Within the Peace programmes we can see the evolution of a certain division of labour – the voluntary sector has assumed, or has been delegated, a key role addressing questions of 'peace and reconciliation' directly at both a transcommunity and transnational level. The sector is seen to be at one remove from territorial government and better placed to network with grassroots organisations on the ground. Indeed, one of the features of our research was the positive views expressed by grassroots project promoters regarding the help provided by voluntary sector intermediate funding body personnel.

Weak institutional frameworks

Whereas the two states, potentially at least, provide strong and durable institutional support for intergovernmental or international cooperation, the institutional support for transnational, cross-border networking is very weak. A skeletal institutional framework for transnational cross-border cooperation does exist, comprising the EU Commission, the SEUPB, the voluntary sector and some cross-border projects at grassroots level. Just as voluntary sector activity within states critically depends on government funding and support, so also transnational voluntary activity needs institutional support. Our respondents underlined the consequences of the stalled, and somewhat fragmented, North–South dimension to the Good Friday agreement, the negative consequences of the gap in funding between Peace I and Peace II, and the long-term inadequacy of short-term projects to tackle long-term issues of peace and reconciliation.

While the EU Commission itself promotes transnationalism and the creation of a common European space of which the island of Ireland is a part, the EU as an entity promotes both internationalism and transnationalism at the same time. However, the great bulk of EU funding is channelled directly through member states rather than through transnational bodies. Indeed, despite the transnational agenda of the commission, there are signs that the balance of influence in the EU is shifting towards the renationalisation of European programmes.[45] The UK government is to the fore in this process in ways which directly impact on the Peace programmes and on any successor to Peace II. The EU Commission official responsible for Peace II noted the contradictory position of the UK government.[46] It is arguing for a renationalisation of the structural funds (of which Peace II was a part) – in other words, it wants to abolish the EU-level distribution system which channels money to needy regions – in favour of a system where national states get their share of the pot and then distribute it internally according to their own criteria. This approach contradicts any arguments that the UK might make for the extension of Peace II on the basis that other member states should recognise Northern Ireland as a special case.[47] Despite its role in rejecting the initial Peace II proposals and its insistence on establishing the 'distinctiveness' of the Peace II programme, the Commission's role has been more 'hands off' than under Peace I. However, it has sought to promote the role of the SEUPB and to work closely with it.

The SEUPB is seen by the Commission as a transnational agency capable of delivering EU-level programmes. It has the potential to support the kinds of transnational voluntary sector activity discussed above. However, apart from the stalled peace process and its initial organisational problems, it too faces the tension between international and transnational approaches and remains in danger of being renationalised, that is, being made subordinate to government departments. A staff member acknowledged that it is working in a very difficult policy environment with the suspension of the North/South Ministerial Council. He suggested that 'there can be no strategic development of policy on the part of our organisation, so that automatically puts us into a management role of the Peace II programme and confines us very much to that box'.[48] Although voluntary sector organisations acknowledge the potential of the SEUPB, they often tend to experience it as just another layer of bureaucracy in the circumstances.[49]

The capacity of the voluntary sector intermediate funding bodies to engage in transnational cooperation is very circumscribed, without direct partnership links to the EU Commission and a strategically oriented SEUPB. Capacity to innovate and promote transnational cross-border projects is also reduced if the voluntary sector is confined to the role of implementing the programmes. Intermediate funding bodies have lobbied for a Peace III on the basis that it should be an EU-wide programme where the promotion of peace and reconciliation through cross-border networking might be normalised and where cross-cultural learning would become possible.

The European Commission has been favourably disposed to multi-level social partnership on the basis that it challenges the territorial paradigm of European politics and provides a new and effective approach to transnational EU-wide socioeconomic problems. On the surface at least, the Peace programmes are an embodiment of the EU commitment to partnership which includes the voluntary sector. These programmes appear to represent a shift from government to governance since they traverse sectoral, communal and state borders; and multiple agents are involved, including the commission, the government departments, local authorities, private sector organisations, intermediate-level voluntary networks, and grassroots voluntary and community groups. Such a transborder network is predicated on an inclusive principle.

The European Conference for Conflict Prevention argued that governments have been reluctant to admit non-state actors to the business of peace and security – a position which runs counter to the growing significance of civil society in other areas.[50] However, in the context of the Peace programmes, the EU Commission has endorsed the involvement of voluntary sector organisations, the business community and research institutions in a partnership for peace building. It remains to be seen, however, whether there will be a significant shift of power from the Commission to the Council of Ministers and the Parliament in an EU with twenty-five members or more, thus reducing the inclusive transnational approach in favour of more discretion for national governments.

Even when states do not directly control activities within their borders, they exert a powerful undertow on the activities of others, including the voluntary sector. This undertow tends to pull everything back into the territorial cage. Such a tendency is magnified in the Irish case by a 'territorial fix' in which both states allow the pace of peace-building to be set by the political representatives of two increasingly separate communities within Northern Ireland. While internal political agreement is critical, peace-building beyond the cage of the national state can create long-term supportive conditions for such agreement. There is a danger, however, in the evolution of an implicit division of labour, whereby government departments charge the voluntary sector with the 'residual' role of tackling peace-building directly while shedding such responsibility themselves.[51]

CONCLUSION

One of the recurring and unsurprising findings of our research was the lack of consensus over the meaning of peace and reconciliation.[52] Some of our respondents suggested that real progress was difficult until there was agreement on the causes of the conflict; others suggested that if there was such agreement, then there would be no need for peace programmes. One of the consequences of voluntary sector involvement in measures like 5.3 has been the production of a literature recognising that peace and reconciliation are processes rather than easily measured products – a viewpoint confirmed in our interviews with project providers. One of the key questions, therefore, concerns the strategies which might be best employed to advance the process. Needless to say, this chapter can offer no easy solutions. However, it does suggest that whatever else the Northern Ireland conflict is about, it is certainly about borders in both a material and metaphorical sense. Therefore, any viable peace and reconciliation strategy must develop a process which confronts the paradoxical nature of borders and seeks to redress the balance between their positive and negative features.

Violence, intimidation, coercion and exclusion are associated with most state borders, even when overt coercion belongs to a distant and largely forgotten past. Yet such borders also have positive functions in facilitating democracy, social inclusion, citizenship, cultural identity and diversity. Northern Ireland is a factory of internal territorial borders, some violently contested, other scarcely visible. They serve as markers of difference and as measures of communal autonomy and control. They also measure shifts in what many perceive as a zero-sum game to claim or control the fixed territory bounded by the state border with the South. The Good Friday agreement promised a transition from violence to politics as a means of pursuing this struggle. However, the struggle, even if non-violent, is unlikely to promote long-term peace and reconciliation or easily overcome the emotions engendered by violent conflicts and how they are remembered. As one of our respondents indicated, in Northern Ireland one side has to 'win'.

State institutions improve conditions for peace-building by reducing inequality and promoting human rights. However, operationally, they are forced to recognise sectarian borders for political and administrative purposes. Moreover, the British state management of the conflict involved caging it within clearly delimited territorial areas, thereby intensifying it in those areas. This, too, was the policy of the Irish state, committed, understandably, to preventing the conflict from spilling over the border. Border stabilisation and maintenance are plausible strategies for limiting or avoiding conflict but they are implausible to the extent that they imagine borders as static entities. In a context where state borders are being constantly reconfigured by economic, political and cultural globalisation, new strategies are being suggested.

In this changing global context, our research suggests that the voluntary sector's promotion of cross-border cooperation can make a distinct contribution to building peace and reconciliation. It allows an escape from state frameworks where borders are contested and viewed in static terms. In the process, it encourages a culture of cooperation – common cross-border organisations, shared goals, discourse, rules, and a focus on positive sum or mutual benefit outcomes. In the case of some unionist groups, it provides a welcome escape from the relentless, conflictual interaction with republicans and nationalists in the North. For some such groups, cross-border links may provide a useful detour on the road to improving links with nationalist or republican communities in the North. For some nationalists, cross-border projects illustrated the need to reduce ignorance, fear and prejudice between nationalists on either side of the border.

The projects we examined varied in the strength of their transnational dimension. Nevertheless, they challenged in a variety of ways the coincidence of cultural and territorial borders so characteristic of the Irish conflict. While cultural and educational activities were the objects of co-operation, they were also the means of developing a culture of cooperative practices. Nevertheless, project-based transnational cooperation, promoted by the voluntary sector, needs a stronger and more durable institutional framework to sustain what is inevitably a long-term process of peace-building and reconciliation. The funds to sustain this framework, even under the Peace programmes, are very limited and time-bound compared to the monies channelled through state and economic organisations.

None of the merits of transnational cooperation detracts from the necessity of inter-state cooperation. The latter has been fundamental to an overall rhetoric of cross-border cooperation which has largely replaced the 'cold war' relationships between the two jurisdictions in Ireland. Transnational cooperation, however, provides a necessary counter-dynamic by transcending and helping to reconfigure borders and by providing an arena for flexible project-based activities organised by the voluntary sector intermediate funding bodies and grassroots groups. Our research demonstrates that such activities combat territorialism by creating a space in which difference can be explored and mutual interests advanced. The voluntary sector can play a key role here but its efforts need to be bolstered by an institutional partnership framework involving a proactive EU Commission, a strengthened SEUPB, and two states willing to support long-term cross-border networking, using innovative methods, embracing grassroots organisations and transcending the borders which define the Northern Ireland conflict.

NOTES

1 Different ways of defining civil society are discussed in chapter 1. All of them involve a particular view of the relationship between state and society. For the purposes of this chapter, the voluntary (including the community) sector is understood as a 'third' or 'non-profit' sector within civil society that is distinct from state institutions on the one hand, and the profit-led economic organisations on the other. Established professional organisations such as the legal, medical and teaching professions, while part of civil society, are here excluded from the voluntary sector. We recognise that the voluntary sector as defined here is largely dependent for its survival on state support.

2 The initial research was funded by the Royal Irish Academy's Third Sector Research Programme and focused largely on measure 5.3 (Peace II) entitled 'Developing cross-border reconciliation and understanding'. It also draws on ongoing research in the Centre for International Borders Research at Queen's University Belfast on the changing significance of state borders and cross-border cooperation in Europe and elsewhere. We used our interviews to explore key themes such as the role of cross-border cooperation in promoting peace and reconciliation, different types of cross-border cooperation, the meaning of partnership, peace-building, and the key issues and problems as perceived by key actors at various levels within the Peace programmes.

3 The impact of the EU in promoting cross-border cooperation has received more attention than that of the USA; see, for example, the EU border conflicts research programme, and K Hayward, *Defusing the conflict in Northern Ireland: pathways of influence for the European Union* (Birmingham: University of Birmingham, 2004) [EU Border Conflicts Series, working paper no. 2]; also available at www.euborderconf.bham.ac.uk/publications/workingpapers.htm [accessed 16-03-2006]. The USA has relied more on supporting private business through the International Fund for Ireland. Comparative studies of EU and US promotion of cross border cooperation suggest that heavy involvement of state institutions at all levels characterises European efforts while US sponsored cross-border cooperation (as in across the US–Mexican border, for example) is focused on private-sector initiatives; see J Blatter, 'From "spaces of place" to "spaces of flows"? Territorial and functional governance in cross-border regions in Europe and North America', *International journal of urban and regional research* 28:3 (2004), pp. 530–48.

4 The specific *raison d'être* of the Peace II programme that has funded the Mapping Frontiers project of which this book forms a part includes 'addressing the legacy of the conflict' and 'taking opportunities arising from the peace'. Like Peace I, Peace II has allocated 15% of its total budget to promoting cross-border co-operation.

5 See J Allister, *Leading for Ulster, speaking for you in Europe: a record of Jim Allister's speeches in the European Parliament July 2004–November 2005* (Belfast: Jim Allister MEP, 2006), p. 64.

6 See, for example, T Diez, S Stetter and M Albert, 'The European Union and the Transformation of Border Conflicts', EU BorderConf Working Paper 1, 2003, www.euborderconf.bham.ac.uk.; J Anderson, L O'Dowd and T M Wilson (eds), *New borders for a changing Europe: cross-border co-operation and governance* (London: Frank Cass, 2003); J Anderson, L O'Dowd and T M Wilson (eds), *Culture and co-operation in Europe's borderlands*, special issue of *European studies: a journal of European culture, history and politics*, 19 (2003); T M Wilson and H Donnan (eds), *Border identities: nation and state at international frontiers* (Cambridge: Cambridge University Press, 1998); and M Anderson, *Frontiers: territory and state formation in the modern world* (Cambridge: Polity Press, 1996).

7 J Nederveen Pieterse, 'Globalization as reworking borders: hierarchical integration and new border theory', paper presented to the Annual Conference of the International Studies Association, New Orleans, 18–22 Mar. 2002.

8 M Albert and L Brock, 'Debordering the world of states', *New political science* 35 (1996), pp. 69–106, at p. 70.

9 C Tilly, *Coercion, capital and European states AD 990–1990* (Oxford: Basil Blackwell, 1990); Z Bauman, 'Soil, blood and identity', *Sociological review* 40:2 (1992), pp. 675–701.

10 Anderson and O'Dowd argue that new forms of globalisation such as the growth of US direct investment and the spread of the mass media played a part in unsettling the border in Ireland, creating new opportunities for contacts between both administrations, stimulating internal tensions within Northern Ireland and providing a means of publicising internationally the grievances of Northern Irish nationalists; see J Anderson and L O'Dowd, 'Contested borders: globalisation and ethno-national conflict in Ireland', *Regional studies* 33:7 (1999), pp. 681–96.

11 The politics of security have come to the fore in the context of the US global 'war on

terror' and new border security arising from the expansion of the EU from fifteen to twenty-five members.

12 D Held, D Goldblatt, T McGrew and J Perraton, *Global transformations: politics, economics and culture* (Cambridge: Polity Press, 1999).

13 I S Lustick, *Unsettled states, disputed lands: Britain and Ireland, France and Algeria, Israel and the West Bank Gaza* (Ithaca: Cornell University Press, 1993), p. 1.

14 Brendan O'Leary notes that 'in the twentieth century borders were moved, re-moved, taken, re-taken, and abandoned, and peoples were moved, re-moved and slaughtered on an epic scale'; see B O'Leary, 'Introduction', in B O'Leary, I S Lustick and T Callaghy (eds), *Right sizing the state: the politics of moving borders* (Oxford: Oxford University Press, 2001), pp. 1–14, at p. 2. In his revised definition of the state (p. 3), he defines it as having a variable border or territory, in contradistinction to Weber's emphasis on a 'fixed territorial boundary'. He suggests that it would be remarkable if the territoriality of states was immune to the variables that have shaped modernity, arguing for a programme of research that examines the causes and consequences of moving borders.

15 See, for example, two working papers by B O'Leary, *Analysing partition: definition, classification and explanation* [IBIS working papers 77]; and *Debating partition: justifications and critiques* [IBIS working paper 78] (Dublin: Institute for British–Irish Studies, UCD, 2006); also available at www.qub.ac.uk/cibr/mappingfrontierswps.htm.

16 One way of conceptualising borders is to see them as barriers (both protective and exclusionary), bridges, resources and symbols of identity; see L O'Dowd, 'The changing significance of European borders', *Regional and federal studies* 12:4 (2002), pp. 13–36.

16 J Coakley and L O'Dowd, *The Irish border and North/South co-operation: an overview* (Dublin: Institute for British–Irish Studies, UCD, 2005) [IBIS working papers 47]; also available at www.qub.ac.uk/cibr/mappingfrontierswps.htm.

17 For a contemporary example, see H Donnan, *Fuzzy frontiers: the rural interface in south Armagh* (Dublin: Institute for British–Irish Studies, UCD, 2006) [IBIS working papers 76]; also available at www.qub.ac.uk/cibr/mappingfrontierswps.htm.

18 Distrust remains among the parties as to their respective commitment to this principle – much of it crystallising in the conflict over the decommissioning of arms. Some unionists have attempted to retreat from this position by arguing that constitutional change should only come about by the agreement of the majority of both unionists and nationalists. This begs the question of whether the double majority requirement should apply to the maintenance of the status quo also or to innovations like the Good Friday agreement.

19 Moreover, plausible speculation might suggest that prolonged interaction with southern governments has persuaded even extreme unionist politicians of the absence of any enthusiastic lobby in southern political circles to 'take over' Northern Ireland, even if they sometimes warn of 'slippery slopes' and creeping unification. Similarly, it might be estimated that prolonged interaction of southern politicians with northern unionists has reduced their enthusiasm for extending the Irish government's responsibility for Northern Ireland.

20 A Blok 'The narcissism of minor differences', *European journal of social theory* 1:1 (1998), pp. 33–56.

21 Hayward, *Defusing the conflict* (2004).

22 L O'Dowd, 'Negotiating the British–Irish border: transfrontier co-operation on the European periphery', Final Report to the ESRC, Grant Number R000 23 3053, April 2004; L O'Dowd, *Whither the Irish border? Sovereignty, democracy and economic integration in Ireland* (Belfast: Centre for Research and Documentation, 1994).

23 A Northern Ireland Council for Voluntary Action (NICVA) document on designing a successor programme to Peace II noted: 'there is no body, architecture or system in place to sustain or to drive North/South co-operation apart from ad hoc arrangements and the joint North/South bodies, which have important, but specific and limited

remits'; see NICVA, *Designing Peace III* (Belfast: NICVA, 2004), p. 8. The potential role of the North/South Ministerial Council has been stymied by suspensions of the agreement's institutions.

24 The emergence of the DUP as the dominant party of unionism is partly due to its ability to persuade the unionist electorate that it has stemmed, and even reversed, the tide of concessions to nationalists.

25 The Commission rejected the initial proposal from the two governments for the Peace II programme for, among other things, imprecision, lack of demonstrable links to peace building, and for insufficiently linking North and South. The voluntary sector argued for a more direct focus on peace and reconciliation, the British government and the Ulster Unionist Party stressed economic cooperation, the SDLP the social dimension and the DUP argued for the stronger presence of elected representatives at the expense of the voluntary and community sector. The revised programme in the end was more heavily geared to economic cooperation than Peace I, although it demanded greater clarity on how the various measures would promote peace and reconciliation; see B Harvey, *Review of the Peace II Programme* (York: The Joseph Rowntree Charitable Trust, 2003), pp. 32–5.

26 Acheson and Milofsky are highly critical of the shift in priorities from Peace I to Peace II. They claim that a definite move has been made to favour macro-economic and political changes as the dominant peace-building strategy over the alternative of further strengthening community-based organisations and the civil society networks they foster. They argue that Peace II money has tended to be channelled to area-based, sectarian community organisations, with more money going to economic and private sector interests and to intermediate funding bodies than to lower-level organisations; see N Acheson and C Milofsky, 'Peace building and participation in Northern Ireland: marginal social movements and the policy process since the "Good Friday" Agreement', paper presented at the Sixth International Conference of the International Society for Third Sector Research, Toronto, Canada, 11–14 July 2004, pp. 3, 11.

27 Hayward, *Defusing the conflict* (2004).

28 Peace I had funds totalling €503m. Peace II was worth approximately €741m, with the EU contributing €531m, national contributions amounting to €177m and private contributions totalling €33m. The proportion allocated to building cross-border partnerships (15%) thus amounted to €79.4m, with €39.7m of that for Northern Ireland (representing 9.3% of the total allocation in Northern Ireland) and €39.7m for the border counties of the Republic of Ireland (representing 37% of the total allocation for the border counties of the Republic).

29 In its 'Ex-post evaluation of Peace I and mid-term evaluation of Peace II' (November 2003) PriceWaterhouseCoopers recommended that funds be transferred to measure 5.3 and measure 2.1 ('reconciliation for a sustainable peace') from the other fifty-four measures of Peace II because both measures related directly to reconciliation and were over-subscribed. The EU commission official responsible for Peace II observed: 'Measure 5.3 is an ideal illustration of what the Peace Programme should be about: making an impact, putting people together at the grassroots level' (interview with DG Regio official, Brussels, 21 April 2004).

30 Although evaluations are now part of the conventional wisdom surrounding such programmes and imply a measure of accountability and criteria for future policy, they remain a highly problematical exercise – especially where the outcome – facilitating peace and reconciliation – is a long-term aim that is relatively intangible and highly contested. It is extremely difficult to measure the impact of short-term projects with limited resources in terms of their contribution to such broad, long-term goals.

31 An EU Commission official dealing with Peace II noted: 'sometimes it's easier to have cross-border rather than cross-community, sometimes it can be the other way around … it's a case by case thing. The important thing is making contact … working with

people from the other side' (interview with DG Regio official, Brussels, 21 April 2004).

32 Interview with Jackie Hewitt, Farset/Inishowen Project, Belfast, 7 May 2003.

33 Interview with John Dean, South Belfast Cultural Society, Belfast 16 May 2003.

34 Interview with John Dean, South Belfast Cultural Society, Belfast 16 May 2003.

35 Interview with Gordon Speer, Border Arts, Castlederg, 10 Sep. 2003.

36 Interview with Derek Reaney, Derry and Raphoe Action, Newtownstewart, 5 June 2003.

37 'Stormontgate' refers to a police raid on the Sinn Féin offices at Parliament Buildings, Stormont, in October 2002. Documents and computers were seized and a number of party workers were arrested on suspicion of subversive activity. In December 2005, charges against the party workers were dropped 'in the public interest'. The following week one of those arrested, Denis Donaldson, admitted that he had been a British agent since the 1980s and denounced Stormontgate as 'a scam and a fiction invented by the police Special Branch' (news.bbc.co.uk/1/hi/northern_ireland/4536826.stm). He was shot dead in April 2006. The 2001 Holy Cross Primary School protest was undertaken by Protestant loyalists because they objected to the route taken by pupils and parents to a Catholic primary school in a 'loyalist area'.

38 Interview with Jackie Hewitt, Farset/Inishowen Project, Belfast, 7 May 2003.

39 Interview with Derek Reaney, Derry and Raphoe Action, Newtownstewart, 5 June 2003.

40 Paddy Logue, ADM/CPA, in focus group hosted by the authors, Belfast, 30 Jan. 2004.

41 Interview with Brian Walsh, Dundalk Newey Museum Project, Dundalk, 9 June 2003.

42 The geographical limiting of the Peace programmes to twelve counties in the Republic of Ireland was criticised by several respondents although occasional derogations were allowed subsequently in order to facilitate links with other counties.

43 This occurred in several measure 5.3 projects, including: Community Visual Images, South Belfast Cultural Society, Ballymacarrett Arts and Cultural Society, Border Arts, the Pushkin Prizes Trust, Cumann Gaelach Chnoc na Ros Doire, Co. Museum Dundalk/Newry and Mourne Museums, and the Downpatrick/Listowel Linkage Group.

44 J Rothman, 'Dialogue in conflict: past and future', in E Wiener (ed.), *The handbook of interethnic coexistence* (New York: Continuum Publishing, 1998), pp. 217–35.

45 The pressure to re-nationalise the structural funds is in part an attempt to limit the claims of the many new underdeveloped regions in central and eastern European accession states on an EU-level redistribution of resources from richer to poorer regions.

46 Interview with DG Regio official, Brussels, 21 Apr. 2004.

47 Interview with DG Regio official, Brussels, 21 Apr. 2004.

48 SEUPB official in focus group hosted by the authors, Belfast, 30 Jan. 2004.

49 The NICVA consultation document on 'Designing Peace III' notes that administration costs have risen from 2% in Peace I to 9% in Peace II. Although it suggests that the SEUPB is valued as a cross-border body, it argues that it should be reconstituted as a smaller, strategic, funding and policy body operating under a partnership model, with a board made up of elected representatives, government and voluntary and community representatives; see NICVA, *Designing Peace III* (2004), p. 22.

50 See papers of European Centre for Conflict Prevention Conference, Dublin Castle, March 2004, at www.gppac.org [accessed 20-10-2006].

51 A leading SEUPB official interviewed by us pointed to this problem, suggesting that if the voluntary sector was to become the sole recipient of future peace and reconciliation funding, it would let the public sector 'off the hook'. He felt that it was essential that government departments, North and South, should be involved in actively promoting peace and reconciliation (interview, Belfast 30 January 2004). The 'good relations' consultation document produced by the Northern Ireland Office seems to indicate some acceptance of this point. However, significantly for the argument advanced in this chapter, it made no reference to promoting cross-border peace and reconciliation.

52 Examples of innovative thinking about peace and reconciliation in the voluntary sector can be found in the following: G Kelly and B Hamber (eds) *Reconciliation: rhetoric or relevant?* (Belfast: Democratic Dialogue, 2005) [Report 17], and B Hamber and G Kelly, *A place for reconciliation? Conflict and locality in Northern Ireland* (Belfast: Democratic Dialogue, 2005) [Report 18].

Part 3

Case studies in the North–South relationship

7

Cooperative projects: the education sector

ANDY POLLAK

INTRODUCTION

The politics of division and partition in Ireland over the past 200 years has usually been mirrored in the island's educational structures, schools and colleges. William Drennan's hopes at the opening of the Royal Belfast Academical Institution in 1814 that 'pupils of all religious denominations should communicate by frequent and friendly intercourse in the common business of education' were soon to be disappointed as the new national school system established in the 1830s took on a strongly denominational character. The religious divide in schools continues on both sides of the border to the present day, with the only significant changes being the emergence of a small integrated or multi-denominational sector in both jurisdictions, and – perhaps more significantly in the longer term – a recent and rapid decline in Catholic vocations and therefore in the Catholic ethos of both teachers and pupils in southern schools.

Education is fundamental to any long-term process of peace and reconciliation on the island of Ireland. At the political level, the new North–South relationships that have emerged since the 1970s – the core theme of this book – are in large part a product of a new partnership between the British and Irish governments developed in response to thirty years of conflict in Northern Ireland. This partnership has been sustained by both states' membership of the EU, and by significant political and financial support from both the EU and the USA. Yet the consolidation of new, more durable and more mutually beneficial relationships between North and South depends in large measure on the development of a related educational dimension that reaches well beyond the elite circles of government policy makers and funders. Strategic educational initiatives can engage younger generations of Irish people, North and South, in a similar way to the education and training programmes which complemented far-reaching political changes to help overcome deep mutual mistrust between the peoples of France and Germany in the fifty years after the second world war.

As this chapter demonstrates, there has been an extraordinary growth in cross-border educational projects between North and South from the late 1980s onwards. However, this cooperation has been based not on any overall educational strategy or programme but on the mushrooming of a very large number of specific projects, driven largely by individual idealism and funded by the EU and other overseas sources. The projects have also had varying durations, content and impacts.

The chapter begins by briefly alluding to the demise of a once-unified Irish educational system and the deep gulf that opened up between North and South following partition. The second section describes the renewal of North–South educational links through the European Studies Project (ESP) for secondary schools and the Wider Horizons youth training project from the late 1980s on. It then outlines the subsequent explosion of new contacts and exchanges in the context of the paramilitary ceasefires and the Belfast or Good Friday agreement, and the injection of EU funds which they engendered. It looks, in particular, at five successful projects: in the areas of primary education exchanges, information and communication technology in education, citizenship education, education for reconciliation, and teacher training. The third section offers a preliminary assessment of the impact of some of the more significant cross-border projects. The chapter concludes with a reflection on the extraordinary growth of cross-border educational cooperation, and the need for some coherent future strategy by governments if such cooperation is to play a constructive role in improving North–South understanding.

THE DEMISE OF A UNIFIED SYSTEM

Education has been a 'core value' for Irish people – North and South, Protestant and Catholic, unionist and nationalist – for at least two centuries. In 1824, according to the Commission of Inquiry into Education in Ireland (before the state became involved in education), there were over 12,000 schools in Ireland, and of those 9,300 were 'hedge schools' catering for very large numbers of people. There was no compulsory attendance or anything like it – these were schools by the people for the people, a 'bottom-up' type schooling movement.[1]

The hedge school system was gradually replaced by the national school system created in 1831, which proved a quite extraordinary success. The nineteenth century saw the rapid growth of a state-supported schools network in Ireland that was way ahead of what was happening in England or Scotland at the time. By 1870 there were 7,000 of these schools catering for a million pupils, again long before compulsory attendance. This was a genuine all-island system, despite its *de facto* denominational structure, with a unified curriculum and a great deal of teacher mobility. Although it was originally designed to promote the education of Catholic and Protestant children alongside each other in mixed schools with a common educational programme, as the system expanded there was in practice increasing segregation along religious lines. By the end of the nineteenth century the original interdenominational blueprint for the system had been effectively undermined, and even the common curriculum was under pressure. The early national school system nevertheless represented a striking expression of an integrated, island-wide approach to primary education.

The distinguished educationalist and antiquarian, P W Joyce – perhaps the most remarkable and least acknowledged figure of nineteenth-century Irish cultural history – can be seen as a symbol of that unitary system. He came from his native county Limerick to work as an organiser of schools in Antrim in the 1850s.[2] Joyce's *A Child's History of Ireland* was a great success when it was published in 1898 and was used widely in schools of all denominations. He was an educational pluralist long before such a term had ever been coined, and strongly emphasised the need for mutual respect, tolerance and affection in the dissemination of Irish history and education. He concluded his introduction to that volume with the following words: 'Perhaps this book … may help to foster mutual feelings of respect and toleration among Irish people of different parties, and may teach them to love and admire what is good and noble in their history, no matter where found.'[3]

Then came partition, and education in Ireland, coming from a common root, sprang apart like a child's catapult, and stayed apart, with an almost 100 per cent 'back to back' separation. In Northern Ireland, primary education came under the control of a newly created Department of Education, but in a major reorganisation of the management system the distinction between Catholic and Protestant schools (which were ultimately to coincide respectively, broadly, with 'maintained' and 'controlled' schools) was accentuated. In the South, the old management system remained undisturbed, but the curriculum was radically reformed in a strongly nationalist direction (with a particular emphasis on the Irish language, and on Irish culture more generally), resulting in a sharp differentiation from the

Northern Ireland system. The distinguished Irish educationalist John Coolahan has said that he trained twice as a teacher in the Republic of Ireland in the 1960s, and 'as far as education in Northern Ireland was concerned it could have been Timbuktu. There was no reference to it, no mention of it – it was just out of one's consciousness.'

THE RENEWAL OF NORTH–SOUTH LINKS

Any serious thought of renewed educational links between the two parts of Ireland would have to wait more than sixty years, until the late 1980s. The wider context for this was a dramatically new one: on the island of Ireland it involved the British and Irish governments working together to seek common solutions to the problems of Northern Ireland; on the continent of Europe it saw the coming together of old enemies in the European Union, stressing education and training as a way of fostering and promoting a common sense of European heritage and unity. In addition to programmes arising out of these priorities, a second wave originated following the paramilitary ceasefires of 1994 and the peace process that began then. These are described in the next two subsections, and some brief comments are then made on their relative significance.

Before the peace process

The European emphasis referred to above led to a multiplicity of exchange programmes – Erasmus, Socrates and Comenius – linking students, teachers and education officials, and bringing together schools and other educational institutions to undertake joint projects and research. In Ireland, the 1985 Anglo-Irish agreement led to the initiation of the first major North–South educational programme, itself firmly embedded in the wider European context: the European Studies Project.

The European Studies Project. This was generously funded by the departments of education in Northern Ireland, the Republic and England in a way that no school-based educational exchange programmes were to be funded subsequently in the later 'peace process' phase from the mid-1990s onwards. In its first six-year phase it had a £3.2 million budget and six full-time field officers in the North, the South and England. It had a junior programme for 11–15-year olds, with schools linked through information and communications technology and occasional visits for the study of history, geography and environmental studies (themes which are common to the curricula of the three jurisdictions); and a senior programme based around the study of contemporary European issues, whether cultural, social, political, technological or economic.

A 1991 report on the junior programme highlighted new 'active learning methods' such as weighing evidence, detecting bias, questioning the validity of sources and students presenting their own considered viewpoints as being particularly suited to dealing with controversial issues in the classroom. Student-centred methods like field trips, role plays and making videos, and the use of information and communications technology – until then little known in Irish schools – were also noted; the first Irish schools to use email on a regular basis were probably schools involved in this programme.[4]

The European Studies Project's firm foundations were shown in the fact that, by 1999, 193 secondary schools (ninety-four in Northern Ireland and ninety-nine in the Republic of Ireland) were involved, and in 2006, twenty years after it started, its website still showed 153 secondary schools (seventy-six in Northern Ireland and seventy-seven in the Republic of Ireland) participating, plus schools from England and seventeen other European countries.[5] One of the project's strongest values is that it has allowed northern Protestant schools to be involved in a North–South link alongside east–west links with England and continental European countries – 'it takes in the wider, safer environment', in the words of one senior Education and Library Board official.[6]

Wider Horizons. A second major programme that dates from the post-Anglo-Irish agreement period in the late 1980s – although it is a youth training rather than a schools-based educational programme – is Wider Horizons. This is run through the main state training organisations, FÁS in the South and the Department for Employment and Learning in the North, and in the period 1987–2006 nearly 15,000 young people, Protestant and Catholic from Northern Ireland, and a cross-section of trainees from the Republic of Ireland, passed through it.[7]

Wider Horizons was established, funded and managed as a training programme for young people aged 18–28 by the International Fund for Ireland (itself a body established after the Anglo-Irish agreement of 1985). Like the International Fund for Ireland itself, the programme has two integrated aims – to promote employability and reconciliation through vocational preparation, training and work experience. These aims are implemented by sending religiously mixed groups of twenty young people from the two jurisdictions abroad for periods of up to two months to countries where they can obtain relevant training and work experience – usually the USA, Canada, Australia, New Zealand or the EU. While abroad, the participants must learn to live and work together as a united group. The aim is that each group should contain both cross-border and cross-community representation in the proportion of one-third northern Catholics, one-third northern Protestants and one-third young people from the South, although in practice the numbers of northern Protestants have sometimes been under the desired quota. There is a preparatory phase in Ireland lasting up to ten weeks, and a return phase where the group as a whole reflects on its experience and looks for work at home. In practice, this last phase has been the weakest in the programme.

The late 1980s also saw the advent of the first significant NGO-run North–South educational exchanges, with the entry into the field of Co-operation North (now Co-operation Ireland). Between 1985 and 1989, 105 different primary and secondary schools completed two-way exchanges organised by Co-operation North. A similar number of youth groups were involved in exchanges, although these were more erratic.[8]

The peace process period

The decade following the announcement of an IRA ceasefire in 1994 may well come to be seen in retrospect as the 'golden age' of North–South educational cooperation. Enhanced activity was due less to the political initiatives of this period – notably the 1998 Good Friday agreement – than being a consequence of the very large injection of EU funds which the Northern Ireland peace process engendered. Moreover, in the first period of funding from the EU Peace I programme in particular (up to 2002), there was an emphasis on funding 'bottom-up' activities which were particularly helpful to school initiatives. It should be noted that comparatively little matching cross-border funding was available for this work from the departments of education in Dublin and Belfast (under 13 per cent according to one recent study), although the former did set up a dedicated North–South unit with a small funding resource.[9]

A Centre for Cross Border Studies scoping study for the Departments of Education in Belfast and Dublin in 2000 estimated that 540 schools on the island – 261 in the North and 276 in the South – were by then involved in a wide range of cross-border programmes and projects, involving either face-to-face or internet contact.[10] This represented nearly 20 per cent of all schools in Northern Ireland, just over 6 per cent of schools in the Republic, and 9.5 per cent of schools in the whole island. When the much smaller number of primary schools is removed, the figures are more striking: in Northern Ireland, over 52 per cent of secondary schools and 59 per cent of voluntary grammar schools reported cross-border links; in the Republic of Ireland, with its larger number of schools (many of them distant from the border), nearly 23 per cent of secondary, vocational and community schools and 35 per cent of fee-paying schools reported such links.

However, the Centre for Cross Border Studies report noted that:

> ... there is a considerable job of work to be done if schools from the less well-off parts of society are to take part in this growing rapprochement. Taking the island as a whole, half the grammar and/or fee paying second level schools in both jurisdictions are involved in cross-border contact, compared to just over a quarter of other second-level schools. There is also a considerable amount to be done to bring more primary and special schools into contact with their counterparts across the border.[11]

A 2000–04 study by the North South Exchange Consortium – made up of Léargas (the Irish agency responsible for managing international cooperation programmes), the British Council and the Youth Council for Northern Ireland – of both school and youth exchanges showed an even more dramatic increase in activities. It concluded that during this five-year period nearly 3,000 school and youth groups had been financially supported, involving more than 55,000 young people.[12] Nearly two-thirds (64 per cent) came from the formal education (schools) sector with one-third (36 per cent) from the informal (youth work) sector. In the formal sector, 57 per cent of those involved came from secondary schools and 25 per cent from primary schools. The North South Exchange Consortium study bore out the somewhat surprising conclusion of the earlier Centre for Cross Border Studies study that participation by northern schools and youth groups from a Protestant background was broadly in line with their proportion of the population of Northern Ireland as a whole.[13] Informally, the North South Exchange Consortium researchers estimated that if one included North–South school and youth exchanges which had not been funded by the EU or other government sources, it was likely that the number of young people participating in such exchanges in this five-year period was around 90,000.

This section will now briefly describe five successful cross-border projects: in primary education, information and communications technology in education, citizenship education, education for reconciliation, and teacher education (their impact is discussed later in this chapter).

Pride of our Place. Primary school exchanges are in the minority, for obvious reasons to do with the requirement to travel and issues of child protection, and they tend to be small-scale. One of the most successful has been the Pride of our Place project, which during the period 2002–6 twinned 9–11-year olds in twelve primary schools in the border counties of Armagh, Down, Louth and Cavan, to carry out studies of a local environmental or historical feature and to share them with a partner school. It was managed by a steering group drawn from the Southern Education and Library Board in Northern Ireland, the Irish Department of Education and Science and the Centre for Cross Border Studies. Funding came from the EU Peace and Reconciliation Programme. This project's main success indicator is that nearly half the schools involved have carried on their cross-border partnership, without EU funding, into joint post-project activities, thus achieving the mainstreaming that is the holy grail of so much cross-border educational project work.

Dissolving Boundaries. The largest and most successful North–South programme in the area of information and communications technology has been Dissolving Boundaries, which is managed and coordinated by the University of Ulster and the National University of Ireland Maynooth, and funded by the two Departments of Education in Bangor and Dublin. It began in 1999 with fifty-two primary, secondary and special schools, taking part in computer conferencing, video-conferencing and emailing on subjects like local history, geography, literature, art, drama, sport, human rights, and the developing world. By 2004 the number of schools which had participated had grown to 172, with 121 schools active in that year. A 2006 research report concluded that participating pupils' learning outcomes included more competent information and communications technology skills, improved social and communication skills, and the transfer of skills from Dissolving Boundaries to other curriculum areas. Nearly 90 per cent of schools reported that they had developed positive relationships with their cross-border partner schools, with many strong friendships emerging.[14]

Civic-Link. The most important organisation in the area of citizenship education is Civic-Link, which grew out of a commitment given by President Clinton's Education Secretary, Richard Riley, to support an Irish cross-border adaptation of a US citizenship education initiative, Project Citizen, which had proved successful in a number of countries. It started in 1999 with a budget of over two million pounds over three years from the US Department of Education, the Irish Department of Education and Science and the Department of Education Northern Ireland. Managed by Co-operation Ireland, it is a pilot initiative that aims to:

> Promote values of mutual understanding, respect and acceptance of diversity; and empower young people to action these values by assuming responsibility for and participation in civic action and

> community building for the mutual benefit of all people on this island, North and South.[15]

Between 1999 and 2002 the number of schools and youth groups involved in Civic-Link's programme of exploring community problems with cross-border partners grew from thirty to 120, and ultimately it involved 160 schools or youth groups in all. The programme drew on two pedagogical approaches: an action learning, public policy focus promoted by the US Centre for Civic Education, and Co-operation Ireland's own North–South relationship-building model. The former encourages and supports students to explore community problems and then devise an action plan to present to policy-makers. The latter emphasises personal contact as a means of tackling inter-group conflict, stereotyping, mutual distrust and prejudice. It is grounded in what is known as the 'contact hypothesis' (which also informed the 'Wider Horizons' project) developed by social psychologists working on issues of prejudice and ethnic relations in the 1950s and 1960s. At the risk of some over-generalisation, this proposes that inter-group prejudice and conflict derive from a lack of knowledge and therefore misinformed stereotypes between members of groups engaged in inter-group hostility and conflict. The solution proposed to such ignorance, and therefore prejudice, is to provide forms of contact that will enable individuals to learn about one another and to realise that they have much in common.

Operationally, Civic-Link combines classroom work, project work to identify and explore the community problem being studied, and a number of residential exchanges with partner schools exploring a comparable problem in the other jurisdiction. It involves second-level students working with their teachers to identify and explore local community problems, and then to devise an action plan to present to policy-makers. Unlike in the USA, this work is not focused in one locality but involves the students using information and communications technology and face-to-face meetings to share their ideas with partner schools and youth groups across the Irish border.

Education for Reconciliation. Dissolving Boundaries and Civic-Link, like the European Studies Project, have benefited from relatively secure funding from Departments of Education in the Republic of Ireland, Northern Ireland, Britain and the USA. They are also all what one of the pioneers of North–South schools cooperation, Aidan Clifford, calls examples of the 'indirect model', where schools come together to work in areas of mutual interest that are not directly related to issues of Irish conflict and identity. The more difficult 'direct model' is rarer: this is where teachers and students take on in the classroom the social, political and religious issues which divide Irish people. According to Clifford, both approaches have value and should exist alongside each other.[16]

Education for Reconciliation, a highly innovative citizenship education project conceived and managed by the Dublin Vocational Education Committee Curriculum Development Unit, is an example of the latter – it has also suffered the financial insecurity experienced by so many smaller projects. In the seven years 1999–2006 it has brought together nearly fifty secondary schools, North and South, to train teachers to deal with the 'hard topics' of reconciliation through the citizenship programmes for 12–15-year olds in both jurisdictions (civic, social and political education in the Republic, and local and global citizenship in the North), and to research and develop a reconciliation module for those programmes.

Despite a glowing report on its first eighteen-month phase (1999–2000), which was funded by the EU Peace I programme, it then experienced a gap in funding and a dispersal of many of its first group of schools and its support team before it was able to re-apply for funding from the same source and start phase two in autumn 2002. There was another gap in funding in 2005, leading to the loss of the project's highly effective manager and research officer. After six months of waiting, grants were forthcoming from the Irish Department of Education and Science (for the first time) and from the EU Peace programme (for the third time). Recruitment of staff for the third phase had to start all over again.

Student Teacher Exchange. Another initiative with a similar stop-go existence, despite high praise from evaluators and senior education officials, is the North–South Student Teacher Exchange project. The first phase of this project (2002–5) was run by the Centre for Cross Border Studies in collaboration with the seven colleges of primary education on the island (four in Dublin, two in Belfast and one in Limerick). It brought eighty trainee teachers to do a significant part of their assessed teaching practice (examined by their college lecturers and forming a central part of their degree course), not in the usual comfort zone of their home place or college locality, but in a primary school in the other Irish jurisdiction. Thus young Protestant trainee teachers from Stranmillis University College found themselves facing classes in Limerick. A young Leitrim Catholic became a particular favourite in 2004 for his project on the *Titanic* with his class in a school in loyalist east Belfast.

Senior Department of Education and Science officials in Dublin said that the project had given a real boost to the Republic's sometimes less than dynamic colleges of education. Department of Education officials in Northern Ireland expressed satisfaction that it had broadened the outlook of the often narrowly focused and provincial graduates of Stranmillis and St Mary's. Yet when the Centre for Cross Border Studies approached a very senior official in the northern department of education for advice about future funding, it was made very clear that the organisers could expect not a penny from a cash-strapped department. In 2006, after a ten-month wait, EU funding was forthcoming for a second phase, incorporating a longitudinal research project to study the exchange's impact on the young trainee teachers' classroom practices and personal attitudes. However, stricter EU regulations on the geographical remit of projects ruled out the participation of the Republic's second largest college of education (because it was in Limerick) and all but one or two southern student teachers from outside the border region.

Three levels of Cooperation

The picture of North–South cooperation involving school students and young people painted here is necessarily only a snapshot; it contains, for example, no data on, or analysis of, the even wider range of cooperation activities in the youth work area. When the origins and scale of funds are examined, three distinct levels of cooperation may be distinguished. Wider Horizons stands alone at the top level with generous funding, largely from the International Fund for Ireland, over nearly two decades, and between 500 and 800 young people passing through its programmes annually. The second level comprises a few relatively well-funded school-based programmes, supported by departments of education, like Civic-Link, the European Studies Project and Dissolving Boundaries. At the third level – at the bottom of the feeding chain – there is a multitude of one- two- and three-year projects kept alive largely by EU Peace funding and unpaid voluntary work. Short-term and 'stop-go' EU funding, regulations ruling out participants from beyond the six southern border counties, and lacking governmental funding, are typical of very many cross-border educational projects. Fund-raising is 'a terrible distraction from the hard work of both education and peacebuilding' in the words of one senior educationalist.[17]

MEASURING THE IMPACT OF COOPERATION

Assessing the impact of any programme designed to overcome deeply held suspicions is particularly difficult, if not impossible, in the short term: such programmes typically need to be in place for many years before their effects are to be felt. This section therefore reviews some of the difficulties in evaluations of this kind, before going on to consider the outcome of such assessments as have been carried out to date. The various programmes are considered in turn.

Project impact

If the funding for North–South and cross-border cooperation in education is uneven, erratic and often non-existent, hard evidence of its impact on peace-building, creating mutual understanding and moving towards that elusive concept, reconciliation on the island of Ireland, is even more sparse. This is a difficult area. Defining and measuring the contribution of time-limited projects to the achievement of long-term societal goals is a very challenging task. Discussions of the impact of school-based projects can also be seen as part of a much broader debate about the relative influence of schools generally in shaping social change compared to familial, peer group, economic and media influences, for example.

The difficulty of assessing the impact of cross-border projects is further underlined by the problems experienced in assessing the impact of cross-community educational work on community relations *within* Northern Ireland. Such work has been going on for far longer than similar work across the border. Almost from the outbreak of the Northern Ireland 'troubles', education has been considered as a possible agent of social change and improved community relations, with much research on the segregation of schooling and experimentation with cross-community contact schemes and other initiatives. The 1989 Education Reform (NI) Order included a range of measures which institutionalised the new concept of Education for Mutual Understanding, formalising joint activities between mainly Protestant (controlled) and Catholic (maintained) schools in the North.

However, although Education for Mutual Understanding and its related area 'Cultural heritage' (focusing on the traditions of the two communities in music, literature and customs) were now statutory, there was no requirement for actual joint activities involving pupils from the two sides. Cross-community contact was encouraged and some funding for it was made available, but schools could, if they wished, teach these themes entirely within their own classrooms without establishing any links with other schools across the divide.[18] Education for Mutual Understanding was also excluded from formal assessment and often taught in a minimalist, cross-curricular manner rather than being integrated into existing subjects. In a deeply segregated society it was often regarded with suspicion, and in the absence of an enthusiast on the staff, the difficult job of coordinating it was sometimes allocated to someone with limited interest or seniority. There were also examples of open antagonism where joint activities involving Catholic and Protestant pupils had to be cancelled because of local protests. For all these reasons, progress in Education for Mutual Understanding was slow, and in recent years government priorities have shifted towards new and broader citizenship programmes. More significantly for the purposes of this chapter, the outcomes of almost a decade of statutory work on this programme were under-researched.[19]

Alan Smith and Alan Robinson, the principal researchers on Education for Mutual Understanding, make a number of points that are also relevant to the evaluation of cross-border projects. They believe that 'despite the inherent attraction of the notion that increased contact and interaction between groups is likely to lead to a reduction in conflict, the empirical evidence to support this notion is limited'. They suggest that the reasons why it is difficult to establish causal links between inter-group contact and attitudinal change range from the lack of sensitivity in research instruments to the possibility that attitudinal changes only emerge over a long period of time. They suggest that there may be merit in:

> ... adopting approaches to evaluation which trace significant numbers of individuals who have participated in a variety of educational and reconciliation programmes during the past 25 years. The aim would be to contrast how individual social attitudes relate to biographical experiences and whether certain formative events are more likely to lead to positive inter-group attitudes than others. However support for this approach to evaluation has been difficult to secure because it is labour intensive and demands a systematic and co-ordinated approach between academic and voluntary agencies over a sustained period of time.[20]

Evaluating the programmes

European Studies Project. Unfortunately this important project has not been externally evaluated since the early 1990s. The 1991 Gleeson evaluation of its junior programme was particularly positive about the pupil-centred 'active learning methods' used and its pioneering use of information and communications technology.[21] A 1992 Coopers and Lybrand evaluation was undertaken from a largely cost-benefit analysis standpoint – concluding that the project was good value for money – and recommended the involvement of more disadvantaged schools.[22]

Wider Horizons. Unlike Education for Mutual Understanding, there is no cross-border educational programme that goes back anything like twenty-five years. However, in its nineteen-year existence, 'Wider Horizons' has worked with a range of target groups with varying degrees of success. Since the early 1990s it has tended to focus on the needs of disadvantaged young people and on a number of disadvantaged areas. The programme has been particularly successful in improving the work motivation of participants, especially young people from deprived backgrounds and employment 'black spots'.[23] A 2002 evaluation – which was conducted through questionnaires and interviews over a period of three years and involved over 700 participants, including trainees, leaders and key administrators – showed that trainees tended to move from part-time to full-time employment and from unskilled to skilled work.[24]

In the area of reconciliation, which is more difficult to measure, Wider Horizons also showed some significant progress. Anton Trant says that:

> ...at a general level it can be said that bringing people together from different sides of the divide in a meaningful, purposeful and non-threatening way has been a very beneficial experience. There is plenty of evidence to show that participants in Wider Horizons projects genuinely look beyond the stereotypes they hold of each other and in many cases actually form close friendships.[25]

He notes that after starting from a position where any attempt to introduce formal reconciliation activities was looked upon warily, with the passing of time four reconciliation elements have been incorporated into the programme. First, as part of their preparation all project leaders are now required to take a formal leadership training course that includes reconciliation. Second, the normal practice is to understand reconciliation in a broad and inter-related manner which will be acceptable to young people, encompassing any issue that tends to divide people, including racism, homophobia and gender discrimination, as well as sectarianism. Third, it became clear that reconciliation – as well as employability –

> ...must be based on what could be called the building up of the individual person. Prejudice is especially difficult to combat when the individuals concerned are themselves vulnerable, fearful and disadvantaged. Hostile attitudes and behaviours towards others derive as much from personal insecurity and low self-esteem as from ignorance and lack of contact. A similar situation exists with regard to employability where studies have found that the young people most likely to

be chronically unemployed usually have little belief in themselves or in their future.[26]

Fourth, Wider Horizons

> ...lends itself particularly well to what could be called institutional reconciliation. The programme not only comprises individual participants but also the various institutions to which these individuals belong and identify with, such as training centres and community and youth organisations. A typical Wider Horizons project requires cooperation from a number of organisations, and this cooperation extends in two directions: cross-community and cross-border. In other words, every project is based on organisations that cater to northern Catholics and Protestants and to people from the South. Several observers of the current conflict in Northern Ireland have pointed to the close connection between the reconciliation of individuals affected by the conflict and the reconciliation of the institutions with which they identify.[27]

The 2002 Wider Horizons evaluation asked whether the programme was succeeding in its task of reconciliation by using three independent assessment measures: (a) friendship and social contact between the participants; (b) participants' perceptions of each other's communities; and (c) the internationally recognised Bogardus social distance scale for measuring tolerance and prejudice.

All three measures showed positive gains. With regard to friendship and social contact, all the participating groups – northern Catholics, northern Protestants and southerners – showed a clear trend of increased cross-border friendship, and at the end of their participation four-fifths of the young people were planning further cross-border visits. Cross-community friendships also increased, with, at the end of the project, over four-fifths of the northern participants planning to make more cross-community social contacts. There was an increase in positive attitudes all around, with all three participating groups impressed by the others' friendliness and fun-loving traits.

The Wider Horizons evaluation used the Bogardus social distance scale as a means of measuring tolerance and prejudice.[28] The results showed that all social distance ratings reduced (that is, improved) following experience of the project: there was a 'significant' change (meaning that there was at least a 95 per cent probability that the change being measured was the result of the Wider Horizons experience) in northern Protestant participants' perceptions of people from the South; and a 'highly significant' change (a 99 per cent probability that the change was the result of participation in the project) in northern Catholic perceptions of northern Protestants, and vice-versa. Thus the most significant change in perceptions following Wider Horizons was the mutual increase in tolerance between the northern Catholic and northern Protestant participants.[29]

Trant concludes that 'the Wider Horizons formula has proved over the years to be a simple, practical and very powerful force for cooperation and integration'. Its uniqueness lies in the way in which the programme integrates its twin aims of reconciliation and employability, so that vocational training and work placements are the vehicle through which people come to know and trust one another – 'it is because the vocational training element of Wider Horizons is perceived to have no ideological threat, that it can be used as a bonding and integrating activity'.[30]

Wider Horizons stands apart from any school-based North–South programme because it is so hugely well-resourced. Up to 2005, it had received £67 million in International Fund for Ireland funding, and its annual budget was running at around £3.5–4.5 million.[31] Nevertheless, the Wider Horizons case study suggests that well-resourced and sustained programmes can reduce intolerance and encourage reconciliation.

Pride of our Place. This impression of significant educational and pedagogical gains from well-conceived, well-run North–South schools projects is reinforced by the conclusions of a very different project, Pride of our Place (2002–6). Project researcher Mary Burke comes to a number of conclusions in her final research report which are of relevance to other cross-border schools projects. She notes that in all but three of the schools, the school leader was a teaching principal and his or her commitment to the project – based on motivations ranging from pride in their schools to belief that they were contributing to the peace process – was a key to its success. Partly because of the small size and rural location of many of the schools, there were also outstanding examples of 'whole staff involvement', as well as participation by parents and governors – another key success factor. She also singles out the important contribution made by the advisory team from Northern Ireland's Southern Education and Library Board in providing guidance, preparing materials and training the teachers to become empowered through the project. Its 'developmental nature' was also crucial 'as the teachers and schools took more ownership as the project grew and developed [over the project's three and a half years] ... Once-off contact is of little use, it must be sustained over a period of time.'[32]

In a comment summarising the experience of Pride of our Place, the project researcher observed:

> This project has been a huge learning process for the participating schools, one which has also brought in the children's parents and grandparents, and the local community. It has been very important for the teachers' development, and they have grown greatly as they have learned to give the initiative to their pupils ... But most important is the impact on the children. They have used a very wide range of activities and methodologies: story, music, art and crafts, drama, ICT, field trips, photographic work, video and animated film, surveys, interviews, studying documents and old artefacts to tell the stories of 'their place'. At one of the most critical times in their lives, this project has given these pupils the ideal context to share their environment, their sense of place and their identity with others. In that sense it is a real 'crossing borders' experience: they have 'invited' others into their own place – 'inviting' is a key word – and through this have gained inter-personal and relationship-building skills that will be critical to them for the rest of their lives.[33]

Dissolving Boundaries. This programme, as we have seen, uses information and communications technology to link teachers and pupils in primary, secondary and special schools in Northern Ireland and the Republic of Ireland. The group of academics at the University of Ulster and the National University of Ireland Maynooth who manage the programme published a report on the project in October 2004.[34] For this they asked the participating teachers for their views on its effectiveness as a means of enhancing and perhaps transforming teaching and learning. The study paid particular attention to the use of information and communications technology in the classroom; the implications of the regular contact between programme schools in the two jurisdictions for North–South understanding; the impact of face-to-face meetings between pupils; and the teamwork within the classroom, and between classrooms of partner schools.

In all, 79 per cent of primary teachers and 70 per cent of secondary teachers considered the programme's computer conferencing 'very beneficial' or 'beneficial' to their pupils; 87 per cent of teachers reported a 'very significant' or 'significant' improvement in their pupils' information and communications technology skills; 68 per cent considered that Dissolving Boundaries had a very significant or significant impact on their pupils' North–South understanding (23 per cent very significant and 45 per cent significant); and 83 per cent felt that Dissolving Boundaries had had a 'very significant' or 'significant' impact on their pupils' curricular learning, including communication skills. The vast majority of teachers reported 'a variety of changes, including more emphasis on information and communications technology, more group work, more field trips, more active learning, more cross-curricular work, more planning'. Teachers regarded face-to-face meetings (involving 63 per cent of participating schools, rising to 92 per cent of the schools in the 2003–4 cohort) as a 'very strong element' in the project.[35]

Civic-Link. For the purposes of comparison with Wider Horizons, it is useful to examine one of the better-funded and longer-running schools-based programmes where similar methods of evaluation were used. Using the same Bogardus social distance scale as in the Wider Horizons evaluation, a 2003 evaluation of Civic-Link found that for the majority of students completing pre- and post-programme questionnaires there was no significant change in social distance between northern Catholics and northern Protestants.[36] The only statistically significant change was among southern Catholics, who reported improved (i.e. reduced) social distance towards 'Protestant people' and 'people from Northern Ireland'. However, somewhat inconsistently, the evaluator also found that the highest proportion of students reporting reduced social distance were the northern Protestants.[37] Another finding was that for all participants – northern Protestant, northern Catholic and southern students – 'the positive effect of Civic-Link participation on reducing social distance … is confined to Civic-Link students attending schools not designated as disadvantaged.'

Given the fact, borne out by other findings in this evaluation, that northern Protestant students in disadvantaged schools are particularly likely to be resistant to any contact with, or understanding of, 'the other side', this is a telling, if not unsurprising, conclusion. Indeed, the evaluator noted 'the greater relevance of Civic-Link for students attending disadvantaged schools who would appear to have fewer opportunities to establish personal relationships on a cross-community basis than their peers attending schools not designated as disadvantaged'.[38] He pointed to the value of 'deepening the engagement' of students from northern Protestant schools in particular and disadvantaged schools in general.[39] The evaluator also stressed that attitudinal changes were more marked among Civic-Link participants experiencing two residential exchanges than among those who had gone on one or no exchanges. Northern Protestants, in particular, 'reported substantially lower levels of social distance towards Catholic people than their peers undertaking just one or no exchanges'.[40] The importance of longer-term exposure to young people from the other Northern Irish community or the other Irish jurisdiction was thus stressed.

The evaluator pointed to a number of studies which had highlighted the limited amount of cross-community contact between children in a segregated education system in Northern Ireland, and the limited impact of many community relations initiatives based on the 'contact hypothesis'.[41] These, he suggested, constitute a particular challenge for Civic-Link in operating to promote mutual understanding and respect among its northern participants, let alone its overall aim of mutual understanding and respect between young people on the island as a whole.

Education for Reconciliation. Work in this area has also been praised for its positive achievements. An unpublished report on this project in 2004 described it as:

> … a superb project, timely and important in the context of the new era of more harmonious relations and moves towards mutual understanding, North and South, brought in by the 1998 Good Friday agreement. It is characterised by excellent leadership, high motivation by the participating teachers, and a courageous effort to grasp one of the most difficult 'nettles' of the post-conflict period in Ireland, the demands of reconciliation.

The report highlighted the project's professional development of participating teachers, giving them the skills and confidence to deal with controversial issues of conflict and identity in the classroom, and its input into key policy documents on citizenship produced by the curriculum councils, North and South.[42]

Student Teacher Exchange. In the North–South Student Teacher Exchange initiative, the focus shifted from students and pupils to trainee teachers. An evaluation of this initiative in 2004 (by the Maynooth educationalist Dr Maeve Martin) was laudatory, calling it 'a courageous, inclusive and groundbreaking exchange' whose 'transformational' effect on the participants 'translates into reality some of the aspirations of the 1998 Belfast agreement'. It noted:

> This teacher exchange project has opened up opportunities for cohorts of student teachers on the island of Ireland to come together in a spirit of sincerity, goodwill and openness with a view to working collaboratively on issues of mutual concern, and in the process to learn from each other. In the absence of this project such an opportunity would not exist. The baseline data prior to the exchange indicate almost total ignorance of the host jurisdiction in aspects that the project addresses: education system, culture and tradition, sociopolitical issues. In contrast the post-exchange data reflect an upbeat enthusiasm from the participants for the learning and insights gained over the exchange period.

The evaluation went on:

> Teachers are extremely influential in the lives of many, and it is therefore very important that they bring to their task accurate information and unbiased orientations. The stakeholders recognise the potential of the project to erode prejudice and ignorance that may have played a destructive or corrosive role in pre-project days. The multiplier effect is also recognised. Young teachers in the long careers that lie ahead of them can influence the attitudes and values of their many cohorts of pupils. This project contributes to the realisation of this desirable outcome by creating conditions to foster mutual understandings, respect and informed insights. It is unlikely that the enrichment that the project brings could be brought about without the lived experience of being a project participant.[43]

Long-term sustainability

The impact of cross-border educational cooperation depends, however, in large part on creating sustainable programmes over long time periods. Even the longer-established programmes in Ireland are of short duration in comparison to similar programmes in Europe. For example, Trant compares Wider Horizons to the not dissimilar Franco-German exchange, a generously resourced youth exchange programme aimed at promoting cooperation and mutual understanding. This was set up over forty years ago with the hugely ambitious aim of effecting a fundamental cultural change in the way the future citizens of those two formerly warring nations viewed each other. Trant cites evidence that this programme

> … has made a substantial contribution towards promoting good relations between the two countries, but this was only discernible after a generation of young people had been given the experience of participating. The lesson for Wider Horizons is clear: if the programme is to make a serious contribution towards reducing prejudice and sectarianism in Ireland, then it must prepare for the long haul.[44]

Unfortunately there will probably be no long haul. The International Fund for Ireland will cease operations in 2010, meaning that the existence of Wider Horizons after that will be in considerable doubt. It thus looks unlikely to last for the twenty-five- to thirty-year period deemed the minimum required to show a lasting beneficial impact in changing the attitudes of the younger generation towards the other community in Northern Ireland and the other jurisdiction in Ireland. One later scenario could see the programme being handed over to its delivery agencies – FÁS and the Northern Ireland Training and Employment Agency (now part of the Department for Employment and Learning) – who are likely to neglect its central reconciliation aim in favour of its much more deliverable employability element, which, after all, is their core business.[45] If it were mainstreamed in this way into a post-2010 phase, the danger of such a 'loss of direction' (the evaluators' phrase) would be far more likely.

Similarly, the evaluators point to one of the problems of Wider Horizons 'from the very beginning – how to link up effectively with the mainline educational and training schemes'.[46] The problems of much smaller but equally highly rated projects like Education for Reconciliation and the North–South Student Teacher Exchange programme in moving towards this mainstreaming have already been noted.

One obvious way to longer-term sustainability for schools-based initiatives is for some incorporation of the 'best practice' materials and methodologies learned from them into mainstream practice in the two jurisdictions, and particularly into the development of teachers. A rare example of this happening is the recent adoption by the departments of education, North and South, of materials on cultural diversity for primary schools developed by a cross-border partnership between the Southern Education and Library Board in Northern Ireland and Trinity College Dublin. The kind of active teaching and learning methodologies which are common to many of these innovative cross-border projects are now seen as international best practice by the OECD and education ministries all over the world.

Active learning and teaching methodologies were at the core of the argument for curriculum-based cross-border education which was the central thesis of the Centre for Cross Border Studies 2000 study *Cross-border school, youth and teacher exchanges on the island of Ireland* (commissioned by the Departments of Education, North and South). It argued that such programmes 'may offer a more sustainable approach to exchange programmes, alongside the face-to-face exchanges which remain the essential tool for lowering barriers and increasing mutual understanding'. Anything that is seen as 'a non-curricular, non-mainstream "add on" will be resisted by schools in these days of increasingly overloaded and examination-oriented timetables'.[47]

Some might argue that this is unrealistic, pointing, for example, to the marginalisation of even a general, single-jurisdiction citizenship programme such as civic social and political education in the South. Tony

Gallagher, an international expert on citizenship education based at Queen's University Belfast, has noted the long struggle in Northern Ireland to achieve a higher status and priority for work in education aimed at promoting reconciliation. He wonders if all the effort and energy has been used to best effect:

> In an abstract sense, these issues are important to the education system. What is less clear is just *how* important they are, or rather, how important they are in relation to other priorities for education. I firmly believe that as long as schools are held to account primarily for academic achievement through base-lining, targets, inspection and development planning, then citizenship education is always going to come lower down, perhaps much lower down, the pecking order.

He suggests that if the *relative* priority of citizenship education and education for reconciliation is likely to remain low, perhaps what is needed is

> … to think of other ways of strengthening and supporting the work of the teachers who are committed to this work. Perhaps now we need to expend some of that effort in a different way, by tackling the potential isolation of citizenship teachers not within, but between schools. Maybe it is time we tried to build effective networks among the committed teachers, rather than hoping the system will catch up with us.[48]

In other words, in this vital area more teacher development is a key way forward, as is the building of networks between those teachers.

Aidan Clifford of the City of Dublin Vocational Education Committee Curriculum Development Unit agrees up to a point. He points out that in a highly prescribed and structured school curriculum and assessment process there are limited methods of entry for innovative curriculum ideas or methodologies – in a single Irish jurisdiction, let alone across a contested border between two. Working with a group of committed teachers personally open to change, as in Education for Reconciliation, was interesting, he says, but the input into the wider school and education system has been limited. He feels that, in the future, North–South innovators will have to put more energy into bringing about change in the system, for example through the policy documents of the National Council for Curriculum and Assessment and the Northern Ireland Council for the Curriculum, Examinations and Assessment. However, this painstaking, long-term kind of movement towards sustaining innovation might not be to the liking of funding bodies, most of whom view sustainability in crude terms of 'take away the funding and the course will continue in the schools anyway'.[49]

CONCLUSION

A major problem in identifying both good practice in North–South education cooperation and ways in which such cooperation might be sustained has been its extraordinarily rapid growth over the past decade. The 2005 North South Exchange Consortium report highlighted a number of features which have emerged from this rich but certainly unsustainable growth. Among its findings were:

- Programmes and projects are funded in very complex ways, and funding routes are unclear (in the northern department of education, six different sections are involved in the funding of cross-border projects). This lack of clarity does not help the efficient or effective transfer of resources to target groups on the ground.
- Core funding to sustain organisations is very limited.
- The requirement of the two largest funders, the EU Peace II programme and the International Fund for Ireland, that funding must go to Northern Ireland and the six southern border counties only (other than in exceptional circumstances), has 'negatively affected wider North–South activity'.
- There is 'a perception among some sections of the Protestant or unionist community that the focus of peace building efforts in this specific region is an attempt to soften or blur the border'.
- There are few organisations promoting east–west activities between schools and youth groups between Britain and Ireland (only a tiny 1 per cent of funding goes to such programmes).
- There are overlaps and duplication between programmes, with the result that some schools and youth groups are participating in several programmes, while the majority are not involved in any activity.
- There is a need for more institutional involvement (less than 10 per cent of cross-border activity is currently through institutional linkages): 'personal relationships developed between group leaders alone cannot sustain a project'.
- 'Proper policy-making structures are needed to provide clarity for future programme development', particularly as funding becomes scarcer, in order to meet the need for a more coordinated, transparent and effective system of oversight and funding.[50]

The report's key policy recommendation is that the current, embryonic North South Exchange Consortium should be developed into a new body, the North South Exchange Trust. This new body would

> ... coordinate and manage the north south programme framework by identifying priority areas for funding, delivering programmes through tenders, developing an overarching monitoring and evaluation framework and developing a corporate plan.

However, in their endorsement of the report's proposals, the two departments of education make it clear that

> ... in the current political context it is not possible to establish such a body at this time, but it is hoped that in the future conditions might arise when the establishment of an independent north south exchange Trust will exist.[51]

When the report was published in late 2005, most observers took this phrase to mean that until there was agreement on returning power to devolved institutions in Northern Ireland, there would be no possibility of setting up a formal North–South body in the area of educational and youth exchanges. However, by the end of 2006 it appeared that the two governments had decided to set up a North South Exchange Trust regardless of progress towards devolution. Nevertheless an obvious question remains: by the time the trust is finally established, will the sizeable funding – most of it from abroad – brought about by the generous international response to the Irish peace process have run out?

The 'short-termism' of politics is not conducive to the long work of reconciliation through education on the island of Ireland. In Anton Trant's words, this is a process which is 'laborious and long-term and demands patience and constant effort'.[52] The social researcher Brian Harvey suggests that the problem of short-termism bedevils cross-border cooperation generally. In a 2005 evaluation of the Centre for Cross Border Studies, he wrote:

> While many people are puzzled at the failure of governments to support the Centre, longstanding commentators on North–South issues point to a historic vacuum in strategies for North–South co-operation, of which the lack of defined funding streams is only a symptom.[53]

It is this absence of any strategies for cooperation by the two governments which is at the heart of the problems facing educational cooperation across the Irish border in the medium to long term. It is perhaps understandable that both governments are nervous about putting forward strategic North–South plans in a historically highly sensitive area such as education. Education, unlike a relatively politically neutral area such as energy, is jealously guarded as a purely national competence by most governments, and in the insecure world of Ulster unionism new North–South structures to promote educational cooperation would be seen as a touchstone for unacceptable moves towards all-Ireland institutions. Even too much fraternising between young people from the two Irish jurisdictions is sometimes seen as distinctly dangerous. More than one school principal in a controlled school in the northern border region has declined invitations to join cross-border projects for fear that strongly unionist parents will protest by sending their children to another school.

However, if the causes of dispelling mutual ignorance and suspicion and promoting greater mutual understanding on the island are to be supported, education will have to play a key role. Two surveys in the past six years indicate that schools from unionist areas of Northern Ireland are participating in cross-border exchanges in line with their proportion of the population of Northern Ireland as a whole. There appears to be no generalised 'chill' factor here, although most unionist parents would probably prefer their children to be participating within the North–South, East–West context laid down as the basis for all future progress by the Belfast agreement.

The era of small, individual, largely unsystematic cross-border education projects is coming to an end anyway with the effective drying up of EU Peace funds for Northern Ireland and the Southern Border Region after 2008. In the words of Co-operation Ireland chief executive Tony Kennedy, it is time for the adoption by the administrations in Dublin, Belfast and London of 'a strategic and developmental approach to the building of a coherent policy for North–South cooperation' – in education as in other key public service areas – which will mean that 'funding truly addresses need, duplication is avoided and models of best practice are developed'.[54] The establishment of a government-sponsored and funded North South Exchange Trust for the systematic future oversight of North–South school and youth exchanges would be a welcome first step.

NOTES

1 J Coolahan, 'Introductory remarks', in Centre for Cross Border Studies, *A report on the North–South school, youth and teacher exchanges conference* (Armagh: Centre for Cross

Border Studies, 2001); available at www.crossborder.ie/pubs/exchangefinal.pdf.
2 Coolahan, 'Introductory remarks' (2001).
3 Quoted in Coolahan, 'Introductory remarks' (2001).
4 J Gleeson, *Final report on the external evaluation of the European Studies Project (11–14), Ireland and Great Britain* (Limerick: Thomond College of Education, 1991).
5 See the project's website at www.european-studies.org.
6 A Pollak, C Ó Maoláin, Z Liston and S McGrellis, *Cross-border school, youth and teacher exchanges on the island of Ireland* (Armagh: Centre for Cross Border Studies, 2000) [unpublished report for the Department of Education (NI) and the Department of Education and Science].
7 The impact of this important initiative on the attitudes of the young participants has been examined in A Trant, S Trant, D Fitzpatrick and J Medlycott, *Evaluation of the Wider Horizons programme of the International Fund for Ireland* (Belfast and Dublin: International Fund for Ireland, 2002) [unpublished report].
8 H Ruddle and J O'Connor, *A model of managed cooperation: an evaluation of Cooperation North's school and youth links scheme* (Limerick: Irish Peace Institute, 1992).
9 North South Exchange Consortium, *Digest* (Dundalk: North South Exchange Consortium, 2005), p. 20 (the digest summarises findings of two research reports that look at the experience of North–South school and youth exchange and cooperative activity).
10 Pollak et al., *Cross-border school exchanges* (2000), p. 6.
11 Pollak et al., *Cross-border school exchanges* (2000), p. 7.
12 R Green, I White, S McGearty and T Macaulay, *Research on the current provision of North South school and youth exchange and cooperative activity 2000–2004* (Dundalk: North South Exchange Consortium., 2004), p. 1.
13 Green et al., *Research* (2004), p. 47.
14 R Austin, M Mallon, A Rickard, N Metcalfe and N Quirke-Bolt, *Dissolving Boundaries: building communities of practice* (Coleraine, Maynooth: Dissolving Boundaries Project, University of Ulster and National University of Ireland Maynooth, 2006); available at www.dissolvingboundaries.org/research/apr2006.doc [accessed 01-01-2007].
15 *Civic-Link resource pack* (Belfast and Dublin: Co-operation Ireland, 2001).
16 Interview with Aidan Clifford, Director of the City of Dublin VEC Curriculum Development Unit, 23 May 2005.
17 The coordinator of another successful initiative, the Horizon project, involving students from a hundred secondary schools in outdoor pursuits, community relations and cross-border team projects, was forced at one point to draw down £6,000 from her pension lump sum to pay an outstanding bill!
18 A Smith and A Robinson, *Education for Mutual Understanding: the initial statutory years* (Coleraine: Centre for the Study of Conflict, University of Ulster, 1996).
19 S Dunn and V Morgan, 'A fraught path – education as a basis for developing improved community relations in Northern Ireland', *Oxford review of education* 25:1–2 (1999), pp. 141–53.
20 A Smith and A Robinson, *EMU in transition* (Coleraine: Centre for the Study of Conflict, University of Ulster, 1996), pp. 77–8.
21 Gleeson, *Final report* (1991).
22 Coopers and Lybrand, *Evaluation of the European Studies Project* (Coopers and Lybrand, 1992).
23 A Trant, 'Promoting peace in Ireland through vocational training and work experience', *International journal of vocational training and education* 11:1 (2003), pp. 84–93.
24 Trant et al., *Evaluation* (2002).
25 Trant, 'Promoting peace' (2003), p. 88.
26 Trant, 'Promoting peace' (2003), p. 89.
27 Trant, 'Promoting peace' (2003), p. 90. He is referring here to S Farren and R Mulvihill,

Paths to settlement in Northern Ireland (Gerrard's Cross: Colin Smythe, 2000), pp. 103–19.

28 The scale measures seven levels of closeness, ranging, for example, from 'part of my family', 'through marriage' and 'close friend' to 'visitor only to my country' and 'expel from my country'. Using this scale, from one to seven, the perceptions of participant groups to each other were measured before and after their involvement in Wider Horizons. The scale has been used extensively in the USA as a means of measuring racial prejudice, as well as in a number of Irish research studies. For a notable example, see M Mac Gréil, *Prejudice and tolerance in Ireland* (Dublin: College of Industrial Relations, 1977); M Mac Gréil, *Prejudice in Ireland revisited* (Maynooth: Survey and Research Unit, St Patrick's College, 1996).

29 Trant, 'Promoting peace' (2003), pp. 89–91.

30 Trant, 'Promoting peace' (2003), pp. 92–3.

31 This reflects the recent finding of the North–South Exchange Consortium study – to the surprise of most informed observers – that the International Fund for Ireland had provided 55% of all funding for North–South school and youth exchanges; see Green et al., *Research* 2004).

32 M Burke, *Pride of our place: draft final research report* (Armagh: Centre for Cross Border Studies, 2007).

33 Interview with Mary Burke, St Patrick's College Drumcondra, 30 May 2005; Ms Burke is also basing her PhD research on the project.

34 R Austin, J Smyth, M Mallon, A Mulkeen and N Metcalfe, *Dissolving boundaries: supporting transformation in the classroom?* (Coleraine, Maynooth: Dissolving Boundaries Project, University of Ulster and National University of Ireland Maynooth, 2004); available at www.dissolvingboundaries.org/Research/sep2004.doc [accessed 14-04-2006].

35 Austin et al., *Dissolving boundaries* (2004), pp. vi–ix, 5, 36–8.

36 T Ronayne, *Learning to live together: an evaluation of Civic-Link* (Belfast: WRC Social and Economic Consultants, 2003) [unpublished report].

37 Ronayne, *Learning to live together* (2003), pp. 8–11.

38 Ronayne, *Learning to live together* (2003), pp. 16–17.

39 Ronayne, *Learning to live together* (2003), p. 48.

40 Ronayne, *Learning to live together* (2003), p. 46.

41 J Hughes and C Knox, 'For better or worse? Community relations initiatives in Northern Ireland', *Peace and change* 22:3 (1997), pp. 330–55; E Cairns and M Hewstone, 'The impact of peacemaking in Northern Ireland on intergroup behaviour', in G Salomon and B Nevo (eds), *Peace education: the concept, principles and practice around the world* (Mahwah, NJ: Lawrence Erlbaum Associates, 1997).

42 M Arlow, A Pollak and T Gallagher, *Evaluation of the Education for Reconciliation (phase two) project – annual report 2003–2004* (Armagh: Centre for Cross Border Studies, 2004) [unpublished report].

43 M Martin, *Evaluation report for phase 2 (2003–2004) of the North/South Student Teacher Exchange Project* (Armagh: Centre for Cross Border Studies, 2004), pp. 23, 25.

44 Trant, 'Promoting peace' (2003), p. 92.

45 Trant et al., *Evaluation* (2002), p. 108.

46 Trant et al., *Evaluation* (2002), p. 107.

47 Pollak et al., *Cross-border school exchanges* (2000), p. 14 and annex, 'Some issues arising from the study'.

48 T Gallagher, 'Good practice in citizenship education', paper given at the SCoTENS (Standing Conference on Teacher Education North and South) conference on citizenship education, Cavan, September 2004.

49 Interview with Aidan Clifford, 23 May 2005.

50 Green et al., *Research* (2004), pp. 40–1, 51–60.

51 Green et al., *Research* (2004), preface.

52 Trant, 'Promoting peace' (2003), p. 92.

53 B Harvey, *Evaluation of the Centre for Cross Border Studies* (Armagh: Centre for Cross Border Studies, 2005); available at www.crossborder.ie/pubs/ccbs2005.pdf [accessed 14-04-2006].

54 T Kennedy and C Lynch, 'Towards an island at peace with itself: an NGO view of North–South co-operation', *The Centre for Cross Border Studies Year 5* (2003), p. 11.

8

Institutional cooperation: the health sector

PATRICIA CLARKE

INTRODUCTION

Health is a fundamental human right with complex medical, philosophical, ethical, socio-economic, political and legal implications, and has long been considered as a key area for cross-border cooperation.[1] As we have seen in chapters 1 and 2, the current context for cross-border cooperation on the island of Ireland, in this as in other areas, is grounded in a series of international and inter-governmental agreements. The last of these agreements, the 1998 Good Friday agreement, saw a new devolved power structure put in place in Northern Ireland and embodied a formal commitment to work towards specific objectives in relation to cross-border cooperation in health. Common health policies and approaches were agreed within the framework of the North/South Ministerial Council (NSMC) but implemented separately in each jurisdiction. Five specific areas for cooperation in health were identified: accident and emergency planning, major emergency planning, procurement of high-technology equipment, cancer research and health promotion. While cross-border cooperation at a ground level pre-dates the agreement, there was a high level of optimism that the project-focused, EU-funded cooperation of the past could be upgraded to include strategic cross-border service development. Since 2000 cross-border cooperation in health has been the subject of a number of influential reports which have evaluated the practical cooperation between health service providers in the immediate border region, reviewed the potential for upgrading all-island health services and examined the benefits of EU membership.[2]

This chapter begins by examining the development of cross-border cooperation between health providers in the border region – the movement of patients across the Irish border for treatment and the enhancement of services. It then assesses the impact of such cooperation from a technical and a political perspective, and concludes by discussing the challenges that may determine future cooperation in health.

DEVELOPING COOPERATION

In assessing progress to date it is important to recall that only twenty years ago cross-border cooperation in health care on the island of Ireland was almost non-existent, apart from isolated ventures involving small numbers of patients travelling for treatments available only in one jurisdiction. There were periodic meetings of ministers that invariably resulted in agreement about the potential for further cooperation, but no facilitating structures existed and the key personnel on the two sides of the border were virtually unknown to one another.

It is notable that cross-border cooperation in health has not become a matter of public controversy across the border or across the 'religious divide' as have suggestions for cross-border working in other fields. This section charts the development of cooperation from the early information-sharing initiatives of health service providers in the border region, to the contracting arrangements which have seen patients travel across the border for care and the development of various institutions which focus on co-operation in health. It deals most extensively with one major initiative for the coordination of service provision, the Cooperation and Working Together (CAWT) initiative, examines recent developments in the area of patient mobility, and considers other recent collaborative initiatives, including the general area of service enhancement.

Cooperation and Working Together

While there was isolated cross-border work involving other agencies, the greater part of the early cross-border collaboration evolved around the CAWT initiative led by service providers located along either side of the border. The CAWT region embraces the whole of the land boundary between the Republic of Ireland and Northern Ireland, serves a population of over one million people and accounts for 25 per cent of the total land area of the island of Ireland. Cross-border relationships between service providers were formalised in 1992 in order to harness the potential community initiative funding opportunities presented by the EU.

In the early stages of CAWT's development (1992–5) the main focus was on establishing relationships and trust between the different partners at senior level. In so doing, this approach has tried to encompass as many areas of health care as possible and to build as many networks as possible. A small number of research projects were undertaken and funded jointly by the health boards. These included research into recruitment practices in both jurisdictions, child care legislation, learning disabilities needs assessment, and social deprivation.

With the securing of EU funding from 1995 onwards, organisational structures and processes were put in place to support the work of CAWT. Between October 1996 and December 2000 CAWT attracted over £5 million in EU funding under measures 3.3a and 3.3b (Cooperation between public bodies) of the Peace I programme. The work of CAWT has been mostly project-focused and very diverse. Project work was developed across a wide range of sectors including acute care, primary care, family and child care, learning disability, health promotion, information technology, human resources, public health and mental health. This work brought people together to gain a better understanding of their professional inhibitions and political difficulties, and extensive networks of contacts have been established in the border region.

Changes in North–South political relationships brought about by the 1998 Good Friday agreement offered CAWT a platform for enhancing its contribution to cross-border health cooperation. As a result, it developed and sought to implement a strategic plan for cross-border health cooperation. It became involved in detailed discussions with the Special EU Programmes Body (SEUPB) and the two departments of health about accessing Interreg III and Peace II funds. Two satellite offices were established along the border and centralised support functions (financial administration, information technology and communications) were secured. The CAWT strategy expanded its role to develop, implement and mainstream practical cooperation in the border region, to agree common cross-border policies and to design quality assurance and evaluation templates for cross-border working.

CAWT has continued to lead the development of cross-border cooperation in health. Indeed it is one of the more prolific cross-border organisations on the island, having been involved in seventy-eight cross-border health activities to date. This work continues to be driven by very substantial EU funding, with CAWT receiving approximately €11.7 million over the period 2000–6. Between 2000 and 2004 CAWT obtained €1.8m for a range of mental health initiatives under the Peace II programme. This funding has facilitated such developments as awareness training in cognitive therapy, a needs assessment of carers, and an examination of the clinical, demographic and social predictors of past suicide behaviour. CAWT was also selected by the two departments of health to deliver the whole €9.9m Interreg 3.2 measure, Health and social wellbeing (2000–6), which has seen the development and implementation of thirty-five projects covering diverse areas such as road safety, sex offenders, fostering care, health impact assessment training, care of diabetes, emergency planning and cross-border GP out-of-hours services.

Patient mobility

Patient mobility has been identified as a key area for cooperation both at North–South level and at EU level. In 1999 a cross-border steering group of senior civil servants was established to report on removing barriers to general mobility on the island of Ireland. In November 2001 the North/South Ministerial Council (NSMC) published the *Obstacles to mobility* report, which includes a section on current health practice on the island of Ireland and its implication for mobility of patients.[3] The report warned of gaps in awareness about the eligibility of frontier workers and posted workers for health care across the border through EU regulations.[4] A series of four health recommendations were made, with the aim of removing obstacles to patient mobility on the island. These recommendations included a proposal for a series of feasibility studies permitting frontier workers to access health services at their nearest hospital; encouraging an increased number of hospitals in the North to accept southern health insurance, and raising awareness of the E128 form for seconded or posted workers through proactive employer contact.[5] The report also called for an objective source of information designed to inform individuals considering a move to either jurisdiction about the changes in their healthcare entitlements. In October 2006 the NSMC began the process of establishing an online one-stop-shop for mobility information; however, the recommendations on feasibility studies have yet to be implemented.

The main impact of early cross-border cooperation could be described as preparing the ground for future, more substantive cooperation initiatives which could be implemented following political endorsement. Although the devolved arrangements in Northern Ireland have been subjected to a series of interruptions, the Irish and British governments, and the EU, have continued to give considerable verbal encouragement to practical cross-border initiatives in health. Despite all these efforts, the level of cross-border services delivery remains very low. In 2004 research under the Europe for Patients project showed that the numbers of patients and professionals crossing the border to receive or deliver healthcare in the other jurisdiction has remained at a low level.[6] Border Ireland shows approximately 3 per cent of the past cross-border health budget spent on such activity.[7] Data on the 2003 cross-border movement of patients provided by the two departments of health, North and South, and the Economic and Social Research Institute in the South show 1,722 patients from the Republic of Ireland treated in Northern Ireland, and 900 patients from Northern Ireland treated in the Republic. The number of patients travelling South to North had increased by 400 since 1996 but there was no increase in the other direction. As expected, most of the 'cross-border' patients were treated in hospitals in the former Eastern Health Board area (which includes Dublin), or those close to the border (formerly the North Eastern and North Western Boards) in the South, and Altnagelvin (Derry), Daisy Hill (Newry) and Erne (Enniskillen) in the North.

The debate on mobility of patients is also linked to a wider set of issues about the future of European health systems. Recent discussions have highlighted a range of ways in which European collaboration can bring concrete benefits to the effectiveness and efficiency of health services across Europe.[8] This includes collaboration to make better use of resources, developing a better understanding of the rights and duties of patients, sharing spare capacity between systems, mobility of health professionals, identifying and networking European centres of reference, and coordinating assessments of new health technologies. It also covers improving information and knowledge about health systems to provide a better basis for identifying best practice, and ensuring universal access to high-quality services.

One of the most useful examples of cooperation has involved contracting (by the health boards in the North and the national treatment purchase fund in the South) for elective surgery to reduce waiting lists within each jurisdiction. In Northern Ireland such initiatives are invariably of short duration because of concerns on the part of the boards that they should be investing resources to maintain the services in their own jurisdiction rather than exporting them. An early example is that of the arrangement between the Royal Group of Hospitals in Belfast and the Southern Health Board (now an area of the Health Service Executive [HSE]) in the Republic of Ireland (covering the area around Cork), to provide hip replacements in order to reduce waiting lists. There are still intermittent initiatives in which health boards in Northern Ireland contract with hospitals in the South, usually employing one-off funds made available by the department to reduce waiting lists. Another example is the provision of ophthalmic services to patients from the old North Eastern Board (now HSE North Eastern area) in the Republic by the Mater Hospital in Belfast. Within the border region there has been a number of temporary contracting arrangements developed under the auspices of CAWT. These include a neonatal intensive care service provided under contract from Altnagelvin (North) to premature or sick babies from Letterkenny (South); patients who had been waiting for hernia surgery for more than eighteen months at Craigavon Area Hospital (North) being treated at Monaghan General Hospital (South); and haemodialysis provided in Daisy Hill, Newry (North) to a small number of people from the Dundalk area (South).

The establishment of the Irish national treatment purchase fund in 2002 enables the health services in the Republic of Ireland to arrange and purchase treatment for qualifying patients in hospitals in Northern Ireland and further afield. Examples of treatments covered under the fund are cataracts, varicose veins, hernias, gall bladders, prostate, tonsils, plastic surgery, cardiac surgery, and hip and knee operations. About 1,000 patients, mostly from Donegal but some from Dublin and elsewhere in the South, have been treated in a private hospital near Derry in the North and approximately 600 patients have travelled to England.

Other initiatives

Other key developments included the establishment by the departments of health, North and South, of the Institute of Public Health in Ireland in 1999 with its priority of reducing health inequalities on the island, and the 1999 signing of a tripartite relationship with the United States National Cancer Institute. The remit of the Institute of Public Health includes providing public health information and surveillance, strengthening public health capacity, programme development and evaluation, and advising on policy. For instance, its 2006 workplan report includes the development of a diabetes population prevalence model and a health poverty index for the island; enhancing the already developed online population health observatory for the island; promoting the implementation of health impact assessment; running its fourth leadership programme; evaluating the all-Ireland 'Decent food for all' project; publication of a men's health directory; and the hosting of a series of major conferences. During the period 1999–2005 it produced over twenty-five publications and reports and worked with a range of partners both on and off the island to promote collective action for sustained improvements in health.[9]

The Ireland–Northern Ireland National Cancer Consortium sponsors six major initiatives to enhance cancer care and research on the island of Ireland: scholar exchange; information technology sharing; clinical trials; cancer registries and epidemiology; nursing; and prevention. This approach is developing evidence, expertise and learning about cancer incidences on the entire island.[10]

Apart from these initiatives, there has been considerable North–South health research, albeit mostly into biomedical or pharmaceutical issues. For instance, the North–South funding programme managed jointly by the Health Research Board in the South and the Department of Health, Social Services and Public Safety in the North gave rise to forty-four collaborative research activities. Border Ireland lists a further forty-seven collaborative activities by academics and practitioners across seven of the nine universities and various major teaching hospitals on the island covering areas such as primary care, dentistry, nutrition, residential care for children, and diabetes, as well as sensor technology and biomedical research. One good example of collaborative working is that of the Healthy Ageing Research Programme, a five-year cross-border project involving the Royal College of Surgeons in Ireland, Trinity College Dublin, the Economic and Social Research Institute and Queen's University, which recently published the first direct comparison of health status and health and social service use by older people resident in the community, North and South.

There are a number of smaller organisations with a sustained interest in developing cross-border healthcare. These include the Derry Well Woman Centre in the north-west region, which has been developing a cross-border network to tackle the issue of women's health in the border region since 1999, the DergFinn Partnership in Strabane, which continues to focus on supporting the capacity of carers, and the Lifestart Foundation in Sligo, which has initiated and developed a home-based pre-school development support for families since 1996.

The remaining health activities are one-off workshops and training events which bring organisations with similar remits together from either side of the border across all areas of the health sector including childcare, learning disability, mental health, counselling and family planning. A good example here is the workshop of the health and safety authorities, North and South, to jointly review fatalities on farms and child safety. The majority of these initiatives were funded under the EU (Peace II) programme.

As in the past, the cross-border agenda continues to emphasise opportunities for joint training, staff development and staff exchanges (for example, in areas of radiotherapy, renal services and major emergencies); exchanges of information (for example, experience of combating drugs); the completion of feasibility studies into areas such as the introduction of Positron Emission Tomography (PET) scanning for cancer patients, and the possibility of first-responder schemes involving local volunteers responding to pre-hospital emergencies in the border region alongside the ambulance service.

Political endorsement of cross-border cooperation has seen the agenda upgraded to address both operational and strategic issues. An example of the former is the development of joint ambulance communications and control arrangements in the border region. The latter include a joint review of the need for renal services in the border region with the establishment of a shared renal information system, and a joint approach towards designing and implementing health promotion initiatives such as the shared folic acid campaign and the public information campaign on physical activity. A Joint Departmental Health Technology Group has been established to draw up protocols for the assessment and evaluation of emerging and new technologies in relation to high-technology equipment. In light of the significant expenditure, North and South, on goods and services, the Regional Supplies Service in Northern Ireland and the Healthcare Material Board in the Republic of Ireland have explored the scope for cooperation in procurement and the achievement of value for money. However the implementation of these latter two initiatives has proved difficult.[11]

ASSESSING THE IMPACT OF COOPERATION

The early efforts at developing cross-border cooperation in the health sector identified several critical factors for success. These may be examined under two broad headings: first, the technical considerations that influence the process of cooperation, and, second, the political dimension.

Technical issues

In previous research studies, respondents have consistently judged work arising out of clinical need, such as the provision of cross-border renal services and dermatology clinics, as the most successful cross-border work. In the early phase of cross-border cooperation there appears to have been only a limited effort to look systematically at border region problems (such as economic and social deprivation, an ageing population, distance from main tertiary centres, and the lack of locally delivered health services) within a health context. More effort needs to be directed to identifying and defining problems which could be better tackled using a cooperative approach.

A number of key factors are conducive to successful cooperation. The first factor is institutional structure. The creation of a separate body such as CAWT has had certain advantages, one of which is the existence of an identifiable focus of responsibility for taking forward cooperation initiatives in the border area. The 2000 evaluation of CAWT clearly showed the contributions that earlier cross-border cooperation (under the auspices of CAWT) has made in terms of improved relationships, inclusive debate, attraction of EU funding, and the creation of pools of expertise in working across jurisdictions. As a separate body dedicated to cross-border cooperation, however, it has an important disadvantage in that it can be seen as distant from the mainstream activities of the agencies involved in routine healthcare. Indeed, the evaluation of CAWT found little evidence that cooperation has become embedded in the routine business of the main service providers. However, the political endorsement of cross-border cooperation and the joint working of health staff from both service provision level and departmental level have seen the cross-border agenda upgraded to address operational issues and to adopt a strategic cross-border approach to the border region.

A second factor is resources. The availability of additional resources, such as those provided from the European Union, is clearly a stimulus to cooperation. Indeed, the securing of EU Peace funding was the stimulus for the initial formalisation of cross-border relationships and the impetus for addressing the more political areas of primary care and acute area. One clear message from the health departments was that the amount that could be achieved and the timescales for progress depend primarily on political determination and leadership, and on putting sufficient resources, both money and people, behind that political will.

A third factor is the removal of identified obstacles. The early years of cross-border cooperation identified a number of barriers which, if tackled, had the potential to enhance the scope of cross-border working. These include different funding arrangements, entitlements, levels of baseline provision, structures and accountability, entrenched professional attitudes, professional accreditation and medical insurance. Previous research called for a concerted effort to identify and dismantle potential barriers to enhanced cooperation, where this is feasible and appropriate, and for guidance for service planners to deal with such barriers.[12] At the level of institutions, restrictive approaches to cooperation had been put in place to ensure that any proposed collaborative developments should not impact negatively on existing services at each individual hospital. This sense of fear could also be seen to be an obstacle to improved patient care.

Political issues

Discussions with key stakeholders identified the overall political context as the most significant factor thought likely to influence cross-border cooperation in healthcare.[13] The pace of development, particularly (but not exclusively) at departmental level, has been closely related to the state of relationships in a broad political sense. Health service providers and government officials from both sides of the border felt that if the cooperative arrangements put in place following the Good Friday agreement could be sustained and built upon, it was likely, as in many other spheres of life, that cross-border and all-Ireland working would become an increasingly accepted and a natural part of the way things are done on the island. There was a strong sense of enthusiasm for such a vision and how it could be achieved under political leadership.

The political endorsement and departmental participation in developing and implementing cross-border collaboration have exposed a number of new constraints. One general difficulty was that of maintaining momentum in the unstable political environment in Northern Ireland where the nationalist Minister of Health was unable to participate in North/South Ministerial Council sectoral meetings over a nine-month period, and then meetings were officially suspended with the placing of the North/South Ministerial Council on a care and maintenance basis. Another general difficulty which has held up progress was the 2001 foot and mouth disease outbreak, which led to the cancellation of all cross-border meetings as the two jurisdictions tightened their border controls in an effort to stop the spread of the disease. A more serious difficulty has been the defining of parameters for acceptable work within the agreed North–South legislation of the Good Friday agreement. For instance, it is very difficult to look at accident and emergency services in isolation from the provision of acute hospital services in general. In addition, the difficulty of phasing cross-border developments in step with national health strategies of the two jurisdictions has proved to be a limiting factor.

CHALLENGES FOR THE FUTURE

There is enduring enthusiasm at political, service provider and community levels for developing future health cooperation. Speaking at the MacGill Summer School in Donegal in July 2006, the Secretary of State for Northern Ireland, Peter Hain, called for 'deeper North–South cooperation which is practical rather than constitutional' and made specific reference to 'patients crossing the border to get treatment where it makes medical sense to do so'.[14]

In setting out a compelling vision of a strong competitive and socially inclusive island economy, a recent British–Irish policy report recommends exploring opportunities for planning and delivering all-island health services.[15] This seminal report comments on the more efficient use of new facilities, better value for money, more balanced regional development and improved access to services and facilities throughout the island that such cooperation could bring. This clarity is particularly welcome at a time when new EU operational funding programmes are being drafted and when, despite the committed efforts of the Dublin and London governments, questions still remain over the full implementation of the Good Friday agreement.[16]

Recent research by the Centre for Cross Border Studies on the planning, development and access to cross-border health services demonstrates strong support in the border community for the development of such services.[17] This research, commissioned by CAWT to assess public willingness to use the planned cross-border GP out-of-hours service, includes feedback from eighty-five community organisations spread along the entire border region and attendees at four public meetings held in the summer of 2006. Furthermore, there continues to be a growing demand for cross-border health cooperation, with Border Ireland documenting a 50 per cent growth in cross-border health activities since 2000.[18]

The rest of this section discusses some of the more important issues which have implications for future North–South cooperation in the health sector. It begins by looking at the main areas of potential future collaboration, setting out in particular how one unique project, the cross-border GP out-of-hours service, is developing solutions to the main obstacles to patient mobility. The key local issues and existing informal practices which bring unique challenges for the future are addressed towards the end of the section.

Key collaborative areas for the future

There are a number of key opportunities for enhancing collaboration in health. The planned GP out-of-hours service is one example of practical cross-border cooperation addressing all of the critical factors needed for successful collaboration. It is first and foremost based on providing patient choice and addressing clinical needs by recognising the unique circumstances that exist in the Irish border region, where 70,000 patients who may need access to primary care outside normal hours would be better served in the other jurisdiction. It is supported by health professionals, politicians and border communities. It is well-resourced and is built on a platform of collaborative primary care expertise developed under the auspices of CAWT over a ten-year period. It is systematically finding solutions to a range of geographical, technical, professional, pharmacy and financial obstacles to cooperation. From January 2007 a six month pilot service is expected to see approximately 400 patients from Donegal and South Armagh crossing the border for GP out-of-hours treatment in the other jurisdiction.

The development of flexible contracting and joint planning arrangements are identified as key factors for enhancing future patient mobility and health. The flexible contracting arrangements negotiated by the national treatment purchase fund in the South and individual hospitals in the North have shown their value in reducing waiting lists for elective surgery. The Europe for Patients case study suggests that, if the two governments were keen to exploit the putative arrangements of cooperation, one option would be to open up competition by creating a fund to facilitate contracting for elective surgery within or across jurisdictions.

Perhaps the greatest potential for cooperation is in secondary care, where there are persistent and growing problems in both jurisdictions in maintaining the viability of small hospitals. Each department of health has a policy favouring raising standards through the concentration of resources. To the extent that the catchment population of hospitals in the border region is unnecessarily restricted by the existence of the border, people there are clearly disadvantaged by receiving a sub-standard service. Ideally hospital rationalisation and planning exercises in both jurisdictions should take account of the possibility of attracting patients from across the border. In the past this has been done only to a limited extent. Applying modelling techniques, public health researchers at Trinity College Dublin have shown theoretically how people living in Leitrim, north Cavan, Donegal, Monaghan, Armagh and Down would currently have quicker hospital access if they could use facilities across the border.[19] The researchers recommend abolishing the 'healthcare border' and formally encouraging cross-border access to hospital facilities between North and South in this region.

The local dimension

However, there are several issues which need to be addressed before the vision of working across boundaries and jurisdictions is achieved in a way which effectively eradicates irrational planning, promotes cost effectiveness and establishes links among the people, service planners and providers.

In resolving current health provision issues for Donegal county in the South, the role of cross-border cooperation has been much debated by groups such as Donegal Action for Cancer Care. While health consultants in Donegal initially expressed a preference to link Donegal cancer treatment services with Galway in the South, the Health Service Executive actively promoted the idea of stronger cross-border cooperation with Belfast in the North. In November 2006 the health ministers from both jurisdictions met and formally agreed to allow cancer patients from Donegal to be treated in the new Radiation Oncology Services at Belfast City Hospital from March 2007.[20] This marks a shift in government policy on cross-border cooperation. In the past, initiatives involving mobility of patients have typically resulted from partnership agreements between individual hospitals. Examples have included the use of Altnagelvin neonatal intensive care facilities (North) for patients from Letterkenny (South) and the conducting of hernia operations for Craigavon patients (North) in Monaghan hospital (South). This recent arrangement on access to radiotherapy services marks an official sustainable agreement led by the two departments of health. The voice of the local community, Donegal Action for Cancer Care, has raised questions about the difficulties of accessing care in Belfast (across the border) given that sharing services across jurisdictions has proved so difficult in the past. Indeed, the work of the cross-border GP out-of-hours project in resolving barriers to mobility has highlighted the inadequacy of recent ministerial announcements on developing cross-border cancer services, as detailed arrangements for this treatment are only being considered following the policy announcement.

In the past there has been a concerted effort to sell non-threatening cross-border cooperation which is sensitive to the feelings of the Irish border communities. A formal agreement on the development of cooperation for acute services between the North Western Health Board (now Health Services Executive – North West area), the managers of Letterkenny General Hospital, and Altnagelvin Health and Social Services Trust contained a number of conditions governing any cooperation between the two hospitals including the following:

- no proposal would undermine the services currently being provided in either hospital; and
- cooperation should be confined to services that a particular hospital could not see itself providing in five to ten years.

These conditions were thought to be necessary because of concerns on the part of politicians and professional staff that Letterkenny General Hospital could otherwise lose out to its dominant neighbour.

The effect of introducing cross-border services in an area where existing local services operate remains a sensitive issue, having been raised in public meetings in both the Donegal and South Armagh areas and in survey responses during research in 2006.[21] Rather than imposing conditions on the development of cross-border services, it would be more prudent to reassure the communities that all patients will be treated equally on the basis of clinical need rather than residence and that any cross-border services are being specifically developed to best meet patient needs in the entire border region (North and South).

Informal practices

The planning of any cross-border service needs to recognise that 'informal' cross-border patient mobility does exist at present, with people having varying degrees of entitlement to dual health service access. Despite the low patient mobility statistics, there are large undocumented movements of patients crossing the Irish border. In 2000 there were an estimated 18,000 EU frontier workers who commuted across the Irish border to work in the other jurisdiction and who could legitimately use the health services in both jurisdictions. However, the experience of this group of health service users, or indeed the large number of unofficial health service users in the South who use an 'accommodation address' in the North to access services illegitimately, have never been officially researched. A brief comparison of the current population and GP registration statistics for the two health boards adjoining the border in Northern Ireland shows over 46,000 patients currently registered with GP practices over and above the official population of these regions.[22] Ironically, one could say that these statistics provide proof of the willingness of patients to avail themselves of cross-border health services. By all accounts this group of unofficial cross-border patients is growing.[23] The public's willingness to use services across EU borders is also reflected in the fact that 1,262,705 European Health Insurance Cards were issued in the South and 359,061 in the North since the launch of the scheme in May 2004 – equating to one in every four people living on the island.

In 2006, public meetings and surveys of the border community suggest that the number of residents living in the southern border counties who use the National Health Service in Northern Ireland without incurring charges is growing. Other EU border regions such as France–Belgium or France–Switzerland have put in place bilateral agreements to include access for dependents of frontier workers. By legitimising this group of 'frontier families' in the Irish border region, any cross-border service would reflect a truer picture of frontier families living and working in this region. A second group of cross-border users who could be rendered legitimate are those people who retire to live in the South after paying National Health Service contributions throughout their working life in the North. This group has been recognised as a key group of cross-border health service users within the France–Belgium border region who should be given dual access to both health systems.

Any cross-border service whose projected use is calculated on the basis, then, of the number of southern residents within a specified distance from the border will need to be mindful that some of these residents have already found an alternative means of accessing healthcare in the North.

CONCLUSION

The reform programmes in the two jurisdictions discussed in this chapter emerged from a number of influential reports.[24] Surprisingly, within the extensive mainstream documentation produced by individual jurisdictions there are few specific references to the implications of change for cross-border healthcare, or the potential that cross-border health care offers. The potential benefits relating to economies of scale, better co-ordination of services and opportunities for specialisation among clinicians that might flow from improved all-island cooperation in health services remain to be examined. Clearly, the concept of cross-border working and planning for health is not yet embedded in the overall policy context of reforming the health services.

The state of the health care system remains at the forefront of debate in politics, North and South, and political support for developing cross-border health arrangements has been apparent in recent years. However, in the past this support does not appear to have been sufficiently translated into a sense of urgent commitment. Political leadership is needed to accelerate what many see as the slow and ponderous process of developing practical, mutually beneficial cross-border health services.

This chapter confirms the harsh reality that implementing practical cooperation in health across borders remains difficult, especially without a detailed North–South policy framework. Reviews of the official strategies and policies of the two departments of health and the North–South institutional framework found no clear rationale for public investment in a cooperation strategy or in individual initiatives.

Cross-border cooperation in the health sector has a long tradition in some EU countries, facilitated by a series of EU directives and frameworks on mobility of professionals, data protection, sharing of confidential information and 'e-health'.[25] This practical experience, which is currently being documented by the European Commission, is very similar to that on the island of Ireland.[26] Typically, health cooperation has emerged as a bottom-up process based on local agreements between providers and purchasers, often within a broader framework of cross-border cooperation and commonly supported by EU (Interreg or Peace) funding programmes. Practical expertise has been developed across other EU borders in relation to the development of shared approaches to quality assurance, continuity of care, information sharing, or compliance with regulatory systems. The development of cross-border health services on the island of Ireland should build on this practical experience and on the renewed interest in the European Commission in facilitating health care across borders.

Since 1998, when the European Court of Justice applied the fundamental principles of free movement of services and goods to healthcare, health policy-makers have been increasingly urged to reflect on how EU law interacts with the management of national health systems. Nevertheless, within the EU, national governments have retained the responsibility for organising and funding health and social care within their own borders. The political reality is that any 'horizontal health issues', such as patient mobility and patient rights to get treatment in different countries, will be constrained by national politics.

Some progress is being made. The announcement of joint government support to provide radiotherapy treatment for Donegal patients in Belfast marks a welcome 'step change' at a policy level in relation to health services. The successful implementation of the cross-border GP out-of-hours service could play an important role in directing future health service delivery on the island. As patients cross the border between the North and the South they simultaneously cross from one health system into another and this border crossing can have important impacts on the systems in each jurisdiction.

To a large extent, health policy remains border confirming rather than border transcending, and despite the many pragmatic reasons for cooperation, the opportunities for economies of scale and better coordination of services on an all-island basis are being overlooked. For now, one could conclude that cross-border health cooperation in Ireland, however impressive and far-reaching, has remained 'project specific' and demands a more proactive political framework.

NOTES

Acknowledgement. The author wishes to acknowledge the fact that this chapter draws on previous joint research completed with Dr Jim Jamison for the Centre for Cross Border Studies, Armagh.

1 Professor S William A Gunn, 'The fundamental human right to health', address upon being conferred a fellowship by special election of the Royal College of Surgeons in Ireland, 5 Dec. 2005.

2 See, respectively, P Clarke and J Jamison, *From concept to realisation: an evaluation of CAWT – Cooperation and Working Together Initiative* (Derry: Cooperation and Working Together, 2001); J Jamison, M Butler, P Clarke, M McKee and C O'Neill, *Cross-border cooperation in health services in Ireland* (Armagh: Centre for Cross Border Studies, 2001), available at www.crossborder.ie; and J Jamison, H Legido-Quigley and M McKee, 'Cross-border care in Ireland', in M Rosemoller, M McKee and R Baeten (eds), *Patient mobility in the European Union: learning from experience* (Brussels: European Observatory on Health Care Systems, 2006), chapter 4.

3 PricewaterhouseCoopers and Indecon Economic consultants, *Study of obstacles to mobility* (Armagh: North South Ministerial Council, 2002).

4 In EU terms a posted worker is a worker who, for a limited period, carries out his or her work in the territory of a member state other than the state in which he or she normally works.

5 From June 2004 the EU simplified procedures for patients, providers and administrations by launching a European Health Insurance Card which replaced all existing paper forms (including the E128) required for occasional health treatment when in another member state. Form E128 was previously used by students and posted workers to certify their entitlements to the full range of healthcare in the country of posting or study. The E128 did not need to be registered in the country of posting or study but was presented at the time treatment was required.

6 The 'Europe for patients' study is an EU 'sixth framework' project researching the ability of patients across the EU to benefit from the cross-border healthcare advantages created by an increasingly integrated Europe. It involves research institutes in Ireland, Britain, Spain, France, Belgium, Slovenia and Estonia.

7 Border Ireland is an online searchable database of cross-border information produced by EU-funded programmes, government departments, academic researchers and other key information providers in Ireland, North and South. This information covers cross-border projects, the publications emerging from these projects and the details of the groups and individuals who have gained cross-border expertise through this work.

8 L Bertinato, R Busse, NK Fahy, H Legido-Quigley, M McKee, W Palm, I Passarani, and F Ronfini, *Policy brief on cross-border health care in Europe* (London: European Observatory on Health Systems and Policies, 2006).

9 Further details on the work of the Institute of Public Health in Ireland are available online at www.publichealth.ie.

10 Further details on the work of the Ireland–Northern Ireland National Cancer Consortium are available online at www.allirelandnci.org.

11 The North/South Ministerial Council Annual Report 2005 refers to little progress being made on cooperation on high technology due to 'emphasis being directed into other areas for cooperation' but outlines its commitment to renewing the focus in this area.

12 Jamison et al., *Cross-border cooperation* (2001).

13 As part of the 2001 research, undertaken by the Centre for Cross Border Studies, on the potential for upgrading cross-border health cooperation a series of interviews were held with government officials, health service providers and other key stakeholders,

North and South.

14 John Hume lecture, MacGill summer school, Donegal, 16 July 2006

15 British and Irish Governments, *Comprehensive study on the all-island economy* (Dublin and Belfast: Department of Foreign Affairs/Northern Ireland Office, 2006).

16 The detailed programmes for two EU funding programmes, the EU Programme for Cross Border Territorial Cooperation and the EU Programme for Peace and Reconciliation 2007–2013, are currently being prepared. These programmes are the successors to the EU Interreg and Peace programmes.

17 P Clarke, E Magennis and J Shiels, *Attitudes to the development of cross-border health services: the case of GP out-of-hours services* (Armagh: Cooperation and Working Together (CAWT), 2007).

18 Border Ireland cross-border information system can be accessed at www.borderireland.info.

19 A Kelly, C Teljeur and I Monleya, 'A rational way to plan health services', in *A picture of health: a selection of Irish health research 2005* (Dublin: Health Research Board, 2005), p. 45; available at www.hrb.ie.

20 The Irish Minister for Health and Children, Ms Mary Harney, TD, and the Northern Ireland Health Minister, Mr Shaun Woodward, MP, met in Belfast on 15 November 2005 and agreed to support arrangements for cancer patients from Donegal to be treated in Belfast Cancer Centre once it formally opens in March 2007. The Belfast Centre is already treating approximately fifty Donegal patients and the new cross-border arrangements will make this service available to a larger number of patients at a centre closer to their homes.

21 Clarke et al., *Attitudes* (2007).

22 Information provided by the Department of Health, Social Services and Public Safety, Northern Ireland.

23 Clarke et al., *Attitudes* (2007).

24 In the South these include the *Audit of structures and functions in the health system* (The Prospectus Report, June 2003), the *Report of the Commission on Financial Management and Control Systems in the Health Service* (The Brennan Report, June 2003) and the *Report of the Task Force on Medical Staffing* (The Hanly Report, October 2003). In the North, reports include the *Independent review of health and social care services in Northern Ireland* (The Appleby Report, August 2005) and the Northern Ireland Executive's *Review of public administration* (November 2005).

25 One the first binational agreements to be signed between neighbouring countries was the health convention of 12 January 1881, between Belgium and France, revised on 25 October 1910, which 'authorised Belgian doctors of medicine, surgery and childbirth established in the Belgian districts bordering France to practise their art in the same way and to the same extent in any neighbouring French district, in which there is no doctor residing', and vice versa.

26 The European Commission has funded a three-year 'Evaluation of cross-border regions in the European Union (Euregio)' project under its public health programme and a three-year research-based 'sixth framework' 'Europe for patients' project.

9

Economic development: the textile and information technology sectors

JOHN BRADLEY

INTRODUCTION

One of the characteristics of economic research on the island of Ireland is that it seldom presents comparisons and contrasts of the two regional economies at the level of very detailed sectors. In part, this is caused by the very different sectoral structure of manufacturing and services North and South. In the Republic, attention is focused on the modern, high-technology sectors of computers, software and pharmaceuticals, and, with the exception of the food processing sector, the remaining sectors are small and attract far less attention. In Northern Ireland the sectoral portfolio of manufacturing and market services is still more traditional, and is less dominated by foreign ownership.[1]

chapter 3 offered a strategic overview of the two economies on the island of Ireland, and examined how they evolved in very different ways before and after 1922. In this chapter we present two case studies of sectoral specialisation on the island, the roots of which lie in the near past in one case, and in the more distant past in the other. After providing a brief overview of the present areas of manufacturing specialisation, we examine a mature or declining sector (textiles and clothing). This sector remains dominant in Northern Ireland but has shrunk to a smaller – mainly specialist – niche in the Republic. In the following section, a modern, high-technology sector – computers and related software – is examined. This sector has grown rapidly during the past decade and a half and has played a crucial role in driving national growth, modernisation and development in the Republic, but plays a much more modest role in Northern Ireland.

At first sight, these case study sectors would appear to be at opposite ends of what Raymond Vernon has called the product life-cycle spectrum: textiles and clothing at the mature or declining stage, and computers and software at the introduction or early growth stage.[2] But appearances can be deceptive. For example, the Irish computer and software complex is narrowly focused on a very specific technology: personal computers, components, peripherals and related software. As will be discussed later, within this segment of the wider electronics and software industry, personal computers appear to be moving towards maturity. So, the case study can be used to reinterpret the product life-cycle framework more flexibly and apply it to niche products within a segment of manufacturing, where future vulnerability might arise because the technologies were not researched and developed in the Republic, but were merely produced and distributed to intermediate and end users.

MANUFACTURING PORTFOLIOS, NORTH AND SOUTH

In this section, attention is drawn to an important aspect of the emergence and characteristics of the portfolio imbalance in Northern Ireland manufacturing, namely the continued existence of a range of traditional labour-intensive sectors in an economy that should have divested itself of these sectors long ago.[3] The performance, structure and market trends characteristics of the textiles and clothing sector of Northern Ireland are examined. Present proposals for addressing the problems are reviewed, and a range of possible future competitiveness strategies is explored.

While we attribute to the clothing and textiles sector many negative characteristics, it should be emphasised that, even in the case of textiles and clothing, the maturity and decline of the sector is neither inevitable nor irreversible. The example of the well-known firm Benetton in northern Italy shows how, in stark contrast to Northern Ireland, a segment of the textiles and clothing sector was developed and transformed into a high-productivity, high-profit success story through a synthesis of process innovations and strategic marketing.[4]

Sectoral specialisation on the island of Ireland

It has been demonstrated in chapter 3 that the textiles and clothing sectors were the largest component of manufacturing in Northern Ireland in the year 1924. In terms of output, they made up 54 per cent in the North, but only slightly above 2 per cent in the South. Over the intervening years, the sector declined in the North, and grew somewhat in the South. For example, in the years 1951 (immediately before the switch to outward policies in the Republic), 1961 (immediately after that switch) and 1967 (immediately before the outbreak of civil unrest in Northern Ireland), the employment composition of manufacturing was as shown in Table 9.1. By 1967, the textiles and clothing sector in the Republic had grown to just over 25 per cent of total employment in manufacturing (its peak), while in Northern Ireland it had continued an inexorable decline to just under 42 per cent.

Although simple matrix techniques can be used to examine portfolios of different businesses, attempts to translate these to the level of an entire country or regional manufacturing sector have not been very successful.[5] In Table 9.2 an attempt at portfolio analysis for Northern Ireland is presented, while an analogous portfolio for the Republic is presented in Table 9.3. Both refer to the period after the ceasefires but before the Belfast agreement (1991–6 for Northern Ireland and 1991–8 for the Republic).[6] Taking Northern Ireland first, the key characteristics of the portfolio of manufacturing sectors in 1996 were as follows:

1. Food processing is the predominant sector in terms of output share (31 per cent), but only second in terms of employment share (19 per cent). In terms of average annual growth over the five-year period 1991–6, it was stagnant in real terms.
2. Textiles and clothing has the second largest output share (13 per cent), but the largest employment share (23 per cent), characterising it as having very low productivity. Average annual real growth is only about 4 per cent, and possibly lower, since price competition is very strong in the sector (see below).
3. Electrical and optical goods is the third largest sector in terms of output (9 per cent), and fourth in terms of employment share (also 9 per cent). This is also a very high-growth sector (about 14 per cent per year in real terms). The characteristics of transport equipment are very similar.
4. For all the other sectors, both output and employment shares are small, ranging from 2 per cent to 8 per cent in the case of output and 3 per cent to 7 per cent in the case of employment, with real growth rates clustering closely about the average of 4 per cent per year.

Turning to the Republic, the key characteristics of the portfolio of manufacturing sectors (see Table 9.3) are very different from Northern Ireland; they are as follows:

Table 9.1. Employment in manufacturing, Republic of Ireland and Northern Ireland, 1951–67

	1951 numbers	%	1961 numbers	%	1967 numbers	%
Northern Ireland						
Textiles	70,658	39.9	47,965	29.3	42,412	26.5
Clothing	27,025	15.3	23,820	14.5	21,959	13.7
Engineering and metal	43,461	24.5	51,508	31.4	49,260	30.8
Food, drink and tobacco	20,802	11.7	25,195	15.4	26,191	16.4
Mineral products	3,143	1.8	4,173	2.5	4,243	2.7
Timber and furniture	3,926	2.2	2,653	1.6	3,252	2.0
Paper, printing etc.	4,500	2.5	4,954	3.0	5,404	3.4
Miscellaneous trades	3,631	2.0	3,612	2.2	7,081	4.4
Total manufacturing	177,146	100.0	163,880	100.0	159,802	100.0
Republic of Ireland						
Textiles	9,535	6.8	15,394	9.8	15,504	8.7
Clothing	28,092	20.0	27,808	17.6	29,729	16.7
Engineering and metal	18,019	12.8	26,407	16.8	33,014	18.6
Food, drink and tobacco	42,038	30.0	46,317	29.4	50,668	28.5
Mineral products	5,029	3.6	6,030	3.8	7,995	4.5
Timber and furniture	8,766	6.2	6,963	4.4	7,726	4.4
Paper, printing etc.	12,343	8.8	14,696	9.3	15,156	8.5
Miscellaneous trades	16,461	11.7	14,007	8.9	17,776	10.0
Total manufacturing	140,283	100.0	157,622	100.0	177,568	100.0

Source: *Report on the census of production for Northern Ireland* (Belfast: Northern Ireland Statistical Agency, various years); *Census of industrial production* (Dublin: Central Statistics Office, various years).

Table 9.2. Sectoral portfolio in manufacturing, Northern Ireland, 1996

	Gross output				Employment,	
	1996 £m.	1996 %	1991 £m.	Growth 1991–6	1996 No.	%
Food, drink and tobacco	2,726	30.9	2,390	2.7	19,370	19.0
Textiles, clothing and leather	1,167	13.2	849	6.6	23,800	23.4
Electrical and optical equipment	829	9.4	384	16.6	9,330	9.2
Transport equipment	742	8.4	652	2.6	10,810	10.6
Other machinery and equipment	671	7.6	328	15.4	6,850	6.7
Chemicals and man-made fibres	600	6.8	450	5.9	3,620	3.6
Rubber and plastics	502	5.7	319	9.5	6,280	6.2
Paper and printing	440	5.0	297	8.2	6,400	6.3
Other non-metallic mineral products	364	4.1	256	7.3	4,360	4.3
Basic metals and fabricated metal products	330	3.7	221	8.3	5,140	5.0
Wood and wood products	286	3.2	192	8.3	2,750	2.7
Other manufacturing n.e.s.	167	1.9	113	8.1	3,180	3.1
Total	8,824	100.0	6,451	6.8	101,890	100.0

Note. Average annual inflation rate of UK manufacturing output (1991–6) = 2.65%.

Source. Northern Ireland Sales and Exports (Belfast: Northern Ireland Economic Research Centre, various years).

1. Electrical and optical equipment is the predominant sector in terms of output share (29 per cent), and in terms of employment share (25 per cent). In terms of average annual growth over the seven-year period 1991–8, it experienced very high real growth of 18 per cent.
2. Chemicals (including pharmaceuticals) and man-made fibres has the second largest output share (24 per cent), but a much lower employment share (9 per cent), characterising it as having low productivity. This was also a very high growth sector (about 21 per cent per year in real terms).
3. Food processing is the third largest sector in terms of output (21 per cent), accounting for a similar proportion of employment, and with growth of about 3 per cent per year in real terms.

Table 9.3. Sectoral portfolio in manufacturing, Republic of Ireland, 1998

	Gross output				Employment,	
	1998	1998	1991	Growth	1998	
	£m.	%	£m.	1991–8	No.	%
Food, drink and tobacco	10,381	21.4	7,807	4.2	47,113	19.5
Textiles, clothing and leather	777	1.6	808	-0.6	15,564	6.4
Electrical and optical equipment	13,831	28.6	3,848	20.1	60,127	24.8
Transport equipment	749	1.5	406	9.1	7,464	3.1
Other machinery and equipment	1,196	2.5	732	7.3	14,668	6.1
Chemicals and man-made fibres	11,728	24.2	2,685	23.4	21,415	8.8
Rubber and plastics	855	1.8	515	7.5	10,476	4.3
Paper and printing	5,018	10.4	1,645	17.3	23,260	9.6
Other non-metallic mineral products	917	1.9	582	6.7	9,977	4.1
Basic metals and fabricated metal products	1,301	2.7	869	5.9	14,960	6.2
Wood and wood products	469	1.0	230	10.7	5,016	2.1
Other manufacturing n.e.s.	1,207	2.5	771	6.6	12,164	5.0
Total	48,429	100.0	20,898	13.4	242,204	100.0

Note. Average annual inflation rate of manufacturing output (1991–8) = 1.86%.

Source. Report on the census of production for Northern Ireland (Belfast: Northern Ireland Statistical Agency, various years); *Census of industrial production* (Dublin: Central Statistics Office, various years).

4. The only other sector with double digit output share is paper and printing (including publishing), with output and employment shares of 10 per cent. This is also a very high-growth sector (21 per cent per year in real terms). Much of the output of the software sector is classified here, including computer manuals and CD-ROMs.
5. For all the other sectors, both output and employment shares are very small, in the range of 1–3 per cent for output and 1–6 per cent for employment, with real growth rates somewhat lower than the average of 11 per cent per year.

In summary, both regions of the island of Ireland display manufacturing portfolios that are strongly concentrated. In the case of Northern Ireland at the time of the negotiation of the Belfast agreement, the two largest sectors were food processing and textiles and clothing, both of which experienced very slow real growth. There was also significant specialisation in a high growth sector, electrical and optical equipment. In the case of the Republic, the predominant specialisation was in two rapid growth high-technology sectors (electrical and optical, and chemicals) and one traditional (but by the mid-1990s, quite capital-intensive) slow-growth sector, food processing. This form of sectoral concentration was continued, and Table 9.4 shows the harmonised data published by InterTrade Ireland for the year 2000.

Table 9.4. Industrial concentration by sector, Republic of Ireland and Northern Ireland, 2000

Sector	Gross output share		Employment share	
	Republic of Ireland	*Northern Ireland*	*Republic of Ireland*	*Northern Ireland*
Electrical and optical equipment	33.8	19.5	27.0	11.1
Chemicals and chemical products	26.3	4.4	9.1	3.6
Food, beverages, tobacco	17.2	29.6	18.8	19.4
Paper, paper products, publishing, printing	10.8	4.1	9.3	6.4
Metal and metal products	2.2	4.9	6.6	7.2
Other manufacturing	1.9	3.1	4.5	4.0
Machinery and equipment	1.8	5.8	5.6	6.7
Non-metallic mineral products	1.6	4.2	4.4	5.7
Rubber and plastic products	1.4	5.2	4.2	7.0
Transport equipment	1.2	8.4	3.8	13.0
Textiles, textile products, leather	0.9	7.6	4.3	13.0
Wood and wood products	0.9	3.3	2.4	2.9

Note: columns report percentages by sector.

Source: *North–South trade: a statistical ground-clearing exercise* (Newry: InterTradeIreland, 2003); also available at www.intertradeireland.com/module.cfm/opt/29/area/Publications/page/Publications [31-12-2006].

CASE STUDY: THE NORTHERN IRELAND TEXTILES AND CLOTHING SECTORS

Overview

In designing strategic industrial policy in Northern Ireland, the clothing and textiles sector poses a major challenge. Although in continual decline, its rate of decline has undoubtedly been slowed by the use of large-scale grant aid to prop up ailing firms whose collapse would have destabilised an economy that was already under siege as a result of civil unrest. In other words, it proved very difficult to attract more modern industries to replace any employment loss from the decline of the traditional specialisation in clothing and textiles. But, unfortunately, the sector itself failed to modernise in a way that might have preserved it from further erosion of competitive advantage.

As part of the most recent major review of industrial strategy in Northern Ireland – *Strategy 2010* – a sectoral working group was set up to examine the textiles and clothing sector.[7] The report examined the underlying structure and characteristics of the sector and attempted to formulate policy recommendations that would preserve a role for it within the future Northern Ireland manufacturing portfolio.

The sector is defined as being made up of business activities involving yarns, fibres, threads, fabric garments, carpets, household furnishings and industrial textiles.[8] It consists of a small number of very large public corporations (the top eight of which are mostly British-owned and account for almost half of total employment in the sector), and a large number of small, mostly family-owned and -run businesses. By the late 1990s, the sector employed about 23,000 people (about a quarter of total employment in northern manufacturing), down from a peak of 70,000 in 1945. Employment was split roughly equally between textiles (10,500) and clothing (12,500).

Table 9.5. Performance in the EU textiles and clothing industries, 1990–7

	Northern Ireland	UK	Republic of Ireland	EU
Production (%)	10	-13	-9	-5.4
Employment (%)	-8	-20	-12	-17

Source: CTWG, Sectoral report (1998), p. 21.

As Table 9.5 shows, production in this sector over the 1990–7 period rose in Northern Ireland, but fell in the UK as a whole, in the Republic and in the EU as a whole. But although northern productivity increased by between 2 per cent and 3 per cent each year, profit margins declined from £2,300 per employee in 1993 to £1,600 per employee in 1996.[9] This represents the lowest level of profitability per employee of any Northern Ireland manufacturing sector, reflecting its traditional nature and its high labour intensity. The sector is mainly oriented to external sales.[10] In 1996, 92 per cent of output was sold outside Northern Ireland, of which three-quarters went to Britain. The main export destinations for the remaining one quarter of external sales were the Republic (one-third of the remainder), Asia (10 per cent), the USA (also 10 per cent), and the residual spread over a wide range of EU and other international markets.

Structure of textiles and clothing subsectors

The textile and clothing subsectors are further segmented, as shown in Tables 9.6 (textiles) and 9.7 (clothing). The carpet subsector is concentrated in a small number of firms, and is the largest segment in the sector. The remainder is divided fairly evenly over six other segments, with household textiles (table linen, furnishing fabric) making up the smallest segment in terms of turnover (7 per cent) but double that as a share of employment (13 per cent). Very few Northern Ireland companies operate in the area of technical textiles, the main company being Dupont (which produces Lycra and Kevlar).

Table 9.6. Textile sector by segment, Northern Ireland, 1996

Segment	Employment	Turnover
Carpets	29	39
Threads, braids, twines	12	16
Weaving	10	12
Spinning	18	10
Household textiles	13	7
Dyeing and finishing	7	4
Miscellaneous	11	12

Note: columns report percentages by segment.

Source: CTWG, *Sectoral report* (1998), p. 10.

Table 9.7. Clothing sector by type of garment, Northern Ireland, 1996

Garment type	Employment	Turnover
Hosiery and lingerie	25	24
Men's outerwear	17	15
Shirts	18	14
Children's wear	10	11
Jeans and leisurewear	5	13
Ladieswear	10	9
Nightwear	7	8
Protective and workwear	3	2
Other	5	4

Note: columns report percentages by segment.

Source: CTWG, Sectoral report (1998), p. 11.

The largest subsector of clothing is hosiery and lingerie (about a quarter of turnover and of employment), but is made up of a range of other garments. What is interesting about this subsector is the nature of its relationship with its main customers. Nearly 60 per cent of the workforce in the clothing subsector is employed on long-term supply contracts to Marks & Spencer. A further 20 per cent work on other non-branded supply contracts, with 20 per cent also working on branded goods. An insignificant proportion (about 2 per cent) is employed on 'cut, make and trim' operations. The firms working on the Marks & Spencer supply contracts tend to be large; the rest tend to be small.

Market trends

This sector has moved through fairly distinctive trends during recent decades.[11] There was buoyant mass-market demand for high-quality goods in the 1970s, requiring capital-intensive techniques, long production runs and strong vertical links in the industry. The 1980s was a period of erratic demand where the market became increasingly dominated by competition between the major UK retailers. Consumer tastes tended to become fashion oriented and segmented. Suppliers needed to be able to respond quickly to fickle changes in tastes and the knock-on fluctuation in demand forced changes on production techniques. During the 1990s, quick response capabilities assumed an even greater importance, and the larger Northern Ireland firms formed close strategic alliances with UK retail chains, particularly Marks & Spencer, leading to mergers and rationalisations.

In the aftermath of the Belfast agreement the sector has faced even more daunting challenges. An immediate problem was the decline in the fortunes of Marks & Spencer, whose supply contracts in Northern Ireland supported almost 60 per cent of employment. Changing lifestyle characteristics of consumers will generate many opportunities for innovation and branding of high-margin products. But the sector does not appear to be well positioned to respond to such demands, since it has functioned mainly as a supply contractor, where design and market research functions have been carried out by retail chains like Marks & Spencer.

Service requirements are also becoming ever more demanding, with continual renewal of styles rather than traditional seasons requiring a radical shortening of supply response capability. However, if the sector continues to operate supply contracts to major UK retail chains, there is a risk that any competitive advantage possessed by the Northern Ireland clothing sector could be eroded by much lower production costs in Central Europe, North Africa and East Asia, where advances in communications technologies and low transport costs could overcome the Northern Ireland advantage of closeness to the UK market. More seriously, the northern textiles and clothing sector can no longer compete as a low-cost producer without massive capital investment.[12] Furthermore, the phasing out of the Multi-Fibre agreement – which had served to protect EU producers from low cost competition – has made the EU and UK markets even more competitive. An alternative strategy – to carry out high added-value design and marketing activities locally and outsource production to low-cost countries – might be feasible, but is likely to place severe strains on the level of technical and marketing expertise.

Future competitiveness strategies

The textile and clothing industry has many of the characteristics of a mature or declining sector. In the absence of exceptional characteristics (such as those displayed by firms like Benetton in northern Italy), the product life-cycle framework of Vernon (see above) would suggest that the sector has very limited options in its present form. Far from displaying any exceptional capabilities, the competitiveness of the Northern Ireland textiles and clothing sector has been deteriorating for many decades. There are only a few large firms that can benefit from scale economies in pursuing low-cost competitive strategies. Local design capabilities were never very strong at any time, but in recent decades have been neglected, as the large firms have engaged in supply contracts with British retail chains. Wage costs have been driven up to British levels, and a relatively low rate of productivity growth has resulted in high unit labour costs. The availability of high rates of subsidy has served to prop up an otherwise ailing sector and reduce the urgency for rationalisation, change and renewal.[13] Finally, the declining nature of the sector precludes any major role for inward foreign direct investment, which is more likely to seek out lower-cost labour in the less developed periphery of the east or south of the EU, or in Asia.

In light of the large size of the textiles and clothing sector in Northern Ireland, it is surprising that the last major review of industrial strategy – *Strategy 2010* – came up with such unfocused and weak proposals.[14] For example, positive aspects of the sector were identified as including strong family firms with professional management, although this has not generated much new thinking or innovation over the past decades. The close partnership with UK retailers was also identified as a strength, an assertion that is open to question (see above). The 'flexible, young workforce' is also counted as a strength, although the sector is characterised by low skills and lack of innovation. Negative aspects of the sector are well known, and include low-cost competition from Eastern Europe, Asia and North Africa, low levels of research and development, over-dependence on a small number of UK multiples, and a 'poor image'. It was suggested that growth in the sector was only likely to be achieved 'by building an international reputation for excellence and specific added-value products or services'.[15] But how was this to be brought about?

There are appropriate end-game strategies for such declining sectors.[16] The conventional strategy suggested by portfolio matrices has been to 'harvest' – to cease any significant investment activity, maximise cash flow, and eventually divest. This was the strategy followed in the Republic, and has led to the decline in importance of textiles and clothing to a minor niche (see Table 9.3 above). However, Harrigan and Porter suggest a less one-dimensional approach to strategy for declining businesses, illustrated in Table 9.8.

1. A market share *leadership* strategy is one where a company attempts to reap above-average profitability by becoming one of the few companies remaining in the industry. Leadership permits more control over the process of decline, but does not reverse it. The tactics of achieving a position of leadership include ensuring that other companies retire more rapidly from the industry, perhaps by reducing their exit barriers or by raising the stakes and forcing competitors to reinvest.
2. The objective of a *niche* strategy is to identify a segment of the declining industry that is likely to maintain stable demand or decay more slowly, but which permits high returns to be made.

3. In a *harvest* strategy, management tries to get the highest cash flow it can from the business, while undergoing controlled disinvestments.
4. Finally, a *quick divestment* strategy is one where the company is sold in the early stages of decline. Divesting quickly will force a company to confront its own exit barriers, such as its customer relationships and corporate interdependencies.

Table 9.8. Strategies for declining businesses

Status of industry structure	Has competitive strengths for remaining demand pockets	Lacks competitive strengths for remaining demand pockets
Favourable industry structure for decline	Leadership or niche	Harvest or divest quickly
Unfavourable industry structure for decline	Niche or harvest	Divest quickly

Source: Harrigan and Porter, 'End-game strategies' (1998), p. 114.

In Table 9.8 a distinction is made between a favourable and unfavourable industry structure for decline. A favourable structure is characterised by low demand uncertainty, low exit barriers, and fragmented rivalry. An unfavourable structure is characterised by high demand uncertainty, high exit barriers, and conditions leading to volatile end-game rivalry. Although this table is designed from an industry perspective, it offers useful insights even in the case of a whole sector in a region like Northern Ireland. The Northern Ireland textiles and clothing sector would appear to have competitive strengths in certain demand pockets and the structure of the industry appears favourable, suggesting a *niche* or *leadership* strategy. The strategy recommendations made by the Clothing and Textiles Working Group appear to suggest moving in that direction.[17] Examples include a continuation of the policy of acting as high-quality, low-cost suppliers to UK and US retail chains; the development of customised products and services; the development of a range of branded products, perhaps in association with the fashion niche in the Republic; and specialisation in a range of technical textile products. A crucial role for government policy is identified, in terms of support for innovation, design, marketing and training.

Summary

Attention has been drawn to the nature of the portfolio imbalance in Northern Ireland manufacturing. While there is some justification for the continued large size of the food processing sector – since the agriculture sector is the largest, in relative terms, of all eleven UK standard regions – the enduring dominance of the textiles and clothing sector is more difficult to explain. Economic logic points clearly to the need to get out of this sector, since the comparative advantage of a high wage region like Northern Ireland is weak at best, and non-existent at worst. The performance, structure and market trend characteristics of the textiles and clothing sector have also been examined, further reinforcing its declining nature. Proposals for addressing the problems as contained in *Strategy 2010* policy review appear to be pious aspirations rather than rational, implementable strategies. The range of possible future competitiveness strategies is not appealing, and includes at best leadership or niche strategies, and at worst, quick divestment. The future of Northern Ireland manufacturing almost certainly lies elsewhere, and not in textiles and clothing. In the next section we turn to the issues that arise in building and sustaining a fast-growing, high-technology sector, a challenge that still faces policy-makers in Northern Ireland.

CASE STUDY: THE IRISH ELECTRONICS AND SOFTWARE SECTORS

Overview

As was apparent in Table 9.3 above, the manufacturing sector in the Republic extends over a much wider area than computers and software. But the computer-related and the pharmaceutical sectors are at the heart of the recent rapid growth and development of the economy, and provide a useful way to examine the capacity of Irish development agencies to design and implement strategies to attract inward foreign direct investment in the high-technology sector generally. This is the main reason for selecting the electronics and software sector as a case study.

In this section, the way in which a complex of computer industries was attracted to the Republic is examined. In particular, the approach of the Industrial Development Authority (IDA) is described and shown to be consistent with the industrial policy frameworks associated with Vernon, Porter and Best.[18] However, the success of IDA strategy needs to be evaluated in the knowledge that the computer–software complex in the Republic is focused on a relatively narrow range of products within the wider electrical and optical sector.[19] It is suggested that this narrow range of products may be about to mature, and that a new approach is needed in order to make the transition to other related manufacturing activities. The section concludes with an examination of how this is being done in the context of changes in modern production processes.

Main characteristics of the computer sector

The main interest here is in the Republic's computer sector, broadly defined. This is primarily a subsector of the manufacture of electrical and optical equipment (NACE 30-33, in the terminology of the general industrial classification of economic activities in the European Community), and is shown in Table 9.9. Using industrial census data, the closest one can get to isolating the core computer subsector, consisting of computer assembly and electronic components, is to combine computers (NACE 3002) with electronic components (NACE 3210), and the result is shown in Table 9.10.[20]

After detailed examination, one can summarise the position as follows.[21] The computer sector in the Republic of Ireland is by no means a homogeneous entity. There are two main categories: computer assembly (NACE 3002) and the manufacture of electronic and computer components (NACE 3210). Within the computer assembly subsector, one finds a

Table 9.9. Manufacture of electrical and optical equipment, Republic of Ireland, 1998

NACE code	Description	Gross output, 1998 (£million)	Employment numbers, 1998
30	Office machinery and computers	8,510	16,049
31	Electrical machinery and apparatus n.e.c.	1,309	14,607
32	Radio, television and communication equipment and apparatus	2,505	13,384
33	Medical, precision and optical instruments, watches and clocks	1,506	15,790
30-33	Electrical and optical equipment	13,831	59,830

Source: Census of industrial production (Dublin: Central Statistics Office, 1998).

Table 9.10. Core computer and component manufacturing subsector, Republic of Ireland, 1998

NACE code	Description	Gross output, 1998 (£million)	Employment numbers, 1998
3002	Computers and other information processing equipment	8,496	15,822
3210	Electronic components	1,603	8,667
Total	Computers and electronic components	10,099	24,489

Soiurce. Census of Industrial Production (Dublin: Central Statistics Office, 1998).

mixture of technologies and processes, ranging from simple assembly operations (often pejoratively referred to as 'screwdriver' operations) to the sophisticated integrated assembly and direct sales operations that are a unique feature of Dell Computers. Within the electronic components subsector one finds the manufacture of state-of-the-art micro-chip processors (Intel being the largest and most sophisticated), computer peripherals (such as disk drives and printers), and simpler electronic components.

The high-technology sector, in particular computers and electronic components, is predominantly foreign-owned. Hence, the forces that drive innovation in products and manufacturing processes tend to originate in the USA rather than in the Republic. It is this feature that presents the most serious threat to the survival and progress of the sector. But to explore further the policy implications of these issues for the future of the Republic's computer sector requires us to step back from data to consider some broader aspects of industrial strategy that brought about the electronics and software agglomeration.

Bringing the US computer industry to Ireland

The success of the 'Celtic tiger' has brought forth many explanations of how it came about. A recent account has been co-written by Padraic White, a former managing director of the IDA, which handled all aspects of industrial promotion prior to 1994.[22] There is always the danger of an element of *post hoc* rationalisation about such accounts, written many years after the key decisions were taken. However, White bases his account of the evolution of the modern Irish manufacturing sector in part on an earlier paper, written before the first major computer company ever decided to locate in the Republic.[23] The story of the IDA is a classic example of a state development agency that mediated between the narrow firm-based concerns of potential investors and the wider social concerns of national policy-makers.

The challenge facing the IDA was how to attract just the right type and scale of foreign investment to fit the Republic's needs. There was a strong planning and research section (headed by Ray McLoughlin), which generated new ideas and concepts that were fully tested against the actual experience of the IDA representatives who were in the field trying to persuade firms to consider locating in the Republic.[24] As McLoughlin tells it, the 'closed loop' system of industrial planning designed by the IDA in the late 1960s had the following components:

1. definition of the national economic and social objectives as outlined by government policy;
2. definition of the criteria for selecting target industries, whether in terms of the Republic's location or its capacity to attract inward investment;
3. identification and targeting of specific foreign companies and detailed assessment of their investment requirements;
4. assessment of the Republic's ability to meet the development needs of those companies; and
5. monitoring of progress in successfully attracting investment projects.

In more informal language, White described the policy goal as 'to target with rifle-shot precision individual companies that met specific criteria, then go directly to them and make the case for locating in Ireland'. Using even more colloquial marketing language, he outlined how 'these armies of cold callers, and the commando-style task forces fanning out across the world, laid the ground for Ireland's dramatic success in getting new industries later in the 1970s'.[25] Since the IDA was a relatively small organisation, the workload to implement all elements of the promotional strategy was phenomenal: 'in the first full year (1971) of the new direct marketing approach, IDA executives made presentations to 105 different target companies. Next year, they increased this to 775 in thirteen countries. And, by 1973, a staggering 2,600 presentations to individual companies were made across the world'.[26]

Even at a very early stage, the IDA had a sophisticated system of scanning the world business horizon, and identified the electronic and pharmaceutical sectors as having desirable characteristics that particularly suited the Republic's situation. The man-made fibre sector had also been targeted, and had been a big success in Northern Ireland. But after an initial period, it was hit by the OPEC oil price shocks of 1973–4, and few firms survived. Clothing and textiles were also targeted, and firms like Wrangler, Bluebell, Farah Jeans and Burlington Industries located in Ireland and created welcome jobs.[27] But with tough price competition from low-wage Asian and Southern European economies, and disruptive changes in fashion, most of them either closed or cut back severely.

The first critical success in attracting a world-class computer firm was Digital Equipment Corporation (DEC), a pioneer in mini-computers. Its presence heavily influenced many other major multinational computer hardware and software companies, encouraging them to locate in the Republic in the following years. By the late 1990s, electronics represented the largest single foreign-owned manufacturing sector. It contributed 30 per cent of total exports and employed about 44,000 people directly (18 per cent of total employment in manufacturing).[28] In addition, a large software sector had grown up around the hardware industry, employing a further 15,000 people directly and producing 40 per cent of all PC package software sold in Europe.[29] Both the hardware and software sectors had further significant impacts on a wide range of other – often traditional – sectors.[30]

It was generally realised by the IDA that their unique selling point, which gave the Republic a crucial advantage in winning inward investment in the high-technology, high-profit sectors, was the low rate of tax on corporate profits (zero on export-related profits initially; changed to a flat rate of 10 per cent after the Republic joined the then EEC in 1973; now a flat rate of 12.5 per cent on all corporate profits). This incentive had some striking virtues. Unlike an incentive system that provided high capital grants and required continuing subventions, the benefit of the tax-based incentive was that it only kicked in when firms were up and running, and actually making profits. It also proved to be a crucial benefit to high-profit firms, who are invariably located at the earlier stages of the product life-cycle and are at the cutting edge of product and process innovation. It was also an incentive that was kept very stable over many decades, and the IDA and the Irish government ensured that it could be fully credible over the usual business investment planning cycles of ten to fifteen years or more. Finally, the tax-based incentive had the great virtue of being very simple, easy to understand and transparent to market.

But the tax incentive, even combined with fairly generous capital grants, would not have been sufficient to stimulate growth from a zero base in new technology sectors. Prior to 1970 there had been no indigenous electronics sector and only a handful of mainly US companies (General Electric, Ecco and Core Memories) in the Republic. It was quickly realised by Ray McLoughlin that the limited supply of electrical engineers and technicians in the Republic would be a major deterrent to selecting the country as a location for industries in this potentially fast-growing niche. By the mid-1970s, Irish universities were producing about 100 electrical engineers and 200 technicians, but a massive increase in supply was called for if the sector was to expand.

The IDA alerted the Irish government to the potential crisis, which could easily have choked off growth. Very quickly, the university sector was expanded and given massively increased resources. By as early as 1979, new and expanded courses in electrical engineering were under way, postgraduate conversion courses were provided to encourage science and other graduates to enter the new field, and a system of sub-degree-level regional technology institutes was planned and introduced over the next decade. When the poor quality of the telephone network was identified as another bottleneck that would impede data transmission, a crash programme was put in place, a new state telecommunications agency was set up, and a fully digital nation-wide system was installed and commissioned by the mid-1980s. This programme was also used as a further incentive to attract inward investment in the telecommunications area.

Just as DEC was the linchpin of the first phase of inward investment in the computer area, the success in attracting Apple to establish its European manufacturing base in the Republic as early as 1980 was the linchpin of a strategy that targeted the new wave of PC-based hardware and software. The IDA approach has been described as follows:

> The IDA electronics division used a see-through model of a computer to identify every component in it. Then, systematically, it canvassed the makers of each individual component, such as keyboards, hard disks, cables, computer mice and sub-assemblies. The decade (1980) closed with Ireland successfully inducing two companies the IDA had pursued for over a decade to locate here – Intel's microprocessor plant and Motorola's communications-products plant.[31]

The high point of the IDA strategy came during the 1990s, when the Republic became the front-runner for most of the sophisticated foreign investment in electronics, computers and software. A virtuous circle had been created, with electronic and computer equipment at its core, a spill-over into PC-related software development and customisation, and a further spill-over into telecommunications-based marketing, customer and technical-support services. This both assisted existing producers located in the Republic and contributed to the creation of a sophisticated international financial services sector.

The future of the computer and software sector

A hint of how the IDA has been dealing with the incipient maturity problem of the computer sector was contained in the review of industrial promotion strategy (Enterprise 2010) prepared by Forfás, the coordinating agency of the IDA, and Enterprise Ireland (a partner agency focusing on developing indigenous Irish industry): 'The emerging new business model is leading to a new pattern of international investment, with corporations selecting the best location for each particular activity, rather than necessarily putting integrated projects in a single location.'[32]

This type of decentralised approach within firms is well known, and was the basis for the success of Dell in creating a high-profit computer firm in an area that looked as if it was reaching maturity in the late 1980s. The nature of operations carried out within the firm range from 'do everything' to 'do nothing'. The nature of inter-firm contacts range from a transactional basis (with many suppliers) to a closed basis (with only a few carefully selected suppliers). The case of Dell illustrated the overriding importance of final assembly, distribution and marketing. In terms of inter-firm contact, a small number of long-term suppliers was used. Ireland was an obvious location for such a company, particularly in the 1990s, since many of the suppliers (including Intel, the supplier of the vital microprocessors) were already located in the Republic, and geographical peripherality was not a serious problem because of good transport and communications infrastructure and (in stark contrast to textiles and clothing) the high 'added-value' density of the final product.

Until recently, sourcing inputs from other countries would have incurred unacceptably high transaction costs (in terms of both inter-firm communications and border controls for intermediate products). However, the dramatic fall in transport and communications costs, as well as the completion of the single European market by 1992, worked strongly in the Republic's favour. But Enterprise 2010 appears to envisage a wider application of global outsourcing, with the Republic at the high added-value core of activities. Porter's framework suggests that this approach would leave the Republic vulnerable to changes in technology, and Best's framework suggests that such an approach will require a high standard of excellence in all aspects of the economy. Either way, the suggested new approach of marketing the Republic as a 'network' location in a type of post-industrial age will be a major challenge.

Summary

There were many different aspects to the success of the IDA in attracting inward investment in high-technology areas. It had a certain independence from government and a separate role in planning strategy at the national as well as the firm level. This meant that it was well equipped to deal both with research into the actual needs of individual industries and with requirements at the national level in terms of basic physical infrastructure, education and training, telecommunications, and transport needs. There was also a realisation that national industrial promotion was a continuously evolving challenge:

> The nature of industry keeps changing – there is a continuous process of decline in some sectors (for example, textiles and mechanical engineering) and growth in others (software and e-commerce). So we can assume that a fair share of the industries we have today will decline and decay in coming years. Thus, we need to be continually searching for the emerging star sectors that are competitive in an Ireland of rising costs compared with others in an enlarged European Union.[33]

Another crucial characteristic of the IDA approach was its proactivity, described provocatively as follows:

> It is IDA policy to gear itself to discharge the total process to the limit of its legislative permit, and while it will not encroach on areas which are clearly the responsibility of other state organisations, it will err on the side of doing rather than not doing where the returns on effort appear to be high.[34]

But, in a curious way, the IDA had a simpler and more direct strategic mission in the Ireland of the dismal 1960s and early 1970s: 'The need to create jobs is even greater now than before. If the jobs aren't there, the advance factories are useless because we can't fill them, the regional plans are useless because there are no jobs to disperse and the selection exercise is useless because there is nothing to select from.'[35]

As the IDA faces into the challenges of the new millennium, and as the existing base of PC-based computers and software matures in the increasingly volatile world of the electronic and communications revolution, a whole new set of complex challenges is presenting itself. But the experience of the past thirty years illustrates that the IDA played a vital role in mediating between the formulation of national industrial policy (interpreted in the very widest sense as including taxation, infrastructure and education) and the requirements of selected sectors and firms within these sectors. The compartmentalisation that appears to characterise the worlds of academic research in economics and in business (where the two groups seldom talk and exchange views) finds no parallel in the IDA's integrated approach to its mission to promote Ireland as a desirable location for high-technology foreign direct investment.

CONCLUSION

Industry in Northern Ireland has yet to develop dynamic, self-sustaining characteristics, especially in terms of clusters of related and supporting industries. It remains heavily subsidised by public funding and is concentrated in the low-technology sectors of traditional industries such as textiles and clothing. The situation in the Republic of Ireland is somewhat healthier, but because industrial development has been so heavily driven by foreign direct investment, which tends not to lay down the full range of developmental roots in the domestic economy, the key interconnections between related firms and industries have yet to take place fully.

Michael Porter has suggested that four interacting characteristics are essential for competitive success: factor conditions, demand conditions, related and supporting industries, and firm strategy, structure and rivalry.[36] First, with regard to *factor conditions*, there is clearly much that could be done to improve the level and quality of education, training, infrastructure and technology on an island basis, in much the same way as the Republic of Ireland has managed to do over the past decade by itself. As Porter emphasises, improved factor conditions do not come about automatically, but as the result of government and companies bringing them about and subsequently sustaining them. What our case study of clothing and textiles in Northern Ireland suggested is that there are serious problems with education and training in these sectors, and in other traditional lines of northern specialisation. In the Republic the problems are less severe, since the educational and training system has been oriented towards serving the factor needs of a range of modern high-technology industries.

Second, *demand conditions* are a clear example of how island-based activity and policy could bring significant economic improvement. What is required is the creation of sophisticated and demanding local buyers who put pressure on companies to meet high standards of product quality, features and services. There is clearly substantial scope for development on this front, even in the Republic, where industrial success is still tightly focused around the activities of multinational companies. There seems to be some evidence that foreign plants are increasingly sourcing their inputs locally and that indigenous industry is responding to the challenges that this presents to them. However, there is certainly potential for further development. The turnaround in performance, documented by O'Malley, and the increased cross-border trading activity of northern small and medium-sized businesses, suggest that circumstances are already changing for the better.[37]

The third determinant of the competitiveness diamond is the need for *related and supporting industries*. In effect, this is the complement of demand conditions, and involves the development of a critical mass of competitive suppliers of specialised components, machinery and services. The relevance of the island economy is that Porter emphasises the importance of geographic proximity and close working relationships for the promotion of the key issue of innovation, involving information flows, technical interchange and the opportunities that exist for sharing. It is in this respect that he presents the case for the importance of *clusters* of related industrial activity, with strong forwards and backwards linkages, both within and between industries. In a long historical context it is clear that the Belfast region had such a cluster of related and supporting industries between the latter part of the nineteenth century and the first third of the twentieth.[38] However, the very success and dominance of sectors such as ship building, clothing and textiles probably made it difficult to break with the past and condemned these sectors to a slow decline (which was terminal in the case of shipbuilding). In the Republic, on the other hand, the high-technology cluster of computers and pharmaceuticals came only towards the end of the twentieth century. International experience has been that regions which have been dynamic in terms of traditional industries often tend to experience serious problems in transforming and restructuring. The inflexibilities are probably more understandable in terms of Olson's collusive coalitions than in terms of any narrow economic calculus.[39]

Fourth is the importance of *firm strategy, structure and rivalry*. Again, the two economies, North and South, would still seem to lack much of what Porter argues for in this regard. For example, he states that companies rarely succeed abroad unless there is intense competitive rivalry at home. In Northern Ireland, competition is limited and cushioned by high levels of public subsidisation. In the Republic, on the other hand, foreign industry does not compete locally and some elements of indigenous industry, at least until recently, operated in partially sheltered markets due to the element of non-traded goods being produced for home consumption.

Intra-island trade on the island has increased in recent years, but there again remains substantial scope for further growth of high-technology two-way trade.

A focus on the North–South axis is perfectly consistent with the fact that the major external markets and sources of inward investment for both regions presently lie, and will continue to lie, outside the island. It is also consistent with the fact that even in the hypothetical situation of a single economy on the island, it would still be one of the most open economies in the world. But openness in terms of trade, in a situation where either island production is dominated by foreign multinational branch plants (as in the Republic), or where the region is dominated by declining sectors (as in Northern Ireland), is not a position of strength.

EU regional comparisons that focus on detailed sectoral performance are revealing in that they show that inter-regional cooperation does not necessarily require extensive harmonisation of economic policies. Rather, cooperative economic activity thrives where policy differences and national preferences are fully understood and are made more transparent against the background of removal of non-tariff barriers to trade through the implementation of the single European market. Such findings suggest that mutually beneficial North–South as well as east–west cooperation could be built along similar lines if contentious political issues could be resolved. Indeed, the Belfast agreement, with its three 'strands', points exactly to this conclusion.

NOTES

1 We make a distinction between foreign ownership and external ownership. Many firms in Northern Ireland are branch plants of British firms, and are thus externally controlled; see *Inward investment in Northern Ireland* (Belfast: Northern Ireland Economic Council, 1992) [NIEC report 99].

2 See chapter 3, and R Vernon, 'International investment and international trade in the product cycle', *Quarterly journal of economics* 80:2 (1966), pp. 190–207 for further details. See also R Vernon, 'The product cycle hypothesis in a new international environment', *Oxford bulletin of economics and statistics* 41:4 (1979), pp. 255–67.

3 It could be held that a major cost to the Northern Ireland economy of the period of civil unrest since 1968 was the slowing down of the normal forces of sectoral restructuring and renewal that operated much more vigorously in Britain and in the Republic. Continuing claims that Northern Ireland be treated as a special case merely prolong the necessary changes.

4 C Pinson and V Tibrewala, *United Colours of Benetton* (Fontainebleau: INSEAD-CEDEP, 1996) [Case Study 597-008-1].

5 P McKiernan, *Strategies of growth: maturity, recovery and internationalization* (London: Routledge, 1992), pp. 115–21.

6 More recent data (up to the year 2004) show that the Republic's portfolio of manufac-

turing sectors has remained very stable, and that the trend decline in the North continued with no break or inflection point. We use the situation in 1996 to represent the facts of economic life that were known to the various participants involved in designing the institutions of the Belfast agreement.

7 Clothing and Textiles Working Group (CTWG), *Sectoral report* (Belfast: Department of Economic Development, 1998) [unpublished background paper to *Strategy 2010*].

8 CTWG, *Sectoral report* (1998), pp. 9–10.

9 CTWG, *Sectoral report* (1998), p. 21.

10 Note that 'external sales' from Northern Ireland are defined as sales outside Northern Ireland itself; 'exports', on the other hand, are sales outside the UK. The distinction is not just semantic. Exports from a region are measured carefully by statistical agencies in the national statistics. Regional external sales – in the above definition – are not.

11 CTWG, *Sectoral report* (1998), pp. 13–14.

12 At the time of the survey (late 1990s), hourly wage costs in textiles (measured in US dollars) for Northern Ireland were in the region of $13, slightly higher than in the Republic ($11) but considerably lower than Germany ($21). However, the figure for Turkey was $2.5, the Czech Republic $2.0, Morocco $1.9 and Bangladesh $0.4. Hourly wage costs in clothing tended to be lower than in textiles in Northern Ireland ($9) but were also relatively lower in a wide range of less developed countries, such as Romania, $1.0 (CTWG, Sectoral report (1998), pp. 71–2). The strong emergence of China, Vietnam and other Asian market economies in the early years of the twenty-first century has made the lack of northern competitiveness in this sector an even more serious challenge. In other words, there was a very serious competitiveness crisis at the time of the Belfast agreement, and things have deteriorated further since then.

13 The average rate of regional preferential assistance to all industry in 1996 was 5.0% of manufacturing GDP in Northern Ireland, but only 1.8% in Wales, 1.1% in Scotland and 0.1% in England.

14 *Strategy 2010: a report prepared by the Economic Development Strategy Review Steering Group* (Belfast: Department of Economic Development, 1999), pp. 92–4.

15 *Strategy 2010* (1999), p. 94.

16 K Harrigan and M Porter, 'End-game strategies for declining industries', in M Porter (ed.), *On competition* (Cambridge, MA: Harvard Business Review Books, 1998).

17 CTWG, *Sectoral report* (1998), pp. 27–42.

18 See Vernon, 'International investment' (1966); M Porter, *The competitive advantage of nations* (London: Macmillan, 1990); M Best, *The new competitive advantage* (Oxford: Oxford University Press, 2001); and for further consideration of the role of strategic business frameworks see chapter 3, above.

19 The sectoral terminology is that of the NACE system (general industrial classification of economic activities in the European Community).

20 NACE 3210 also includes valves and tubes, but these are likely to be insignificant throwbacks to the pre-transistor and pre-microchip age.

21 Further details are available in J Bradley, 'The computer sector in Irish manufacturing: past triumphs, present strains, future challenges', *Journal of the Statistical and Social Inquiry Society of Ireland* 31 (2001), pp. 25–70.

22 R MacSharry and P White, *The making of the Celtic tiger* (Cork: Mercier Press, 2000). Organisational changes in the wake of the 1992 review of Irish industrial policy split off the task of attracting inward foreign direct investment from the very different task of promoting development in locally owned manufacturing. The former is now handled by a more focused IDA, and the latter by a new agency, Enterprise Ireland.

23 R McLoughlin, 'The industrial development process: an overall view', *Administration* 20:1 (1972), pp. 27–36.

24 On a personal note, in the year 1986 the author – in the process of compiling a lecture for development ministers from less-developed countries explaining the Irish experi-

ence of foreign direct investment – had occasion to call the IDA research section in order to check out the extent to which IDA policy analysts had made use of Vernon's product life-cycle framework in selecting attractive sectors. To his surprise, he was told that nobody had ever heard of Raymond Vernon or of the product life-cycle! However, Vernon had been 'in the air', and may have been a subliminal guide!

25 MacSharry and White, *Celtic tiger* (2000), p. 231.

26 MacSharry and White, *Celtic tiger* (2000), p. 232.

27 MacSharry and White, *Celtic tiger* (2000), p. 274.

28 Detailed data for the electronics subsector of NACE 30–33 (electrical and optical equipment) is taken from the annual census of industrial production.

29 Once again, on a personal note, the author was coordinator of a meeting in Bucharest in 1997, with collaborators from a range of EU and former Communist states. At this meeting he noticed that the laptop computers, whose purchase had been funded by the European Commission for the teams working on the project, were all Dells, assembled in Limerick, and that their local (foreign-language) versions of Windows had been customised in Dublin!

30 For example, the packaging and printing industry – largely locally owned – supplies sophisticated products and services to the hardware and software sectors. Only some of the activities of the software sector fall within the classification of 'manufacturing', and are included in the census of industrial production. Further data are available from the IDA website: www.ida.ie.

31 MacSharry and White, *Celtic tiger* (2000), pp. 288–9.

32 *Enterprise 2010: a new strategy for the promotion of enterprise in Ireland in the 21st century* (Dublin: Forfás, 2000), p. 2.

33 MacSharry and White, *Celtic tiger* (2000), p. 313.

34 McLoughlin, 'Industrial development process' (1972), p. 30.

35 McLoughlin, 'Industrial development process' (1972), p. 36.

36 Porter, *Competitive advantage* (1990).

37 E O'Malley, 'The revival of Irish indigenous industry 1987–1997', *Quarterly economic commentary, April* (Dublin: Economic and Social Research Institute, 1998).

38 C Ó Gráda, *Ireland: a new economic history 1780–1939* (Oxford: Clarendon Press, 1994).

39 M Olson, *The rise and decline of nations: economic growth, stagflation and social rigidities* (New Haven: Yale University Press, 1982). What Olson discovered was that the behaviour of individuals and firms in stable, inward-looking societies leads to the formation of dense networks of collusive, cartelistic and lobbying organisations that make economies less efficient and dynamic.

10

Competitive sports: the territorial politics of Irish cycling

KEVIN HOWARD

INTRODUCTION

This chapter presents an account of the way in which territorial disputes associated with partition have had an impact on the organisation of a particular sporting activity, competitive cycling. As was shown in chapter 4, the partition of Ireland has had a varying impact on the associational life of the island, and indeed of the archipelago. There are numerous examples of the mismatch between the boundaries both of Ireland and of Britain, and of the territorial reach of their respective 'Irish' and 'British' civil society organisations. In Ireland, the key question relates to the distinction between the borders of the state of Ireland and the island of Ireland. Similarly, in the UK, the territorial parameters of British civil society organisations might be confined to the island of Great Britain, but, alternatively, they might include Northern Ireland and/or some, or all, of the adjacent crown dependencies (Jersey, Guernsey and the Isle of Man), or indeed encompass the entire archipelago.

The practical difficulties in answering these questions are acute for those competing in the international sporting arena. In short, what is the national territory? The answers are all the more intensely contested in the context of Northern Ireland. Is Northern Ireland part of the UK or of Ireland? Its status varies according to the sporting discipline and the type of sporting event. For example, Northern Ireland is part of Ireland for rugby, though not for soccer; it competes independently in the Commonwealth Games; but it is part of the UK for the Olympic Games. Moreover, as this chapter shows, Northern Ireland's status has also varied over time. In the field of competitive cycling, its location has been unsettled: it has been independent, it has been part of the UK, and by 2007 it has been incorporated into a nine-county Ulster governing body (Cycling Ulster) that is part of the all-island federation, Cycling Ireland.[1] This history has been marked by suspicion, misunderstanding and conflict, but finally agreement was reached on a compromise that combines all-island practicalities of scale with the recognition and accommodation of opposing identities. In this way, competitive cycling's territorial organisation mirrors at the micro-level the contested legacy of political partition.

The chapter begins by locating cycling within the wider context of the territorial politics of sport in Ireland. The second section outlines the complex evolution of early divisions in competitive cycling and their relationship to political divisions. The third section describes the impact of the sport's international governing body's decision to recognise one governing body for the island of Ireland and is followed by a section detailing a unionist campaign to reverse this policy. The penultimate section brings the story up to date by assessing the impact of the new political context (post the Good Friday agreement) on cycling divisions and the eventual resolution of the issue in December 2006. The conclusion briefly highlights the practical difficulties involved for the organisation of cycling in a situation where the territorial boundaries of Great Britain and Ireland are defined as variable and problematical.

SPORT AND TERRITORY

Territorial disputes about cycling should be understood in the context of the territorial politics of Irish sport generally. The bulk of the literature on this topic deals with three main sporting activities and their associated organisations: Gaelic games with the all-Ireland Gaelic Athletic Association; soccer with the twenty-six-county Football Association of Ireland and the six-county Irish Football Association; and rugby with the all-island Irish Rugby Football Union. Explicitly or otherwise, each of these relies on a particular territorial conceptualisation:

- Gaelic games and the Gaelic Athletic Association's organisational structure can be understood as a form of ***boundary-denying*** thirty-two-county nationalism.
- Soccer, whether in its southern (Football Association of Ireland) or northern (Irish Football Association) guise, can be understood as expressing forms of ***boundary-reinforcing*** twenty-six-county and six-county nationalism.
- Rugby can be understood as a form of ***boundary-transcending,*** all-island trans-nationalism.

Boundary-denying nationalism is characterised by regarding partition as an illegitimate and ultimately unsustainable imposition; it is paradigmatically irredentist and it ignores rather than accommodates ethnic difference. Boundary-reinforcing nationalism also ignores rather than accommodates ethnic difference; it is the inward-facing, insular nationalism characteristic of state consolidation. Boundary-transcending nationalism, on the other hand, acknowledges and seeks to accommodate difference within an overall national framework; it is the nationalism characteristic of federations and multi-ethnic states in which differences are both enduring and legitimated. These are ideal types, and they apply imperfectly to the dynamics of territorial politics of cycling analysed below. Nevertheless, the framework is useful and its parallels with the wider political dynamic on the island are clear. The analysis presented here shows the conflictual process in the move over time from a boundary-denying, through a boundary-reinforcing, to a boundary-transcending style of territorial organisation. In this way it makes a valuable and novel addition to the existing literature that deals specifically with territorial politics and sport in Ireland and, more generally, with the impact of partition on associational life on the island of Ireland.

Although it may lack the high profile of Gaelic football, soccer or rugby, competitive cycling offers important evidence of the ubiquity of the territorial issue. The international profile of Irish cycling was at it highest during the period when its territorial organisation in Ireland was most bitterly disputed. Any discussion of Irish cycling has to at least mention the two towering figures of Irish cycling in the 1980s and 1990s, Stephen Roche and Sean Kelly, who raised the international profile of Irish cycling, or at least of cyclists from Ireland. The most important manifestation of this international prestige was in 1998, when the *Tour de France* (the world's largest annual sporting event) began in Dublin and spent three days racing through Ireland; it did not cross the border. Similarly, the Nissan Classic, a five-day road race, an integral part of the high-profile professional calendar, stayed solely within the state of Ireland.

In looking at the case of competitive cycling in Ireland, we return once more to John Whyte's preliminary assessment of the impact of partition on associational life already discussed in chapter 4.[2] As we saw in that chapter, Whyte highlighted the Byzantine complexity of the organisation of sport on the island of Ireland. In attempting to give some shape to this complexity, he hypothesised that sporting bodies founded on an all-island basis have generally remained that way. Moreover, this was even more likely if the participant base of these sports was 'middle class' – his primary example being rugby. On the other hand, Whyte categorised cycling as a 'proletarian' sport. He suggested that proletarian sports were less likely to be organised on an all-Ireland basis, and he identified cycling as being organised separately on either side of the border. This was indeed true at the time of Whyte's study, which drew on databases from the early 1970s, but only partially so. As can be seen from Table 10.1, the organisation of Irish cycling is more complicated than the initial data suggested. At the time when Whyte was writing there were three organisations: one all-Ireland body, one twenty-six-county body, and a third, six-county body; it was the two boundary-reinforcing organisations that figured in Whyte's research. The third, the boundary-ignoring National Cycling Association, established in 1932, did not figure in his original, preliminary overview. The story of how these three bodies contested competitive cycling's jurisdiction tells us much about the changing significance of the Irish border both for cycling and for the organisation of sport in general on the island of Ireland.

Table 10.1. Territorial structure of organised competitive cycling in Great Britain and Ireland, 1932–2007

Cycling organisation	Dates	Territorial reach	UCI sanctioned
National Cycling Association (NCA)	1932–88	all-Ireland	no
Irish Cycling Federation (ICF)	1954–88	26 counties	yes
Northern Ireland Cycling Federation (NICF)	1949–84 1984–2007	6 counties	yes no
Federation of Irish Cyclists (FIC)	1988–2000	all-Ireland	yes
Cycling Ireland (CI)	2000–	all-Ireland	yes
Ulster Cycling Federation (UCF)	1988–2000	9 Ulster counties	yes
Cycling Ulster (CU)	2000–	9 Ulster counties	yes
British Cycling Federation (BCF)	1959–95	Great Britain	yes
	1995–2000	United Kingdom	no
	2000–	Great Britain	yes

Note: the British Cycling Federation also has jurisdiction over organised competitive cycling in three adjacent crown dependencies (Jersey, Guernsey and the Isle of Man), which are neither part of Great Britain nor of the United Kingdom, but are nevertheless described as 'British'.

COMPETITIVE CYCLING AND EARLY DIVISIONS

In the middle of the twentieth century, cycling's international governing body, the Union Cycliste International (UCI), recognised two separate 'national' organisations in Ireland, each operating exclusively on its own side of the border: the Northern Ireland Cycling Federation (NICF, founded in 1949) and the Irish Cycling Federation (ICF, founded in 1954). Alongside these, however, there co-existed the National Cycling Association (NCA, founded in 1932), which regarded the island of Ireland as its territory. The UCI deemed the Irish–UK border as the proper boundary for the sport's two national governing bodies and refused to recognise the boundary-ignoring NCA. Hence, the NCA could not compete in UCI-sanctioned events (such as the amateur Olympic Games and the professional world championships). Rather inconsistently, the UCI allowed that for international events the 'Ireland' team could be drawn from both the twenty-six-county ICF and the six-county NICF.

In the early 1950s, in response to its international isolation, the NCA organised the Rás Tailteann, an island-wide stage race that for the first twenty years of its existence was used explicitly to promote an all-Ireland nationalist agenda. The nationalist symbolism surrounding this race was consciously promoted. The very name served to associate the race, its organisers and participants, with the Tailteann Games, a form of pre-Christian, 'Celtic Olympics'.[3] Class as well as an urban–rural dimension characterised the differences between the NCA and the ICF. The NCA was strong in the countryside and regarded the Dublin-based, internationally orientated ICF as pro-British and as having sold out on core nationalist principles. Tom Daly quotes Joe Christle, one of the NCA's leading figures and ideologues, as saying that 'in the field of sport we could never be denied complete independence. No doubt, we could lose certain privileges by maintaining that independence, but we prefer national honour to international dishonour.'[4]

In Rome in August 1955, in pursuit of 'national honour', four members of the NCA disrupted the start of the men's road race at the UCI's world cycling championships. Italian police arrested four NCA members after a scuffle had broken out at the start line.[5] The animosity evident in Rome in 1955 reached its nadir nearly two decades later at the 1972 Munich Olympics. The northerner Noel Taggart (an NICF-affiliated rider) was riding for the Ireland Olympic team and was pulled from his bike by the NCA-affiliated Kerryman John Mangan who, incredibly, had breached whatever security arrangements were in place and infiltrated cycling's blue-ribbon Olympic event, the men's road race. Far from bringing national honour, the international outcry at this politically motivated disruption to a sporting event, coming within a few days of the murder of Israeli athletes by Palestinian paramilitaries at the same Olympics, was regarded in Ireland as a national disgrace.

The international opprobrium associated with the Olympic incident was such that it bolstered those within the NCA who were seeking to repair the rift in Irish cycling. While initially attitudes within the NICF and ICF hardened against the NCA, it was clear that some kind of *rapprochement* was needed. Under the auspices of the Sports Council for Northern Ireland, a tripartite agreement between the three organisations was reached in 1978. It was formalised at a special conference in Dublin on 11 November 1979, in the presence of the UCI's secretary-general. Under the agreement, each association committed itself to recognise the other associations' affiliated members for the purposes of domestic competition in Ireland, while at the international level 'one unified team shall participate in the world championships'. Although the Irish Tripartite Cycling Commission monitored this agreement, it was accepted that 'each of the [national] bodies will preserve its sovereignty and its independence'. The period in which the national governing bodies of cycling worked together under the umbrella of the tripartite commission (1979–84) is regarded as a kind of golden age of associational and organisational harmony. The acrimony between the NCA and ICF had declined, and the northerners, organised into the NICF and the NCA's Ulster region, cooperated under the tripartite committee's umbrella.

ONE GOVERNING BODY, ONE COUNTRY?

For the UCI the relative autonomy of the tripartite committee's constituent entities was, in the long term, untenable. In 1984 the UCI declared that henceforth it would only recognise 'one governing body per country'. It was to be through this national governing body that internationally approved licences providing access to international events would be issued. However, the UCI ruled that it was the island of Ireland that constituted one country, which by definition required an all-island organisation; this was to be a federated organisation made up from a federation of the three hitherto autonomous entities – with one president. The tripartite commission that had coordinated the sport for the previous five years was to be wound up, and replaced by a ten-member board, to oversee the transition to the new all-island organisation. As far as the international governing body was concerned this new organisation would be the recognised authority for the governance of cycling on the island of Ireland. As for the NICF, it was proposed that it would merge with the Ulster Council, the northern region of the NCA, thus becoming the Ulster Cycling Federation, the nine-county northern component of the proposed all-island federation. In other words, after nearly forty years of independent existence the governing body for cycling in Northern Ireland was being asked to disappear into an Ulster-based entity governed ultimately from Dublin. For the purposes of organising competitive cycling it was proposed that Northern Ireland's boundary would disappear.

The proposal to amalgamate the Ulster Council of the old NCA with the NICF was put to the NICF's annual general meeting in November 1987. This proved to be a tumultuous and divisive meeting. On the one hand, a majority of NICF members (fifty-six delegates out of eighty-five) were willing to follow the same logic as their southern counterparts forty years before, when the ICF had been set up to comply with the edicts of the world governing body, thereby ensuring the sanctioning of racing events and access to racing licences needed for participation in domestic and international competition. This time, however, rather than following the UCI's earlier prescription that the border had to be observed, Ireland's cyclists were required to organise into a single, boundary-transcending all-island body. Key figures in the NICF, particularly from the North Down club, initiated a High Court action to prevent this, on the grounds that the two-thirds majority required by the organisation's constitution had not been achieved. The High Court accepted this argument, granted an injunction, and suggested that the vote be re-taken. The NICF reconvened the meeting in February 1988, when a slightly larger majority rejected the motion to amalgamate with the Ulster Council (fifty-five for, twenty-nine against, one abstention) – still falling short of the constitutionally required two-thirds majority. So, the proposal to merge was defeated because of this constitutional provision, even though a majority of NICF members were in favour of being subsumed within the federation.

Nevertheless, voting with their feet, clubs withdrew unilaterally from the NICF and in March 1988 they joined the clubs of the NCA's northern region to create the Ulster Cycling Federation, which then affiliated with the all-island body. Later that year, in Seoul, cycling's world governing authority endorsed the all-island Federation of Irish Cyclists (FIC) as the governing body for cycling in the whole island of Ireland. The statutory-based Sports Council for Northern Ireland followed suit, withdrawing its recognition of the NICF and affirming that in future any grant aid would go to the nine-county Ulster Cycling Federation, not the six-county NICF. However, rather inconsistently, the Northern Ireland Commonwealth

Games Council continued to endorse the NICF as the province's official governing body. So, at the end of 1988, two officially recognised entities governed cycling in Northern Ireland. For the purposes of the Commonwealth Games it was the six-county NICF; for all other international purposes it was the Ulster Cycling Federation, the nine-county, regional body of the all-island federation.

MOBILISING UNIONISM

It is clear that the primary catalyst for the subsequent territorial dispute in Irish cycling was the international governing body's ruling regarding 'one national governing body per country'. The formation of the all-island FIC necessitated the disappearance of the all-Ireland NCA. However, suspicion that the FIC was merely the irredentist NCA under another name was given some credence in the run-up to the NICF's 1987 annual general meeting by the comments in the *Irish Times* by one former NCA official to the effect that 'the promotion of [all-Ireland] nationalism was more important than the promotion of cycling'.[6] In other words, the disappearance of the stalwart NCA was acceptable if it meant international recognition for an alternative, albeit less 'green', thirty-two-county entity.

The symbolism of an internationally endorsed all-island body subsuming a Northern Ireland-based organisation was obvious, and the NICF sought to tap deep-rooted unionist fears of nationalist encroachment. In January 1989, the NICF wrote to all of Northern Ireland's twenty-six district councils asking for their assistance in stemming 'the progress of the 32-County Body'; it conveyed to unionist councillors its view that the newly formed nine-county Ulster Cycling Federation was:

> In fact a new name for the Ulster Council of the National Cycling Association, a body which from 1933 had been expelled from International Recognition because of its Nationalistic claim on both parts of Ireland ... the NCA ... has never accepted the 6 County border, of British Northern Ireland ... The Dublin based Federation of Irish Cyclists is ... a new name for the National Cycling Association and The Ulster Cycling Federation its 9 County Ulster Council.[7]

The councils' responses fall into three categories: one, outright support of the NICF; two, acknowledgement but no action; and three, outright rejection. Only one local authority, Moyle Borough Council, took the third option. Craigavon fudged the issue, passing it on to the Sports Council of Northern Ireland. The majority of local authorities (nineteen) took the second option, mainly on the grounds that it was not their policy to adopt resolutions agreed by other local authorities. However, five were unequivocal in their support for the NICF. Significantly, these included the largest and most important local authority, Belfast City Council.[8] Unionists on Belfast City Council argued that 'it would be ridiculous for a Unionist controlled council like our own to sit down and let this discrimination continue against an organisation whose basic principles are the same as our own'.

The NICF also sought to mobilise unionist sentiment amongst members of the British Cycling Federation (BCF). The UCI affirmed that Northern Ireland's cyclists could as individuals obtain racing licences through the British body, though fundamentally it continued to insist that the FIC remained the solely national governing body for the island of Ireland. But the FIC interpreted this concession as a direct challenge to its sovereignty. It suspected that the British Cycling Federation was covertly attempting to extend its jurisdiction: 'Members of the FIC board have been aware for some time now of your ambition to obtain control of the Northern part of our area of jurisdiction. It would appear now that you have realised that ambition.'[9] The British Federation's response to this charge is reminiscent of the seminal declaration that Britain had 'no selfish strategic or economic interests' in Northern Ireland:

> Nobody in the BCF has any ambition to expand into Northern Ireland if the interests of the riders are properly catered for by another organisation or organisations ... The formation of the single [all-island] Federation of Irish Cyclists has obviously not had universal acceptance. This is a pity, but not surprising in the political context ... I do not believe that the British Cycling Federation should refuse the requests for licences from British nationals whether they happen to live in Belfast, Bristol, or Birmingham. That said ... the BCF has no objection to riders opting to have an FIC licence ... I do not believe that we can abdicate our responsibility as a national organisation, although ... [someone in our organisation] considers that our being 'kneecapped' is a possibility ... How tragic ... We are talking about sport aren't we? ... many of my colleagues in the BCF will consider we are in a 'No Win' situation.[10]

The problem, as the British Cycling Federation saw it, was that the international governing body had, initially, shown a remarkable lack of political sensitivity in recognising the FIC as the sole governing authority. By so doing it had:

> ... ignored a major dispute on national borders that has remained unsolved ... the current unhappy situation with regard to cycle sport in Northern Ireland proved that the border dispute can't be ignored ... we have no ambitions in Northern Ireland other than a service for British riders who do not wish to join an organisation they (the riders) consider politically unacceptable ... We would, however, far rather you all came to an agreement.[11]

The tone of the British federation's observations mirrors the hegemonic self-understanding of the British in relation to the obdurate and violent Irish. The British are 'honest brokers' who in the absence of Irish ability or willingness to sort out their own mess are honour-bound to support those people in Ireland who regard themselves as British. For the FIC the matter was simple: the internationally recognised sovereignty of an all-island federation (which contained the majority of Northern Ireland's cyclists from both traditions) was being challenged by the separatist NICF and was doing so with British backing, despite British claims to be merely arbitrators.

In the event, the FIC also went some way in accepting this compromise, temporarily lifting its ban against the participation of NICF teams and riders with British licences for the coming (1991) racing season in Ireland. This was of significance given that 1991 was the UN-designated year of sport; the concession meant that NICF individuals could participate in the 1991 Northern Ireland Milk Race, a prestigious UCI-sanctioned six-day stage race sponsored by the British Dairy Council. For the NICF, however, this 'temporary concession' meant little. It once again made representations to Northern Ireland's twenty-six local authorities, this time asking them not to support the race because of what it regarded as the ongoing discrimination against its riders on the part of the Dublin-based body. Larne Council was the first to respond, announcing that it was withdrawing its (admittedly modest £500) financial support for the Milk Race. The DUP councillor Bobby McKee accused the FIC of seeking to enforce the Irish Republic's constitutional claim to Northern Ireland in the cycling world; they should be told to 'get on their bikes'.[12]

However, as far as the NICF was concerned, its best protection from being subsumed in the all-island body would be if it was incorporated into the British Cycling Federation. In other words, it would welcome an outcome in which the British Federation, whether with international backing or unilaterally, extended its jurisdiction to include Northern Ireland. At the British Cycling Federation's annual general meeting in December 1991, Scottish supporters of the NICF reworked notions of the 'innate' difference between Northern Ireland and the South, and the natural affinity of the former to Great Britain. However, the motion to extend the BCF's jurisdiction was again defeated – but this time by only one vote.[13] From the perspective of the NICF the narrowness of the vote vindicated their view that there was a groundswell of support within the British organisation that would see the NICF incorporated into a UK-wide entity sooner rather than later. These hopes were deflated when a year later the British Federation once again formally recognised the FIC as the sole governing body on the island of Ireland. So, by 1993, the UCI, the British Cycling Federation and the Northern Ireland Sports Council (effectively, an arm of the government) all recognised the authority of the all-island FIC.

The NICF was nothing if not determined. Through 1994 it continued to lobby both the UCI and the British Cycling Federation. The concession that individual NICF members could take out British racing licences was used as a kind of 'no taxation without representation' argument, or, more accurately, an argument that taxation should entitle representation. NICF members contributed to the British Federation's coffers; therefore they should be entitled to a voice in the BCF's deliberations. Their doggedness paid off. At the British Cycling Federation's annual general meeting in December 1995, the North London and East Midlands divisions put forward two proposals to the effect that the federation grant the NICF the same status as that enjoyed by the Scottish Cyclists' Union and the Welsh Cycling Union, and, crucially, that the Federation amend the constitutional definition of its jurisdiction by replacing the words 'Great Britain' with the words 'United Kingdom'. Quite disingenuously, an accompanying note claimed that the NICF was the cycling body affiliated to the Northern Ireland Sports Council, and stated that any agreement between the British federation and the NICF would not affect any existing agreements between the former and the FIC. Perhaps because of this inaccurate depiction of the context and the misleading assessment of the impact of the proposed changes, the proposals were carried. The BCF amended its constitution, unilaterally re-casting its territorial jurisdiction to include Northern Ireland. From the perspective of the NICF, this expansion was regarded as a triumph; it had seen off the all-island FIC and its continental ally, the UCI.

THE GOOD FRIDAY AGREEMENT: A NEW CONTEXT

This change of position by the British Cycling Federation turned out to be a miscalculation, and the FIC and the UCI reacted vigorously. By 1998 the BCF had decided to retrench once again to the island of Great Britain and the crown dependencies. But the NICF's response to this threat pushed this relatively minor dispute over the territorial jurisdiction of a sporting activity to the centre of the political stage. Two motions were proposed for the British Cycling Federation's 1998 annual general meeting: to remove the expression 'United Kingdom' from the constitution and replace it with 'Great Britain', and to withdraw the voting and speaking rights of the NICF. However, 1998 was also the year of the Good Friday agreement. The *Belfast Telegraph* drew a contrast between the agreement's guarantee that 'Northern Ireland should remain part of the UK as long as that is the will of the people' and the British cycling body's proposed abandonment of the NICF. The NICF managed to secure a cross-party motion in the House of Commons signed by twenty MPs supporting the NICF's entitlement to remain part of the British cycling organisation, and referring to the British Olympic Committee's charter, which defines Great Britain as the United Kingdom of Great Britain and Northern Ireland. More importantly, Northern Ireland's newly announced First Minister-designate, David Trimble, personally intervened, writing both to the British Cycling Federation and the UCI to state that for him 'it is inconceivable that British citizens in Northern Ireland, who belong to the Northern Ireland Cycling Federation and who wish to be affiliated to their British parent body, would be prevented from doing so'.[14] In response to this overt political pressure the retrenchment motions were withdrawn.

For the FIC, Trimble's intervention was seen as possibly perpetuating the divisions within Irish cycling which, by its own lights, it had done so much to heal. The FIC wrote to Trimble outlining effectively the anti-democratic nature of the NICF's campaign.

> The Ulster Cycling Federation ... has in excess of double the membership of the NICF. The members of the UCF are from both sides of the religious and political divide in Northern Ireland and have no problem whatsoever in being part of an all Ireland Federation ... The emergence of the FIC contributed a great deal to the breaking down of political and religious hatred within cycling, both in Northern Ireland and in the Republic. It is very unfair to the vast majority of cyclists in this Island, that a small number of cyclists who would appear to have more of a political, than a cycling agenda

> can cause so much upset to the smooth running and development of cycling in Ireland ... you should also listen to representatives of the majority of cyclists in Northern Ireland and hear their views, bearing in mind that it is very much a multi political and multi racial group.[15]

The UCI's response to such a high-profile intervention on the part of the Nobel-prize winning First Minister-designate was to seek a meeting to set out the UCI's and the FIC's position. The BCF urged Trimble to agree, while reiterating its own position that individual NICF members could and would continue to be able to avail themselves of federation membership.

> The only point at issue, is whether the NICF should itself be permitted to ... contravene the constitution of the UCI which permits only one governing body per territory. For Northern Ireland, and for the Republic of Ireland, the UCI recognises the Federation of Irish Cyclists ... an All-Ireland body that draws its membership from all sections of the community in both Northern Ireland and the Irish Republic ... I can assure you that neither I, nor the Executive Board, nor the National Council of the BCF wish to do anything whatsoever that might permit this matter to affect the wonderful progress that has been made in bringing the Peace Process so far ... Please note that I am also seeking some guidance on this matter from the UK Sports Council, who are, as you know effectively our link to the Government.[16]

The First Minister agreed to meet the UCI's president and its chief legal adviser. The meeting took place in late January 1999 and was also attended by two representatives of the NICF. According to the UCI's report of the meeting, the First Minister-designate began by questioning the validity of the world governing body's decision in 1988 to recognise the FIC as the 'one governing body' for Ireland. We recall the dispute over the NICF vote on whether or not to amalgamate with the NCA's Ulster Council to form the Ulster region of the FIC. At best, the interpretations of that decision-making process are contested. Trimble, however, accepted the NICF interpretation that the formation of the FIC was the irredentist NCA in another guise. The UCI, in this view, had endorsed this organisation and penalised those cyclists in Northern Ireland – cyclists who sought to resist being subsumed in an Irish nationalist entity. The UCI was left in no doubt as to how sensitive Unionists were in relation to perceived nationalist encroachment. The Good Friday agreement from the Unionist perspective had 'copper-fastened' partition. To facilitate an all-island entity in incorporating a Northern Ireland organisation that wanted to remain British flew in the face of what Unionists had achieved in the agreement:

> [The First Minister's] basic approach was that Northern Ireland is part of the United Kingdom and this has been recognized by the Irish Republic in the Good Friday agreement. The Irish Republic has abandoned its claim (written down in the constitution) on Northern Ireland. In conformity with that agreement, FIC and NICF should be on the same basis in Northern Ireland.[17]

The meeting concluded with the First Minister-designate's assistant suggesting that some kind of resolution using the Good Friday agreement as the template could be worked out. In response, the UCI president suggested that the NICF could take the FIC to court and let the judges decide jurisdiction one way or the other, indicating perhaps that the UCI had no effective solution to offer.

The intervention of the First Minister-designate on behalf of the NICF represents a high-water mark of its political influence. While the NICF continued to have the backing of unionist and unionist-minded MPs in the House of Commons, the suspension of the Assembly from October 2002 weakened its political support. That same year, the UCI's congress passed another resolution reaffirming the all-island jurisdiction of the FIC (in 2000 the FIC was renamed Cycling Ireland) and calling on the British Cycling Federation to reverse its 1995 decision to unilaterally incorporate Northern Ireland. It was at this point that the pressure from the UCI on the British federation finally told. In what was one of its most tempestuous annual general meetings, in December 2002 it agreed to amend its constitution once again, to redefine its territorial parameters as Great Britain and the crown dependencies.

While the decision of the BCF to retrench healed the rift between the British and Irish national governing bodies, and reconciled the former with the UCI, it meant the effective abandonment of the NICF. Confirmation, for the purposes of cycling, that Ireland means the island of Ireland and Britain means Great Britain and the crown dependencies was formally agreed in September 2004 under the UCI's auspices:

> Cycling Ireland (CI) is the internationally recognised National Cycling Federation for the island of Ireland. The British Cycling Federation (BCF) undertakes that it will not seek to extend the area of its own control into the recognised territory of Cycling Ireland (CI) ... The BCF may issue membership and licences to individual

> British citizens resident in Northern Ireland provided such persons do not wish to take out a CI membership and/or licence. However, only one licence may be held at any one time.[18]

This accommodation of British identity is not quite as expansive as that in Article 1 (vi) of the Good Friday agreement, which allows people in Northern Ireland 'to identify themselves and be accepted as Irish or British, or both, as they may so choose'. On the other hand, the Good Friday agreement signals the confirmation of British territorial sovereignty, with built-in safeguards for Irish identifiers. The British–Irish agreement in cycling represents a confirmation of Irish sovereignty.

For the best part of the next two years, the NICF studiously ignored Cycling Ireland's existence and that of its regional body, the nine-county Cycling Ulster. A visitor to the NICF's website was given no indication that the organisation resided on an island in which cycling is actually governed by a different and much larger all-island federation. Behind the scenes, however, the NICF's support base, its membership, was crumbling, even within its most stalwart clubs, such as those in North Down and Ballymena. The context of Northern Ireland had of course changed dramatically since the mid-1990s, when the BCF had responded to NICF pressure and unilaterally extended its jurisdiction. Finally, in December 2006, prompted by Ballymena Road Club's decision to join the FIC from January 2007, the NICF accepted the inevitable. Following representations from Cycling Ulster, it opened negotiations on amalgamation; on 14 December 2006 its member clubs voted twenty-nine to two in favour of joining the all-island body.[19]

The contrasting interpretations of this event are revealing. On the one hand, Cycling Ulster was entirely upbeat and stressed how this presented no challenge to political identities: 'This is an historic occasion and will see the Ulster region become the strongest of the four provincial federations … members will still be able to opt for their preferred nationality code and thus no-one's identity is compromised.'[20] By contrast, the NICF's tone was fatalistic rather than enthusiastic in explaining why amalgamation with the Ulster Cycling Federation was now acceptable nearly twenty years after it was first proposed. As its chairman put it:

> As we had become increasingly marginalised, we thought it would be an opportune time to enter into talks. Our position was weakened a couple of years ago when the UCI instructed British Cycling to remove 'UK' from its constitution … the NICF Executive, though not all of them, thought it best to enter into [amalgamation] negotiations

> while there was still something left to offer. The deal is the best we could come up with, but in reality we are running out of funds and haemorrhaging individual members and clubs at an unsustainable rate.[21]

In contrast to the earlier agreement of December 2004, any cyclist on the island of Ireland who wants a racing licence has to have one issued by the FIC. The FIC will continue to organise racing events in Northern Ireland, but from 1 January 2007 the choice of either a British or Irish licence for individual cyclists was removed. The only concession granted was that the nationality criterion was relaxed to allow cyclists to declare as Irish or British. The NICF became effectively a member of the FIC. Poignantly, and tellingly, there was no mention on the BCF's website of the *de facto* demise of the Northern Ireland Cycling Federation.[22]

CONCLUSION

The example of cycling shows the relevance of John Whyte's warning of the ease with which political implications can be read into what appears at first sight to be an entirely apolitical activity. This case study shows how the territorial reorganisation of cycling was interpreted as boundary-ignoring thirty-two-county irredentism in disguise. From the British Federation's perspective, this was largely the result of the world governing body's insensitivity to the legacy of partition. But it was the British governing body's own resistance to the UCI's ruling concerning 'one country, one governing body' that further raised the political stakes. The demand by the UCI that the British body accede to its request was treated as if Northern Ireland was being ejected from its natural home and being forced into the NCA in disguise. The intervention of Northern Ireland's first ever First Minister-designate was a high-water mark in the politicisation of this dispute. It is an intriguing question as to how effective the NICF's political support would have been if the northern Assembly had not been suspended.

What emerges clearly from any assessment of the legacy of partition is that the boundaries of Ireland and of Britain are ambiguous. As we have seen, this ambiguity presents practical difficulties in clarifying what constitutes a national organisation in the British–Irish context. Moreover, the way in which territorial entities are structured or named, even those concerned with the seemingly most innocuous of activities, can be laden with political resonance. The tangled story of how competitive cycling has been organised on the island of Ireland combines both dimensions. For practical reasons, the lack of international endorsement, cyclists in the Republic organised into a boundary-reinforcing twenty-six-county entity. It was the UCI's insistence on an all-island, boundary-transcending, governing body that led to the amalgamation of the twenty-six-county ICF, the all-Ireland NCA and a majority of clubs from the six-county NICF; pragmatism reigned.

However, as we have seen, the suspicion that all-island bodies are merely guises for Irish irredentism can be easily aroused. Local unionist politicians became involved in a dispute over an association's structure, name and procedures, recasting it as emblematic of British resistance to Irish irredentism. Yet, as Whyte argued, people can participate in all-island or all-archipelago associational life and keep their politics separate. This raises interesting questions as to the extent, if any, to which all-island integration in one domain influences the acceptance of all-island structures in others. The *de facto* demise of the NICF in 2007 suggests that the organisation of associational life on an all-island basis that respects the identities of its constituent members need have no political resonance at all. Ireland the island is the country that can represent people from all ethnic backgrounds and none.

NOTES

1 I wish to express my thanks to Jack Watson, of Bangor, Co. Down, formerly of the Northern Ireland Cycling Federation and currently Honorary Secretary of cycling's all-island governing body Cycling Ireland (until 2000, known as the Federation of Irish Cyclists) for allowing me access to his archive of material upon which this chapter is largely based. This is referred to in the notes below as the 'Watson archive'.

2 J H Whyte, 'The permeability of the United Kingdom–Irish border: a preliminary reconnaissance', *Administration* 31:3 (1983), pp. 300–15.

3 T Daly, *The Rás* (Cork: Collins, 2003) p. 15. The fledgling Irish state in the 1920s engaged in a similar project of legitimacy building through association with the ancient version of the games by staging an event that combined sporting and cultural activities and calling it the Tailteann Games.

4 Daly, *The Rás* (2003), p. 20.

5 These included Mick Christle, the brother of the above-mentioned Joe. The Italian police detained Mick Christle for five days; he was then released, tried in his absence and sentenced to six months' imprisonment. Ten years later, a fine notice for £14 from the Italian authorities arrived at Christle's home in Drimnagh, Dublin. He chose not to pay!

6 E Cregan, *Irish Times*, 27 Oct. 1987.

7 I Hendry, Northern Ireland Cycling Federation, to Unionist Councils 9 January 1989 (Watson archive).

8 The other four were Ballymena, North Down, Larne and Antrim Borough Councils.

9 J Watson, FIC, to B Cookson, BCF, 20 July 1990 (Watson archive).

10 B Cookson, BCF ,to J Watson, BCF, 9 Oct. 1990 (Watson archive).

11 Brian Cookson, BCF, to J Watson, FIC, 30 Oct. 1990 (Watson archive).

12 *Larne Times*, 11 Jan. 1991; *Larne Guardian*, 16 Jan. 1991. The issue of licences was partly resolved in March 1991 at a meeting in Banbridge between FIC and NICF officials. The sentiments of the Good Friday Agreement were foreshadowed in the concession that 'cyclists in Northern Ireland have a choice of an FIC or a BCF licence or both', FIC press release 3 Mar. 1991 (the press release is part of the Watson archive).

13 *Cycling Weekly*, 21–28 Dec. 1991.

14 First Minister-designate to Brian Cookson, British Cycling Federation, and Heini Verbruggen, UCI, 30 October 1998 (Watson archive). There is perhaps an element of hyperbole in all this given that the British Cycling Federation had been the NICF's 'parent body' for a mere three years. David Trimble continued to be First Minister-designate until December 1999, when he assumed office on completion of an all-party deal.

15 J Watson, FIC, to First Minister-designate, 24 Nov. 1998 (Watson archive).

16 B Cookson, BCF, to First Minister-designate, 12 Nov. 1998 (Watson archive). However, the UK Sports Council did not want to get further involved. As far as it was concerned the question of which national governing body had jurisdiction in Ireland was a matter for the UCI.

17 H Verbruggen, UCI, to P McQuaid, FIC, and J Hendry, BCF, 1 Feb. 1999 (Watson archive).

18 Agreement between Cycling Ireland and British Cycling Federation, www.cyclingireland.ie/html/documents/Agreement [accessed 20-06-2005].

19 'NICF Members vote for change', www.nicycling.homestead.com [accessed 20-12-2006].

20 'NICF Vote for Change', www.cyclingulster.com/index [accessed 20-12-2006].

21 *Ballymena Times*, 13 Dec. 2006.

22 However, the leading UK cycling publication *Cycling Weekly* quoted a response from the BCF President to the news of the amalgamation: 'I'm delighted that there seem to have been positive developments ... I'm sure British Cycling will want to be supportive, in the best interests of our sport'; BCF President in *Cycling Weekly* 20 December 2006 available online at www.cyclingweekly.co.uk/news/NICF_switch_ [accessed 21-12-2006].

11

Public policy cooperation: the 'common chapter' – shadow or substance?

EOIN MAGENNIS

INTRODUCTION

Public policy cooperation has been an element in North–South relationships dating back at least to the mid-1960s, with plans for joint tourism promotion and energy supply cooperation.[1] However, while practical cooperation in some areas of public policy has been achieved, this has often proved to be fragmentary, of limited duration and poorly resourced. Different methods have been used to try to achieve the goal of ongoing public policy cooperation. Intergovernmental agenda-setting, as in the period of the Anglo-Irish agreement or, more recently, in the work of the British–Irish Intergovernmental Conference, is one method. Establishing North–South institutions with budget lines and legislative remits has been another. A third way has been the 'common chapter' which, as will be shown below, incorporates many elements of the first two methods. This chapter will seek to assess how successful this 'common chapter' has been since 2000, and asks whether it is the substance of public policy cooperation or its shadow.

The 'common chapter' takes its name from the fact that, since 1994, the respective development plans in Northern Ireland and the Republic of Ireland for EU structural funds have included a common chapter or agreed text. This has been intended to act as a strategic statement or framework for agreed cooperation, particularly in the economic development field. As the 2007–13 structural fund plans will repeat the exercise it is timely to ask whether the common chapter is contributing at all to closer North–South cooperation or economic integration.[2] This chapter begins by describing the origins of the 'common chapter', and this is followed by a second section on its connections with wider economic cooperation. The third section details how the 'common chapter' has been operating in the period up to 2003 (the latest year for data). The penultimate section considers the future prospects for the 'common chapter' in structural fund plans for 2007–13, and this is followed by a concluding assessment of this element of North–South cooperation.

ORIGIN OF THE 2000–6 'COMMON CHAPTER'

The agreed text which makes up the 'common chapter' is described as a 'strategic framework' for cooperation.[3] In the jargon of the public sector, this is described as a strategy which will inform both the priorities and process for cooperation.[4] The 1994–9 common chapter is usually referred to as aspirational, something that the 2000–6 framework was meant to build upon and extend. In the 1994–9 period, transport, tourism and energy were stressed as key areas for cooperation, following the priorities laid down in the Interreg II programme in respect of the two jurisdictions. However, progress in joint planning or implementation of projects was painfully slow, except at the level of local authorities and other organisations in the border region. For 2000–6 cooperation was seen as being in three directions: between Northern Ireland and the southern border counties (or along the border corridor); North–South within the island; and east–west between the island of Ireland, Great Britain and Europe. These North–South and east–west perspectives betray the fact that the 'common chapter' was very much a product of the Good Friday agreement period.

The agreed text for 2000–6 outlined the context in which it was envisaged and composed, which explains something of the high hopes for the 'common chapter'. The political context was provided by the Good Friday agreement, the establishment of the North/South Ministerial Council (NSMC) in 1999, and the creation of the six North–South implementation bodies in the same year. The key North–South bodies with a role in economic development were InterTrade Ireland, Waterways Ireland, the Loughs Agency and the Special EU Programmes Body (SEUPB). The east–west direction was not forgotten in this political context, as the text also referred to the new British–Irish Council and expressed the hope that Northern Ireland would 'progressively develop and increase its degree of involvement in wider European and international networks of cooperation'.[5]

The economic and social context for the 'common chapter' was provided by the 'improved economic performance' on both sides of the border in the 1990s. Falling unemployment and other indicators meant that North and South had converged enough with the rest of the EU to become regions in transition rather than having so-called 'objective one' status (where GDP is less than 75 per cent of the EU average and the region is entitled to special assistance). The exception to this was the Border, Midlands and Western region (created in 1999, and bringing together the six border counties with the rest of Connacht and four north-western counties of Leinster), which retained this status. The agreed text also recognised sub-regional disparities, especially in Northern Ireland and the border region (which provided the particular focus of the Peace II and Interreg IIIA programmes).

The third part of the context for the 'common chapter' was the development of opportunities for future cooperation using the steps taken in 1994–9. The text noted significant developments at the level of 'local authorities, non-government organisations, business and central government, especially in implementing EU programmes'.[6] Examples of this progress were the work of organisations such as the Centre for Cross Border Studies in Armagh, the three cross-border local authority networks, and the Irish Business Employers Confederation – Confederation of British Industry Joint Business Council. The agreed text also outlined opportunities for future development in 2000–6 in nine different areas. Six of these (agriculture, education, environment, health, tourism and transport) were those agreed as areas of cooperation to be driven forward by the NSMC.[7] Three other areas of cooperation were identified which did not fall under the charge of the NSMC: energy, 'e-commerce' and information and communications technology, and human resources development.[8]

Implementation and promotion were seen as 'fundamental to the impact of cross-border development in the European context over the period 2000–06'.[9] The lead role for this work was given to the new SEUPB and it was to be provided with a budget to 'identify and alleviate constraints' to cooperation. The common chapter was now to 'receive structured, focused and ongoing attention' and to be 'actively promoted with the Community structural fund Monitoring Committees, North and South, on which the SEUPB will be represented'.

THE 'COMMON CHAPTER' AND ECONOMIC COOPERATION

Cross-border economic cooperation on the island of Ireland is the key priority area in the 'common chapter'. In the first place, the EU structural funds (which give rise to the development plans in which the 'common chapter' can be found) are designed to bring about economic cohesion in the EU at both transnational and national levels. Second, while the structural funds are supposed to be about improving social conditions, this is seen as being largely dependent on getting economic conditions right. Third, and most importantly for this chapter, cross-border economic cooperation is often regarded as a shorthand way of describing North–South public policy cooperation.

This is not to say that, in the North–South relationship, cooperation has been restricted to the economic field (even if we add agriculture and tourism to this). The Interreg and, in particular, the Peace programmes have prioritised educational and cultural initiatives, with the 'third sector' playing a very significant role in progressing these (see chapters 7 and 12). Infrastructure, from roads to ports and sewerage works to health services, has also been supported by these programmes. Nevertheless, economic cooperation has been the area which has been most developed and stressed by governments and other commentators.

One obvious reason for this emphasis is that economic cooperation is seen as mutually beneficial to North and South. Indeed, its very practical and 'non-political' nature (the fact that it is not obviously linked to the thorny constitutional questions raised by the Irish border) is stressed at every turn. Recent government pronouncements from either the Northern Ireland Office or Dublin tend to emphasise the shared benefits of North–South cooperation in this area and the desirable aim of creating an 'island economy'. One of the major stories of the last fifteen years has been the enthusiasm of most northern political leaders for all-island cooperation in the economic sphere. The position of the DUP remains ambivalent, however, with the Reverend William McCrea arguing that the South and North are rivals, not potential collaborators, though Peter Robinson was keen to talk about practical opportunities for cooperation at the September 2004 Small Firms Association conference in Dublin.[10] This growing recognition of the opportunities offered by economic cooperation was noted by one academic in the late 1990s; he put it down to the economic growth in the South while the North's 'chronic Mezzogiorno-like' dependence on the British subvention continued.[11]

At the same time, it is important to ask, as one conference speaker recently (mis)put it, is all this talk a case of 'more breath than depth'? There are those, and not all of them unionists, who question the credibility of this talk of an 'island economy'. The sceptics generally come to a shared conclusion – that the two economies are structurally completely different, with different historical trajectories. In chapter 3, John Bradley argues that the North has suffered from a failure of industrial policy (both with regard to inward investment and indigenous industry), with the effect that the North is entirely structurally different from the South and needs to undergo painful restructuring.[12] Another sceptic, Esmond Birnie, is much less pessimistic about the North, though he does see the two economies as structurally different. Instead he argues that they are as integrated now as they are likely to be, and that the North's future lies in closer links with the UK, with which it shares a similar economic structure.[13] Among those who are less sceptical there is still a note of caution, as we are not yet sure of the factors that either motivate cross-border collaboration or would act as influence on the competitiveness of an 'island economy'.[14]

One final question about cross-border economic cooperation which is crucial to the 'common chapter' is whether it leads to other integrative or cooperative spillovers. The international literature on this debate is a large one and, in Ireland, the cudgels have been taken up by Etain Tannam and Jonathan Tonge.[15] In essence there is no clear answer to the question because of the vagueness of the evidence of what the spillovers might be, and how or whether these lead to further cooperation or integration. In other research, Henderson and Teague critically scrutinise the efficacy of the link between cross-border cooperation in the tourism industry and public policy generally.[16] This perspective could provide the backdrop for any assessment of the impact of the 'common chapter'. However, as we shall see, official assessments of the operation of the 2000–6 'common chapter' have been largely confined to detailing public expenditure associated with it.

THE 2000–6 'COMMON CHAPTER' IN OPERATION

Reporting on the 'common chapter'

Leaving aside the background to the 'common chapter', this section will assess how it has worked in practice in the period 2000 to 2003. Information on its performance is difficult to acquire, as the progress reports commissioned by the SEUPB remain unpublished. The data for this chapter have come from these unpublished reports, from research carried out in the Centre for Cross Border Studies for the Border Ireland website, and from various annual reports of the North–South bodies.[17] For structural fund programmes, mid-term evaluations have been used to assess their findings on the extent of North–South cooperation. The structural funds in the South were laid out in the National Development Plan, which encompasses five different operational programmes: three state-wide ones (Economic and Social Infrastructure, Education and Human Resource Development, and the Productive Sector) and two regional (Southern and

Eastern Regional operational programme, and Border, Midland and Western Regional operational programme). In the North, the overarching structural fund programme is entitled Building Sustainable Prosperity. The mid-term evaluations of all these programmes were completed by the end of 2003 and published in 2004.

When assessing the operation of the 'common chapter' it is as well to recognise that the agreed text shrewdly included the phrase 'sufficiently flexible' three times in ten pages. This has proved useful given the changed context since the two structural fund plans were released. The political context for North–South cooperation remained largely positive until October 2002 but has been in a state of stalemate ever since. The suspension of the Northern Ireland Assembly and Executive has meant that the role envisaged for the NSMC has ended. The North–South bodies, including the SEUPB, are run under a provision of 'care and maintenance' which has basically ended any policy entrepreneurship (see chapter 2).

Given this brake on the process of cooperation, the heady hopes expressed in 2000 might be expected to be largely unfulfilled. The 'common chapter' is still referred to in an aspirational manner by northern nationalist politicians when speaking about extending the agenda for North–South cooperation.[18] The SEUPB has (at least periodically and publicly) maintained an interest in progress made on this front. At an institutional level the body is represented on the two monitoring committees for the structural funds. Before the suspension of the devolved institutions in 2002, an intergovernmental committee of Department of Finance officials and the SEUPB drew up terms of reference for the monitoring and promotion of the 'common chapter'. However, the intergovernmental working group has operated in a very low-key manner since late 2002. It did commission a report in mid-2004 on the operation of the 'common chapter' in the 2002–3 period and this was completed in April 2005. It has remained unpublished since that date. A report on the 2004–5 period was commissioned in the autumn of 2006 and there are plans to publish this when it has been completed.

For reporting on and promoting the 'common chapter' the SEUPB has identified four main areas into which North–South and cross-border activity falls:

1 EU-supported programmes including Peace II, Interreg IIIA, Leader+, Equal and Urban II.
2 Structural fund operational programmes including those incorporated under the National Development Plan and Building Sustainable Prosperity.

3 The work of the North–South implementation bodies.
4 Activity in each of the six areas of cooperation.

It might be expected that the first two of these areas would be most important to cross-border cooperation given the budgets allocated to them for 2000–6. The combined National Development Plan and Building Sustainable Prosperity budgets is almost €58 billion, while the various EU programmes have a combined allocation of over €900 million. However, very little of this money was actually specifically allocated to cross-border cooperation. Interreg IIIA is the only dedicated cross-border programme, while elements of Peace II and Leader+ were also to be spent on collaboration, perhaps amounting to €260 million in total. Beyond that, the 'common chapter' urged joint action in the EU and structural fund programmes, but no specific budgets were set aside for this work.

Indeed, it has been the EU programmes and the North–South bodies which outweigh the others in terms of activity. The work of the North–South bodies has been tightly controlled by legislation, and their progress has not been helped by the suspension of October 2002. However, their work has become well-established over time and their combined budgets have amounted to over €450 million between 2000 and 2005. The set of EU programmes managed by the SEUPB is the other area where cross-border cooperation is strongest. The Peace II and Interreg IIIA programmes have been particularly strong, and have funded over 650 cross-border initiatives since 2000. The dependence on these two programmes can be seen by the fact that over 80 per cent of all projects begun since 2000 have been funded by Peace or Interreg monies.[19] The challenge of sustaining such cooperation becomes clear given the small budgets for these EU programmes compared to other structural fund programmes, noted above, and the fact that the SEUPB will be in control of declining amounts of money in the 2007–13 period.

The attempt to measure the sums of money involved is important, because progress on the 'common chapter' has been measured until now by expenditure amounts only. In May 2005 the Chief Executive of the SEUPB, Pat Colgan, referred to over €600m of expenditure for 'common chapter' activities.[20] At the time the speech did not make clear which period this referred to, but it is clear from the 'common chapter' progress reports commissioned by the SEUPB that it refers to expenditure on North–South activities in 2002–3. The 2002–3 report gives an expenditure total of €685 million, which can be broken down into €255 million for inter-governmental activity and €430 million for EU programmes of various kinds.

The unpublished SEUPB reports provide some further detail about where this €685 million was spent. The EU-supported programmes only account for €22.6 million of expenditure. This relatively small amount is due to the slowness of the programmes getting under way. Almost 95 per cent is due to the Peace II programme as the Interreg IIIA had barely begun, while the other programmes were contributing little beyond some networking activities by monitoring committees. For the structural fund programmes almost €410 million expenditure is reported for 2002–3, with 88 per cent of this coming from one operational programme – Economic and Social Infrastructure (in the South's National Development Plan). The €410 million seems massive when compared to the €22.6 million noted above but is a very small proportion of structural fund expenditure on the island for 2002–3, which was €18.1 billion.[21] Road-building programmes on the two sides of the border, some joint tourism marketing, sectoral training, travellers' education, fishery development and film industry marketing were all noted in the 2002–3 report.

The North–South bodies obviously provided some scope for reporting activity and expenditure as all seven (if we count two under the heading of the North–South Language Body) were fully active in carrying out their duties. As a result, €101 million in expenditure was reported for 2002–3. A surprising fact, on first glance, was that expenditure in the six 'areas of cooperation' in the same years came to over €153 million. Tourism was to the fore due to the role of Tourism Ireland Ltd (which in reality is another executive North–South body), but so too was transport, which accounted for 41 per cent of the total expenditure in this fourth area.

Assessing the North–South content

The unpublished reports on the 'common chapter' have been deficient in several ways in that they tend to both understate and overstate the extent of overall cooperation. In terms of understating, they have ignored several sectors and areas where cross-border and North–South cooperation exist. This may reflect the emphasis on economic cooperation in the agreed text of 2000. Some of the cross-border work which has fallen outside this reporting template includes:

- Cross-border programmes supported by other funding sources such as the International Fund for Ireland or the Department of Foreign Affairs' own reconciliation fund.[22]
- Cooperation within the agreed 'areas of cooperation' which falls outside the remit of the NSMC.[23]
- Designated areas within the 'common chapter', such as energy

cooperation, which appear not to have reporting templates designed for them and are thus not included.[24]

- Non-designated sectors with high levels of cooperation activity (such as the arts and sports) or cooperation between other public bodies (such as the two human rights commissions).

On the other hand, official reporting also overstates the extent of genuine cross-border cooperation, which is a more serious problem for the 'common chapter'. In the case of both the EU-supported programmes and the structural fund operational programmes, the phrases 'actions in one jurisdiction with an impact on the other' or 'actions carried out on one side of the border but which benefit communities on the other side' recur. In the 2002–3 SEUPB report on 'common chapter' activity, this category of expenditure, which accounted for 93 per cent of the €410 million total for the structural fund programmes, is devoted to activities which were said to have an impact on the other side of the border. There is no doubt that the Dundalk by-pass in County Louth or the Newtownstewart by-pass in County Tyrone make travelling in the border region easier, but the absence of joint planning of these works, or joint financing, makes cooperation extremely indirect. The inclusion of these projects and their expenditure as cross-border ones seems quite misleading.[25]

The mid-term evaluations of the various structural fund operational programmes paint an even bleaker picture – one of minimal cooperation. The evaluation for the largest of these programmes, the South's Economic and Social Infrastructure Programme, has only one mention of North–South cooperation, and that is a passing one in the introduction. The consultants presumably found little evidence of cooperation, or thought that it was not significant enough to mention again. In the original programme document written in 2000, cooperation was envisaged in the major road-building and public transport projects but, until 2003, this seems to have fallen by the wayside.[26] The evaluation for the Education and Human Resources Development Programme notes that there is some evidence of North–South cooperation but the consultants were unable to find out what expenditure was involved. Cooperation seems to have been confined to generic exchanges of information, joint provision of training and courses being open to participants from the North. The extent of this is not assessed.[27] A third evaluation, for the Productive Sector Programme, also recorded no expenditure but noted that there was progress towards a programme for cross-border research and support for joint film industry projects.[28]

The evaluation for the Southern and Eastern Regional Programme reports over €1 million spent mainly by Waterways Ireland or in aquaculture and childcare projects. The sense is given of a region far removed from Northern Ireland and with no strong element of North–South project development.[29] The other regional programme, for the Border, Midland and Western region, should have had fewer problems in project development given the proximity to the border and the links built up during the 1994–9 period. The evaluation was unable to provide any expenditure figures for this region but does offer a clear picture of unmet commitments on North–South cooperation.[30] Indeed, the consultants are (unusually for an official evaluation) critical of all concerned for not making cooperation more of a priority. The evaluation details the arrangements for cooperation where the Regional Assembly (as managing authority) could act in tandem with the SEUPB to promote activity.[31] The absence of results was put down to there not being a 'central driver … to undertake work with measures'. Without this driver, the evaluation concluded that the 'scope for using the structures established under the Peace II and Interreg IIIA initiatives to increase cross-border cooperation should be explored'.[32]

The practical results of cooperation are hard to find in the Border, Midland and Western evaluation but three features do stand out. First, most cooperation extends only to northern representatives sitting on management committees (for example, Ulster Architectural and Heritage Society staff assist in the management of the Urban-Village Renewal sub-measure) or information and best-practice sharing (for example, representatives of Dúchas, the Republic's heritage agency, working with the Environment and Heritage Service of Northern Ireland on habitat protection). Second, where joint projects are reported they usually turn out to have been funded by the Peace II or International Fund for Ireland programmes. This is particularly true for the tourism and aquaculture sub-measures, while in the social inclusion and childcare sub-measures the consultants reported that there were few cross-border projects and 'this impression is reinforced when the same activities are reported on a number of different occasions'.[33] Finally, the evaluation consultants tended to lay the blame for unmet North–South commitments at the door of vague 'statements of intent' from the original programme documents. This is supported by comments from Border, Midland and Western Assembly staff:

> We were shooting for the stars back then [in 2000]. The new [North–South] bodies were up and running and it seemed like co-operation was made an integral part of every measure and sub-measure in the operational programme. It's hard to know if we were too unrealistic or we have had enough to be doing working on

> our side of the border. The lack of any political impetus from either side of the border has to be recognised as well.[34]

As with the Border, Midland and Western programme, one might expect that Northern Ireland's operational programme, Building Sustainable Prosperity, would show a strong element of North–South cooperation given the North's infrastructural deficit and also the desire for economic cooperation. However, the news is not much better, as this programme's evaluation described the 'common chapter' as 'rudderless' and having 'little additional impact' on the delivery of the structural funds North or South.[35] The evaluation reported that by September 2003 there had been zero expenditure which had a North–South dimension.[36] To assess why so little cooperation occurred, the consultants surveyed the 138 promoters of the 489 Building Sustainable Prosperity projects which had begun by mid-2003. When asked how many 'sought to promote' North–South cooperation, 43 per cent of the promoters said they did. To another query 42 per cent said they were undertaking specific North–South actions. Finally, 40 per cent said that funding from this source allowed them to place more emphasis on cooperation than would have been the case otherwise. Of the fifty-eight promoters who said they were specifically undertaking North–South activity, thirty-five said they were either establishing new networks or building on older ones. These tended to be at the personal level, involving information exchange of some sort, which may explain the lack of expenditure noted in the evaluation. Another striking fact about North–South cooperation in the Building Sustainable Prosperity programme was that most of the fifty-eight promoters were 'third party' organisations rather than central government bodies.[37] The dependence on these 'third party' actors as the key to cross-border cooperation is worrying, as they only account for 25 per cent of overall structural fund expenditure. This position is underlined by the perception that much of their work is judged by various EU governments to be marginal to overall structural fund aims.[38]

FUTURE PROSPECTS

The operation of the 'common chapter' between 2000 and 2003 raises two key (inter-connected) issues for the rest of the 2000–6 period and for the drafting of any new 'common chapter' in the 2007–13 development plans, North and South. First, it seems that talk of money being made available for North–South cooperation does not automatically translate into initiatives and programmes of work. To go further, even the allocation of set amounts of funding under various 'areas of cooperation' or priorities in funding programmes can mean little without the commitment of government and other intermediaries to find suitable initiatives to support. Second, the 'common chapter', for all its emphasis on being a strategic framework for cooperation, particularly in the economic development field, has not, so far, delivered anything like a vision for either the 'island competitiveness' that is to be at the heart of any targets in the development plans for the 2007–13 period or for other areas of development.[39]

The reports on 'common chapter' activity and the evaluations of the operational programmes reveal that, while expenditure is an important indicator of activity, it does not tell us much about the *extent* of cross-border or North–South cooperation, or how far it has been embedded either in overall government operations or policy. Talk of huge sums of money, particularly sums in the millions or billions, can dazzle people. The reference to €600 million being spent on supporting cooperative actions under the current 'common chapter' is a good example of this. The sum is huge, but this chapter shows that the figure overstates how much has actually been spent on joint North–South actions.[40]

The same dazzling rhetoric surrounds the figure of €100 billion which has been referred to on many different occasions by the most senior Irish ministers as well as by Northern Ireland Office ministers.[41] This sum of money seems to be the cumulative money from the new structural funds, North and South, and government financing of social and economic infrastructure over the next decade. The question of how much of this €100 billion will be 'renationalised' (or spent in each jurisdiction in a back-to-back manner) has not been resolved. Certainly the current experience of the 'common chapter' would suggest that more would need to be done to embed cooperation in the operational programmes beyond the enthusiastic, but vague, agreed text of 2000.

So what could be done to embed North–South cooperation in any new 'common chapter'? There are reports that the Irish government will provide money to support infrastructure north of the border, including the restoration of the Ulster canal and facilities at Altnagelvin hospital.[42] In 2000 there was certainly a desire to move beyond the aspirational nature of the 1994–9 'common chapter' and the spirit of the agreed text was then carried into programme documents, such as the Border, Midland and Western regional programme or the Building Sustainable Prosperity programme. The problems faced by managing authorities in living up to the original commitments, as revealed in the evaluations and in interviews for this chapter, may stem from the failure to identify specific cross-border actions or actors linked with clearly defined funding allocations. A recent report, *Spatial strategies on the island of Ireland*, released at the start of June 2006, gives some idea as to how this might be done.[43] It provides models of cooperation from Europe and the USA in 'regional' and cross-border spatial planning and also identifies indicative actions that might form part of any future 'common chapter'. However, even here, there is a reluctance to attribute North–South or cross-border 'actions' to responsible 'actors', and thus the same old doubts will arise once more.[44]

A second major issue concerns the extent to which the 'common chapter' can deliver 'island competitiveness' or perhaps non-economic developments through North–South cooperation. Whether or not there have been socio-economic policy spillovers from the kinds of initiatives supported under the 'common chapter' is something that has not been tested. Scepticism on this point was noted earlier in this chapter.[45] However, there is a more fundamental issue of how seriously the 'common chapter' is taken as a framework for cooperation. Certainly it is ambitious in conception and covers most (if not all) areas in which cooperation is likely to happen (see above for examples of cooperation not included in the 'common chapter' in fields such as reconciliation, the arts and sport). It also offers a biennial reporting structure to the SEUPB on the state of North–South cooperation. So far, however, this reporting procedure has not served to promote the various kinds of ongoing practical cooperation evident in fields from energy policy to education exchanges. There are important examples of North–South and cross-border activity being funded that break new ground. The work of the North–South bodies and the projects funded under Peace II and Interreg IIIA are pushing out the boundaries for cooperation. However, the emphasis on expenditure figures when reporting progress in the 'common chapter' obscures any policy or programme innovation that might have actually taken place in cross-border cooperation.

CONCLUSION

Future North–South cooperation is likely to be informed by the new study on potential economic collaboration published in October 2006 by the British and Irish governments.[46] This British–Irish Intergovernmental Conference study has identified a number of proposals for enhancing cooperation in key areas such as research and development, skills enhancement, joint investment opportunities and support for trade development. If laid alongside the talk of one billion euro being invested by the Irish government in a cross-border peace dividend in the 2007–13 period, then both the policy and funding background for a continuation of this approach appear to be more promising.[47]

However, the experience of the 2000–6 'common chapter' would seem to suggest a few extra steps that the two governments must take in ensuring that ambitious plans are implemented. In the first place, an agreed vision for such a shared approach (and for North–South economic cooperation in general) is necessary. The British–Irish Intergovernmental Conference study contains this (at least with regard to economic cooperation), and offers two tests before any cross-border policy measures are included. The first of these is that market failure or public utility must be in evidence; the second is that it must be clear that a 'border effect' lies behind the market failure or is a block to public service provision. These could just as easily be applied to the measures which aim to have a beneficial impact on the other side of the border. However, there has been some debate over their relevance, given the differences in economic structures and policy challenges on either side of the border.[48] A more obvious weakness, however, is that there is no clear framework for cooperation proposed in the British–Irish Intergovernmental Conference study beyond the fact that all of the proposals are combined in the same document.

The 2000–6 experience would suggest that there is no guarantee of rhetoric translating into action. In some cases, according to the evaluations for the operational programmes, there was a problem of identifying suitable projects for cooperative activity. In other cases, a major obstacle seems to be the institutional inertia of territorially bounded institutions. An example of this was where a northern economic development agency used structural fund monies to support a financial assistance scheme offering mixed grant and equity support to small and medium-sized enterprises. Similar schemes are run at both local and state-wide levels in the South. However, when looking into the potential for North–South cooperation, the Building Sustainable Prosperity consultation was told that the programme had 'no scope for cross-border collaboration'. Whether this answer betrays a lack of knowledge or political will is unclear, but it does provide a good example of institutional inertia. Most important of all, surely, is the loss of political momentum in North–South cooperation and the peace process more generally.

In conclusion, it is fair to say that much useful North–South cooperation does exist. However, the overall picture remains fragmented, obscure and confusing to most people. The 'common chapter' should offer a means by which cooperation can be planned, implemented and then evaluated and promoted. This chapter has looked closely at the 'common chapter'

2000–2006 to explore the extent to which the new North–South relationship has led to public policy cooperation. It is meant to be more than the sum of these various parts and something that can act as a framework for proactive North–South policies and initiatives. As it has not yet become such a framework, the current 'common chapter' has to be judged to be more shadow than substance.

NOTES

The research for this chapter was completed in 2006 while the author was working on the Border Ireland and Mapping Frontiers projects in the Centre for Cross Border Studies. The author would like to thank Andy Pollak and Michael Kennedy for their advice.

1 M Kennedy, *Division and consensus: the politics of cross-border relations in Ireland, 1925–1969* (Dublin: Institute of Public Administration, 2000), chapter 10.

2 The role of the EU was seen as central to the common chapter given that structural fund monies were to be the main driver behind the cooperative process. The Peace, Interreg and International Fund for Ireland (which received funds from the EU) programmes were all noted as being critical also for cross-border cooperation.

3 Much of the detail and occasional quotations in this section are taken from the agreed text found in Department of Finance, *Ireland: National Development Plan, 2000–2006* (Dublin: Stationery Office, 2000), chapter 9, and Department of Finance and Personnel, *Northern Ireland Structural Funds Plan, 2000–2006* (Belfast: Stationery Office, 2000), chapter 9.

4 It is intriguing to note that this understanding is giving way to the phrase 'whole organisation' framework, where the processes and priorities are to become part and parcel of an organisation's *raison d'être*. I don't believe that this is what the 'common chapter' is intended to be, but it might be an interesting way of embedding cross-border cooperation (through mainstreaming, targeting, benchmarking and engagement) in the work of various public and voluntary sector bodies. For recent research which uses this 'whole organisation' framework approach, see P Watt and F McGaughey (eds), *Improving government service delivery to minority ethnic groups: Northern Ireland, Republic of Ireland and Scotland* (Armagh: Centre for Cross Border Studies, 2006).

5 *National Development Plan, 2000–2006*, p. 179.

6 *National Development Plan, 2000–2006*, p. 180.

7 In these six areas for cooperation the sectoral remits agreed by the two governments in 1999 were repeated with one major addition: in transport the aim for 2000–6 was declared to be the achievement of better cooperation between private and public sector organisations in order to create a more sustainable transport and logistics plan for the island as a whole (*National Development Plan, 2000–2006*, pp. 181–2).

8 In the case of energy, the creation of an EU internal market was seen as the driver for cooperation in opening up the two energy markets and the joint development of new supplies including the Corrib gas field. The 'e-commerce' and information technology area was presented as a key element to underpin North–South cooperation through assistance to the intergovernmental North–South Digital Corridor working group, the digital strategy for the North West and a study for an Armagh–Monaghan digital corridor. In the area of human resources development, cooperation was to build upon joint work between the training agencies Fás and the Department of Employment and Learning in the 1994–9 period.

9 *National Development Plan, 2000–2006*, p. 186.

10 For McCrea and Robinson contributions see 'DUP anger over Ahern speech at Northern Ireland conference', *The Newsletter*, 1 Sep. 2006, and speech downloaded from www.peterrobinson.org.

11 J Anderson, 'Integrating Europe, integrating Ireland: the socio-economic dynamic', in J Anderson and J Goodman (eds), *Dis/Agreeing Ireland* (London: Pluto Press, 1998), p. 78.

12 See also J Bradley, 'North/South economies far apart', *Irish Times*, 27 Oct. 2006.

13 E Birnie, 'The island economy: a meaningful concept?' in J Bradley and E Birnie, *Can the Celtic tiger cross the Irish border?* (Cork: Cork University Press, 2001), pp. 47–89. Cross-border trade patterns also lead some economists to wonder whether more integration will happen as trade is growing in volume and value terms but becoming less important proportionately to the trade patterns of North and South. See C Ó Gráda and B Walsh, *Did (and does) the Irish border matter?* (Dublin: Institute for British–Irish Studies, 2006) [IBIS Working Paper no. 60]; also available at www.qub.ac.uk/cibr/mappingfrontierswps.htm.

14 S Roper, *Cross-border and local cooperation on the island of Ireland: an economic perspective* (Dublin: Institute for British Irish Studies, 2006) [IBIS Working Paper no. 57]; also available at www.qub.ac.uk/cibr/mappingfrontierswps.htm. This is also true for non-economic cooperation where there has been no benchmark either of the extent of public and voluntary sector cooperation or of the factors which drive it.

15 Tannam has been the key author on this debate over the applicability of the 'neo-functionalist' model of cooperation on the island of Ireland. Her work has consistently argued that cooperation is assisted less by economic or EU integration and more by intergovernmental actions; see E Tannam, *Cross-border cooperation in the Republic of Ireland and Northern Ireland* (London: Macmillan, 1999); E Tannam, 'Cross-border cooperation between Northern Ireland and the Republic of Ireland: neo-functionalism revisited', *British journal of politics and international relations* 8:2 (2006), pp. 256–76. Jonathan Tonge has questioned this argument by laying more emphasis on the EU's role and casting doubt on the importance of the intergovernmental activities or the importance of most of the North–South implementation bodies; see J Tonge, 'Resolving conflict through functional cooperation: the EU and cross-border activity in Ireland', paper delivered to European Consortium for Political Research joint sessions of workshops, Uppsala, 13–18 Apr. 2004.

16 J Henderson and P Teague, *The Belfast Agreement and cross-border economic cooperation in the tourism industry* (Dublin: Institute for British–Irish Studies, 2006) [IBIS Working Paper no. 54]; also available at www.qub.ac.uk/cibr/mappingfrontierswps.htm.

17 This research was partially funded by the Higher Education Authority through the Mapping Frontiers project.

18 For examples see Social and Democratic Labour Party, *North South makes sense* (Belfast: SDLP, 2005), p. 5, and Sinn Féin, *A green paper on Irish unity* (Dublin: Sinn Féin, 2005), p. 10.

19 These figures are taken from the Border Ireland database held by the Centre for Cross Border Studies.

20 Presentation to the conference 'The North–South bodies five years on', Institute for British–Irish Studies, UCD, 27 May 2005.

21 Figures provided by National Development Plan evaluation office and the Department of Finance and Personnel (Northern Ireland).

22 In some cases these funds have provided 'match funding' for initiatives which are supported by EU programmes, but there are examples also of reconciliation projects and programmes that are supported by the Department of Foreign Affairs or International Fund for Ireland only.

23 A good example in the health sector is the work of the all-island Institute of Public

Health, which is funded by the two departments of health and has been active in areas such as health inequalities and health impact assessments (see chapter 8).

24 The development of the 'all-island energy market' is often cited as a success story of cooperation, albeit one provoked more by EU reforms than by either commercial pressures or inter-governmental action. It has been a slow and complex process with a recent postponement of the opening of the market for wholesale electricity trading from July 2007 to the end of 2007; see *Irish Times*, 9 Aug. 2006. The regulation of the all-island telecommunications market, or at least the ending of UK–Ireland roaming charges, has recently been finalised; see *Irish Times*, 28 Mar. 2006. In this case it was government pressure on the telecommunications companies that seems to have worked, and this has allowed the Irish government to hold up this cross-border action as a model for the EU more generally.

25 It is fair to report that subsequent to 2003 the authorities North and South have come together to jointly manage the connection of the Newry–Dundalk road to the extent that the National Roads Authority in the Republic and the Roads Service of Northern Ireland jointly issued and adjudicated the contract for building the new road.

26 Indecon Group, *Mid-term evaluation of the Economic and Social Infrastructure Operational Programme* (Dublin: Department of Finance, 2003).

27 Fitzpatrick Associates, *Mid-term evaluation of the Education and Human Resources Development Programme, 2000–2006* (Dublin: Department of Finance, 2003). In the original programme document €10 million was mentioned as being available for North–South cooperation but one Department of Enterprise, Trade and Employment official told this author that much of the ongoing cooperation is 'box ticking'. This situation seems odd given the extent of cooperation between the Republic's training agency, FÁS, and its Northern equivalent, the Training and Employment Agency (now part of the Department of Employment and Learning) under the Peace I (1994–99) programme, where they led the way in cross-border public sector cooperation.

28 Indecon Group, *Mid-term evaluation* (2003). The SEUPB reports €4.8 million of expenditure for 2002–3 (of which €4.7million is direct cooperation). The film industry work is interesting as Irish language medium projects appear to have been the main beneficiaries or the keenest participants. Another key participant is Teagasc, the Republic's agriculture development agency, whose 'research stimulus fund' has been encouraging North–South research bids.

29 Farrell Grant Sparks, *Mid-term evaluation of the Southern and Eastern Region Operational Programme* (Dublin: Department of Finance, 2003). The SEUPB reports €3.5 million of expenditure for 2002–3 and €2.8 million is direct cooperation through Waterways Ireland, with a small sum for the Dundalk-based Cross Border Centre for Community Development.

30 The 2002–3 report for the SEUPB gives a total of €16 million (of which €6 million is direct expenditure and the rest indirect).

31 Fitzpatrick Associates, *Mid-term evaluation of the Border, Midlands and Western Region Operational Programme* (Dublin: Department of Finance, 2003). The Border, Midland and Western Assembly has had a North–South working group made up of councillors and other social partners which has met regularly since 2001.

32 Fitzpatrick Associates, *Mid-term evaluation of the Border, Midlands and Western Region* (2003), p. 225.

33 Fitzpatrick Associates, *Mid-term evaluation of the Border, Midlands and Western Region* (2003), p. 168.

34 Interview with Border, Midland and Western Assembly staff, 30 May 2006.

35 DTZ Pieda, *Mid-term evaluation of the Building Sustainable Prosperity operational programme* (Belfast: Department of Finance and Personnel, 2003). In an interview one Department of Enterprise, Trade and Investment (NI) official noted that there was a 'commitment to work the common chapter' but that by 2001 it was judged to have

'intangible targets and impacts'. Since then (especially in the absence of NSMC input) it had 'drifted along in a directionless manner'.

36 In contrast, the SEUPB reports €31.6 million in expenditure for 2002–3 (of which €4.6 million is direct cross-border expenditure).

37 One case study included in the evaluation is of the Citizen's Advice Northern Ireland which referred to cross-border cooperation with Comhairle, the Republic's citizens' advice agency. This has been ongoing since the 1990s but has been dependent on Peace I and II funding to support it rather than any direct support from the Building Sustainable Prosperity programme.

38 B Harvey, *The illusion of inclusion: access by NGOS to structural funds in the new EU member states* (Brussels: ECAS, 2004).

39 The development of 'island competitiveness' has been a central focus of two recent British–Irish policy documents: see Department of the Taoiseach, *Lisbon Agenda: national reform programme for Ireland* (Dublin: Department of the Taoiseach, 2005), Annex 1, 'Common contribution by the British and Irish Governments'; *Comprehensive study on the all-island economy* (Dublin and Belfast: British and Irish Governments, 2006); available at www.nics.gov.uk/press/ofmdfm/final271006.pdf [accessed 07-12-2006].

40 An additional problem is that there is a significant amount of double counting in the 2002–3 'common chapter' report for the SEUPB. For example, there are roads projects which are counted both under the structural fund operational programmes and the transport 'area of cooperation'.

41 The first mention of this sum was by An Taoiseach, Bertie Ahern, speaking at the Institute for British–Irish Studies conference in Dublin (May 2005), followed by Minister for Foreign Affairs, Dermot Ahern, at an all-island infrastructure conference in Dundalk (November 2005) and Brian Cowen on Radio Ulster's *Good Morning Ulster* programme (Jan. 2006).

42 'State to invest in North under new plan', *Irish Times*, 12 Jan. 2007.

43 The genesis of this report is interesting as it reveals something of how North–South policy-making can develop. The report was commissioned by InterTrade Ireland in a piece of policy entrepreneurship as the body 'to examine the potential for infrastructural development required to promote trade between Ireland and Northern Ireland and report to the two governments'; see Enterprise Strategy Group/Forfás, *Ahead of the curve* (Dublin: Forfás, 2005), p. 101. The authors of *Spatial strategies on the island of Ireland* come from the International Centre for Local and Regional Development, which links northern and southern universities with Harvard-based academics. The report was originally envisaged as a way of linking the largely disconnected or 'back-to-back' spatial strategies, North and South, which both mentioned cross-border gateways (Derry–Letterkenny and Dundalk–Newry) but lacked an island-wide view. However the report caught the mood of the times by tying its 'strategic framework' to the discussion of €100 billion in infrastructural spending. When an advance copy of the report was provided to the newspapers it was reported under the headline 'Call for all-island spending strategy', showing, once again, that money talks much more loudly than any policy statement; see *Irish Times*, 20 May 2006.

44 Brian Scott, 'Framework for collaborative action for spatial development strategies on the island of Ireland or it's good to cooperate!', *First Trust Bank economic outlook and business review* 21:3 (Sep. 2006), pp. 18–20.

45 For examples of this scepticism see Henderson and Teague, *Belfast Agreement* (2006), and Bradley, 'North/South economies' (2006).

46 British and Irish Governments, *Comprehensive study* (2006).

47 'Dublin to spend €1bn in North under new National Development Plan', *Sunday Business Post*, 22 Oct. 2006.

48 British and Irish Governments, *Comprehensive study* (2006), pp. 14–19; Bradley, 'North/South economies' (2006).

12

Sustaining cooperation? The public, private and civil society sectors

LIAM O'DOWD, CATHAL McCALL AND IVO DAMKAT

INTRODUCTION

By the end of the twentieth century there seemed to be a new dynamic in the relationships between the two parts of Ireland (see chapter 1). New forms of interaction and cooperation now spanned the border, reversing a pattern of increasing separation and 'back to back' development which had characterised the first fifty years of partition. Preceding chapters have examined the emergence of new cross-border relationships in politics and the public sector, the economy (the private sector) and civil society, and have also explored specific sectors of cooperation. In this chapter, we adopt a 'case study' approach to cross-border cooperation, selecting case studies which embrace all three domains and some of the relationships between them. Given that the flowering of cross-border cooperation is relatively recent, and a response to a particular configuration of circumstances, we concentrate here on exploring a central question – how sustainable are these new patterns of cooperation? While we cannot pretend to predict the future vagaries of political and economic development, we can identify at least some of the factors which currently serve both to support and to undermine sustainable North–South cooperation.

Case studies are conceived here as illustrations of how the actual process of cross-border cooperation works within a changing macrostructural framework which both enables and constrains action. A qualitative case study approach takes into account the perceptions and experiences of practitioners themselves and the ways in which they perceive, and respond to, changing political and economic conditions. Our objective was not to construct detailed and highly specific research profiles of each case studied – we lack the range of specialist expertise required to undertake this task. Rather our aim was to identify generic factors shaping cross-border cooperation – factors identified in earlier research carried out singly and collaboratively by the authors.[1] We have used interviews to examine the significance of these factors and how they are perceived and addressed by practitioners actively involved in promoting cross-border projects.[2] Our case studies were framed by the wider research literature on Northern Ireland, and the impact of European integration on the island of Ireland, while drawing on the international border studies literature. They were also shaped by the research project on which this book is based.[3]

In Ireland, the study of cross-border cooperation has tended to cluster around two poles. The first is macro-level analysis of political and economic cooperation produced by academics.[4] The second is a diffuse and much less public literature associated with the practice of cross-border cooperation and with the monitoring and evaluation of specific projects. This tends to be produced by consultants and organisations working on the ground.[5] This chapter is partially aimed at bridging the gap between these two poles by drawing on a series of case studies in cross-border cooperation. We concentrate on one theme, or module, from our data – sustainability – now emerging as a critical issue alongside signs that the current phase of funded cooperation appears to be coming to an end. Over the last two decades, the dynamic behind cross-border cooperation was driven, *inter alia*, by the search for a settlement of the conflict and by a generous transnational funding regime. The former has been only partially realised; the latter is diminishing.

We begin the chapter with a brief outline of the macrostructural supports for, and constraints on, cross-border cooperation. In the second section we provide an outline description of the research project on which this chapter is based and of the ten case studies undertaken – including the four that we select to illustrate most clearly the issues under discussion. The third section addresses the significance of various meanings of sustainability and the factors which shape it. It draws on our interviews in order to examine what sustainability might mean to practitioners within the main societal sectors – the state, economy and third sector – and in partnerships which bridge these sectors. In the final section, we advance some tentative conclusions from the research and we explore their implications for cross-border cooperation more generally.

MACRO-STRUCTURAL SUPPORTS AND CONSTRAINTS

The remarkable growth of a new interdisciplinary field of border studies since the early 1990s points to three macrostructural factors which have served to reconfigure North–South relationships in Ireland and international borders generally.[6] First, accelerated economic globalisation has made borders more permeable to flows of capital and information, exposing national economies to more intense market competition; second, transnational blocs such as the EU have emerged to regulate the global markets on a macroregional basis; and third, interstate wars have been largely, if not completely, replaced by intrastate wars. The latter are typically rooted in conflicts between existing states and ethnonational groups demanding greater autonomy or independence. All these factors have impacted in complex ways on the development of cross-border cooperation in Ireland.

The effect of the Northern Ireland conflict on cross-border cooperation was both constraining and enabling. It limited socio-economic cooperation while eventually encouraging a close political partnership between the British and Irish governments (and eventually the US government) in the search for a settlement. The other dominant influence on cross-border cooperation has been the process of European integration. Both of these influences have become increasingly interwoven since the mid-1990s. Until the 1980s, the European Community, in contrast to the Council of Europe, carefully avoided border-related issues which were deemed to be internal matters for member states.[7] With the creation of the single European market and the gradual abolition of non-tariff barriers, the EC/EU began to support regional cross-border cooperation and transfrontier regions (or Euroregions) at its internal and external borders. The main vehicles used to promote regional cross-border cooperation were the Interreg initiatives beginning in 1989. The broader effect of the single market and the more region-specific impact of Interreg have provided a significant and sustained stimulus to cross-border economic collaboration in Ireland in ways which are often not directly linked to the search for a political settlement.

Research carried out between 1991 and 1994 in the Irish border region underlined the importance of Interreg for stimulating local economic initiatives and the rhetoric of cross-border economic cooperation.[8] While initial cross-border cooperation was more rhetorical than substantive, the strengthening of a discourse of cooperation was an important counterbalance to the contemporary discourse of conflict and division around the political violence, military fortifications, and closure of border roads. A survey of local councillors in all the local authorities contiguous to the border revealed a high degree of support for cross-border cooperation.[9] Even among unionist councillors – supportive of road closures and border fortifications, and traditionally sceptical of cross-border links – there was a surprising degree of support for economic cross-border cooperation provided it had no 'political' agenda. They were far more favourably disposed to Interreg, which they saw as politically neutral, than they were to the International Fund for Ireland, which they saw as part of the political agenda of the Anglo-Irish agreement.[10]

The EU as a whole, however, was gradually moving toward a more comprehensive borders policy which added political and security concerns to its earlier focus on cross-border economic cooperation. This shift was encouraged by the EU expansion eastwards in the wake of the collapse of the Soviet bloc, and the increasing prominence of intrastate divisions and wars in the Balkans and the states bordering Russia. Commitment to expanding the free market brought with it a political focus on security threats linked to crime, illegal immigration and terrorism, all of which became important items on the agenda of the EU and its member states.[11] This changing international context bolstered the rationale for the EU's sponsorship of the two Peace programmes, 1994–9 and 2000–6, although British–Irish intergovernmental support was critical to their introduction.

The result of sustained levels of intergovernmental cooperation and the evolving process of European integration has helped stimulate a variegated panoply of cross-border links, projects and organisations, operating at different geographical, sectoral and political levels. At intergovernmental and local government levels, the scale of formalised cross-border cooperation since the mid-1980s contrasts dramatically with the previous sixty years of largely back-to-back state-building. Alongside the International Fund for Ireland (to which the EU also contributed), EU funding initiatives have stimulated business and third sector cross-border networking on an island-wide basis and beyond. The various funding sources have helped construct a new twelve-county region incorporating the six counties of Northern Ireland and the six border counties of the Republic (including the five counties contiguous to the border, and Sligo). The bulk of Interreg and Peace funding has been concentrated in this region.

Etain Tannam argues that the key driver of the upturn in cross-border cooperation has been increased political cooperation between the British and Irish governments rather than spillover from European economic integration (see chapter 5). This intergovernmental relationship is very different from the one that existed prior to 1973. Katy Hayward, in summarising her research into the impact of the EU on the Irish conflict, sees the EU not as an independent actor, but more as a framework which enables and facilitates cross-border connections.[12] Jon Tonge sees the EU as having a role in conflict management in Northern Ireland even if it has functioned as an economic agent rather than an overt political manipulator.[13] Hayward rejects the notion, however, that the

EU can offer an alternative form of identity to unionist and nationalist identities in Northern Ireland, and suggests that the EU cannot transform the conflict, in so far as it is a deep-rooted identity conflict.

Clearly, a more sustainable political framework for British–Irish intergovernmental cooperation has emerged since the mid-1980s. The Good Friday agreement underpinned the constitutional recognition of partition and appeared to put North–South links on a firm footing, embedding them within a broader complex of relationships linking the two main communities in Northern Ireland, and linking the island of Ireland with Britain. A supportive and sustained transnational funding regime has sought to underpin the peace process and consolidate the agreement. The outworkings of the single European market provided a rationale for cooperation to improve economic integration and competitiveness on the island.

Nevertheless, it is easy to exaggerate the degree of commitment to building sustainable cross-border networks. Only 15 per cent of the total Peace I and Peace II budget has been allocated to the cross-border dimension. Although ostensibly cross-border, Interreg I and II were characterised by a preponderance of back-to-back projects; Interreg IIIA, however, has reflected a move towards more genuinely cross-border activities. Overriding all of this is the stark fact that the overall resources provided for cross-border cooperation are a tiny proportion of the public expenditure in the two jurisdictions. While the relationship between the British and Irish government remains close at several levels, this does not necessarily translate into an effective and dynamic environment for developing cross-border cooperation on the ground.

The Good Friday agreement has proved to be the high-water mark for the development of a policy framework linking cross-border cooperation to ameliorating violent political conflict. Nevertheless, several factors have threatened the sustainability of such cooperation. These factors include the continuation of the ethnonational conflict in political mode within Northern Ireland, and the painful stop-start process of fully implementing the agreement. After the 2002 suspension of the Northern Ireland Assembly and North/South Ministerial Council, intergovernmental cooperation did not extend to actively developing a joint overall strategy for cross-border cooperation through the North–South implementation bodies or by other means.[14]

Peter Smyth has noted how the lack of ministerial direction inhibited progress after 2002, particularly in the areas of cooperation as designated under the Good Friday agreement, while the implementation bodies survived on a 'care and maintenance' basis.[15] While John Coakley has advanced a number of reasons why the implementation bodies will survive (because of human resources committed, the policy niches they fill, and the political cost of ending them), his analysis scarcely envisages a strategically dynamic future for these bodies either.[16]

In this vacuum there is a danger of regression to the old regime of missed opportunities and back-to-back developments in areas such as spatial planning, 'community' or 'good relations', and the reform of public administration, especially in health and local government. The danger of regression is underlined by the imminent decline in the current funding regime for cross-border cooperation. Both the International Fund for Ireland and the Peace programmes are likely to end, or significantly diminish, in the near future. While Interreg will continue, the EU's policy on borders is increasingly focused on the new member states and the urgent priorities of their transformed external borders to the east and south. Moreover, pressures to limit and 'renationalise' the EU budget, and the stalling of the momentum behind the continued deepening of European integration, mean that the general environment for promoting cross-border cooperation is less favourable than it has been for the last decade. On the other hand, there remains the possibility that the British and Irish governments will pick up the baton and run with a cross-border agenda at elite and grassroots levels.[17] Many cooperative projects have been initiated and a body of practitioners has emerged that is knowledgeable about the potential for, and obstacles to, cross-border cooperation. It is against this background that our case studies have been undertaken.

THE CASE STUDIES

Outline of the research project

Our case studies were undertaken in ten areas: vocational training, local authority cooperation, health, waterways, women's issues, energy, business and enterprise, rural development, tourism and sport (see Table 12.1). Interviews were carried out with thirty-five key individuals, and additional information was collected from published and unpublished documentary material in the areas examined.

While these case studies are not intended to be in any sense representative of the whole spectrum of cross-border cooperation, they were selected to include:

1. examples of cooperation within the three main societal sectors: the state or public sector, the economy or profit-motivated sector, and civil society or third sector;[18]
2. a range of different cross-sector partnerships;

3. areas covered by the Good Friday agreement implementation bodies, designated areas of cooperation under the agreement and areas not covered by the agreement;
4. cooperation confined to the twelve border counties designated by the main funding programmes, as well as examples of all-island cooperation; and
5. cooperation which was established prior to the agreement, and as a consequence of it.

Data were collected via taped semi-structured interviews, between December 2004 and December 2005, organised in four main modules for each case study: (1) the history, nature and context of the cross-border cooperation involved, (2) funding, (3) issues of sustainability, and (4) the views of the individuals interviewed on the relationship between cross-border cooperation and the promotion of peace and reconciliation. In this chapter, we focus on just one of the four main modules in our data – the issue of sustainability.

Four illustrative cases

For the purposes of the following discussion, we will draw mainly on four of our ten case studies while citing evidence from the other six as appropriate (see Table 12.2). The four cases chosen for more detailed scrutiny are: Border Horizons, a decentralised, area-specific unit of the Wider Horizons programme funded by the International Fund for Ireland; Co-operation and Working Together (CAWT), an initiative originating in the four health boards (two on either side of the border) covering counties close to the border; the Irish Central Border Area Network (ICBAN); and Coolkeeragh, which refers here to a series of actions: a successful campaign to save the Coolkeeragh Power Station in Derry from closure under the privatisation of energy generation in Northern Ireland, the initial management–union buyout, and its eventual redevelopment and acquisition by an arm of the Republic's electricity body, ESB International.

Border Horizons is a vocational training programme aimed at the young unemployed drawn from the two main communities in Northern Ireland and the two sides of the border. Its territorial remit includes the counties of Donegal, Derry and Antrim. Its principal funder is the International Fund for Ireland, supplemented by the two training agencies, FÁS (the training and employment authority in the Republic) and the Department of Employment and Learning (Northern Ireland). As well as receiving some support from Peace I, Border Horizons continues to attract financial

Table 12.1. Overview of case studies in North–South cooperation

Case	Origin	Geographical target area	Primary sector involved	Main funders
Vocational training (Border Horizons)	pre-1998	border counties	state/ economy/ third sector	International Fund for Ireland
Waterways (Waterways Ireland)	post-1998	island-wide	state	government departments
Health (CAWT)	pre-1998	border counties	state	Interreg/ Peace
Local authority (ICBAN/East Border Region)	pre-1998	border counties	state	Interreg/ local authorities
Rural development (ROSA)	pre-1998	border counties	third sector	Peace
Women's sector (WEFT/Derry Well Woman Centre)	pre-1998	island-wide/ border counties	third sector	Peace
Tourism (Greenbox/Sliabh Beagh)	post-1998	border counties	third sector/ economy	Peace/ Interreg
Business/Enterprise (Confederation of British Industry (Northern Ireland Branch) and Irish Business and Employers' Federation Joint Business Council Border Visions)	pre-1998	island-wide/ border counties	economy	business/ Interreg/ Peace
Energy (Coolkeeragh)	pre-1998	island-wide/ border counties	economy	business/EU structural funds
Sport (IRFU)	pre-1998	island-wide	third sector	self-funding

Note: 'Pre-1998' and 'post-1998' identify whether the initiative originated before or after the Good Friday agreement. The designation 'border counties' is applied to the twelve northerly counties on the island, where the bulk of cooperation funding has been targeted.

Table 12.2. Four selected case studies in North–South cooperation

Case	Border Horizons	CAWT	ICBAN	Coolkeeragh
Date of origin	1999	1992	1995	1992
Content	Vocational training for young unemployed	Improving health services in border region	Socio-economic development in central border region	Redevelopment of power station as new gas-fired facility in Derry
Partners	FÁS, Department of Education and Learning (Northern Ireland), business (outside Ireland)	Western Health and Social Services Board Southern Health and Social Services Board, (Northern Ireland); North-Western Health Board, North-Eastern Health Board (Republic)	Ten local authorities (Northern Ireland, Republic)	Coolkeeragh Plc, British and Irish governments, ESB
Political/ adminis-trative support	US government (via International Fund for Ireland), Republic/ Northern Ireland training agencies, international companies, donations, fundraising	state agencies	Northern Ireland Executive; EU Commission	Northern Ireland Executive; British and Irish governments; EU Commission

support based on donations and fundraising, particularly in the US and Canada, which gives it extra flexibility. Its novel training dimension lies in its placement of trainees in overseas companies, especially in North America, in order to improve their job prospects, while building cross-communal and cross-border relationships among the trainees. Our Border Horizons interviewees recognised that the International Fund for Ireland was looking for an exit strategy as it gradually reduced its funding. The second big threat to sustainability originated in the economy, in the falling unemployment rates in both jurisdictions and the fall-off in applicants because of the 'Celtic tiger' boom in the Republic.

CAWT also represents a sustained exercise in cross-border cooperation (see chapter 8). Formed when the chief executives of the health boards in the border corridor came together in 1992, it aims to improve the level of healthcare in its area. It has developed through a series of stages, establishing reciprocal relationships across the border, creating cross-border organisational structures via a secretariat and development centre and attracting support from the EU Peace and Interreg programmes.[19] Senior staff from the health boards support and coordinate the work of CAWT in the secretariat on a part-time basis, while the development centre is staffed by employees seconded from the northern and southern health services. Although the health boards provide financial and in-kind assistance to CAWT, as an initiative it remains heavily dependent on EU funding, notably on Interreg IIIA, and to a lesser extent on Peace II. It promotes a diverse range of about thirty-three projects valued at £8m. While CAWT personnel develop strategic frameworks for cross-border health service provision, our interviewees underlined the difficulty of sustaining and mainstreaming projects which are dependent on short-term EU funding: 'accessing European funding ... drives you down the road of projects'.[20]

Another interviewee suggested that not everything was dependent on funding. She pointed to the importance of good personal relationships across the border in sustaining the project. However, she noted the challenge of health service reorganisation on both sides of the border: 'the thing is with the changes in the south, and the proposed changes in the north ... we may need to reinvent the relationships'.[21] For CAWT to be sustained and to develop in a more strategic manner, the potential problems arising from over-dependence on EU funding for short-term projects and from the increased centralisation of health services on both sides of the border need to be overcome.

Since its inception in 1995, ICBAN has sought to forge a role for itself as a 'strategic broker and facilitator for development within the (mid-border) region and for the allocation of resources within the region'.[22] It was funded initially by a levy on its local authority members. In acting on behalf of ten local authorities in the mid-border region, it complemented the two pre-existing cross-border local authority networks, the North West and Eastern border regions. Interreg III, a much more decentralised initiative than its predecessors and with a more pronounced cross-border component, is crucial to ICBAN (and to the other local authority networks) in that it is now an officially designated delivery agent for Interreg monies that fund a great variety of projects and networks. ICBAN's strength lies in its base in local government and its ability to promote and become involved in cross-border networks that include elected representatives, officials, business interests and the third sector. Its remit is diffuse – ranging from broadband access, minor border roads, civic and community networking, cross-border company clusters in the food area, fisheries boards, water maintenance, independent living for people with intellectual disabilities, and cultural heritage. In the wake of the Good Friday agreement, it is funded through SEUPB and has acted as a coordinator for intraregional lobbying and policy development. Threats to its sustainability include the possible diminution of EU funding, the radical local government reforms proposed for Northern Ireland, the mismatch of competencies with local authorities in the southern border counties and tensions in the relationship between unionist and nationalist councillors.

The Coolkeeragh project is rather different from the other three case studies in that it represents a clearly defined and time-limited project to save the Derry power plant from closure in the context of the privatisation of energy generation in Northern Ireland and moves to establish an island-wide energy market linked to the British energy network. As a relatively inefficient oil-fired plant, in the early 1990s, Coolkeeragh was mooted for closure by 2002 at a time when it employed more than 300 workers.[23] When put up for sale in the sell-off of Northern Ireland generating stations to the private sector, it failed to attract a buyer. Subsequently, a management–employee team bought out the company in 1992 with the help of venture capitalists. From 1993 onwards the new management launched a campaign to prevent the closure of the station. This mobilised a very broad coalition with the aim of bringing gas to the north-west and ensuring the survival of the sole generating station in the region. It involved all the political parties at local authority level as well as officials, two key Northern Ireland government ministers, Mark Durkan and Reg Empey, ministers and civil servants in the British and Irish governments, the Joint Business Council of the Irish Business and Employers' Federation and the Confederation of British Industry (Northern Ireland Branch), the trade union movement in Britain and Ireland, and the EU Commission.[24]

As an exercise in cross-border cooperation, the Coolkeeragh project was distinctive in the context of our overall study. It represented by far the most inclusive, multi-level mobilisation of support networks – a disparate coalition mobilised behind a clearly defined objective. The campaign was successful in that it led to the buyout of Coolkeeragh by ESB International, the redevelopment of the plant as a modern gas-fired facility with a reduced workforce of forty, the building of a gas connector pipeline across the border, and a successful joint approach by the British and Irish government to the EU for structural funds to support the project. As a measure of what coordinated action can accomplish, the Coolkeeragh project provides a salutary example for cross-border cooperation in general. However, in the shifting context of the energy market, its sustainability is threatened by a dramatic rise in gas prices which has caused it to run at a loss since it opened (it only began generating electricity in March 2005). While cross-border cooperation was thus facilitated by the privatisation of the electricity industry, its future may well depend on how the two states on the island regulate the energy market in the context of the dynamics of the global energy market.

THE SIGNIFICANCE OF SUSTAINABILITY

The sectoral meanings of sustainability

The meaning of sustainability varies across the main societal sectors within which cross-border cooperation is organised. Our selected case studies are drawn from the three main sectors, the state, the third sector and the economy, and they also provide examples of a variety of cross-sectoral partnerships in cross-border cooperation.

Sustainability or survival is not a major problem for much of the state sector. Given the stability of state institutions on either side of the border, they provide, potentially at least, the most durable basis for long-term cross-border cooperation from an institutional and financial perspective. However, the institutional imperatives of the territorial state are more prone to consolidate the border as a line of division rather than as a bridge across which coordinated and harmonised cooperation might occur. The huge variation among states in terms of their size, origins, development and priorities ensures the material importance of state borders as markers of difference. The Irish border is no exception. The limits to cross-border cooperation associated with the state sector are reinforced by mismatched competencies of state agencies on either side of the border and excessive bureaucratic regulation and centralisation. When such factors co-exist with a legacy of interstate and intercommunal antagonism as in Ireland, the barriers to cooperation are even greater.[25] As Tannam (in chapter 5 of this volume) and Smyth, among others, have pointed out, political direction from elected representatives is crucial in advancing cooperation; but the short-term perspective, limited territorial constituencies and conflicting political ideologies of elected representatives can inhibit or preclude sustained support for long-term cross-border cooperation.[26]

Sustainability in the profit-motivated economy is of a different order. The criteria of profitability and economic self-interest provide an in-built measurement of sustainability, although a tension remains between short-term profitability and long-term strategic considerations. This sector promises an underlying rationale for cooperation which lies outside politics and is blind to communal divisions. It is particularly attractive to those who are wary of politicians' involvement in cross-border cooperation or of the political implications of cooperation.[27] The extent of cooperation may be constrained by the imperatives of competition and the vagaries of local, national and global economies. Nevertheless, advocates of social capital and the value of embedding economic relationships in cooperative relationships continue to insist on the mutual interdependence of cooperation and competition.

For the third sector, the issue of sustainability is omnipresent due to its uncertain and multiple sources of funding. Over the last five years, imminent changes in state and EU funding have promoted an intense concern with sustainability, although little attention has been paid to cross-border cooperation as such in this context.[28] The third sector has demonstrated a potential to mobilise cross-border cooperation at grass-roots level and to identify practical projects which are of mutual benefit to groups on either side of the border. The sector is also capable of identifying and responding to gaps in social provision and the consequences of market failure. Under the Peace programmes, its relative distance from the state and profit-motivated sectors has led it to take the lead in directly tackling issues of peace building and reconciliation in particular. Its flexibility and mobilising potential is limited, however, by funding constraints, notably the difficulty of maintaining core funding, duplication and overlap of projects, the capacity of volunteers to commit their time and effort, and the extent to which the third sector itself mirrors the communal division in civil society and the different orientations of the two jurisdictions.

In practice, however, cross-border cooperation has frequently involved two or more sectors, a process encouraged by EU promulgation of the concepts of 'partnership' or 'networking'. For example, the third sector and the state have worked closely together on EU-funded programmes with periodic involvement from the profit-motivated sector. Similarly, much funding has been directed to partnership between government and the private economic sector.

Five factors affecting sustainability

Our case studies and interviews helped us to identify five key factors affecting the sustainability of cross-border cooperation. These include:

1. Political, administrative and funding context: the orientation of the two national governments (and of the Northern Ireland Assembly when operational) as one of the overarching factors affecting sustainability. Here the priority and commitment accorded to cross-border cooperation is critical, as is the extent to which the two governments will compensate for the decline in EU and International Fund for Ireland funding.
2. Demand: the interest in cooperation among the target population, the commitment to continue to cooperate once a cooperative project is established, and the ability of a project to meet demand in ways which ensure its sustainability.
3. Experience and effectiveness: the relevant experience and effectiveness of project personnel and of personal networks.
4. Institutionalisation: the degree and nature of institutionalisation as measured by consolidation of funding arrangements, routinisation or mainstreaming of cooperative activities, embeddedness of cross-border agencies in wider networks of institutions on either side of the border, and declining reliance on individual champions of cross-border cooperation.
5. Grassroots support and legitimacy: the degree to which cross-border cooperation is underpinned by durable grassroots relationships capable of generating trust and viable, fundable projects.

In what follows we will illustrate the effects of these five factors from our case studies. While we remain largely focused on the four case studies in question, we also draw on the other six to enhance the illustration.

Political and administrative context

At a general level, many of our respondents singled out the Good Friday agreement as improving the environment for cooperation, noting the encouraging attitude of the two administrations. A trade unionist prominent in the campaign to save Coolkeeragh was adamant that it would not have succeeded without the existence (at the time) of the power-sharing Northern Ireland Executive and the support of key local ministers.[29] Likewise, a southern respondent from Greenbox, a relatively new cross-border ecotourism project, emphasised that ministerial direction was crucial to cross-border cooperation, suggesting that very few government or semi-state agencies have succeeded in bringing forward effective cross-border projects without being told to do so by a government minister or ministers. He complained about excessive administrative regulation and centralisation as inhibiting effective cooperation and argued that senior managers, policy makers, chief executives of agencies, or secretaries-general of government departments have low expectations of cross-border projects. They have 'a very patronising view … they do not expect them to deliver'. This respondent felt that few cross-border projects had been really successful and laid the blame on institutional culture:

> … the conservative, short-sighted, very reactionary constipated culture of so many institutions, in fact both North and South, that really inhibited any form of genuine healthy engagement, or exploration of synergy between North and South. There is a huge impediment there, that impediment is the cultures within individual organisations, within government departments, within development agencies, etc. It's culture, culture, culture.[30]

Government departments were singled out for qualified criticism by an ICBAN official who commented:

> I personally believe that there are elements in central government who would rather not have the inconvenience of having cross-border partnerships involved in deciding on funding. There is still a sense that you're coming from the local government sector … you get a sense sometimes that you are regarded as hicks who do not actually really understand things and that, if you are raising a concern, that is because you are parochial and regional and everything else. Obviously that perception is beginning to change.[31]

As far as the involvement of politicians was concerned, some respondents favoured an approach which kept them at arm's length. Respondents in Border Horizons and CAWT saw politicians as an obstacle to cross-border cooperation: 'The best bet is to keep the politicians out of it. As soon as they are involved, the argument of politics or religion is put … it is doomed.'[32] In the health sector, this respondent saw administrative cooperation between the health boards and hospitals on either side of the border as the best way forward. While local politicians played a key role in ICBAN, our respondents saw ICBAN as filling a niche which avoided political controversy at the level of 'high politics' and diplomacy.[33]

Our respondents in CAWT, a cross-border health project representing an established area of social provision, emphasised the importance of practical administrative cooperation on the ground. They saw the interests of the two governments as benign, but felt that the ideas for cooperation developed at a local and regional level among the four health boards involved. They suggested that health provision in the border area was not a top priority for the Dublin and Belfast administrations, but they welcomed official endorsement via the Interreg initiative, the cross-border local authority networks and the Institute of Public Health.

In all cases, we were struck by the extent to which very different partnerships and networks were dependent on International Fund for Ireland or EU funding and the degree to which the initiation of cross-border networks depended on the availability of such funding. Obviously, the implication is that the diminution or elimination of such funding sources will seriously test the survival capacities of these projects.

The demand for cooperation projects

The more high-profile and durable projects we examined were those which developed a niche role for themselves – they identified demands not being met by other bodies. For CAWT, this niche was responding to the needs of border residents (especially in the north-west) for access to hospitals and other health services. For Border Horizons, it was to address in an innovative way the training needs of unemployed young people who had under-achieved in the formal education system. The local authority networks such as ICBAN met a demand from the EU for more decentralised delivery of the Interreg programme through genuine cross-border structures. 'Demand', however, should not be construed as something that merely pre-exists, an opportunity waiting to be discovered, or as automatically or naturally coming into existence in response to abstract notions of the market or social need. Part of the potential of cross-border cooperation may be the ability to create its own 'demand', and to provide benefits successfully to people on either side of the border.

Nor can narrowly construed and short-term market demand be adopted as the sole criterion of sustainability, as our Coolkeeragh and Greenbox case studies demonstrate. There may be multiple reasons for supporting projects that seem unsustainable when viewed within narrow administrative or short-term market parameters. State support may remain critical, either in terms of market regulation, administrative support or short-term subsidies. Of course, a demand for cross-border cooperation has also been generated by the availability of EU and International Fund for Ireland funds, but here the level of demand may decline with the diminution in these funds over time. There seems to be a role here for individuals and organisations to act proactively as persuaders for new forms of cross-border cooperation while pointing to their potential benefits.

Project personnel and personal networks

Our most active and durable projects were those which contained active champions of cross-border cooperation, with experience of working in, or with, the two jurisdictions, and with personal networks which spanned the state, market and third sectors. In this respect, the cross-border cooperation activities of the last fifteen years have produced a considerable human resource of individuals with experience of working on either side of the border. Increased cross-border contact in funded projects has generated experiences and knowledge of dealing with people and organisations in the 'other' jurisdiction.

In the case of Border Horizons, which dealt with young unemployed people from deprived and sharply divided communities, cooperation depended on support from influential people with extensive networks in these areas. Those involved in the initiation and further development of ICBAN, CAWT, Border Horizons and Greenbox were either adept at generating new networks or were already connected to important networks of influence. Derry Well Woman Centre had in retrospect benefited from the work of the manager of the cross-border project who had been elected as the chair of the Western Health Board. The development and design of the Greenbox project was ascribed to an individual with a long track record in many cross-border projects and with experience of working in the two jurisdictions. One of our respondents underlined the importance of personal networks, seeing them as vital to successful cooperation:

> When it comes to cross-border cooperation … it really has to do with personal networks. I know people, people trust me, I trust them, I know what I am capable of doing. I know if I want a problem solved, or if I want to propose an idea, I just have to phone them up, and I can talk it through with them. And that, if it is to our mutual benefit, we would do it. So, it is all to do with personal networks. If there is any

> message that I get through to you today: what is the key asset that will drive cross-border cooperation, is the ability of individuals on the ground to network effectively with counterparts of the other jurisdiction.[34]

Degree and nature of institutionalisation

Personal networks or the existence of a cadre of cross-border workers, however, cannot be sustained over the medium and long terms without effective institutionalisation. Even with established state institutions, employees are moved between jobs in ways which may impact on the organisation's commitment or experience of cross-border cooperation. Institutionalisation may be measured by the existence and/or consolidation of core funding arrangements, the routinisation or mainstreaming of cooperative activities, and the embeddedness of cross-border agencies in wider networks of institutions on both sides of the border. In this respect, one of the more successful examples of institutionalisation is InterTrade Ireland, established as one of the North–South implementation bodies under the Good Friday agreement. Its remit involves improving the business environment on an all-island basis and it has taken up and developed many of the concerns of the Joint Business Council of the Irish Business and Employers' Federation and the Confederation of British Industry.[35]

The weakness and uncertain future of the funding base is the overriding factor which affects the institutionalisation of cross-border cooperation generally. Much cooperation still constitutes niche activity for the organisations involved. It tends to be marginal rather than central to institutional priorities, an add-on because of the availability of funding, one which will be dispensed with when funding runs out. On the basis of our work to date, we would hypothesise that cross-border cooperation ranks higher on the agendas of northern than of southern organisations. While political commitment to cooperation is reiterated regularly by government ministers in the South, the institutional arrangements for cross-border cooperation are less impressive. One of our respondents in a southern government agency involved in cross-border cooperation articulated this issue in pointing out that cross-border cooperation was outside the mainstream interests of his agency: 'so, it can hinder your career development, you are on a side walk. You are on a backwater, and nobody really knows about what goes on in this [cross-border] unit.'[36] In some respects, the differential emphasis of northern and southern organisations on cross-border cooperation is understandable given the relative size of the two jurisdictions and the fact that funding for cross-border cooperation is relatively more significant in the North. Similarly, while British ministers frequently endorse North–South cooperation, the resources allocated to it are dwarfed by the annual British financial subvention to Northern Ireland.

Our interviews with projects dealing with women's issues demonstrated the other side of the niche problem. Women's issues span a broad spectrum both in terms of general policy and in terms of day-to-day concerns. Therefore, they could hardly be termed niche issues. On the other hand, weak institutionalisation of these concerns on either side of the border limits the scope and sustainability of cross-border cooperation. In one project in Derry, one of our respondents pointed out that she had success in raising consciousness of women's issues at the beginning of the project but over time organisational commitment waned. She also pointed to the problem of the personnel changes within organisations creating problems of continuity in cross-border cooperation.

Grassroots support and legitimacy

In the last two decades, even though the financial resources allocated to cross-border cooperation have been relatively small, there has been a mushrooming of cross-border projects, networking and organisations across a broad spectrum of activities at local, regional and national levels. It remains difficult to estimate the degree to which such cooperation has influenced popular perceptions and generated durable grassroots relationships capable of promoting trust and viable cross-border projects in the future. Evidence from our respondents confirms the findings of previous research that there are many examples of cross-communal support within Northern Ireland for cross-border cooperation (such as Border Horizons, Coolkeeragh and ICBAN). Many unionists are prone to be sensitive or sceptical, however, about the relationship between political and economic cooperation, unlike northern nationalists, who actively welcome both. Although there are several individual champions of cross-border cooperation on the southern side of the border, there are also signs of apathy and lack of interest, notably within state institutions.

Our respondents emphasised the extent to which the Good Friday agreement, initially at least, created positive support for cross-border cooperation that percolated down to grassroots level. The subsequent divisions and impasse over the full implementation of the agreement has made it more difficult to sustain popular support. There is a danger that the conflictual zero-sum thinking characteristic of the post-agreement period will attenuate the positive-sum dimension of cross-border cooperation. A malign scenario could develop – rooted in a combination of unionist scepticism, southern and British disinterest and northern nationalist frustration. A fragmented, low-profile and non-dynamic field of cross-border cooperation, associated with such a scenario, has the potential to erode the peace process and inhibit socio-economic development on the island. One of the characteristics of the Peace programme, in particular, is that it has engaged with, and encouraged, cross-border cooperation at grassroots level. When the programme ends, there is a danger that cross-border cooperation will revert to being an elite-dominated, intergovernmental activity again. The difficulty of building popular support and legitimacy for this type of cooperation is analogous to the problems of popular legitimacy facing the European integration process as a whole. The cooperation of elites generates constituencies of committed cross-border networkers, but excludes large sections of the people, who remain ignorant, apathetic and potentially hostile.

CONCLUSION

Macro-structural shifts characterised by economic globalisation, European integration and the evolution of a joint British–Irish intergovernmental response to the Northern Ireland conflict have clearly generated new opportunities and rationales for cross-border cooperation. The Good Friday agreement and its North–South components, the North/South Ministerial Council, cross-border implementation bodies and areas of cooperation, have provided a supportive framework and a political space for a great variety of cross-border projects.

Against this background, we have used a qualitative case study approach to explore the issue of sustaining forms of cooperation developed over the last two decades. Our aim here has not been to evaluate the effectiveness or desirability of particular projects or of the programme of cooperation in general. Rather we have attempted to explore, in a number of different contexts, the factors affecting sustainability and what it might mean within and across the main sectors – the state, economy and third sectors. Our findings would suggest that the sustainability issue is understood differently and treated with different degrees of urgency within the different sectors. As much cross-border cooperation is cross-sectoral, a key question is which understanding of sustainability will prevail in such projects. What criteria are to be employed and over what time-scale? Criteria might include, for example, crude 'value for money' or 'market-demand' ones; calculations of social need, public interest or political acceptability; availability of funds; and zero-sum calculations of which community or jurisdiction benefits most. It seems clear from our case studies that none of these sustainability criteria are self-evident; they have to be advanced by actors and organisations willing to act as persuaders and publicists for the strategic, long-term benefits of cross-border cooperation. This means, among other matters, highlighting the costs and disadvantages of non-cooperation.

Sustaining cross-border cooperation, therefore, is in the widest sense of the term a political task. Our case studies suggest that declining EU and IFI funds, lack of political direction, institutional inertia and poor institutionalisation of existing cooperation all undermine the prospects for sustainable cooperation in the medium and long term. While low-profile bureaucratic and technocratic forms of cooperation may avoid political controversy, they have great difficulty in combating the institutional centralisation, inertia, and the back-to-back nature of the state sector in the two jurisdictions. This would appear to confirm the importance of active and innovative political direction.

From our work to date, it would appear that those activities capable of maintaining flexible partnerships across the three main sectors are better placed to survive. Even then, however, much depends on the general political environment, personal networking and the capacity to institutionalise cooperation effectively. Perhaps even more important is whether the two governments are willing to increase the resources for cross-border cooperation, at both the elite and grassroots levels, to compensate for the diminution of transnational funding in the process. There is also a question mark over the degree of their *strategic* commitment to developing a cross-border approach in areas such as public administration, community relations and spatial planning.[37] A substantial human resource has developed, consisting of workers with a history of commitment and experience in cross-border working. One of the main dangers is that this resource will be dissipated under a restructured cross-border funding regime.

Our interviewees explicitly and implicitly underlined the deep-rooted nature of divisions within Northern Ireland as well as the problems of bridging two separate jurisdictions. There is a keen awareness among practitioners at all levels that these divisions will not be tackled effectively by short-term expedients or projects. There is a parallel awareness of the threats to sustaining existing initiatives arising from uncertain funding, difficulties in fully implementing the Good Friday agreement, institutional inertia and the short-termism associated with political or market imperatives.

Taking a more long-term perspective, it seems likely that the current phase of cross-border cooperation dating from the late 1980s to the present may be coming to an end. A maturing, if incomplete, peace process and a decline in transnational funding will place more responsibility on the two governments (and the power-sharing administration in Northern Ireland) to institutionalise and mainstream cross-border cooperation. There is a sense in which the discourse of cross-border cooperation, as represented in our interviews, breaks from the zero-sum thinking which has characterised much political debate within Northern Ireland. It is a discourse that stresses mutual benefit, peace-building and the value of cooperation in order to compete more effectively in the global economy. In these senses, it is both outward- and forward-looking. Obstacles remain, rooted in the separate development of two sets of state institutions, their different policy agendas and priorities, and their associated mindsets as represented in official, media and popular perceptions. This research indicates, however, that there are different dynamics at work in the political, economic and civil society domains with respect to cross-border cooperation and its sustainability. In practice, cooperation often involves networks which span these domains as well as the border itself. The challenge is to establish a viable understanding of cooperation and sustainability within such networks that will embed a flexible and innovative culture of cross-border cooperation within key institutions and organisations in the two jurisdictions.

NOTES

1 L O'Dowd, 'Negotiating the British–Irish border: transfrontier cooperation on the European periphery', Final Report to the Economic and Social Research Council, Grant Number R000 23 3053, April 1994; L O'Dowd, J Corrigan and T Moore, 'Borders, national sovereignty and European Integration', *International journal of urban and regional research* 19:2 (1995), pp. 272–85; L O'Dowd and C McCall, *From Peace I to Peace II: promoting voluntary sector activity in the Irish border region* (Dublin: Third Sector Research Programme, Royal Irish Academy, 2003).

2 The bulk of the interviews for this project were carried out by Ivo Damkat.

3 The design of this project was shaped in part by the division of labour among colleagues within the broader project. For project working papers, see www.qub.ac.uk/cibr/mappingfrontierswps.htm.

4 M D'Arcy and T Dickson (eds), *Border crossings: developing Ireland's border economy* (Dublin: Gill and Macmillan, 1995); E Tannam, *Cross-border cooperation in the Republic of Ireland and Northern Ireland* (Basingstoke: Macmillan, 1998); M Anderson and E Bort (eds), *The Irish border: history, politics, culture* (Liverpool: Liverpool University Press, 1999); M Kennedy, *Division and consensus: the politics of cross-border relations in Ireland, 1925–1969* (Dublin: Institute of Public Administration, 2000); J Bradley and E Birnie, *Can the Celtic tiger cross the border?* (Cork: Cork University Press, 2001); K Hayward, *EU BorderConf: Ireland/Northern Ireland: final report* (Belfast: School of Politics and International Studies, Queen's University, 2005); D Hamilton, 'Economic integration on the island of Ireland', *Administration* 49:2 (2001), pp. 73–89.

5 Examples include the output of third-sector organisations involved in cross-border cooperation such as Co-operation Ireland, Area Development Management/Combat Poverty Agency (ADM/CPA), the Centre for Cross Border Studies and the Special EU Programmes Body (SEUPB), as well as monitoring and evaluation reports commissioned by individual projects. A major source for this material is the BorderIreland.Info project developed by the Centre for Cross Border Studies (see www.crossborder.ie). For an example of a report which links the concerns of a specific project to wider structural factors see B Harvey, A Kelly, S McGearty and S Murray, *The emerald curtain: the social impact of the Irish border* (Carrickmacross: Triskele Community Training and Development, 2005).

6 See, for example, the bibliography on the Centre for International Borders Studies website, www.qub.ac.uk/cibr; J Anderson, L O'Dowd and TM Wilson (eds), *Cross-border cooperation*, special issue of *Administration* 49:2 (2001); J Anderson, L O'Dowd and TM Wilson (eds), *Culture, cooperation and conflict at international borders in Europe*, special issue of *European studies: a journal of European culture, history and politics* 19 (2003); J Anderson, L O'Dowd and TM Wilson (eds), *New borders for a changing Europe: cross-border cooperation and governance* (London: Frank Cass, 2003); J Coakley (ed.), *The territorial management of ethnic conflict*, 2nd edn. (London: Frank Cass, 2003); JF Helliwell, *How much do national borders matter?* (Washington, DC: Brookings Institution Press, 1998); H van Houtum, O Kramsch and D Ziefhofer (eds), *Bordering space* (Oxford: Ashgate, 2004); TM Wilson and H Donnan (eds), *Border identities: nation and state at international frontiers* (Cambridge: Cambridge University Press, 1998).

7 L O'Dowd, 'Transnational integration and cross-border regions in the European Union', in J Anderson (ed.), *Transnational democracy: political spaces and border crossings* (London: Routledge, 2002), pp. 111–28.

8 O'Dowd, 'Negotiating the British–Irish border' (1994); O'Dowd et al., 'Borders' (1995).

9 O'Dowd, 'Negotiating the British–Irish Border' (1994).

10 The International Fund for Ireland is a transnational fund established in 1986 by the British and Irish governments to underpin the Anglo-Irish Agreement. It has allocated over €750 million since 1986 to socio-economic development in Northern Ireland and the six border counties of the Republic. Its budget for 2006 is €36 million. It has recently changed its focus from supporting economic development to a more explicit concentration on reconciliation, cross-community and cross-border links. The main contributor has been the US government; the EU and the governments of Canada, Australia and New Zealand have also contributed to the Fund (Irish Department of Foreign Affairs, Press Release 18 Jan. 2006; available at foreignaffairs.gov.ie/Press_Releases/20060118/1961.htm [accessed 29-11-2006].

11 C McCall, 'Creating border space: an EU approach to ethno-national threat and insecurity', in J Anderson and W Armstrong (eds), *Europe's borders and geopolitics: expansion, exclusion and integration in the European Union* (London: Routledge, 2007, pp. 61–77).

12 Hayward, *EU BorderConf* (2005).

13 J Tonge, *The EU and the Irish border: shaping aid and attitudes* (Belfast: Centre for International Borders Research, Queen's University, 2005) [(CIBR) Working Paper Series, WP05/1].

14 While the SEUPB, with the active support of the EU Commission, has provided an administrative and financial management framework for EU funds, it has not been able to develop a strategy framework for future cross-border development; for an early discussion of the SEUPB, see B Laffan and D Payne, *Creating living institutions: EU cross-border cooperation after the Good Friday Agreement* (Armagh: CCBS, 2001) [Report for the Centre for Cross Border Studies in association with the Institute for British–Irish Studies, May 2001].

15 P Smyth, *North–South cooperation since the agreement* (Dublin: Institute for British–Irish Studies, UCD, 2005) [IBIS working papers 52]; also available at www.qub.ac.uk/cibr/

mappingfrontierswps.htm.

16 J Coakley, *The future of the North–South bodies* (Dublin: Institute for British–Irish Studies, UCD, 2005) [IBIS working papers 53]; also available at www.qub.ac.uk/cibr/mappingfrontierswps.htm.

17 Attempts to restore the power-sharing Assembly stimulated a renewed rhetoric of inter-governmental cooperation. On 26 October 2006 the two governments introduced a 'comprehensive study' on the all-island economy and signalled their intention to initiate a work programme based on the study. The areas identified for cross-border 'coordinated policy intervention' went beyond the economy sector. They included health and educational services, as well as energy, transport and telecommunications infrastructure provision, trade and investment promotion, and enterprise and business development. See *Comprehensive study on the all-island economy* (Dublin and Belfast: British and Irish Governments, 2006); available at www.nics.gov.uk/press/ofmdfm/final271006.pdf [accessed 01-11-2006].

18 The state sector includes political parties and government, including bureaucratic state administration. The economy covers the profit-motivated sector (such as private companies, corporations and market transactions between individuals). The third sector or social economy includes non-governmental organisations such as charities, community and voluntary groups, credit unions and cooperatives.

19 P Clarke and J Jamison, *From concept to realisation: an evaluation of CAWT* (Armagh: Centre for Cross Border Studies, 2000).

20 Interview with CAWT principal officer, 15 Dec. 2004.

21 Interview with finance official, Southern Health and Social Services Board (Northern Ireland), 1 Feb. 2005,

22 Interview with Catriona Mullan, ICBAN programme manager, 14 Feb. 2005.

23 Interview with Micky Creswell, trade union representative, 1 Dec. 2005.

24 A detailed account of the sequence of events was provided by Richard Sterling, the ex-managing director of the station under the buyout, at the SDLP conference on North–South cooperation in Derry, December 2005. Mr Sterling kindly provided Liam O'Dowd with a copy of his presentation and agreed to be interviewed subsequently.

25 Of course, even the most barrier-like state border is permeable. All states (including the UK and the Republic of Ireland) are connected by both international and transnational networks. As Michael Mann points out, the formation of modern states has involved a 'social caging' of pre-existing transnational networks; see M Mann, *The sources of social power, volume II* (Cambridge: Cambridge University Press, 1993). Globalisation and European integration have multiplied international and transnational networks and, hence, enhanced the opportunities and incentives for cross-border cooperation. In some cases, European integration has revitalised old transnational networks that are a legacy of imperial Europe. One example in Ireland is the renewed interest in southern Irish participation in the First World War, a development which has been the subject of some funded North–South peace projects.

26 Smyth, *North–South cooperation* (2005).

27 The Joint Business Council of the Irish Business and Employers' Federation and the Confederation of British Industry (Northern Ireland Branch) has put pressure on the two governments to improve the general business environment in relation to telecommunications, energy, waste management, business education linkages, transportation, supply management, logistics and cross-border labour mobility. One of our interviewees in the Joint Business Council noted that for individual companies, the issue was less cross-border cooperation *per se*, but the aim of increasing competitiveness on the island and internationally.

28 See, for example, recent discussions in Northern Ireland about the sustainability and resourcing of its large third sector, which demonstrate the territorial boundedness of

the third sector in Northern Ireland: *Joint government/voluntary and community sector forum, voluntary and community sector panel* (Belfast: NICVA, 2003) [Issues paper for the Taskforce on Sustainability of the Voluntary and Community Sector]; and *Pathways for change: position paper by the Taskforce on Resourcing the Voluntary and Community Sector* (Belfast: Department of Social Development, 2003). For an exception that directly addresses the sustainability of cross-border cooperation see P Logue, 'Cross border reconciliation and development', in *Taking 'calculated' risks for Peace II* (Belfast: Community Foundation Northern Ireland, 2003), pp. 86–91. The Centre for Cross-Border Studies, specifically established in 2000 to promote cross-border cooperation, has faced periodic financial crises because of the difficulty of accessing core funding as distinct from project-related funding (see evaluation reports on www.crossborder.ie). For such organisations, sustainability pressures are a continuous concern.

29 Interview, Micky Cresswell, 1 Dec. 2005.

30 Interview, Western Tourism Development Board official, 1 Feb. 2005.

31 Interview, Catriona Mullan, ICBAN Programme Manager, 14 Feb. 2005.

32 Interview, Paul Maguire, Senior Administrative Officer, former North Western Health Board (Republic of Ireland), 15 Dec. 2004.

33 Interview, David Clarke, former ICBAN Chief Executive Officer, 22 July 2005.

34 Interview, Western Tourism Board official, 1 Feb. 2005.

35 For further information see www.intertradeireland.com. InterTrade Ireland also supports the activities of bodies such as the International Centre of Local and Regional Development (ICLRD), a North–South –US partnership specialising in all-island spatial planning. (see: www.iclrd.org/ns/index.html)

36 Interview, FÁS project officer, 15 Sep. 2005.

37 For example, it is difficult to find any systematic or explicit recognition of the cross-border dimension in the administrative reform of the health services in the South, or in the ongoing review of public administration in the North.

Part 4

Conclusion

13

Conclusion: the Irish border in the twenty-first century

JOHN COAKLEY AND LIAM O'DOWD

INTRODUCTION

Although the local impact of the Irish border is now much less visible than it used to be, many older people will still empathise with the reaction of the celebrated travel writer Henry Morton when he first encountered this new frontier less than a decade after its creation:

> As I approached Strabane, which is one of Northern Ireland's frontier towns, the Free State customs stopped me, groped about in the car for contraband goods, smiled at me in a friendly way when they discovered that I was not a smuggler, and took me into a tin hut to settle the one serious annoyance which faces the motorist in the Free State. If you take a car into this country you have to deposit a third of its value with the customs, and similarly if you remove it from the country, as you do technically when you take it over the border into Northern Ireland ... What a queer sight it was, this North-and-South Border line. Five or six cars were halted by the road-side waiting to be searched. An omnibus came along. It pulled up. Its passengers got out. Their brown paper parcels were prodded ... the Irish Boundary has all the elements of a game – 'Come on, let's play at being foreigners; you be French and I'll be German'.[1]

In the middle decades of the twentieth century, local communities were all too aware of the role of the Irish border as an obstacle to free movement – an obstacle which varied in intensity depending on circumstances, and one whose impact began to diminish only towards the end of the century. But borders are not merely barriers. Their location and the form they take express the changing relationships between political entities and their populations. In general, the various contributions to this book suggest that the Irish border will be a rather different phenomenon in the twenty-first century from the one it was for most of the twentieth. Our contributors demonstrate the extent to which the parameters governing cross-border relationships have changed, particularly since the early 1970s, and most notably since the Good Friday agreement of 1998. On the other hand, the story that emerges here is scarcely unilinear or developmental, nor is it easily captured in terms of a crude process of economic and social development. Factors pointing to the increased permeability of the border and to a closer integration of the two parts of the island are counterbalanced by enhanced patterns of separate development which serve to reinforce the border as a barrier. This book is also a reminder that politics and public administration, however central to cross-border relationships, co-exist and interact with the domains of the economy and civil society. Although the changes in these domains may operate on longer time scales than those of politics, they remain critically important to the development of North–South relationships in the twenty-first century.

Politically, the story that emerges from the foregoing chapters may contain some unwelcome surprises for both traditional nationalist and conventional unionist perspectives on partition. The constitutional and institutional confirmation of the integrity of the border since 1998 does not presage its disappearance in the foreseeable future. While this might provide comfort to unionists, the associated reconfiguration of North–South and British–Irish relationships suggests that nationalists will have a much enhanced influence on the terms under which partition and the union operate. In sum, the traditional political mantras of uniting Ireland or maintaining the union have lost much of their conviction – or, alternatively, they may now be capable of more diverse and creative definition. More generally, however, the findings reported here challenge not only the political slogans of nationalists and unionists, but also the various forms of denial practised by all the main protagonists of the Irish border question. We may summarise these findings under three broad headings, which constitute the three sections into which this chapter is divided: evolving orientations towards the border on the part of the main interested parties, the changing significance of the border over time and in particular sectors, and assessments of the role of cross-border interaction in recent years in modifying some of its more jagged edges.

SHIFTING PERSPECTIVES ON THE BORDER

For much of the twentieth century, British and Irish governments were in denial about their role in creating and maintaining partition. Typically, successive British governments represented the issue as one for the people in Ireland to resolve, while Irish governments laid responsibility at the door of the British. Despite strong support for Ulster unionists in prominent British political circles at the time of partition, British governments in general were never the most ardent supporters of the division of Ireland as such, as we have seen in chapter 1. With the political upheavals in Northern Ireland from the late 1960s onwards, however, they were forced to face the consequences of their *de facto* support for and endorsement of a particular form of partition over the previous fifty years. This new awareness has continued to inform British support for power sharing and for the forging of a new and closer partnership with the Irish government in the search for a settlement to the Northern Ireland conflict.

Irish governments, rhetorically anti-partitionist, have been forced to recognise the extent to which they too have supported the border, even if the border-reinforcing consequences of their state- and nation-building policies were unintended (see chapters 1 and 2).[2] There appears also to be a dawning recognition among policy makers of the degree to which Irish governments have a vested interest in the maintenance of the border. The constitutional recognition of its democratic legitimacy by the Irish government in the Good Friday agreement not only acknowledges the unionist position, but also that government's own interest in maintaining it, at least in the medium term.

Northern unionists, the most committed advocates of partition historically, saw the border as essential to preserving their collective identity and as a form of protection against the threat of Catholic and nationalist domination on the island. However, they found themselves denying to the nationalist minority in Northern Ireland the rights of self-determination that they claimed for themselves.[3] This denial was compounded by the manner in which the boundary between North and South was drawn, as well as by its location. Their strong identification with Great Britain encouraged unionists to obscure the ways in which their relationship to nationalists on both sides of the border constituted an integral part of their own position and identity.

Northern nationalists, historically the most committed opponents of the border, were also the group most divided internally by its creation. Border nationalists and militant republicans attempted, at different times, to ignore, boycott or attack the border and the Northern Ireland administration, driven by overlapping beliefs that they could not, and should not, last. The parliamentary opposition of constitutional nationalists between 1921 and the late 1960s proved to be ineffectual and largely symbolic. At the end of the 1960s, however, a more coherent political mobilisation of nationalists and republicans emerged, aimed at reforming, or radically opposing, Northern Ireland from within. This, combined with a new capacity to mobilise support well beyond the borders of Northern Ireland, provoked militant resistance from unionists, eventually forcing all the main political protagonists to re-engage with, and re-think, the basis of the partition settlement. An important part of this re-thinking was the emergence of concepts such as the 'Irish dimension' (associated with the short-lived Sunningdale agreement in 1973) and 'strand two' (dealing with new North–South relationships in the peace process negotiations leading up to the Good Friday agreement of 1998). This book delineates a changing political landscape indicative of a gradually more realistic and accommodating appreciation of the border and of North–South relationships. Nevertheless, it also highlights the persistence of some forms of denial as well as the potential dangers of recidivism to older attitudes and practices.

Of course, the reconfiguration of North–South relationships is not merely a consequence of political dynamics within Northern Ireland, or within the island generally. At a global level, national borders, while they continue to proliferate, have become increasingly permeable and spanned by ever denser cross-border networks. Changes in the global environment have encouraged the traditional protagonists of the Irish border issue to re-think and reconfigure cross-border relationships, and to register the costs of denying the material realities of the border. These changes include the restructuring of the global economy and its manifestations on the island of Ireland, the central significance of foreign direct investment, the development of the EU (notably its decision to actively promote the single market and regional cross-border cooperation from the late 1980s onwards), the direct and indirect influence of the US government on the peace process, and the emergence of the 'Celtic tiger' in the South in the 1990s. These changes have not just facilitated the intergovernmental partnership between Britain and Ireland; they have also encouraged a perception of the island of Ireland as an economic and geographical region in an increasingly competitive global marketplace.

As our contributors indicate, however, there is much scope for debate about the extent to which the reconfiguration of North–South relationships adequately reflects the changed global environment, or indeed changes within Northern Ireland (see, for example, John Bradley's assessment of manufacturing industry in chapters 3 and 9). The foregoing chapters indicate that institutions and groups involved vary considerably in their willingness and capacity to respond to global and local transformations. Indeed, academic researchers themselves, perhaps too reliant on fixed state boundaries to define their units of analysis, have also been very slow to examine the changing material realities of the Irish border and North–South relationships.[4]

DIMENSIONS OF CHANGE

In this book, we have set out to assess North–South relationships from both a temporal and a cross-sectoral perspective. The temporal perspective traces the evolution of cross-border relationships through three phases, each characterised by defining events: first, the partition of Ireland in 1920–1 and its long aftermath; second, the dramatic changes between the late 1960s and the 1990s associated with the Northern Ireland conflict, the fall of Stormont, the development of a British–Irish intergovernmental partnership and membership of the EU; and, third, the changes consequent on the Good Friday agreement of 1998 and its aftermath. The cross-sectoral perspective explores North–South relationships in three domains: politics and public administration, the economy and civil society. These domains are interrelated but not reducible to each other, and taken together they help to reveal the complex and ambiguous relationships which exist between the two parts of the island.

The temporal dimension: alternative benchmarks

An historical perspective is essential in appraising the scale and significance of changing North–South relationships. Much depends, however, on where we set the benchmark in assessing cross-border developments. If we select a recent date – say, the suspension of the Northern Ireland Executive in 2002 – then we get a relatively negative picture, one of decline in the immediate aftermath of a post-agreement surge in activity: loss of momentum, political stalemate, disappointed expectations, funding gaps, and problems of sustainability in the North–South relationship, as we have seen in chapters 2, 7, 11 and 12.

If, however, we adopt the early 1970s as our starting point, evidence of positive change is more striking. A much more stable and consistent British–Irish intergovernmental partnership has developed. The combined impact of European integration, the 'Celtic tiger' in the South, and transnational funding for cross-border cooperation have also greatly improved the climate for building North–South relationships. Of course, the main benchmark employed in this book is the partition of Ireland itself in 1921, as we have seen in chapter 1. Contemporary developments viewed in the light of almost ninety years of partition are a reminder of a number of key themes.

First, powerful border-reinforcing dynamics were set up by the establishment of two jurisdictions in Ireland in 1920–1. These dynamics were not necessarily all consciously intended by the parties to the partition settlement, but they developed a momentum of their own arising from the policies and institution-building strategies of the British and Irish governments and of the pre-1972 Northern Ireland administration. For much of this period, the global consolidation of the inter-state system, the experience and aftermath of world war, and the retreat of empire, all supported a logic of separation between North and South.

Second, accelerated forms of globalisation and membership of the EU stand out clearly as major influences: they promote a border-transcending dynamic which encourages the reconfiguration of the island of Ireland as a shared regional space conducive to the emergence of cross-border co-operative networks. These networks have elastic boundaries within the island, but they also span Britain and Ireland generally, as well as the rest of Europe and North America.

Third, most nationalists on the island of Ireland have shifted their focus away from the bilateral and often antagonistic relationship with Britain towards a much more differentiated engagement with the wider world. This has had the somewhat paradoxical effect of facilitating British–Irish relationships at intergovernmental level, while at the same time diverting public interest in the South in a new direction and arguably leading to diminished popular interest in the Northern Ireland issue.

Fourth, one of the factors affecting North–South relationships has been the shift in the communal balance of power within Northern Ireland itself. The relatively powerless position of northern nationalists, the main political losers in the 1921 settlement, has substantially altered. Recent radical political and administrative reforms (in the areas of policing, human rights and equality legislation) have helped to transform their political position. The changing demographic balance within Northern Ireland has also been striking. As the Catholic proportion of the population has increased to about 45 per cent, there are clear signs that the trend is towards demographic parity.[5] Nationalist and republican influence on local government has increased, most notably in the border counties – the four 'chequered' counties discussed in chapter 1. It seems likely that, by giving them a more substantial stake in the system, this will redirect northern nationalists more strongly towards actively supporting and influencing any devolved Northern Ireland administration, while also encouraging a more active emphasis on cross-border relationships.

If the historical benchmark for assessing contemporary developments is set in the 1950s – towards the end of the first major post-partition phase (1921–72) – then the transformation in North–South relationships appears truly remarkable. As indicated in chapter 1, the 1950s in many respects marked the widest gulf politically, economically and socially between the two parts of the island. The reversal in the relative economic fortunes of the North and the South culminating in the 'Celtic tiger' phenomenon of the 1990s, the ending of mass emigration, and the growth in population and immigration in the South – these are changes which might be regarded as almost epochal in nature in the context of the last 150 years of Irish history. In many respects, it is too early to assess the full impact of these developments on North–South relations, given the slow pace at which they necessarily operate in transforming attitudes and behaviour.

The functional dimension: three sectors

The temporal dimension described above illustrates how choice of particular benchmarks or key events can shape perceptions of change. For good reason, these benchmarks tend to be overwhelmingly drawn from one domain, politics and public administration, where sharp changes of direction are immediately visible and critical points may easily be identified. While this domain is central to any discussion of North–South relationships, it should not obscure the two other domains discussed in this book, the economy and civil society. These have a certain autonomy of their own, even if they are strongly influenced by political and administrative change, but they should not necessarily be measured on the same timescale as politics and public administration.

In terms of the economy, for example, it is imporant to start considering the North–South relationship well before partition, beginning at the latest in the mid-nineteenth century. At this time we see the first clear signs of the emergence of what Bradley (in chapter 3) calls a viable industrial district centred on Belfast. This was incorporated into the British and imperial economy in a very different way from the deindustrialising, overwhelmingly agricultural economy centred on Dublin. It might be suggested that the zenith of Northern Ireland's regional economy had actually passed by the time Ireland was partitioned. Thereafter, it was marked by regular periods of mass unemployment and eventually by deindustrialisation between 1960 and 1980. The northern economy followed a different but nevertheless generally more successful trajectory than its southern counterpart for much of the twentieth century. From the late 1960s, however, the balance of economic power on the island began to shift southwards. The economic crisis of the southern economy in the 1950s led to the abandonment of protectionism, and through a series of stages the Republic became transformed into one of the most open and globalised economies in the world. By contrast, Northern Ireland was slow to replace its declining traditional industries. The outbreak of the conflict made it extremely difficult to attract foreign direct investment, and as the conflict deepened local politicians were deflected from paying attention to economic development issues. By contrast, electoral politics in the South followed the more conventional route of a society in transition, where issues of economic policy were central to political debate. Thus the two economies followed rather distinctive paths, despite being faced with common challenges associated with European integration and the restructuring of the global economy.

In chapters 3 and 9, John Bradley concentrates on the different structures and developmental pathways of manufacturing employment on either side of the border, dwelling also on the problem of competitiveness facing the island as a whole. In chapter 3, he points to the economic consequences of asymmetrical competencies of the two administrations. In changing its economic course, the Republic was able to exploit its fiscal autonomy in a way that was simply not open to Northern Ireland, even before 1972. Northern Ireland was not just a component part of the UK politically; it was also a peripheral UK region economically, and could do little to emulate the kinds of policies that were so important for maximising economic growth in the Republic. Of course, lack of autonomy, and economic peripherality within the UK, brought their benefits. High levels of public expenditure served to maintain living standards, even if they did little to stimulate a competitive private sector.

Bradley's analysis suggests that Northern Ireland has been slow to escape the legacy of its declining traditional sectors. The Republic, on the other hand, has been able to develop modern industrial clusters, and these have fuelled rapid economic growth. Bradley acknowledges that these clusters may now be reaching maturity. North and South thus face a shared dilemma of dealing with rather different forms of economic dependence: the North on subvention from the British exchequer, the South on foreign (largely US) direct investment. This places a premium on developing new industrial clusters on an island-wide basis – a challenge rather different from that of harmonising economic policies. In Bradley's view, however, political, administrative and business frameworks seem ill-suited to promoting a policy of maintaining and enhancing competitiveness on an all-island basis. The unwillingness of the British government to reduce corporation tax in the North to southern levels is only one of the many factors which influence the capacity to attract foreign investment and build a coherent, island-wide economic strategy. Neither is this process assisted by the fact that the Republic, oriented to a much wider global economy, may see the North as relatively unimportant in developing future economic strategy.

This argument is underscored in chapter 11 by Magennis's analysis of the 'common chapter' in the development plans of Northern Ireland and the Republic. He implies that the two governments have failed to provide a coherent and substantive strategic framework for developing a supportive infrastructure for economic development on an island-wide basis. This is all the more important in circumstances where existing patterns of North–South trade do little to stimulate an all-island economy. Limited in scale, they are largely restricted to traditional sectors, as we have seen in chapter 3. Thus, there is no all-Ireland market which could serve as a proving ground for Irish firms seeking to hone their competitiveness in the global marketplace. The relatively small degree of cross-border inter-firm cooperation on the island, notwithstanding the prospects it holds out of developing economies of scale, is underlined by Tannam in chapter 5, and the impressive work of InterTrade Ireland has been described in chapter 2. This has been one of the most active North–South implementation bodies, building cross-border partnerships, information and trust networks among firms on either side of the border. Similarly, the acquisition of Coolkeeragh power station by the southern Electricity Supply Board demonstrates what can be achieved when management and workers, unionists and nationalists, work in tandem with the policies of the two governments and the European Commission, as chapter 12 has shown.

The economic domain clearly does not map precisely onto existing political and administrative borders; nor does its temporal development coincide with the political events that have shaped the partition of Ireland. Economic issues and relationships clearly transcend political borders, especially under the contemporary conditions of accelerated globalisation. However, the contributions to this book underline the importance of a supportive political, administrative and business environment in maximising the synergies which might arise from 'the formation and development of deeply embedded, interconnected and supportive island industrial activity', as Bradley points out in chapter 3.

Neither does the domain of civil society coincide precisely with the political and administrative border. If civil society is understood in terms of associational life, then it, too, displays a degree of autonomy in respect of jurisdictional frameworks. As Kevin Howard shows in chapter 4, there has been a strong tendency for national organisations founded before partition to continue with a thirty-two-county organisational structure after that date. Since the most important areas of life are also those where organisations are likely to appear earliest, there has been a tendency for important pre-partition, thirty-two-county bodies to survive. Howard's survey of more than 600 organisations shows precisely this tendency. In areas such as the churches, other religious organisations, youth bodies, sporting organisations and cultural and scientific associations, all-Ireland organisations – remarkably, from a comparative perspective – are more common than separate organisations on the two sides of the border. But in organisations where the relationship with the state is more important, as in the case of professional bodies, voluntary organisations, trade associations and trade unions, although many all-Ireland bodies continue to exist, there is a tendency towards the formation of separate organisations in the Republic and in Northern Ireland, though there are also many organisations which operate throughout Great Britain and Ireland (see also chapter 1). As Howard notes, 'the imposition of the political boundary and the evolution of different legal, regulatory and social administrative environments on either side have had a curling effect – associations have reorientated towards the centre of political and administrative power in their respective jurisdictions'. In other words, many 'Irish' associations of this kind retracted to the South after partition, with an important sporting body, the Irish Football Association (which became the representative organ for soccer in Northern Ireland), as a major exception in retracting instead to the North.

In chapter 6, O'Dowd and McCall point to the development of a new role by voluntary organisations in promoting peace and reconciliation in Northern Ireland and on the island as a whole. Pollak also draws attention in chapter 7 to the prominent role of this sector in promoting educational links across the border. These chapters highlight the close relationship between the voluntary sector and state institutions, and the leading role taken by the former in addressing issues of peace-building and reconciliation directly from the 1980s onwards – an area where voluntary organisations have depended heavily on the EU and on other forms of transnational funding. The endemic precariousness of their funding base, the lack of a clearly sustainable cross-border framework for their activity, and the vulnerability of the voluntary organisations to communal division and political crises inhibit their work. Kevin Howard's case study of cycling in chapter 10 underlines the problematic intersection of politics and voluntary activity on the island of Ireland, but also shows how political divisions can be overcome for pragmatic reasons of competition and co-operation within an international setting. Sport, in particular, provides some flexible models for both recognising and transcending political boundaries. Rugby offers a particularly good example of intersecting and overlapping frameworks, with its club, provincial, all-Ireland, and British and Irish teams, and its participation in competitions at the all-Ireland, Celtic League, European club and 'six nations' levels.

The voluntary organisations of civil society have been successful in promoting popular grassroots involvement in cross-border activity in a multitude of activities and projects (see chapters 4, 6, 8 and 10). Here, they draw on a long tradition of religious and cultural organisations which have built networks that have in many cases predated partition. Voluntary associations offering new forms of service delivery are more tightly caged within their respective jurisdictions by their reliance on state funding and partnership with state agencies. Nevertheless, they have benefited from the EU's active promotion of a transnational civil society, particularly through the Peace programmes. The relatively limited funding that their activities has attracted does not reflect the significance of their contributions to cross-border activities on the island.

CONTRASTING ASSESSMENTS OF CROSS-BORDER COOPERATION

Woven through the various chapters in this book, then, is the story of how North–South relationships have changed over time, and how they have been expressed in the distinct, if related, domains of politics and administration, economics and civil society. Not surprisingly, the evidence adduced does not all point in the same direction. There is much support for a rather sceptical view of progress in cross-border cooperation, just as there is countervailing evidence for a more positive assessment. We may consider these perspectives in turn.

The sceptical view

There are signs that in Ireland cross-border cooperation suffers from the drawbacks and public *ennui* that characterises such cooperation in the EU generally, as chapter 2 has suggested. Thus, it is technocratic, excessively dependent on consensus, heavily bureaucratic, and largely confined to elite circles of practitioners and enthusiasts. Socially disadvantaged communities are less willing, or less well-positioned, to develop cross-border links in areas such as education (see chapter 7). Similarly, grassroots Protestant involvement is more tentative, even if it has increased over time (see chapters 6 and 7). The initial political impetus for cross-border cooperation had diminished considerably, with the suspension of the North/South Ministerial Council and the placing of the North–South implementation bodies on a form of life support, as we have seen in chapter 2. While the two governments have continued to express strong rhetorical support for an all-island economy and for North–South cooperation, the scale of targeted action does not match the good intentions articulated.

At a deeper structural and less conscious level, border-reinforcing patterns persist. The territorial imperative of electoral politics and administration tends to prioritise sharply defined territorial units. Despite some devolution in Great Britain, Northern Ireland remains highly centralised, as does the Republic. Areas such as fiscal policy, education (see chapter 7), health (see chapter 8) and welfare encourage a logic of separation and distinctiveness, and do not prioritise the specific needs of peripheral or marginalised border regions. Studies of regional cross-border cooperation in the EU invariably reach a striking conclusion: cooperation is more successful in states where regions and municipalities have devolved power than in centralised states where they have less discretion.[6] There is little sign that reform of public administration and health structures on either side of the border – whether planned or implemented – has taken any account of the possible benefits of cross-border cooperation. The active involvement of cross-border networks of local authorities in areas such as health (as Clarke shows in chapter 8) has been enhanced by EU support, but it has been diminished by weak and mismatched competencies of local government authorities on either side of the border. As in other such contexts, bureaucratic structures in each jurisdiction work to reproduce themselves and, in the absence of active political direction, develop conservative cultures not prone to creating innovative cross-border links. In sum, there is a deep-rooted territorial imperative in public institutions, especially in centralised states, which is border reinforcing – particularly in areas which are not directly influenced by transnational regulation at European level.

Advocates of cross-border cooperation in Ireland have typically emphasised two rationales: the case for an all-island economy to enhance the competitiveness of the island as a whole in the European and global economy, and the promotion of peace and reconciliation on the island. The first of these constitutes a particular challenge. Indeed, it might be argued that the deep-rooted economic divisions between the two jurisdictions have now emerged in a new form which has reduced the incentive for building economic linkages across the border. On the one hand, living standards north of the border are sustained by massive public sector subsidy rather than by a competitive private sector. In the South, on the other hand, extra-island linkages may seem more important than North–South ones to planners and entrepreneurs. In this respect, John Bradley's conclusion in chapter 3 is noteworthy: his assessment is that the Good Friday agreement marked a missed opportunity to forge a competitive and articulated all-island economy.

The second main rationale for cross-border cooperation is its potential to enhance peace and reconciliation on the island. This has been central to the peace process and the Good Friday agreement. Yet, on the evidence of the research presented in this book, relatively few of the resources allocated to cross-border cooperation were directly linked to peace building and reconciliation. Moreover, much of the responsibility for direct engagement with this question was left to the voluntary sector, while, at the same time, much business and state sector cooperation across the border was only loosely linked to difficult questions of reducing mutual ignorance and building cultural bridges. The discussion of the voluntary and educational sectors in chapters 6, 7 and 12 provide examples of the real potential of cross-border cooperation in this area, but also recognises that the short-term projects which characterise it are in themselves inadequate for pursuing the long-term goal of overcoming the legacy of the recent conflict in Northern Ireland, not to mention centuries of political and cultural division on the island.

Notwithstanding the progress towards North–South cooperation that we have witnessed in recent years, the curve of development has been slow if it is measured by the expectations of many – and particularly nationalists – who signed up to the agreement. By far the biggest difficulty has been the crisis brought about by the suspension of Northern Ireland's devolved institutions in 2002. The North–South bodies were established in an atmosphere of optimism or even excitement, and initially made rapid progress. A good deal of dynamism was needed to meet the various challenges associated with building new institutions: overcoming different legal regimes, administrative systems and cultural expectations on the two sides of the border, for instance, as described in chapter 2 in respect of the language body. The process survived the short-term difficulties posed by tensions within the Ulster Unionist Party (which resulted in one suspension of the devolved institutions, a long prohibition on participation in meetings of the North/South Ministerial Council by Sinn Féin ministers, and the resignation of the First Minister, as we have seen in chapter 2). It also survived even the passive opposition of the Democratic Unionist Party, which also placed a strain on the system.

But the long-term uncertainty that prevailed after 2002 had a debilitating effect on the North–South relationship. The governments, for understandable political reasons, made only the bare minimum number of decisions needed to keep the implementation bodies alive. But several chapters (2, 6, 11 and 12) highlight the negative effects of a prolonged vacuum at the political level where implementation bodies require direction, in the absence of which there is loss of momentum and decline in morale. This political vacuum and the focus of the two governments on re-establishing the executive has also had a disabling effect on proactive intergovernmental cooperation and on promoting new developments in the domains of the economy and civil society.

A second important difficulty has been a big gap between the enthusiasm of the top rank of leaders (including senior politicians and civil servants in Dublin and London) and middle-level officials. As Tannam points out in chapter 5, the Irish and British governments were responsible for promoting a very high level of administrative cooperation while the institutions were up and running, but this was not necessarily reflected at political or civil service level within Northern Ireland. Indeed, given the challenges of working across the border, the level of commitment required on either side to ensure that new institutions can function probably requires more powerful and sustained commitment than the passive acceptance which is the most that can realistically be expected of middle-level officials.

Third, even the long-term focus of the two governments on Northern Ireland will inevitably be open to question, as they, too, move on to other challenges. In chapter 12, O'Dowd, McCall and Damkat note that the close relationship between the British and Irish governments does not necessarily translate into an 'effective and dynamic environment for developing cross-border cooperation on the ground'; furthermore, they detect little evidence of an all-Ireland dimension in the thinking of the two governments in major planning areas (such as public sector reform in Northern Ireland and health system reform in the Republic). Indeed, there may be some tendency for cooperation to be higher on the agenda of northern than of southern agencies, with officials in the latter often giving this sector low priority and writing it off as a dead end, and as possibly damaging to their careers. chapter 2 uses the example of the Tourism Brand Ireland incident (which exposed deep-rooted southern resistance to compromise with Northern Ireland even on minor matters) as an indicator of unwillingness on the part of the South to cooperate at island level.

The research findings in this book, then, provide substantial material for a rather critical audit of contemporary cross-border relationships. Overall cross-border cooperation remains patchy, project-specific and lacking a viable strategic framework, as we have seen in chapters 8, 11 and 12. It depends heavily on external funding, notably from the International Fund for Ireland and the EU, and even then most money from these sources is spent in separate tranches within each jurisdiction rather than within active cross-border partnerships. Funded projects have been mainly confined to the twelve northern counties of the island, thereby largely marginalising linkages with some of the more dynamic centres on the island, such as Dublin, Cork, Limerick and Galway. With the ending of violence and the enlargement of the EU, external funding sources are, in any case, a rapidly diminishing asset, with limited capacity to compensate for the restricted level of cooperation in other areas.

A positive appraisal

The sceptical view of North–South cooperation can muster formidable empirical support and will be embraced by those opposed to such cooperation, or at least lukewarm as to its merits. Nevertheless, our contributors are also able to point to much counter-evidence, illustrating many path-breaking developments particularly over the last thirty years. As suggested above, criticisms of the obstacles to cross-border cooperation since 2002 appear in a different light when placed in a longer time frame dating from the 1970s or even earlier.

Many sceptics point to the fact that the relatively limited funding allocated to cross-border cooperation has not matched the apparently substantial verbal commitment to it. Certainly, the financing of North–South cooperation pales into insignificance compared to that devoted to running the institutions within the two jurisdictions. But talk, or rhetoric, is important in its own right, particularly when it is talk about reducing mutual ignorance, promoting shared benefits, and cooperating to meet global challenges. More specifically, it marks a constructive alternative to the rhetorical hostility which marked the long 'cold war' between the two parts of the island for much of the post-partition period. The hostility between unionist and nationalist Ireland intensified during the Northern Ireland conflict. Just as that conflict appeared to be approaching stalemate in the early 1990s, and as the border became increasingly militarised and fortified, the EU's promotion of the single market, and the ideology of economic cross-border cooperation, stimulated a more positive countervailing rhetoric in the border region, among business organisations North and South, and between the British and Irish governments. This also helped to legitimate cross-border links in the areas of education (chapter 7), health (chapter 8), and peace-building (chapters 6 and 12). It has also encouraged an evolution in EU-funded programmes (Interreg and Peace) from promoting projects which were only nominally cross-border to more genuinely integrated ones.

As Tannam's analysis of party manifestoes in chapter 5 shows, early starkly opposed perspectives on institutional cross-border cooperation within Northern Ireland have softened. On the one hand, the Democratic Unionist Party has moved gradually to a position of acceptance of cooperation via the implementation bodies, provided they are appropriately answerable to a Northern Ireland assembly. Sinn Féin has also become less insistent on the notion that the bodies provide a path towards Irish unity. The kind of contact with which the bodies are associated is likely to resemble the patterns of cooperation set in place by EU programmes: as chapters 6 and 7 argue, the positive effects of such contact are likely to be noticeable only in the long term. There is a sense in which EU membership has helped to normalise the border as an internal one like other increasingly permeable national borders within the EU.

The enshrining of North–South relationships within the Good Friday agreement has further legitimised cross-border cooperation, integrating it with new east–west arrangements between the two islands and cross-communal institutions within Northern Ireland. It would be difficult to overstate the long-term effects of the sea change in political attitudes that has led the vast majority of Irish nationalists to offer constitutional and institutional recognition to the Irish border as democratic under the Good Friday agreement. This removes one of the main objections of unionists to closer North–South links, undermining their image of an aggressive southern constitutional claim on Northern Ireland and the perception that North–South links mark a slippery slope to realising that claim. It seems likely that more regular unionist–nationalist interaction across the border has begun to convince unionists of the lack of enthusiasm among southern politicians for abolishing the border in the medium term, and of the reassuring limits to their interest in Northern Ireland. This may create more scope for cooperation in the domains of the economy and civil society.

The case for economic cooperation and for supportive political and administrative arrangements on an island-wide basis continues to be made and to be practically advanced by North–South bodies such as InterTrade Ireland, Tourism Ireland and Waterways Ireland. While civil society organisations may in many respects be the poor relations of North–South cooperation, organisations such as Co-operation Ireland, Democratic Dialogue, the Institute for British–Irish Studies, the Centre for Cross-Border Studies and the Cross-Border Consortium (embracing Border Action, the Community Foundation of Northern Ireland and Co-operation

Ireland) have become repositories for exploring and promoting new thinking on cross-border developments.

Finally, conditions and influences external to the island of Ireland have been overwhelmingly favourable to enhancing North–South links. Devolution in Britain contains the promise of more flexible and symmetrical regional cooperation between parts of Britain and the two Irish jurisdictions, a development supported by a Scotland–Ireland strand in the proposed Interreg IV territorial programme. As several of our contributors show, the EU has played a large role in actively supporting North–South links, as have the US government and a variety of international non-governmental organisations interested in conflict resolution and peace building. The challenges posed by an ever more competitive global economy, and by the global issues associated with energy and the environment, all strengthen the rationale for all-island cooperation lodged within a supportive east–west and EU framework.

CONCLUSION

How, then, are we to weigh positive appraisals of North–South cooperation against the more sceptical assessments described above? Evidence from the domain of politics and administration points to a positive, medium and long-term transformation in North–South relationships, albeit one not yet fully embedded in post-agreement Northern Ireland. New cross-border institutions, a close British–Irish intergovernmental partnership, increased cross-border interaction and the increased legitimacy of such contacts all underline the progress that has taken place. While developments in economic and civil society cooperation have not been as visible, much innovative cross-border activity has taken place in these domains. It has been heavily dependent, however, on external funding sources, even if these have been largely channelled through existing state agencies.

Several chapters in this book illustrate the potential benefits of new forms of cross-border cooperation in economic development, health, education, planning, and in promotion of peace and reconciliation. In so doing they implicitly distinguish between the functional and territorial dimensions. The functional domain refers to the set of networks that transcend the territorial border. These networks themselves have elastic boundaries that encompass the border region and the island as a whole as part of the wider transnational space of the EU and beyond. With their roots in the economy and civil society, such networks build trust, undertake specific projects for mutual benefit and break down barriers of ignorance and prejudice. Perhaps most significantly, they hold out the promise of new positive-sum relationships capable of being of mutual benefit to people on either side of the Irish border.

Territory, on the other hand, is more the realm of politics and administration. It involves the sharply demarcated boundaries of elected politicians, voters, civil servants and their respective organisations. Such boundaries are the *sine qua non* for representative democracy, political control, public accountability and the functioning of modern states. In Ireland, and elsewhere, their paradox lies in their less than democratic and often violent and coercive origins. When, as in Northern Ireland, the central material and symbolic issue in politics is the very territory of the state, politics takes a chronic zero-sum form, expressed in competition between protagonists to claim and control territory.[7]

Much of the project-based cross-border cooperation described in this book indicates the potential of cross-border networks to counterbalance the zero-sum politics of territorialism. However, several chapters also point to the importance of interstate and intergovernmental cooperation in its own right. The latter serves to confirm existing territorial borders but, in so doing, it can ameliorate the conflicts associated with them by adequately supporting border-transcending networks, and by specifying how existing borders can be 'democratically' maintained or altered. This is a rather fine balancing act and a particularly difficult one in contested political jurisdictions like Northern Ireland.

The sceptical view of the current state of North–South relationships represented in this book suggests that the potential of cross-border networks is not being realised, and that they are not being adequately supported by state institutions. Lacking an overall strategic framework, they are too dependent on individual champions of cross-border cooperation and on short-term external funding from the EU and elsewhere. They run the risk of being marginalised with the diminution of external support and the failure of governments to provided adequate compensatory funding.

Some of the evidence adduced here implies that there has been a widespread political tendency to devalue and minimise the role of North–South relationships for promoting peace, reconciliation and a political settlement on the island. chapter 12, for example, raises serious doubts about the sustainability of even existing levels of cross-border cooperation. A future malign scenario remains possible, where such cooperation remains fragmented, low-profile and non-dynamic, thereby losing its capacity to advance the peace process and to promote socio-economic development on the island. A plausible political context for this scenario might be a combination of unionist scepticism, southern uninterest, British detachment and northern nationalist frustration. In this eventuality, it would seem likely that North–South cooperation would simply become another stake in the zero-sum communal politics of Northern Ireland, undermining its potential to enhance the positive-sum aspects of an enduring political settlement.

Of course, the waterfront of North–South relationships is far too wide to cover in one book. We are conscious, for example, that we pay relatively little attention here to questions of culture, identity, the mass media, law and order, or the extensive, localised and often illegal economy directly dependent on the border. The dynamics and legacy of nearly thirty years of violent conflict in Northern Ireland have been analysed exhaustively elsewhere; they remain a major influence on the reshaping of North–South relationships described and analysed by our contributors. The continued impact of the multi-faceted legacy of the 'troubles' on cross-border relationships deserves much more scrutiny that we have been able to accord it. Certainly, many of the developments described in this book, the new British–Irish intergovernmental relationship and the Good Friday agreement may be understood as a response to sustained violent conflict in Northern Ireland. Thus, while the conflict stimulated new departures in North–South relationships, there is a sense in which the legacy of that conflict continues to alienate both parts of the island while making the recognition of common interests more difficult.

The evidence advanced by our contributors suggests that the jury is still out on whether the potential of North–South cooperation will be realised, and over what time period. The detailed scrutiny of the North–South dimension advanced here signals the many weaknesses and obstacles which threaten its development, at least in the short term. On the other hand, this book is replete with contemporary illustrations of the positive aspects of North–South cooperation. Moreover, its account of the changing historical parameters and international context of Irish politics suggests a more optimistic evaluation of the prospects for cross-border relationships in the twenty-first century. We began this book by referring to the spectacular East lighthouse on Rathlin Island, run from Dublin by the Commissioners of Irish Lights, as a symbol of the complexity of relations between North and South, and between Great Britain and Ireland. We close it by returning to this symbol. It is true that, politically and legally, Ireland's lighthouse network highlights the case for island-level and British–Irish integration. But it also illustrates the extent to which functional cooperation in areas as vital as marine safety comfortably sidelines political sensitivities, suggesting that in the long term it is the logic of efficient service delivery rather than the emotive baggage associated with Ireland's serpentine border that will determine popular acceptance of systematic cooperation, institutional and informal, North and South.

NOTES

1 HV Morton, *In search of Ireland*, 9th edn. (London: Methuen, 1934), p. 230 [first published 1930].

2 Clare O'Halloran argues convincingly that the 1937 constitution, and specifically articles 2 and 3, represented 'a further retreat from reality into the refuge of hollow rhetoric and pragmatic partitionism'; see C O'Halloran, *Partition and the limits of Irish nationalism: an ideology under stress* (Dublin: Gill and Macmillan, 1987), p. 177. This is not incompatible with de Valera's own pragmatic attitude towards partition – he regarded Irish unity as 'inevitable but postponable'; see J Bowman, *De Valera and the Ulster question, 1917–1973* (Oxford: Clarendon Press, 1982), pp. 305–15. This process seems to have accelerated since the 1970s; see J Coakley, 'Conclusion: new strains of unionism and nationalism', in J Coakley (ed.), *Changing shades of orange and green: redefining the union and the nation in contemporary Ireland* (Dublin: UCD Press, 2002), pp. 149–52.

3 As Michael Laffan put it eloquently, 'Anglo-Irish–Ulster relations can be compared to a nest of Russian matryoshka dolls, one doll enclosing another. Britain tried to dominate Ireland. The Irish majority tried to dominate Ulster. The Ulster majority tried to dominate the Ulster minority. The northern Catholics were the smallest and innermost doll, with no one else to envelop or dominate. They were the ultimate victims of partition'; M Laffan, *The partition of Ireland 1911–1925* (Dundalk: Dundalgan Press, 1983), p. 113.

4 David Rottman has argued that 'scholars in one part of the island operate through mind sets that render the structures and processes of the other part irrelevant to understanding and explaining'; see DB Rottman, 'Problems of, and prospects for, comparing the two Irelands', in AF Heath, R Breen and CT Whelan (eds), *Ireland North and South: perspectives from social science* (Oxford: Oxford University Press, 1999) [*Proceedings of the British Academy*, vol. 98], pp. 1–33, at p. 24. Rottman suggests that social psychological barriers between scholars on the two sides of the border resulted in each of them adopting different comparative reference points, an observation echoed in J Bradley, 'The history of economic development in Ireland, North and South', in Heath et al., *Ireland* (1999), pp. 35–68, who comments on the limited contact between researchers in Northern Ireland (whose focus was on Britain) and those in the South (whose focus was on European and world arenas). Reluctance to engage in comparative work was matched by the paucity of analysis of actual cross-border relationships. For example, the border region (where everyday cross-border relationships were strongest) was *terra incognita* for academic researchers until the early 1990s.

5 This figure is an estimate based on the allocation of professed non-believers or those not indicating their religion to an assumed cultural background.

6 L O'Dowd 'Transnational integration and cross-border regions in the European Union', in J Anderson (ed.), *Transnational democracy: political spaces and border crossings* (London: Routledge, 2002), pp. 111–28.

7 The politics of zero-sum territorialism was exacerbated in Northern Ireland in the post-Agreement period by political controversies over parades, peacelines and tensions in interface areas. But such controversies are also evident in the South, for example, in the intense local conflicts over the location of hospitals and hospital services – a factor which also impinges on cross-border cooperation in the health services (see Patricia Clarke's account in chapter 8).

Glossary: Selected bodies and programmes dealing with North–South matters

Note. This glossary lists only a selection of institutions and structured activities associated with the North–South relationship. Cross-references to other entries are in bold lettering. For more comprehensive information on Northern Ireland-related bodies, see the directory produced by CAIN in the University of Ulster (cain.ulst.ac.uk/othelem/organ).

Anglo-Irish Agreement. agreement signed by Taoiseach Garret FitzGerald and Prime Minister Margaret Thatcher on 15 November 1985; provided for a formal Irish government voice in the affairs of Northern Ireland, to be exercised through an **Anglo-Irish Intergovernmental Conference** with a permanent secretariat; replaced by the British–Irish agreement incorporated in the **Good Friday Agreement**, which came into effect on 2 December 1999; text: www.dfa.ie/uploads/documents/angloirish agreement 1985.pdf.

Anglo-Irish Intergovernmental Conference. Arrangement under the **Anglo-Irish Agreement** for regular meetings between British and Irish government ministers to discuss aspects of the government of Northern Ireland and North–South relations; established in 1985 under the umbrella of the **Anglo-Irish Intergovernmental Council**; had a permanent secretariat in Maryfield, Belfast; superseded by the **British–Irish Intergovernmental Conference** on 2 December 1999.

Anglo-Irish Intergovernmental Council. Arrangement agreed in talks between Taoiseach Charles Haughey and Prime Minister Margaret Thatcher in 1981 to provide for regular meetings between British and Irish government ministers to discuss matters of common interest; superseded by the **British–Irish Intergovernmental Conference** on 2 December 1999.

Belfast Agreement. See **Good Friday Agreement**.

Boord o Ulstèr-Scotch. See **Ulster-Scots Agency**.

Border Action. Partnership between Pobal (founded in 1992 as Area Development Management to manage certain EU programmes, and reconstituted under its new name in 2005) and the Combat Poverty Agency (founded in 1986); in existence since 1995, but formally renamed in 2005; acts as an intermediary funding body to implement Peace and Interreg measures in the border region; has also joined with the Community Foundation of Northern Ireland in a cross-border consortium to implement Peace programme measures; based in Monaghan; web: www.borderaction.ie.

British–Irish Council. Intergovernmental organisation comprising the Irish and British governments, the Scottish, Welsh and Northern Irish executives, and the governments of Jersey, Guernsey and the Isle of Man; created on 2 December 1999 in conformity with a British–Irish agreement on 8 March 1999 and the **Good Friday Agreement**; web: www.british-irishcouncil.org.

British–Irish Intergovernmental Conference. Arrangement under the **Good Friday Agreement**, formally approved in a British–Irish agreement on 8 March 1999 and coming into effect on 2 December 1999, for regular meetings between British and Irish ministers to discuss non-devolved aspects of the government of Northern Ireland and North–South relations; has a permanent secretariat in Belfast; supersedes the **Anglo-Irish Intergovernmental Conference** and the **Anglo-Irish Intergovernmental Council.**

British–Irish Inter-Parliamentary Body. Consultative assembly of British and Irish parliamentarians proposed by Taoiseach Charles Haughey and Prime Minister Margaret Thatcher during talks in 1981, and further agreed in the **Anglo-Irish Agreement** of 1985; established in 1990; originally comprised twenty-five members each from the Irish and British parliaments; in 2001 five members each from the Scottish parliament and the Welsh and Northern Irish assemblies, and one each from the legislatures of Jersey, Guernsey and the Isle of Man, were added; meets twice yearly; web: www.biipb.org.

Centre for Cross Border Studies. Organisation established in 1999 by Queen's University Belfast, Dublin City University and the Workers Educational Association to promote cross-border cooperation and policy research on cross-border issues; based in Armagh, with an office also in Dublin City University; web: www.crossborder.ie.

Commissioners of Irish Lights. Body responsible for the supervision and maintenance of the lighthouses around the Irish coast; founded in 1786 as the 'Corporation for preserving and improving the Port of Dublin'; given responsibility for all lighthouses around the Irish coast in 1810;

given its present name in 1867 when the port and lighthouse functions were separated; planned to become an agency of the **Foyle, Carlingford and Irish Lights Commission**, but legal difficulties (the fact that its operation was governed by UK legislation rather than by legislation in a devolved sector) prevented this; based in Dun Laoghaire; web: www.cil.ie.

Common chapter. Identical text, agreed by the British and Irish governments, dealing with island-wide planning, first adopted in the northern and southern development plans of 1994–9; adopted in the Republic's National Development Plan and Northern Ireland's Structural Funds Plan for the period 2000–6 (chapter 9 of each document); overseen by the **Special EU Programmes Body**; text: ndp.ie/documents/publications/ndp_csf_docs/ndp_complete_text.pdf.

Cooperation and Working Together. Cross-border body established in 1992 by regional health boards in the Republic and Northern Ireland to promote cooperation between health and social service workers in the border area; based in Derry/Londonderry; web: www.cawt.com.

Co-operation Ireland. Organisation committed to encouraging North–South contact with a view to promoting peace; founded in 1979 as Co-operation North; name changed to present one in 1998; offices in Dublin, Belfast, Armagh, Cork, USA and Great Britain; web: www.cooperationireland.org.

Council of Ireland. (1) Interparliamentary assembly proposed by the **Government of Ireland Act**, 1920; it was to comprise forty members, drawn equally from Northern Ireland and Southern Ireland, with thirteen from each House of Commons and seven from each Senate; never came into existence; formally abandoned in 1925 by agreement between the northern, southern and UK governments. (2) North–South body proposed by the **Sunningdale Agreement**, 1973; it was to comprise a Council of Ministers, made up of seven ministers from the Irish government and the same number from the Northern Ireland executive, with 'executive and harmonising functions' but acting by unanimity, and a Consultative Assembly, made up of thirty members of the Dáil and thirty members of the Northern Ireland Assembly; never came into existence; became a dead letter on the collapse of the Northern Ireland executive on 28 May 1974 following the Ulster Workers' Council strike.

East Border Region Committee. Cross-border network linking local authorities in the eastern border area to promote development in agriculture, industry, commerce and tourism; includes councillors from the county councils of Louth, Meath and Monaghan in the Republic, and from the district councils of Ards, Armagh, Banbridge, Craigavon,

Down, Newry and Mourne, and North Down in Northern Ireland; established 1976; based in Newry; web: www.eastborderregion.com.

Food Safety Promotion Board. See **Safefood.**

Foras na Gaeilge. Agency established as one of the two components of the **Language Body**, which came into existence on 2 December 1999 under the terms of the **Good Friday Agreement**; responsible for promoting the Irish language throughout Ireland; incorporated an existing public body, Bord na Gaeilge, and other bodies in the Republic; based in Dublin, with an office in Belfast; web: www.forasnagaeilge.ie.

Foyle Fisheries Commission. North–South body established by the Irish and Northern Irish governments in 1952 to manage the fisheries in the Foyle area; incorporated in the **Foyle, Carlingford and Irish Lights Commission** on 2 December 1999.

Foyle, Carlingford and Irish Lights Commission. Implementation body established under the **Good Friday Agreement**, and under the terms of a British–Irish agreement of 8 March 1999, coming into formal existence on 2 December 1999; it was intended that it would operate through two agencies, the **Loughs Agency** and the Lights Agency; the former was duly created, but the latter, intended to subsume the **Commissioners of Irish Lights**, was never brought into existence because of legal complexities.

Good Friday Agreement. agreement between most Northern Ireland parties and the British and Irish governments on 10 April 1998, also known as the Belfast agreement; comprised both an agreement between parties (the multi-party agreement) and between governments (the British–Irish agreement); provided *inter alia* for various changes to the government of Northern Ireland, for the establishment of a **North/South Ministerial Council** and **North–South implementation bodies**, for a **British–Irish Council** and for a **British–Irish Intergovernmental Conference**; came into effect on 2 December 1999, superseding the **Anglo-Irish Agreement**, 1985; text: www.nio.gov.uk/agreement.pdf.

Government of Ireland Act, 1920. Act of the UK parliament which superseded the Government of Ireland Act, 1914 (the 'home rule' act), devolving authority separately to two states into which Ireland was partitioned, Northern Ireland and Southern Ireland; came into effect in 1921; made provision for certain all-Irish institutions, including a **Council of Ireland**; superseded in Southern Ireland by the Anglo-Irish treaty of 1921.

Great Northern Railway Company. Private company which managed a network of railways, including the Belfast–Dublin line; taken over by the Irish and Northern Ireland governments in 1953 and operated as a North–South body; partitioned in 1958 between the railway authorities of Northern Ireland and the Republic.

IBEC/CBI Joint Business Council. Committee established in 1991 jointly by the Irish Business and Employers Confederation and the Confederation of British Industry in Northern Ireland to stimulate cross-border trade and to make business on the island of Ireland more competitive; web: www.cbi.org.uk/pdf/jbcflier.pdf.

Institute of Public Health in Ireland. North–South body established in 1999 by the health departments in Northern Ireland and the Republic to promote cooperation in the area of public health; offices in Belfast and Dublin; web: www.publichealth.ie.

International Fund for Ireland. Body established in 1986 by the British and Irish governments under the **Anglo-Irish Agreement**, 1985, to promote economic and social development and to encourage reconciliation between nationalists and unionists throughout Ireland; funded by the British, Irish, American, Canadian, Australian and New Zealand governments, and the EU; offices in Belfast and Dublin; web: www.internationalfundforireland.com.

Interreg programme. EU-funded programme designed to promote regional development across national borders in Europe, introduced initially to help regions adjoining such borders; Interreg I covered the period 1990–3, Interreg II, 1994–9, and Interreg III 2000–6; managed by the **Special EU Programmes Body**.

InterTrade Ireland. Implementation body established under the **Good Friday Agreement**, and under the terms of the British–Irish agreement of 8 March 1999, coming into formal existence on 2 December 1999; originally known as the Trade and Business Development Body; responsible for the promotion of trade and business on an all-island and cross-border basis; based in Newry; web: www.intertradeireland.com.

Ireland. (1) Traditional name of the island. (2) Official English-language name of the southern state according to the 1937 constitution, in which article 4 stated that 'The name of the state is *Éire*, or, in the English language, *Ireland*'; it succeeded the Irish Free State, established in 1922 under the terms of the Anglo-Irish treaty of 1921, which itself succeeded Southern Ireland, established in 1921 under the terms of the **Government of Ireland Act**, 1920; given the additional 'description' (but not name!) Republic of Ireland in 1949; after accession to the EU in 1973, increasingly accepted by the British as the name of the state; formally accepted in 1998.

Irish Association for Cultural, Economic and Social Relations.

Association founded in 1938, largely on the initiative of unionists in Northern Ireland, to encourage good relations between North and South, and between unionists and nationalists; web: www.irish-association.org.

Irish Central Border Area Network. Cross-border network linking local authorities in the central border area to address the area's unique social needs; includes councillors from the county councils of Donegal, Cavan, Monaghan, Sligo and Leitrim in the Republic, and from the district councils of Armagh, Cookstown, Dungannon, Fermanagh and Strabane in Northern Ireland; established 1995; based in Enniskillen; web: www.icban.com.

Irish Congress of Trade Unions. Umbrella body linking trade unions on both sides of the Irish border; established in its present form in 1959, succeeding an older organisation established in 1894; has a separate Northern Ireland Committee; web: www.ictu.ie.

Irish Republic. (1) Name of the revolutionary state proclaimed in 1916 and partly established by the first Dáil in 1919; superseded by the Irish Free State in 1922, though one strand of militant nationalism continues to recognise it until the present. (2) Name used in the past, along with 'Eire', in official British circles to describe the Republic of Ireland with a view to avoiding implications of a territorial claim on Northern Ireland.

Language Body. Implementation body established under the **Good Friday Agreement**, and under the terms of a British–Irish agreement of 8 March 1999, coming into formal existence on 2 December 1999; operates through two agencies, **Foras na Gaeilge** and the **Ulster-Scots Agency**.

Leader programme. EU-funded programme designed to encourage rural development; Leader I covered the period 1991–4, Leader II, 1994–9, and Leader+, 2000–6.

Loughs Agency. Agency established as one of the two intended components of the **Foyle, Carlingford and Irish Lights Commission**, which came into existence on 2 December 1999 under the terms of the **Good Friday Agreement**; responsible for managing marine matters (including fisheries and aquaculture) in Lough Foyle and Carlingford Lough; incorporated and assumed the functions of the **Foyle Fisheries Commission;** based in Derry/Londonderry, with an office in Carlingford; web: www.loughs-agency.org.

North South Exchange Consortium. North–South body, linking the British Council, Léargas (the Republic's youth agency) and the Youth Council for Northern Ireland, established in 2002 to advise the education departments in Northern Ireland and the Republic on North–South school and youth exchanges; based in Dundalk; web: www.nsec.info.

North West Region Cross-Border Group. Cross-border network linking local authorities in the northwestern border area to promote local economic development; includes councillors from Donegal county council in the Republic and from the district councils of Derry, Limavady and Strabane in Northern Ireland; established 1979; based in Derry/Londonderry.

North/South Ministerial Council. Intergovernmental body linking the Irish government and the Northern Ireland executive, meeting in plenary format (involving the Taoiseach, First Minister, Deputy First Minister and other ministers), sectoral format (involving ministers from specific areas) and institutional format (a residual technical category) to supervise the work of the North–South implementation bodies and areas of cooperation defined in the **Good Friday Agreement**; formally provided for in a British–Irish agreement on 8 March 1999; came into existence on 2 December 1999; met first on 13 December 1999; most recent meeting on 8 October 2002; has a permanent secretariat in Armagh; web: www.northsouthministerialcouncil.org.

North–South implementation bodies. Set of six bodies agreed as part of the **Good Friday Agreement**; given legal basis in a British–Irish agreement on 8 March 1999; came into existence on 2 December 1999; web: www.northsouthministerialcouncil.org/index/north-south-bodies.htm.

Peace programme (European Union Special Programme for Peace and Reconciliation). Predominantly EU-funded programme designed to promote peace and reconciliation in Northern Ireland and in the six border counties of the Republic of Ireland; Peace I covered the period 1995–9, and Peace II the period 2000–6; managed by the **Special EU Programmes Body**.

Safefood. Implementation body established under the **Good Friday Agreement**, and under the terms of the British–Irish agreement of 8 March 1999, coming into formal existence on 2 December 1999; originally known as the Food Safety Promotion Board; responsible for promoting information and awareness of food safety issues throughout the island of Ireland; based in Cork, with an office also in Dublin; web: www.safefood.eu.

Shannon–Erne Waterway Promotions Ltd. Limited company established by the Irish and British governments in 1993 to promote the newly opened Ballinamore–Ballyconnell canal and associated waterways; incorporated in **Waterways Ireland** on 2 December 1999.

Special EU Programmes Body. Implementation body established under the **Good Friday Agreement**, and under the terms of the British–Irish agreement of 8 March 1999, coming into formal existence on 2 December 1999; responsible for managing and overseeing EU funds, the **Common Chapter**, and related matters; based in Belfast, with offices also in Omagh and Monaghan; web: www.seupb.org.

St Andrews Agreement. agreement between Northern Ireland parties and the British and Irish governments on 13 October 2006; modified certain of the provisions of the **Good Friday Agreement**; text: www.nio.gov.uk/st_andrews_agreement.pdf

Sunningdale Agreement. agreement signed by Taoiseach Liam Cosgrave, Prime Minister Edward Heath and the leaders of the Ulster Unionist Party, the SDLP and the Alliance Party at the civil service college at Sunningdale, Berkshire, on 9 December 1973; proposed to build on a power-sharing executive within Northern Ireland by linking Northern Ireland and the Republic through a **Council of Ireland**; text: cain.ulst.ac.uk/events/sunningdale/agreement.htm.

Tourism Ireland Ltd. Publicly owned limited company formally established on 27 October 2000 following several years of planning which predated the **Good Friday Agreement**; corresponds to one of the six 'areas of cooperation' in the agreement, the only one where a body of this kind has appeared; based in Dublin, with an office in Coleraine; web: www.tourismireland.com/corporate.

Ulster-Scots Agency. Agency established as one of the two components of the **Language Body**, which came into existence on 2 December 1999 under the terms of the **Good Friday Agreement**; also known as Tha Boord o Ulstèr-Scotch; responsible for promoting awareness of Ulster-Scots cultural issues; based in Belfast; web: www.ulsterscotsagency.com.

Waterways Ireland. Implementation body established under the **Good Friday Agreement**, and under the terms of the British–Irish agreement of 8 March 1999, coming into formal existence on 2 December 1999; responsible for the management of Ireland's navigable rivers and canals.; based in Enniskillen, with offices also in Carrick-on-Shannon, Scarriff and Dublin; web: www.waterwaysireland.org.

Bibliography

PUBLICATIONS

Acheson, N., B. Harvey, B. Kearney and A. Williamson, *Two paths one purpose: voluntary action in Ireland, north and south* (Dublin: Institute of Public Administration, 2004)

Akenson, D. H., *Education and enmity: the control of schooling in Northern Ireland 1920–1950* (Newton Abbot: David and Charles, 1973)

Albert, M. and L. Brock, 'Debordering the world of states', *New political science*, 35 (1996), pp. 69–106

Allister, J., *Leading for Ulster, speaking for you in Europe: a record of Jim Allister's speeches in the European parliament, July 2004–November 2005* (Belfast: Jim Allister MEP, 2006)

Anderson, J. and L. O'Dowd, 'Contested borders: globalisation and ethno-national conflict in Ireland', *Regional studies*, 33:7 (1999), pp. 681–96

Anderson, J., L. O'Dowd and T. M. Wilson (eds), *Cross-border cooperation*, Special Issue of *Administration*, 49:2 (2001)

Anderson, J., L. O'Dowd and T. M. Wilson (eds), *Culture, cooperation and conflict at international borders in Europe*, special issue of *European studies: a journal of European culture, history and politics*, 19 (2003)

Anderson, J., L. O'Dowd and T. M. Wilson (eds), *New borders for a changing Europe: cross-border cooperation and governance* (London: Frank Cass, 2003)

Anderson, M., *Frontiers: territory and state formation in the modern world* (Cambridge: Polity Press, 1996)

Anderson, M. and E. Bort (eds), *The frontiers of Europe* (London: Pinter, 1998)

Bairner, A. (ed.), *Sport and the Irish: histories, identities, issues* (Dublin: UCD Press, 2005)

Barry, F. and J. Bradley, 'FDI and trade: the Irish host-country experience', *Economic journal*, 107:445 (1997), pp. 1,798–811

Barton, B., 'Northern Ireland, 1925–39', in J. R. Hill (ed.), *A new history of Ireland: VII: Ireland, 1921–84* (Oxford: Oxford University Press, 2003), pp. 199–234

Baumann, Z., 'Soil, blood and identity', *Sociological review*, 40:2 (1992), pp. 675–701

Best, M., *The new competition: institutions of industrial restructuring* (Cambridge: Polity Press, 1990)

Best, M., *The new competitive advantage* (Oxford: Oxford University Press, 2001)

Bew, P. and G. Gillespie, *Northern Ireland: a chronology of the troubles* (Dublin: Gill & Macmillan, 1999)

Bew, P., K. Darwin and G. Gillespie, *Passion and prejudice: nationalist/unionist conflict in Ulster in the 1930s and the origins of the Irish Association* (Belfast: Institute of Irish Studies, Queen's University Belfast, 1993)

Bew, P., P. Gibbon and H. Patterson, *Northern Ireland 1921–1996: political forces and social classes*, rev. edn. (London: Serif, 1996)

Billig, M., *Banal nationalism* (London: Sage, 1995)

Birrell, D. and A. Murie, *Policy and government in Northern Ireland: lessons of devolution* (Dublin: Gill and Macmillan, 1980)

Blatter, J., 'From "spaces of place" to "spaces of flows"? Territorial and functional governance in cross-border regions in Europe and North America', *International journal of urban and regional research*, 28:3 (2004), pp. 530–48

Blok, A., 'The narcissism of minor differences', *European journal of social theory*, 1:1 (1998), pp. 33–56

Booth, C., 'Economic distribution of population in Ireland', in Department of Agricultural and Technical Instruction (ed.) *Ireland: industrial and agricultural* (Dublin: HMSO, 1901), pp. 54–62

Borooah, V., and K. Lee, 'The regional dimension of competitiveness in manufacturing: productivity, employment and wages in Northern Ireland and the United Kingdom', *Regional studies*, 25:3 (1991), pp. 219–29

Bowman, J., *De Valera and the Ulster question, 1917–1973* (Oxford: Clarendon Press, 1982)

Bradley, J. (ed.), *Regional economic and policy impacts of EMU: the case of Northern Ireland* (Belfast: Northern Ireland Economic Council, 1998) [Research Monograph 6]

Bradley, J. and D. Hamilton, 'Strategy 2010: planning economic development in Northern Ireland', *Regional studies*, 33:9 (1999), pp. 885–902

Bradley, J. and E. Birnie, *Can the Celtic tiger cross the border?* (Cork: Cork University Press, 2001)

Bradley, J., 'Economic aspects of the island of Ireland: an overview of the two economies', in J. Bradley (ed.), *The two economies of Ireland: public policy, growth and employment* (Dublin: Oak Tree, 1995), pp. 7–34

Bradley, J., 'Foreign direct investment: implications for Irish economic development and wider lessons', *Rassegna economica: quaderni di ricerca*, 3 (2000), pp. 97–138

Bradley, J., *An island economy: exploring long-term consequences of peace and reconciliation in the island of Ireland* (Dublin: Forum for Peace and Reconciliation, 1996)

Bradley, J., 'The history of economic development in Ireland, North and South', in A. F. Heath, R. Breen and C. T. Whelan (eds), *Ireland North and South: perspectives from social science* (Oxford: Oxford University Press, 1999), pp. 35–68 [Proceedings of the British Academy, volume 98]

Bradley, J., 'The Irish economy in comparative perspective', in B. Nolan, P. O'Connell and C. Whelan (eds), *Bust to boom* (Dublin: Institute of Public Administration, 2000), pp. 4–26

Bradley, J., *The island economy: past, present and future* (Cork: Cork University Press, 2001) [*Cross currents* series]

Bradley, J., 'The computer sector in Irish manufacturing: past triumphs, present strains, future challenges', *Journal of the Statistical and Social Inquiry Society of Ireland*, 31 (2001), pp. 25–70

British and Irish Communist Organisation, *The economics of partition*, 4th edn. (Belfast: British and Irish Communist Organisation, 1972)

British and Irish Governments, *Comprehensive study of the all-island economy* (Dublin and Belfast: Department of Foreign Affairs and Northern Ireland Office, 2006)

Cairns, E. and M. Hewstone, 'The impact of peacemaking in Northern Ireland on intergroup behaviour', in G. Salomon and B. Nevo (eds), *Peace education: the concept, principles and practice around the world* (Mahwah, NJ: Lawrence Erlbaum Associates, 1997)

Cannadine, D., *Ornamentalism: how the British saw their empire* (London: Penguin, 2002)

Castells, M., *The rise of the network society* (Oxford: Blackwell, 1996)

Cathcart, R., *The most contrary region: the BBC in Northern Ireland 1924–1984* (Belfast: Blackstaff Press, 1984)

Central Statistics Office, *Statistics for North–South trade* (Cork: Central Statistics Office, 2004)

Clayton, P., *Enemies and passing friends: settler ideologies in twentieth century Ulster* (London: Pluto Press, 1999)

Coakley, J. (ed.), *The territorial management of ethnic conflict*, 2nd edn. (London: Frank Cass, 2003)

Coakley, J., 'Conclusion: new strains of unionism and nationalism', in J. Coakley (ed.), *Changing shades of orange and green: redefining the union and the nation in contemporary Ireland* (Dublin: UCD Press, 2002), pp. 132–54

Coakley, J., *The North–South institutions: from blueprint to reality* (Dublin: Institute for British–Irish Studies, University College Dublin, 2002) [IBIS Working Paper, no. 22]

Coakley, J., 'Religion, national identity and political change in modern Ireland', *Irish political studies*, 17:1 (2002), pp. 4–28

Coakley, J., 'The North–South relationship: implementing the agreement', in Coakley, J., 'Northern Ireland and the British dimension', in J. Coakley and M. Gallagher (eds), *Politics in the Republic of Ireland*, 4th edn. (London: Routledge, 2004), pp. 407–29

J. Coakley, B. Laffan and J. Todd (eds), *Renovation or revolution? New territorial politics in Ireland and the United Kingdom* (Dublin: UCD Press, 2005), pp. 110–31

Cooke, P. and K. Morgan, *The associational economy: firms, regions, and innovation* (Oxford: Oxford University Press, 1998)

Coyle, D., W. Alexander and B. Ashcroft (eds), *New wealth for old nations: Scotland's economic prospects* (Princeton: Princeton University Press, 2005)

Cradden, T., *Trade unionism, socialism and the labour movement in Northern Ireland, 1939–53* (Belfast: December Publications, 1993)

Cronin, M., *Sport and nationalism in Ireland: Gaelic games, soccer and Irish identity since 1884* (Dublin: Four Courts Press, 1999)

Crotty, R., *Ireland in crisis: a study of capitalist colonial underdevelopment* (Dingle: Brandon Press, 1986)

Daly, M.E., *Social and economic history of Ireland since 1800* (Dublin: Educational Company of Ireland, 1981)

Daly, T., *The Rás: Ireland's unique bike race, 1953–2003* (Dublin: The Collins Press, 2003)

D'Arcy, M. and T. Dickson (eds), *Border crossings: developing Ireland's border economy* (Dublin: Gill & Macmillan, 1995)

Davies, N., *The Isles* (London: Macmillan, 1999)

Department of Economic Development, Northern Ireland, *Strategy 2010, a report prepared by the Economic Development Strategy Review Steering Group* (Belfast: Department of Economic Development, 1999)

Dunn, S. and V. Morgan, 'A fraught path – education as a basis for developing improved community relations in Northern Ireland', *Oxford review of education*, 25:1–2 (1999), pp. 141–53

Etzioni, A., *The spirit of community* (London: Fontana, 1993)

Farley, N., 'A comparative analysis of the performance of the manufacturing sectors, North and South: 1960–1991', in J. Bradley (ed.), *The two economies of Ireland: public policy, growth and employment* (Dublin: Oak Tree Press, 1995) [Irish Studies in Management]

Farren, S. and R. Mulvihill, *Paths to settlement in Northern Ireland* (Gerrard's Cross: Colin Smythe, 2000)

Farrington, C., *Models of civil society and their implications for the Northern*

Ireland peace process (Dublin: Institute for British Irish Studies, 2004) [IBIS Working Paper no. 43]

Fitzgerald, G., *Ireland in the world: further reflections* (Dublin: Liberties Press, 2005)

Fitzgerald, G., *Towards a new Ireland* (London: Charles Knight, 1972)

Forfás, *Enterprise 2010: a new strategy for the promotion of enterprise in Ireland in the 21st century* (Dublin: Forfás, 2000)

Gallagher, M., *The Irish Labour Party in transition, 1957–82* (Dublin: Gill & Macmillan, 1982)

Gibbon, P., *The origins of Ulster unionism* (Manchester: Manchester University Press, 1975)

Guelke, A., 'Civil society and the Northern Ireland peace process', *Voluntas*, 14:1 (2003), pp. 61–78

Gwynn, D., *The history of partition, 1912–1925* (Dublin: Browne and Nolan, 1950)

Hamber, B. and G. Kelly, *A place for reconciliation? Conflict and locality in Northern Ireland* (Belfast: Democratic Dialogue, 2005)

Hamilton, D., 'Economic integration on the island of Ireland', *Administration*, 49:2 (2001), pp. 73–89

Harrigan, K. and M. Porter, 'End-game strategies for declining industries', in M. Porter (ed.), *On competition* (Cambridge, MA: Harvard Business Review Books, 1998)

Harvey, B., *Review of the Peace II Programme* (York: Joseph Rowntree Charitable Trust, 2003)

Harvey, B., *Rights and justice work in Ireland: a new base line* (York: Joseph Rowntree Charitable Trust, 2002)

Hassan, D., 'Sport, identity and Irish nationalism in Northern Ireland', in A. Bairner (ed.), *Sport and the Irish: histories, identities, issues* (Dublin: UCD Press, 2005), pp. 123–39

Held, D., D. Goldblatt, T. McGrew and J. Perraton, *Global transformations: politics, economics and culture* (Cambridge: Polity Press, 1999)

Helliwell, J. F., *How much do national borders matter?* (Washington, DC: Brookings Institution Press, 1998)

Hennessey, T., *Dividing Ireland: World War 1 and partition* (London: Routledge, 1998)

Hodges, M., *European integration* (Harmondswoth: Penguin, 1972)

Hughes, J. and C. Knox, 'For better or worse? Community relations initiatives in Northern Ireland', *Peace and change*, 22:3 (1997), pp. 330–55

Isles, K. S. and N. Cuthbert, *An economic survey of Northern Ireland* (Belfast: HMSO, 1957)

Jamison, J., H. Legido-Quigley and M. McKee, 'Cross-border health care in

Ireland', in M. Rosemoller, M. McKee and R. Baeten (eds), *Patient mobility in the European Union: learning from experience* (Brussels: European Observatory on Health Care Systems, 2006)

Jamison, J., M. Butler, P. Clarke, M. McKee, and C. O'Neill, *Cross-border co-operation in health services in Ireland* (Armagh: Centre for Cross Border Studies, 2001)

Johnson, D. S, *The interwar economy in Ireland* (Dundalk: The Economic and Social History Society of Ireland, 1985) [*Studies in Irish economic and social history*, 4]

Kay, J., 'Economics and business', *Economic journal*, 101 (1991), pp. 57–63

Kay, N., 'Multinational enterprises: a review article', *Scottish journal of political economy*, 30:3 (1983), pp. 304–12

Keane, J., *Civil society: old images, new visions* (Stanford: Stanford University Press, 1998)

Kelly, G. and B. Hamber (eds), *Reconciliation: rhetoric or relevant?* (Belfast: Democratic Dialogue, 2005)

Kennedy, D., *The widening gulf: Northern attitudes to the independent Irish state, 1919–1949* (Belfast: Blackstaff Press, 1988)

Kennedy, L., *The modern industrialization of Ireland, 1940–1988: studies in Irish economic and social history*, 5 (Dundalk: Economic and Social History Society of Ireland, 1989)

Kennedy, M., *Division and consensus: the politics of cross-border relations in Ireland, 1925–1969* (Dublin: Institute of Public Administration, 2000)

Kirk, J. M., 'Ulster Scots: realities and myths', *Ulster folk life*, 44 (1998), pp. 69–93

Krugman, P., 'Good news from Ireland: a geographical perspective', in A. Gray (ed.), *International perspectives on the Irish economy* (Dublin: Indecon Economic Consultants, 1997), pp. 38–53

Laffan, B. and D Payne, *Creating living institutions: EU cross-border co-operation after the Good Friday Agreement* (Armagh: Centre for Cross-Border Studies, 2001)

Laffan, M., *The partition of Ireland 1911–25* (Dundalk: Dundalgan Press, 1983)

Lawrence, R. J., *The government of Northern Ireland: public finance and public services 1921–1964* (Oxford: Oxford University Press, 1965)

Logue, P., 'Cross border reconciliation and development', in Community Federation for Northern Ireland, *Taking 'calculated' risks for Peace II* (Belfast: Community Foundation of Northern Ireland, 2003), pp. 86–91

Lustick, I. S., *Unsettled states, disputed lands: Britain and Ireland, France and Algeria, Israel and the West Bank Gaza* (Ithaca: Cornell University Press, 1993)

Mac Gréil, M., *Prejudice and tolerance in Ireland* (Dublin: College of Industrial Relations, 1977)

Mac Gréil, M., *Prejudice in Ireland revisited* (Maynooth: Survey and Research Unit, St Patrick's College, 1996)

Mac Poilín, A., (1999) 'Language, identity, and politics in Northern Ireland', *Ulster folk life*, 45 (1999), pp. 108–32

MacSharry, R. and P. White, *The making of the Celtic tiger* (Cork: Mercier Press, 2000)

McCall, C., 'Creating border space: an EU approach to ethno-national threat and insecurity', in J. Anderson and W. Armstrong (eds), *Europe's borders and geo-politics: expansion, inclusion and integration in the European Union* (London: Routledge, 2007, pp. 61–77)

McCarthy, C., *Trade unions in Ireland 1894–1960* (Dublin: IPA, 1977)

McClain, L. and J. Fleming, 'Some questions for civil society revivalists', *Chicago-Kent Law Review*, 75:2 (2000), pp. 301–54

McGarry, J. and B. O'Leary, *Policing Northern Ireland: proposals for a new beginning* (Belfast: Blackstaff Press, 1999)

McGarry, J., 'Europe's limits: European integration and conflict management in Northern Ireland', in J. McGarry and M. Keating (eds), *European integration and the nationalities question* (London: Routledge, 2006), pp. 273–9

McKiernan, P., *Strategies of growth: maturity, recovery and internationalization* (London: Routledge, 1992)

McLoone, M. and J. Macmahon (eds), *Television in Irish society: 21 years of Irish television* (Dublin: RTE, 1984)

McLoughlin, R., 'The industrial development process: an overall view', *Administration*, 20:1 (1972), pp. 27–36

Mann, M., *The sources of social power, volume II* (Cambridge: Cambridge University Press, 1993)

Mansergh, M., *Cross-border bodies and the North–South relationship: laying the groundwork* (Dublin: Institute for British–Irish Studies, University College Dublin, 2001) [IBIS working paper, no. 12]

Mansergh, N., *The Irish Free State: its government and politics* (London: Allen and Unwin, 1934)

Mansergh, N., *The government of Northern Ireland: a study in devolution* (London: Allen and Unwin, 1936)

Meenan, J., *The Irish economy since 1922* (Liverpool: Liverpool University Press, 1970)

Miller, D., *Don't mention the war: Northern Ireland propaganda and the media* (London: Pluto Press, 1994)

Montgomery, M., 'The position of Ulster Scots', *Ulster folk life*, 45 (1999), pp. 86–107

Motyl, A. J., *Imperial ends: decay, collapse and revival of empires* (New York: Columbia University Press, 2001)

Munck, R., *The Irish economy: results and prospects* (London: Pluto Press, 1993)
Northern Ireland Council for Voluntary Action (NICVA), *Joint government/voluntary and community sector forum, voluntary and community sector panel* (Belfast: NICVA, 2003) [Issues paper for the Taskforce on Sustainability of the Voluntary and Community Sector]
Northern Ireland Council for Voluntary Action (NICVA), *Designing Peace III* (Belfast: NICVA, 2004)
Northern Ireland Economic Council (NIEC), *Inward investment in Northern Ireland* (Belfast: NIEC, 1992) [Report no. 99]
Northern Ireland Economic Council (NIEC), *The implementation of Northern Ireland's development strategy in the 1990s: lessons for the future* (Belfast: NIEC, 1999) [Report no. 131]
Ó Corráin, D., *The Irish churches and the two states in Ireland, 1949–73* (Manchester: Manchester University Press, 2006)
Ó Gráda, C., *A rocky road: the Irish economy since the 1920s* (Manchester: Manchester University Press, 1997)
Ó Gráda, C., *Ireland: a new economic history 1780–1939* (Oxford: Clarendon Press, 1994)
O'Donnell, R. and P. Teague, 'The potential limits to North–South economic co-operation', in P. Teague (ed.), *The economy of Northern Ireland: perspectives for structural change* (London: Lawrence and Wishart, 1993), pp. 240–70
O'Dowd, L., *Whither the Irish border? Sovereignty, democracy and economic integration in Ireland* (Belfast: Centre for Research and Documentation, 1994)
O'Dowd, L., 'Development or dependency? State, economy and society in Northern Ireland', in P. Clancy et al. (eds), *Irish society: sociological perspectives* (Dublin: IPA, 1995), pp. 132–77
O'Dowd, L., 'The changing significance of European borders', *Regional and federal studies*, 12:4 (2002), pp. 13–36
O'Dowd, L., 'The great reversal: nationalism and unionism, 1950–2000', in M. P. Corcoran and M. Peillon (eds), *Ireland unbound: a turn of the century chronicle* (Dublin: IPA, 2002), pp. 260–77
O'Dowd, L., 'Transnational integration and cross-border regions in the European Union', in J Anderson (ed.), *Transnational democracy: political spaces and border crossings* (London: Routledge, 2002), pp. 111–28
O'Dowd, L., J. Corrigan and T. Moore, 'Borders, national sovereignty and European Integration', *International journal of urban and regional research*, 19:2 (1995), pp. 272–85
O'Dowd, L. and J. Corrigan, 'Buffer zone or bridge: local responses to cross-border economic cooperation in the Irish border region', *Administration*, 42:4 (1994–5), pp. 335–51

O'Dowd, L. and J. Corrigan, 'Securing the Irish border in a Europe without frontiers', in L. O'Dowd and T. M. Wilson (eds), *Borders, nations and states: frontiers of sovereignty in the new Europe* (Aldershot: Avebury, 1996), pp. 117–33

O'Halloran, C., *Partition and the limits of Irish nationalism: an ideology under stress* (Dublin: Gill & Macmillan, 1987)

O'Hearn, D., 'Global restructuring and Irish political economy', in P. Clancy et al. (eds), *Irish society: sociological perspectives* (Dublin: IPA, 1995), pp. 90–131

Ohmae, K., 'Putting global logic first', in K. Ohmae (ed.), *The evolving global economy* (Cambridge, MA: Harvard Business Review Books, 1996), pp. 129–37

Ohmae, K., *The invisible continent* (London: Nicholas Brealey, 2000)

O'Leary, B., 'Introduction', in B. O'Leary, I. S. Lustick and T. Callaghy (eds), *Right sizing the state: the politics of moving borders* (Oxford: Oxford University Press, 2001), pp. 1–14

Ollerenshaw, P., 'Industry, 1820–1914', in L. Kennedy and P. Ollerenshaw (eds), *An economic history of Ulster, 1820–1939* (Manchester: Manchester University Press, 1985), pp. 62–108

Olson, M., *The rise and decline of nations: economic growth, stagflation and social rigidities* (New Haven: Yale University Press, 1982)

O'Mahony, D., *The Irish economy: an introductory description* (Cork: Cork University Press, 1964)

O'Malley, E., 'The revival of Irish indigenous industry 1987–1997', *Quarterly economic commentary, April* (Dublin: Economic and Social Research Institute, 1998)

Phoenix, E., 'Michael Collins: the northern question 1916–1922', in G. Doherty and D. Keogh (eds), *Michael Collins and the making of the Irish state* (Cork: Mercier Press, 1998), pp. 92–116

Pollak, A. (ed.), *A citizens' inquiry: the Opsahl Report on Northern Ireland* (Dublin: Lilliput Press, 1993)

Porter, M., *The competitive advantage of nations* (London: Macmillan, 1990)

Porter, M., *On competition* (Cambridge, MA: Harvard Business Review Press, 1998)

Portes, A., 'Social capital: its origins and applications in modern sociology', *Annual review of sociology*, 24 (1998), pp. 1–24

Powell, F. and D. Guerin, *Civil society and social policy: voluntarism in Ireland* (Dublin: A & A Farmar, 1997)

Powell, F. and M. Geoghegan, *The politics of community development: reclaiming civil society or reinventing governance?* (Dublin: A & A Farmar, 2004)

Putnam, R., *Making democracy work: civic traditions in modern Italy* (Princeton:

Princeton University Press, 1993)

Putnam, R., *Bowling alone: the collapse and revival of American community* (New York: Simon and Schuster, 2000)

Quinlivan, E., *Forging links: a study of cross-border community co-operation in the Irish border region* (Belfast: Co-operation Ireland, 1999)

Rolston, B., *War and words: the Northern Ireland media reader* (Belfast: Beyond the Pale Publications, 1996)

Rothman, J., 'Dialogue in conflict: past and future', in E. Wiener (ed.), *The handbook of interethnic coexistence* (New York: Continuum Publishing Co, 1998), pp. 217–35

Rottman, D. B., 'Problems of, and prospects for, comparing the two Irelands', in A. F. Heath, R. Breen and C. T. Whelan (eds), *Ireland North and South: perspectives from social science* (Oxford: Oxford University Press, 1999) [Proceedings of the British Academy, vol. 98], pp. 1–33

Rowthorn, B. and N. Wayne, *Northern Ireland: the political economy of conflict* (Cambridge: Polity Press, 1988)

Sheehy, M., *Divided we stand: a study of partition* (London: Faber and Faber, 1955)

Smith, A. and A. Robinson, *Education for mutual understanding: the initial statutory years* (Coleraine: Centre for the Study of Conflict, University of Ulster, 1996)

Social Democratic and Labour Party [SDLP], *North South makes sense* (Belfast: SDLP, 2006)

Stigler, G., 'The division of labor is limited by the extent of the market', *Journal of political economy*, 59 (1951) pp. 185–93

Tannam, E., *Cross-border cooperation in the Republic of Ireland and Northern Ireland* (Basingstoke: Macmillan, 1999)

Tannam, E., 'Cross-border co-operation between Northern Ireland and the Republic of Ireland: neo-functionalism re-visited', *British journal of politics and international relations*, 8:2 (2006), pp. 256–76

Tilly, C., *Coercion, capital and European states AD 990–1990* (Oxford: Basil Blackwell, 1990)

Tonge, J., 'The EU and the Irish border: shaping aid and attitudes' (Belfast: Centre for International Borders Research, Queen's University, 2005) [CIBR Working Paper Series, WP05/1]

Trant, A., 'Promoting peace in Ireland through vocational training and work experience', *International journal of vocational training and education*, 11:1 (2003) pp. 84–93

van Houtum, H., O. Kramsch and D. Ziefhofer (eds), *Bordering space* (Oxford: Ashgate, 2004)

Vernon, R., 'International investment and international trade in the prod-

uct cycle', *Quarterly journal of economics*, 80:2 (1966), pp. 190–207
Vernon, R., 'The product cycle hypothesis in a new international environment', *Oxford bulletin of economics and statistics*, 41:4 (1979) pp. 255–67
Whyte, J. H., 'The permeability of the United Kingdom–Irish border: a preliminary reconnaissance', *Administration*, 31:3 (1983), pp. 300–15
Whyte, J. H., 'Reconciliation, rights and protests, 1963–8', in J. R Hill (ed.), *A new history of Ireland: VII: Ireland, 1921–84* (Oxford: Oxford University Press, 2003), pp. 309–16
Wilford, R. and R. Wilson, *A democratic design? The political style of the Northern Ireland Assembly* (London: Constitution Unit, University College London, 2001)
Wilson, R. (ed.), *No frontiers: North–South integration in Ireland* (Belfast: Democratic Dialogue, 1999)
Wilson, T. M. and H. Donnan (eds), *Border identities: nation and state at international frontiers* (Cambridge: Cambridge University Press, 1998)
Yadowski, S., 'The new orientalism and the democracy debate', in J. Beinin and J. Stork (eds), *Political Islam* (London and New York: Taurus, 1995), pp. 33–51

WORKING PAPERS

The following working papers, produced as part of the project, *Mapping Frontiers, Plotting Pathways: Routes to North–South Cooperation in a Divided Island*, on which this book is based, have been used as background in the production of the text. Ancillary papers 1–7 also appeared respectively as IBIS working papers 40–42 and 50–53; working papers 1–3 appeared also as IBIS working papers 47–49, and working papers 4–28 as IBIS working papers 54–78. All the papers are also available at: www.qub.ac.uk/cibr/mappingfrontierswps.htm.

Ancillary papers

1. Tannam, E., 'Cross-border co-operation between Northern Ireland and the Republic of Ireland: neo-functionalism revisited' (2004)
2. Rankin, K. and Schofield, R., 'The troubled historiography of classical boundary terminology' (2004)
3. Coakley, J., 'Ethnic conflict and the two-state solution: the Irish experience of partition' (2004)
4. Ahern, B. (An Taoiseach), 'The future of North–South cooperation' (2005)

5. O'Connor, T., 'The establishment of the North/South Ministerial Council and the North–South bodies' (2005)
6. Smyth, P., 'North–South co-operation since the agreement' (2005)
7. Coakley, J., 'The future of the North–South bodies' (2005)

Working papers

1. Coakley, J. and O'Dowd, L., 'The Irish border and North–South co-operation: an overview' (2005)
2. Rankin, K., 'The creation and consolidation of the Irish border' (2005)
3. Anderson, J. and O'Dowd, L., 'Imperial disintegration and the creation of the Irish border: imperialism and nationalism 1885–1925' (2005)
4. Henderson, J. and Teague, P., 'The Belfast agreement and cross-border economic co-operation in the tourism industry' (2006)
5. McCall, C. and O'Dowd, L., 'The significance of the 'cross-border dimension' for promoting peace and reconciliation' (2006)
6. Coakley, J., Ó Caoindealbháin, B. and Wilson, R., 'The operation of the North–South implementation bodies' (2006)
7. Roper, S., 'Cross-border and local co-operation on the island of Ireland: an economic perspective' (2006)
8. Todd, J., 'A puzzle concerning borders and identities: towards a typology of attitudes to the Irish border' (2006)
9. Pollak, A., 'Educational co-operation on the island of Ireland: a thousand flowers and a hundred heartaches' (2006)
10. Ó Gráda, C. and Walsh B., 'Did (and does) the border matter?' (2006)
11. O'Dowd, L., McCall, C. and Damkat, I., 'Sustaining cross-border co-operation: a case study approach' (2006)
12. Howard, K., 'Diasporas and ambiguous homelands: a perspective on the Irish border' (2006)
13. Magennis, E., Clarke, P. and Sheils, D., 'Study of funding support for cross-border and North–South co-operation on the island of Ireland, 1982–2005: a summary' (2006)
14. Cividin, A., 'Irish cross-border co-operation: the case of the North-West region' (2006)
15. Meehan, E., 'Borders and employment: opportunities and barriers' (2006)
16. Howard, K., 'Nationalist myths: revisiting Heslinga's 'The Irish border as a cultural divide'' (2006)
17. Rankin, K. J., 'Theoretical concepts of partition and the partitioning of Ireland' (2006)
18. Ó Caoindealbháin, B., 'Citizenship and borders: Irish nationality law

and Northern Ireland' (2006)
19. Hayward, K., 'Contention, competition and crime: newspapers' portrayal of borders in the north-west of Ireland' (2006)
20. Howard, K., 'Continuity and change in a partitioned civil society: Whyte revisited' (2006)
21. Howard, K., 'Territorial politics and Irish cycling' (2006)
22. Bradley, J., 'An island economy or island economies? Ireland after the Belfast agreement' (2006)
23. Bradley, J., 'Industrial development in Ireland North and South: case studies of the textile and information technologies sectors' (2006)
24. Anderson, J., 'Irish border communities: questioning the effects of state borders and ethno-national identities' (2006)
25. Kennedy, M., 'The realms of practical politics: North–South cooperation on the Erne hydroelectric scheme, 1942 to 1957' (2006)
26. Donnan, H., 'Fuzzy frontiers: the rural interface in South Armagh' (2006)
27. O'Leary, B., 'Analysing partition: definition, classification and explanation' (2006)
28. O'Leary, B., 'Debating partition: justifications and critiques' (2006)

Index